Colonial Situations

HISTORY OF ANTHROPOLOGY

Colonial Situations

ESSAYS ON
THE CONTEXTUALIZATION
OF ETHNOGRAPHIC KNOWLEDGE

Edited by

George W. Stocking, Jr.

HISTORY OF ANTHROPOLOGY
Volume 7

THE UNIVERSITY OF WISCONSIN PRESS

The University of Wisconsin Press
114 North Murray Street
Madison, Wisconsin 53715

3 Henrietta Street
London WC2E 8LU, England

Printed in the United States of America

Library of Congress Cataloging-in-Publication Data
Colonial situations: essays on the contextualization of ethnographic
knowledge / edited by George W. Stocking, Jr.
348 pp.   cm. — (History of anthropology: 7)
Includes bibliographical references and index.
ISBN 0-299-13120-3
1. Ethnology—History.   2. Ethnology—Philosophy.
3. Ethnocentrism—Europe.   4. Imperialism—History—Case studies.
I. Stocking, George W., 1928-   .   II. Series.
GN308.C64   1991
305.8—dc20   91-50327
CIP

HISTORY OF ANTHROPOLOGY

EDITOR
George W. Stocking, Jr.
Department of Anthropology, University of Chicago

EDITORIAL BOARD

Talal Asad
Department of Anthropology, New School for Social Research

James A. Boon
Department of Anthropology, Princeton University

James Clifford
Board of Studies in the History of Consciousness,
University of California, Santa Cruz

Donna J. Haraway
Board of Studies in the History of Consciousness,
University of California, Santa Cruz

Curtis M. Hinsley
Department of History, Northern Arizona University

Dell Hymes
Department of Anthropology, University of Virginia

Henrika Kuklick
Department of History and Sociology of Science,
University of Pennsylvania

Bruce G. Trigger
Department of Anthropology, McGill University

INFORMATION FOR CONTRIBUTORS

Normally, every volume of *History of Anthropology* will be organized around a particular theme of historical and contemporary anthropological significance, although each volume may also contain one or more "miscellaneous studies," and there may be occasional volumes devoted entirely to such studies. Since volume themes will be chosen and developed in the light of information available to the Editorial Board regarding research in progress, potential contributors from all areas in the history of anthropology are encouraged to communicate with the editor concerning their ongoing work.

Manuscripts submitted for consideration to *HOA* should be typed twenty-six lines to a page with 1¼-inch margins, with *all* material double-spaced, and documentation in the anthropological style. For exemplification of stylistic details, consult the published volumes; for guidance on any problematic issues, write to the editor. Unsolicited manuscripts will not be returned unless accompanied by adequate postage. All communications on editorial matters should be sent to the editor:

George W. Stocking, Jr. (HOA)
Department of Anthropology
University of Chicago
1126 E. 59th St.
Chicago, Illinois 60637 U.S.A.

All communications relating to standing orders, orders for specific volumes, missing volumes, changes of address, or any other business matters should be addressed to:

Marketing Department
The University of Wisconsin Press
114 North Murray Street
Madison, Wisconsin 53715

Contents

Contents

Colonial Situations

COLONIAL SITUATIONS

Twenty-five years ago, the relation of anthropology to colonialism/imperialism became for the first time a burning issue for anthropologists. As several of the articles in this volume testify, an awareness of its colonial context was by no means then a completely new phenomenon in anthropology. But in the aftermath of political decolonization (Holland 1985), the voices of national liberation rang louder in the academy (Fanon 1961), and access to traditional fieldwork sites now in the control of independent "new nations" became problematic. The exposure of Project Camelot (the covert attempt by the United States Department of Defense to organize counter-insurgency research in Latin American countries) raised serious questions about the ethical and political implications of government support (Horowitz 1967; Beals 1969). The publication of Malinowski's field diaries (1967) helped to focus emerging concerns about the interaction of ethnographers with their subject peoples (Nash & Wintrob 1972). And all of this took place in the shadow of United States involvement in the culminating phase of a quarter century of postcolonial warfare in Vietnam—in which the role of anthropologists was to become a controversial issue (Wolf & Jorgenson 1970). By 1970, anthropology was sometimes spoken of as the "child" or "daughter" of "western imperialism" (Gough 1968; Lévi-Strauss 1966), and as a form of "scientific colonialism" (Galtung 1967; Lewis 1973). In the context of a more general reaction against "structural-functionalism" and other forms of "positivism" in the social sciences (e.g., the "systems" theory that was built into the conception of Project Camelot), some began to speak of a "crisis of anthropology" and to call for its "reinvention" (Scholte 1971; Hymes 1972; cf. Stocking 1982).

The timing and pattern of discussion varied in the several hegemonic anthropological traditions. Abortively foreshadowed in the United States in the aftermath of World War II (Kennedy 1945; Kimball 1946; Gregg & Williams 1948), a more systematic critique developed first in France in the early 1950s in the context of independence movements and colonial warfare in Indochina and Algeria (Leiris 1950; Balandier 1951). It later took a somewhat different form in Britain, where the focus was on the implications of colonial involvement for anthropological theory (Banaji 1970; Goddard 1969), and in the United States, where the ethical and political involvement of the ethnographer was the center of concern (Berreman 1968). But in the five years after

1968, these tendencies came together in a number of articles and book-length works, culminating in several sessions at the International Congress of Anthropological and Ethnological Sciences in Chicago (Asad 1973; LeClerc 1972; Huizer & Mannheim 1979).

The critique of colonialism and anthropology met resistance in many quarters—especially among those who, having acted in good liberal faith, now felt the moral basis of their careers to be under attack (Loizos 1977). By the mid-1970s, the discussion had somewhat died down (Stocking 1982). The "crisis of anthropology"—which many did not regard as such—was by then in the process of domestication, as radicals of the 1960s became established in the academy, where some were to become more concerned with the deconstruction of hegemonic texts than the reconstruction of relations of dominance in the real world. Positions that had once seemed radical became merely fashionable (and even passé): the assumption that anthropology was linked to Western colonialism became as much a commonplace of disciplinary discourse as the ignoring (or compartmentalizing) of that relationship had once been. But if colonialism was finally incorporated into the subject matter of anthropology (e.g., in the emergence of a genre of "colonial ethnography"), serious interest in the history of anthropology in colonial context was somewhat attenuated (cf., however, Kuklick 1978).

A kind of schematized outline history of the relationship of anthropology and colonialism—the residue of the discussion of the "crisis" period—is of course readily available today. It hinges on the emergence of functionalism after World War I. Before that, in the expansive phase of Western colonialism, evolutionism in anthropology was both the reflection of and the justification for the invasion, appropriation, and subjugation of the "savage," "barbarian," or "semicivilized" regions of the earth by the representatives of European "civilization"—the actors being conveniently color-coded in racial terms. But with the establishment of European colonial power, what was required was no longer simply the justification of dominance in terms of difference, but the more detailed knowledge of functioning societies that would facilitate and maintain an economical and trouble-free colonial administration—with a stress on the values of traditional native culture or social organization serving as a counterweight to urbanizing progressive natives who identified too closely with European models of equality and democracy (Maquet 1964; cf. Asad 1973; Stauder 1980).

In this simplifying scenario, the diffusionism of early-twentieth-century anthropology tends to be obscured by evolutionism and functionalism on either side. On the farther side of evolutionism one may glimpse the "preanthropology" and the "precolonialism" of the Enlightenment (LeClerc 1972), and beyond that "the conquest of America" (Todorov 1982). On the hither side of functionalism there is decolonization and the "crisis"—blending into the neocolonial, postmodern anthropological present (Marcus & Fischer 1986).

Within such an archetypal diachronic plot, one may distinguish equally archetypical synchronic moments (cf. Stocking, in this volume, on the "primal scene" of first encounter). During anthropology's "classical" functionalist phase, the archetypal moment was that characterized by Georges Balandier in 1951 as the "colonial situation." As subsequently described by Jacques Maquet in an influential essay on "Objectivity in Anthropology," the "existential situation of anthropologists in the colonial system" was that of "scholars whose material and professional interests lay in their home countries but who participated in the privileges of the dominant caste during their stay." Members of the white minority, "they lived according to the same patterns, spoke the same language, and were assigned a certain status within the European group"—that of "middle level specialists." Their existential situation was perfectly compatible with holding progressive views, and with the participant-observer attitude some of them adopted in their fieldwork, but it "depended on the stability of the European domination system." These "objective" conditions of the colonial situation were in turn "reflected in the mental productions" of anthropologists as a group (Maquet 1964). Fortified by a more recent discourse on the relations of knowledge and power (Foucault 1977), some such ideal-typical conception of the colonial situation of the ethnographer might still appeal to many today.

Whatever its adequacy as historical generalization, that conception is, however, a somewhat problematic one from the point of view of a history of anthropology concerned also with the activities of particular anthropologists in specific ethnographic locales. Such a historiography demands a pluralization of the "colonial situation" concept. Going beyond ideal-[stereo?-]typicalization, it would explore in greater depth a variety of differing "colonial situations," the range of interaction of widely differing individuals and groups within them, and the ways in which these situational interactions conditioned the specific ethnographic knowledge that emerged. Although there were some ventures in this direction during the "crisis" period (cf. several of the essays in Asad 1973 and Diamond 1980), by and large the promise of such pluralization has not been followed up, despite a recent interest in the problems of "ethnographic authority" and the "poetics and politics of ethnography" (Clifford 1988; Clifford & Marcus 1986; cf. however, Fardon 1990, which examines a number of "regional traditions of ethnographic writing").

It is in the interest of pursuing this pluralizing and deepening agenda that the essays gathered here have been selected. To be sure, it is not possible in a volume of this sort to deal comprehensively with so broad a topic. There are any number of "colonial situations" that might have been included here, but were, for varying reasons, unrealizable: Evans-Prichard among the Nuer in the aftermath of a British punitive expedition in the late 1920s; Franz Boas among the Kwakiutl on Vancouver Island during the off-seasons at the canneries in the 1890s; George Grey in New Zealand in the wake of Maori "rebellion" in the 1830s; François Peron in Australia on an expedition to counter British influence in the region during the Napoleonic era; and beyond that, the broad expanse that may be epitomized by Las Casas and the tears of the Indians—to mention only a few such unrealized "colonial situations" scattered along axes of time and space.

The ones that we have succeeded in corralling are, however, distributed fairly broadly along both these axes: from Oceania through southeast Asia, the Andaman Islands, and southern Africa to North and South America, and from the middle of the nineteenth century to the end of the twentieth. By illustrative example if not by systematic interpretation, they cover the range of modern ethnography in its major phases, from its emergence in the activities of scientific travellers to its formalization among academic field-workers, to its hoped-for transformation by certain ethnographic activists. Viewed as exemplary types, these "colonial situations" also cover a fairly broad range: from first contact through the establishment of colonial power, from District Officer administrations through white settler regimes, from internal colonialism to international mandates, from early "pacification" to wars of colonial liberation, from the expropriation of land to the defense of ecology. And the motivations and responses of anthropologists are equally varied, ranging from the romantic resistance of Maclay and the complicity of Kubary in early colonialism, through Malinowski's advertising on behalf of academic anthropology, through Speck's advocacy of Indian land rights, through Schneider's grappling with the ambiguities of rapport, to Turner's facilitation of Kayapo cinematic activism.

Although far from exhausting the possibilities, we hope that this volume may at least open up again a serious historical consideration of the varying "colonial situations" in (and out of) which the ethnographic knowledge so essential to anthropology has been produced.[1]

1. The choice of verb here is a charged one: "discovered" or "constructed" would each have given the phrase a different epistemological/ideological spin; the decision to avoid either was deliberate. So also, the use of the word "knowledge." This, despite the fact that by and large the accounts in this volume might suggest that what is at issue is rather error, or ideology, or opinion, or representation, or some other more obviously contingent category than "knowledge" customarily implies. Although its contributing impulses vary, the guiding spirit of HOA is not intended to be systematically subverting of the ethnographic (or the anthropological) enterprise. That the contents of any volume, or more generally of much of the recent historiography of anthropology, might nevertheless sustain that impression is itself an interesting problem in the sociology of this field of knowledge—which may perhaps be considered in a future volume of this series.

Acknowledgments

Aside from the editor, members of the editorial board, the contributors, and Betty Steinberg and the staff of the University of Wisconsin Press, several other individuals have contributed significantly to the preparation of this volume. Ira Bashkow, John Comaroff, and Raymond Fogelson offered helpful advice, and Andrea Lee-Harshbarger served as editorial assistant. Most important, Talal Asad played a substantial editorial role, and graciously agreed to offer concluding reflections from the perspective of a major participant in the earlier discusssion of colonialism and anthropology, and in its evolution during the last two decades.

References Cited

Asad, T., ed. 1973. *Anthropology and the colonial encounter.* London.

Balandier, G. 1951. The colonial situation: A theoretical approach. In *The sociology of black Africa: Social dynamics in central Africa,* trans. D. Garman, 34–61. New York (1970).

Banaji, J. 1970. The crisis of British anthropology. *New Left Rev.* 64:71–85.

Beals, R. L. 1967. *The politics of social research: An inquiry into the ethics and responsibilities of social scientists.* Chicago.

Berreman, G. 1968. Is anthropology alive? Social responsibility in anthropology. *Curr. Anth.* 9:391–98.

Clifford, J. 1988. On ethnographic authority. In *The predicament of culture: Twentieth-century ethnography, literature and art,* 21–54. Cambridge, Mass.

Clifford, J., & G. Marcus, eds. 1986. *Writing culture: The politics and poetics of ethnography.* Berkeley.

Diamond, S., ed. 1980. *Ancestors and heirs.* The Hague.

Fanon, F. 1961. *The wretched of the earth.* New York (1963).

Fardon, R., ed. 1990. *Localizing strategies: Regional traditions of ethnographic writing.* Edinburgh.

Foucault, M. 1977. *Power/knowledge: Selected interviews and other writings, 1972–1977.* New York.

Galtung, J. 1967. Scientific colonialism. *Transition* 30:11–15.

Goddard, D. 1969. Limits of British anthropology. *New Left Rev.* 58:79–90.

Gough, K. 1968. New proposals for anthropologists. *Curr. Anth.* 9:403–7.

Gregg, D., & E. Williams. 1948. The dismal science of functionalism. *Am. Anth.* 50:594–611.

Holland, R. F. 1985. *European decolonization, 1918–1981: An introductory survey.* New York.

Horowitz, I. L., ed. 1967. *The rise and fall of Project Camelot: Studies in the relationship between social science and practical politics.* Cambridge, Mass.

Huizer, G., & B. Mannheim, eds. 1979. *The politics of anthropology: From colonialism and sexism toward a view from below.* The Hague.

Hymes, D., ed. 1972. *Reinventing anthropology.* New York.

Kennedy, R. 1945. The colonial crisis and the future. In *The science of man in the world crisis,* ed. R. Linton, 306–46. New York.

Kimball, S. 1946. The crisis in colonial administration. *Appl. Anth.* 5(2): 8–16.

Kuklick, H. 1978. The sins of the fathers: British anthropology and African colonial administration. *Research in the Sociology of Knowledge, Science and Art* 1:93–119.

LeClerc, G. 1972. *Anthropologie et colonialism: Essai sur l'histoire de l'africanisme.* Paris.

Leiris, M. 1950. L'ethnographe devant le colonialism. *Les temps mod.* 6:357–74.

Lévi-Strauss, C. 1966. Anthropology: Its achievements and its future. *Curr. Anth.* 7:124–27.

Lewis, D. 1973. Anthropology and colonialism. *Curr. Anth.* 14:581–97.

Loizos, P., ed. 1977. [Special number on colonialism and anthropology.] *Anth. Forum* 4(2).

Malinowski, B. 1967. *A diary in the strict sense of the term.* New York.

Maquet, J. 1964. Objectivity in anthropology. *Curr. Anth.* 5:47–55.

Marcus, G., & M. Fischer. 1986. *Anthropology as cultural critique: An experiemental moment in the human sciences.* Chicago.

Nash, D., & R. Wintrob. 1972. The emergence of self-consciousness in ethnography. *Curr. Anth.* 13:532–42.

Scholte, B. 1971. Discontents in anthropology. *Soc. Res.* 38:777–807.

Stauder, J. 1980. Great Britain: Functionalism abroad. A theory in question. In S. Diamond 1980:317–44.

Stocking, G. W. 1982. Anthropology in crisis? A view from between the generations. In *Crisis in anthropology: View from Spring Hill, 1980,* ed. E. A. Hoebel et al., 407–19. New York.

Todorov, T. 1982. *The conquest of America: The question of the Other.* New York (1984).

Wolf, E., & J. Jorgenson. 1970. Anthropology on the warpath in Thailand. *N.Y. Rev. Books,* November 19:26–35.

MACLAY, KUBARY, MALINOWSKI

Archetypes from the Dreamtime of Anthropology

GEORGE W. STOCKING, JR.

One of the functions of history, by traditional accounts, is to demythologize — myth being taken in the negative sense of a self-interestedly or naïvely fabulous or archetypal account of origins (cf. McNeill 1986). But as Malinowski long ago maintained (1926a), myth can also have a positively empowering cultural function; and from this perspective, the historian may be justified in treating it in a less dismissive fashion. Especially, perhaps, the historian of anthropology. Other disciplines, of course, have their empowering (and inhibiting) myths — but not so easily as does anthropology (cf. Halpern 1989; Bensaude-Vincent 1983). Counting responses to a questionnaire may have a certain mythic susceptibility; but to define the condition of humanity in the encounter with the exotic "other" at the boundaries of civilization is, in that bare statement, already a mythic activity.

Beneath, behind, beyond, above, and within the history of anthropology, there is a mythic realm in which the European anthropological encounter with "otherness" is enacted, again and again (cf., among others, Baudet 1965; Todorov 1982; Torgovnick 1990). A set of archetypal situations and experiences, residues of several thousand years of Western history — including the Garden of Eden, the Rousseauian natural state, and the Columbian first encounter — define a kind of anthropological "primal scene" in terms of which the experience of fieldwork is pre-experienced in imagination. Its myth, like any other, will vary with the teller, but every hearer will recognize the plot: the anthropologist venturing bravely across the sea or into the jungle to encounter an

---

George W. Stocking, Jr., is Stein-Freiler Distinguished Service Professor of Anthropology and Director of the Morris Fishbein Center for the History of Science and Medicine at the University of Chicago. He is currently at work on a sequel to his book, *Victorian Anthropology* (1987), entitled *After Tylor: The Reformation of Anthropology in Post-Victorian Britain, 1888 to 1938.*

9

untouched people, there to be stripped of the defensive trappings of civilization and reborn in the study of a simpler culture, and returning with a grail
of scientific knowledge and a vision of alternative cultural possibility. A myth
of modernity, it does not tell so well in the postmodern world; but if we no
longer (or never did) really believe, we do not easily give up the fantasy. The
most sober positivist or the most ardent reinventor must recognize this mythic
vision of anthropology, even as they seek either to deny or to transcend it.
Worldly wise and cynical professors glimpse it in aspiring graduate students
and recall it in themselves; it is what makes anthropology exciting to the general public; it defines an image against which any "truer" history of the venture must be written. In a word, one might say that this mythic vision inspires
the history of anthropology, both as enacted and recounted (Sontag 1966;
cf. Stocking 1989b:208).

There are, of course, other mythic inspirations. Against the Garden may
be posed the Fall; against Rousseau, Hobbes; against Columbus, Cortez. Like
European dominance, anthropology has at times been inspired also by variations on the theme of fallen man—the uplifting of savages lapsed into idolatry
and indolence, who must be taught to worship God and to earn their bread
by the sweat of their brow (cf. Lovejoy & Boas 1935; Pagden 1982; Smith
1973). And it is not simply a matter of inspiration: both the softer and the
harder primitivistic myths are enacted (interactively) in "real" historical settings, the most powerfully charged of which is now often (mythically?) encompassed in the phrase "the colonial situation" (Balandier 1951).

From the beginning of the modern fieldwork tradition, anthropology was
characteristically enacted under an umbrella of European colonial power (cf.
Asad 1973; LeClerc 1972). This fact was implicitly acknowledged in 1913 by
William Rivers, at that time the leading spokesman for the new mode of "intensive study" in British anthropology. The "most favorable moment for ethnographical work," Rivers suggested, was from ten to thirty years after a people had been brought under "the mollifying influences of the official and the
missionary"—long enough to ensure the "friendly reception and peaceful surroundings" that were "essential to such work," but "not long enough to have
allowed any serious impairment of the native culture," or to have witnessed
the passing of a generation who had participated in any "rites and practices"
that might have "disappeared or suffered change" (1913:7). Although colonialism threatened to destroy (by transformation) the object of anthropological
inquiry, it was at the same time a condition *sine qua non* of ethnographic
fieldwork.

Rivers' pragmatic acknowledgment of the enabling aspect of colonialism
stands in sharp contrast to the treatment of colonialism by others among the
early cohorts of professionalizing anthropologists. This is not to say that colonialism itself was never acknowledged. Coming to anthropology in the early
1890s, Rivers' Cambridge colleague A. C. Haddon found the map of the world

splotched with "the red paint of British aggression," whose victims would "be less than men if they did not rebel"; it was in this context that Haddon first envisioned an Imperial Bureau of Ethnology that would both soften the effects and reduce the cost of "maintaining our ascendance" (ACHP: manuscript on imperialism, c.1891). Here, however, the enabling relationship moved in the other direction, from anthropology to colonialism. And in the ethnographic accounts which might presumably have served that enabling purpose, the colonial system was characteristically unmarked and invisible (cf. Stocking 1983).

Preeminent among the generation of Haddon and Rivers' students—though formally a student of neither—was, of course, Bronislaw Malinowski. He was the one who most self-consciously, systematically, and successfully applied Rivers' "General Account of Method" to what Haddon called "the intensive study of a restricted area," in order to carry out a "revolution in anthropology." That it was with his name that an emerging style of fieldwork was henceforth to be associated no doubt reflected the excellence of Malinowski's own ethnography, as well as his institutional and pedagogical role. But as the disillusion following the publication of his field diaries attests, it also reflected the more or less self-conscious mythicization by which, in a book full of mythic resonance, he had made himself the archetype of "the Ethnographer." For the opening chapter of *Argonauts of the Western Pacific* was not simply a methodological prescription; in the terms of Malinowski's later anthropological theory, it was a "mythic charter" for what was to become the central ritual of social anthropology. A motivating myth for "apprentice ethnographers," it reassured them that a difficult and even dangerous task was possible, that those who would follow in Malinowski's charismatic methodological footsteps could in fact "get the work done"—even to the point where it would become a matter of disciplinary routine (cf. Stocking 1983).

Malinowski's epoch-marking fieldwork in the Trobriand Islands came within the optimal period Rivers had defined—a decade after a permanent government station, a decade and a half after the last internal fighting and an abortive attempt at violent resistance to colonial power, two decades after the Methodist Overseas Mission headquarters had been established at Losuia (Weiner 1976:33–34; Seligman 1910:664–65). Such facts, however, went unrecorded in *Argonauts*, where the methodological stage is set in terms of the classic anthropological mythos ("imagine yourself set down . . . alone on a tropical beach close to a native village . . . "), and the European colonial presence is reduced to annoying archetype (the "neighboring white man, trader or missionary") from whom the ethnographic novice is urged quickly to absent himself (1922b:4; cf. Payne 1981; Thornton 1985). The present essay is, among other things, an attempt to contextualize that mythicizing erasure.

To do so, it will help to consider Malinowski's fieldwork in relation to that of prior ethnographic ventures in the western Pacific, in somewhat different colonial situations than his own. Two earlier ethnographers, Nikolai Miklouho-Maclay and Jan Kubary, are of special interest, because their names occur, somewhat cryptically, at a critical point in Malinowski's Trobriand diary, when he was explicitly contemplating problems of ethnographic method:

> Yesterday while walking I thought about the "preface" to my book: Jan Kubary as a concrete methodologist. Mikluho-Maclay as a new type. Marett's comparison: *early ethnographers as prospectors.* (1967:155)

Posed here against some undefined "new type," the "concrete method" was Rivers' special contribution to ethnographic methodology; and Malinowski had begun his Melanesian fieldwork under Rivers' ethnographic aegis. But as he elsewhere indicated, Malinowski sought not just to emulate Rivers but to transcend him: "Rivers is the Rider Haggard of anthropology; I shall be the Conrad" (R. Firth 1957:6). In this context, we are perhaps justified in combining these statements into an archetypal programmatic proportion: "as Mikluho-Maclay was to Kubary, I shall be to Rivers." No longer surveying like a mere ethnographic prospector, Malinowski, as he suggested elsewhere in his diary, would dig down below the surface of difference to the native's "essential deepest way of thinking" (1967:119).

In relating himself to Miklouho-Maclay and Kubary, Malinowski chose two ethnographers who shared with him a connection with partitioned Poland, and who, although working in other areas of the western Pacific, had both briefly visited the Trobriands. The ethnographic biographies of all three men resonate to issues that have been much in the forefront of professional concern in the quarter century since publication of Malinowski's diaries sent shock waves of reluctant recognition through the anthropological world. In the context of a heightened awareness of the colonial situation of modern anthropology, we may read those biographies today with greater sensitivity to issues of reflexivity and responsibility, of ethics and of power in the practice of ethnography. As we shall see, the implicit programmatic proportion attributed here to Malinowski bears only a rather tenuous symbolic reference to what may be known of the ethnographic biographies of the three men, in the context of their differing relationships to the differing colonial situations of their ethnography. But by placing the ethnographic careers and changing colonial situations of all three anthropologists in juxtaposition, we may perhaps nevertheless illuminate that murky realm in which myth and history interact, and in the process cast light on the emergence of modern anthropology, both as a specific historical phenomenon and a generalized experiential archetype.[1]

1. Colleagues in the Fishbein Workshop in the History of the Human Sciences at the University of Chicago, to which a penultimate version of this essay was presented, questioned my use

Tamo Russ: Defender of Paradise

Nikolai Miklouho-Maclay was born in 1846 in a village in the Russian province of Novgorod, son of a petty nobleman and engineer with the Cossack surname Miklouho. Glossing it as Maclure, one source has suggested that the family descended from Scottish craftsmen brought to Russia by Peter the Great (Greenop 1944:20)—which may have encouraged young Maclay to adopt a more recognizably Scottish name (perhaps that of his grandmother) when

---

of the notion of "myth," and I have no doubt that it is questionable, from at least three different points of view. From the perspective of a more systematic literary historical myth analysis, my references to the Garden and the Fall may seem casual and undeveloped (cf. Frye 1957; Gould 1981; Smith 1973). From the perspective of the deconstructively inclined (of whom there were several in the Workshop), the implication that there might be a defensible distinction between "myth" and "history" seemed not only questionable in itself, but counter to the thrust of the essay, insofar as it tended, deconstructively, to reduce a certain version of the "history" of British social anthropology to the status of "myth." Finally—though they were not represented in the Workshop—I am aware of a reaction to my work on the part of senior British social anthropologists, students of Malinowski, who tend at times to see me as simply another deconstructionist doubter. Thus Edmund Leach, speaking on behalf of those "few surviving British anthropologists who knew Malinowski in the flesh"—for whom he was "a great hero"—associated me with those who view Malinowski as "a fraud, a man who preached the gospel of 'participant observation' but did not practice it" (Leach 1990:56).

   Regarding the issue of systematicity: I waver between, on the one hand, feeling that a more capable myth analyst, and perhaps even I myself, might develop the mythical parallels of the Garden and the Fall more systematically, and, on the other hand, feeling that those parallels are better left as unsystematized resonances, for readers to augment if they are so inclined—on the grounds that it is as resonances that such ideas are present in the minds of anthropologists and echo through the history of anthropology. Regarding the myth-history distinction: while I am conscious of its epistemologically problematic status, I am committed to a notion of the historian's craft which assumes that a distinction between myth and history, or between more and less mythical views of history is worth attempting in the practice of historiography—at the same time that one recognizes that much of what we deal with as historians is perhaps at some level irreducibly "mythistorical" (cf. McNeill 1986). Regarding Malinowski's contribution: I would appeal (as, apparently unnoticed, I have done before) to Malinowski's own notion of the empowering charter function of myth, which makes it possible to "get on with the work" of that highly problematic process of participant observation, and to produce ethnographies, which although of varying quality, are many of them at least as valuable and permanent contributions to our knowledge and understanding of the variety of humankind as the efforts of those who would deconstruct them (cf. Stocking 1983:112). Of these, surely among the most valuable and most permanently interesting were those of Malinowski.

   I am aware that this ambiguous, ambivalent, and epistemologically problematic historiographical posture may limit the present history in various ways—and perhaps even facilitate further criticism. Myth is far from being the only interpretive theme that I would apply to the history of anthropology. But the mythic element in anthropology seems to me a diffusely powerful one, and an appropriate interpretative frame for the historical specificities of this essay. I can only hope that the latter may be of interest even to those who would have framed them differently—as I will, too, in other places (cf. Stocking, in process).

he was twenty-one.[2] Left fatherless at ten, Maclay was much influenced by his widowed mother, who was of Polish origin and apparently had some connection to the revolutionary circle of Alexander Herzen (Tumarkin 1982a:4). During adolescence Maclay was also inspired by Nikolai Chernyshevsky, another leader of the democratic movement, and at fifteen he was arrested in a student demonstration and briefly jailed. In 1864, he was expelled from St. Petersburg University and forced to seek his education abroad.[3]

After studying natural science and political economy at Heidelberg, Maclay migrated to Leipzig and to Jena, where he worked under the leading German Darwinist, the zoologist Ernst Haeckel. In 1867, he accompanied Haeckel on a field trip to the Canary Islands, after which he journeyed alone through North Africa on foot. During a subsequent marine zoological trip to Sicily and the Red Sea, Maclay became interested in the anthropological variety of the latter region (in which, like such other nineteenth-century anthropological notables as Richard Burton and William Robertson Smith, he travelled in Arab dress).

Maclay's incipient anthropological interests were further stimulated after his return to Russia in 1868, when he came under the influence of Russia's leading scientist, Karl von Baer. World-renowned as zoologist and embryologist, Von Baer was also active as an ethnographer and physical anthropologist. An ardent monogenist, he had proposed the need for more detailed study of the relations of the Papuans to other races in order to confirm the unity of the human species against the arguments of Anglo-American polygenists (Tumarkin 1982b:10–11). Although Von Baer was anti-Darwinian, the racial affinities of the Papuans were also an issue to evolutionary writers, including Alfred Russel Wallace, whose account of The Malay Archipelago drew a sharp distinction between the Malayan and the Papuan races. Wallace assumed the latter were remnants of the aboriginal population of a subsided continent, which the British geologist Phillip Sclater had called Lemuria, and which Haeckel suggested was "the probable cradle of the human race" (Webster 1984:

2. The transliteration of Maclay's name has been quite various: Miclucho, Mikloucho, Miklouho, Mikluka, Miklukho; Maclay, Maklai, Maklay. I have used the spelling adopted by the Institute of Ethnography of the Soviet Academy of Sciences, which was renamed for Maclay in 1947.

3. The most reliable biographical source is Webster 1984, which includes references to a number of secondary accounts. Although Soviet writers have had access to materials unavailable in the West, they emphasize the heroic egalitarian aspect of Maclay's persona, and minimize his authoritarian Kurtzian side, rendering him more comfortably "progressive" than perhaps he was (Tumarkin 1982a, 1982b, 1988; cf. Butinov 1971). As a result, the accounts of several critical episodes come across quite differently than in Webster's account (cf. Webster 1984:250–52; Tumarkin 1982b:38). A similar idealizing tendency may also be at work in postindependence New Guinea publications (Sentinella 1975; cf. Webster 1984:350).

Miklouho-Maclay (seated) with Ernst Haeckel, at Lanzarote, in the Canary Islands, on their marine zoological field trip of 1867. (From *Ernst Haeckel im Bilde: Ein physiognomische Studie zu seinem 80. Geburtstage, herausgegeben von Walther Haeckel mit einem Geleitwort von Wilhelm Gölsche* [Berlin, 1914], pl. 6.)

28, 30; Stocking 1987:100). Maclay had already been planning to do zoological researches in the Pacific when he read Wallace's book in 1868, and he now thought of pursuing anthropological questions as well, hoping perhaps to find Lemurians still living in the interior of New Guinea. Having brought himself to the attention of the president of the Russian Geographical Society (the Grand Duke Konstantine, brother of the tsar), Maclay was able to obtain free transport to the Pacific on the naval corvette *Vitiaz*.

After a ten-month voyage around Cape Horn, Maclay was set ashore in September 1871 at Astrolabe Bay on the north coast of New Guinea, still weak from illness he had suffered while at sea. He had brought with him two servants, a Swedish seaman named Will Olsen, and a Polynesian Maclay spoke of simply as "Boy," whom he thought would somehow serve as his intermediary with the Papuan natives. Boy soon died from malaria, and Olsen proved a constant burden. Maclay thus found himself virtually alone among previously uncontacted and totally "untouched" groups of the sort whose racial characteristics he had planned to study—an ethnographic situation often imagined in archetype, but rarely achieved in practice.

For the next fifteen months, Maclay made his home in a cabin built for him by the corvette's crew before their departure. He had chosen a site ten minutes walk from a nearby native village, for reasons that illuminate his ambivalent and ambiguous ethnographic situation: lacking the natives' language, he was unable to ask their permission to settle within the village; fearing that he would be annoyed by the noise if he did, he felt more comfortable remaining outside. This mixture of panhuman tact and strongly asserted personal identity defined for Maclay a position in the Papuan world that was at once intimate and distanced. Although the salvos fired in honor of the Grand Duke's birthday and the swaths cut through the jungle by the corvette's crew from the beginning set Maclay somewhat above the natural course of Papuan existence, his considered policy was to bring himself close down to, though still above it—simultaneously asserting a common humanity and a powerfully alien identity. Going unarmed into the village, he faced arrows shot to see if he would flinch. His response was to put down his mat in the village square and go to sleep—using a natural human function to assert a more than natural strength of will (Tumarkin 1982b:82–83). From that time on, Maclay let the natives' curiosity lead them to his cabin, confident that in a moment of crisis the shotgun and revolver he kept hidden from them would set a "big crowd of natives fleeing" (126). Following a "policy of patience and tact" (112), he regularly blew a whistle before coming into the village of Gorendu, so that the men would know he did not come to spy and the women would have time to hide—until one day the women were all introduced to him, in order that henceforth life could go on normally in his presence.

At points, Maclay spoke of himself as "becoming a bit of a Papuan" (Tumarkin 1982b:187)—as when on impulse he caught a large crab and ate it raw. By disposition, however, he seems to have savored solitude, and when he was drawn forth from it, he preferred to be "a mere spectator and not an active participant in whatever is going on" (173). He never gave up his boots and gaiters, or moved into the village, and in several instances his considered policy clearly contributed to setting him apart from—and above—Papuan normality. To keep secret Boy's death—which would have belied the prevailing notion of the intruders' immortality—Maclay threw the weighted body into the sea at night, leaving the natives to believe that he had enabled Boy to fly to Russia, which in their minds soon became equated with the moon. Amazing them by burning alcohol and by the power of his "taboo" or shotgun, curing people who had been abandoned to death, refusing proffered sexual partners ("Maclay does not need women!" [225]), never allowing "any expression of familiarity" (388), he came to be "regarded as a really extraordinary being" (229). Rather than answer their direct question as to whether he himself could die—and unwilling to lie to them—Maclay offered his body for the natives to test; their unwillingness to do so became proof of his immortality (388). At once god and man, Maclay seems to have created for himself a remarkable position of trust and power, one which might well have been assumed to provide the basis for Malinowski's ethnography of a new type.

In retrospect, however, the anthropological purposes to which Maclay employed his unusually privileged position seem remarkably time-bound. They are suggested by a grisly operation he coolly performed on the still-warm body of Boy. Maclay—who at one point planned a five-volume work on the comparative anatomy of the brain—wanted "to preserve Boy's brain for research purposes." But lacking a "vessel large enough to contain a whole brain," and fearful that the natives might arrive at any moment, he removed only the speech apparatus—thus fulfilling a promise to his German professor of comparative anatomy, Carl Gegenbaur, to bring back "the larynx of a dark man with all the muscles" (Tumarkin 1982b:129). As a student of Haeckel and disciple of Von Baer, Maclay held research interests that were "anthropological" in the nineteenth-century continental European sense: it was, at least in the first instance, the physical characteristics of man that preoccupied him, and "ethnological" questions were to him those of "racial" relationship (cf. Stocking 1989a).

While Maclay seems to have avoided taking positions on many of the major anthropological issues of the day (Webster 1984:343), his sympathies were in general monogenist. He rejected the notion that living races were closer anatomically to animal forebears; his purpose in collecting so many samples of Papuan hair was to show that it "grows in precisely the same way as ours, . . . and not in groups or tufts as one reads in anthropology textbooks" (Tumarkin 1982b:142). On the other hand, his dissections of executed criminals in Australia suggested that there were "peculiarities of by no means trifling import" in the brains of different races, and he was inclined to attribute his own inability to pronounce certain sounds in New Guinea languages to a racial difference in vocal organs (Webster 1984:240, 343, 350; cf. Sentinella 1975:291). But if Maclay could be naïvely ethnocentric in evaluating Papuan physical beauty, and took for granted an evolutionary view of their social development, he also felt that, at bottom, Papuan natives were just like Europeans—practical, hardworking, ready to "adopt and use European instruments at the first opportunity" (Tumarkin 1982b:214).

Maclay spent a great deal of time sketching—physical types, costumes, material culture, local settings. Indeed, he seems in general to have stayed at the surface of things, and to have expressed relatively little interest in penetrating the subtleties of religious life and social organization. While this clearly reflected the limitations of the anthropological perspective he brought from Europe, Maclay's focus on what was easily described from the outside may also have expressed a sensitivity to the extremely problematic character of any attempt to get beneath the surface. Although his background, personal history, and surviving correspondence indicate a facile multilingualism like that of Malinowski—who is said to have made his way in eleven languages— Maclay's diaries suggest also an acute sense of the difficulties of language learning in a pristine contact situation, in which there was not a single bilingual intermediary. After two months, he still did not know the Papuan words for "yes" and "no": "Anything that cannot be pointed at remains unknown, unless I learn the word by chance" (Tumarkin 1982b:117). It was only after five months that he finally figured out the word for "bad" (by giving the natives all sorts of salty, bitter, and sour substances to taste), and then by opposition, the word for "good"—having been for some time misled by the word for "tobacco" (150–51). Even then, it turned out that the word he had learned was specific to food preparation (491). Had he carried with him the "genealogical method," on which Rivers' "concrete method" was founded, Maclay could scarcely have made use of it, since he did not learn the words for "father" and "mother" until the eighth month (219).

Maclay's focus on readily observable surface phenomena can thus be interpreted not only in terms of conceptual predisposition but also as a reflection of methodological restraint. It was only toward the end of his first visit, when after fifteen months he had won the natives' "complete trust" and had a "pretty good command" of one dialect, that he felt that "he had cleared the ground" for the many years of research it would take to "get a real knowledge of these men's way of thinking and way of life" (Tumarkin 1982b:271). Even then, in promising that he would return, he could not tell them that it would be "many months," because he had not yet learned a word for "many" (278).

In December 1872, Maclay—whose death had been rumored at home—boarded a Russian clipper that had been sent in search of him by the Grand Duke Konstantine. When he took a group of natives on to the ship "for a bit of sightseeing," they were so frightened by the many Europeans and the "various devices whose purpose they did not know" that their clinging to him made movement impossible; wrapping a rope around his middle, he left the ends free for them to hold as he walked about the deck (Tumarkin 1982b: 277). At this time, northern New Guinea had barely been touched by the expansive processes of European colonialism, and it was unfamiliarity rather than prior experience of contact that terrified them. But forces were already in operation that were to engulf Maclay's New Guinea Garden in the larger colonial situation of the southwestern Pacific. The first permanent mission had just been established on Murray Island in the Torres Straits, and in a few months Captain John Moresby was to discover the harbor which became Port Moresby (Biskup et al. 1968:20, 29). Australian interest in New Guinea had already been stirred by rumors of gold, which had led to the formation of a short-lived New Guinea Prospecting Association (Joyce 1971a:9). By this time the labor traffic to supply the plantations of Queensland, Samoa, and Fiji had already begun, and "blackbirders" were regular intruders in the region (Scarr 1969; Docker 1970). The consequences of such intrusions into his primal ethnographic scene were soon to distract Maclay from any systematic social anthropological goals he might have entertained.

After a circuitous trip—during which he made a three-day anthropometric study of Philippine Negritos he thought might be related to the Papuans—Maclay disembarked in Java, where he spent seven months as the guest of Governor-General of the Dutch East Indies, recuperating from the debilitation of his New Guinea experience. Early in 1874, he was off again, this time to the same southwestern Papuan coastal area Alfred Russel Wallace had refrained from visiting two decades before, because the natives were rumored to be "bloodthirsty" (Sentinella 1975:226). What Maclay found during two months in the area were groups of Papuans similar to those he knew already. Concluding that their differences in nasal structure were of no significance, he suggested that it was only "anthropologists who have never left Europe and divide the human race into races from their comfortable armchairs" who regarded the nose as a "characteristic feature" (Tumarkin 1982b:322). The "wretched" nomadic life led by these groups had been forced upon them by the recurrent raiding of Malay slave traders; their "treachery" toward strangers —which he himself on one occasion narrowly escaped—was a perfectly understandable human response.

This experience with a Papuan population suffering from culture contact seems to have heightened Maclay's awareness of the external political and social forces impinging on untouched Papuan life—which more and more took on an aura of Noble Savage innocence. But in the case of these already contaminated Papuans, his response was to suggest a more active European intervention. If his friend the Dutch Governor would not agree to found a "military settlement" sufficiently strong "to enforce law and order," Maclay was willing himself to return "with a few dozen Javanese soldiers and one gunboat" provided he was given "complete independence of action, including the right to decide matters of life and death regarding my subordinates and the natives" (Tumarkin 1982b:442, 445).

When his offer was refused, Maclay undertook instead two difficult expeditions in the Malay Peninsula, measuring the heads of mountain Negrito aboriginals he thought might be related to the Philippine and Papuan groups he had previously studied, as well as the local representatives of those Malay pirates who had ravaged the Papuan coast. Ironically, it was in relation to the latter· that, according to one source, he now adopted the policy of principled silence which, in the context of a developing activist commitment, was drastically to limit his published ethnographic output. Aware that the English were try-· ing to extend their influence north from Singapore, and having enjoyed the hospitality of Malay rajahs only after assuring them he was "not an Englishman," Maclay felt it would be dishonorable to "communicate any information under the guise of benefit to science"—the Malays who trusted him would rightly have called "such behaviour espionage" (Sentinella 1975:231; cf. Webster 1984:368, n. 167).

When Maclay returned to Singapore late in 1875 from his second expedition into Malaya, the newspapers were debating the problem of British annexation of the eastern half of New Guinea, which Australians were pressuring the London government to do (Jacobs 1951b; Legge 1956:7–18). Determined to do what he could to forestall "the *terribly pernicious* consequences for the black population of their encounter with European colonisation" (Tumarkin 1982b:25), Maclay decided the time had come to keep his promise to return to the northeast Papuan coast to which he had given his name. This time, however, he would come "*not just* as naturalist, but also as the '*protector*' of my black friends" (447). Once there, he intended to proclaim the independence of the "Papuan Union of the Maclay Coast"; if the attempt should prove abortive, at least his scientific studies would partly "compensate" him (26).

In February 1876, Maclay began his return trip to Astrolabe Bay aboard a vessel captained by the notorious David O'Keefe, a flamboyantly aggressive American trader who was later to style himself Emperor of Yap. While at Yap, Maclay made ethnographic notes on a hierarchical society for which he had a very limited empathy; he had even less for the natives of Kubary's Palau, whom he saw as corrupted by a long experience of European trade. Imagining them as once Noble Savages among whom the first white men walked "as gods," he dismissed their present warfare as "all ruses, deceptions and ambushes." Moving from the trade center of Korror to the larger island with which it was often at war, Maclay seems completely to have misunderstood the transferral of allegiances involved when he acquired two parcels of land on which he thought he might someday settle. But he willingly accepted another gift offered "to bind the white man's loyalty": the twelve-year-old niece of a native dignitary, who went on with him to Astrolabe Bay—but as one of three native servants, rather than as "temporary wife" (Webster 1984:180–85, 191).

Maclay's second sojourn in Astrolabe Bay (June 1876–November 1877) is less well documented, and it has been suggested that his journal entries were "short and fragmentary precisely for the reason that he did not want to facilitate . . . the 'appropriation' of this part of New Guinea by foreign invaders" (Tumarkin 1982b:29). Despite his status as *Tamo-boro-boro* (big, big man) his scientific work apparently did not go well: "secretiveness and superstitious fear"—along with continuing linguistic difficulties—forced him to become "a spy for science." Employing "strategems to witness ceremonies 'accidentally,'" he learned "next to nothing" of "the natives' thoughts and beliefs" (Webster 1984:188, 194). Several attempted explorations into the interior and along the coast, undertaken in part to enlarge the area of his political influence, revealed instead the limits of his authority. Relying on his reputation for magical power, he never really understood the local disputes in which he became entangled. He did, however, become aware that his own activities (including the illicit trade his servants carried on in goods stolen from his stock) were doing quite a bit to modify the pristine contact situation, and by the time he left in November 1877, he had decided that he would do "positively nothing, either directly or indirectly, to facilitate the establishment of communication between whites and Papuans" (Tumarkin 1982b:29). Before his departure, he called together representatives of nearby villages to warn them against other white men, with hair and clothing like his own, who might come in ships and take them into slavery—and gave the Papuans signs by which they could tell potential "friends from foes" (30).

Maclay's subsequent travels in New Guinea were all motivated as much by political as by scientific concerns. Settling in Australia, he was befriended by several prominent Scotsmen with scientific interests (one of whose daughters he was subsequently to marry). In March 1879, he undertook a ten-month voyage through the New Hebrides and the Solomons, combining scientific work with the attempt to gather more first-hand information on the "blackbirding" trade. After stopping briefly in the Trobriands on his return, he sailed along the southeastern coast of New Guinea on the London Missionary Society steamer, measuring heads and striking up an acquaintance with the missionary James Chalmers, who was to be an ally in the defense of native land rights and the opposition to labor recruitment.

By this time Maclay's exploits had given him a considerable public notoriety. Referred to as "Baron" in the Australian and European press, he tacitly accepted the title, and as "Baron de Maclay" spoke out publicly in defense of Papuan interests. He sent several open letters to Sir Arthur Gordon, the British High Commissioner of the Western Pacific, calling on the Imperial Government to "recognize the right of the aborigines to their own soil." Arguing on the basis of his own researches that every single piece of land on the Maclay Coast was already "entirely owned by different communities engaged in tilling the soil," he insisted that the natives had no understanding of "parting with their land *absolutely*" (Tumarkin 1982b:449, 453; Webster 1984:221).

When the killing of ten Polynesian teachers of the London Missionary Society at a village in southeastern New Guinea provoked a punitive expedition in 1881, Maclay wrote to the British naval commander of the southwest Pacific, Commodore John Wilson, suggesting that such "massacres" were to be understood as a response to the blackbirding trade. In this case, however, his friend Chalmers was inclined to blame "sheer blood lust"; and although both he and Maclay were taken along as mediators, the outcome was a shooting affray in which, quite by chance, the village chief was killed (Webster 1984: 250–52; cf. Tumarkin 1982b:38).

Later that year, however, Maclay wrote an "open, but very confidential" letter to Commodore Wilson attempting to enlist his support for a more ambitious plan for the controlled acculturation of the Maclay Coast. Politically, it involved the formation of a "Great Council," with Maclay himself as foreign minister and general advisor, in order to bring the Papuans gradually to a "higher and more general stage of purely native self-government" extending over a large area. Economically, Maclay proposed the establishment of plantations in which the natives would be employed at "reasonable remuneration and under fair treatment." After "having been for some time under the direction of competent overseers," they would "gradually acquire habits of greater industry" and "become possessed of sufficient knowledge to work for themselves." To raise the necessary capital of £15,000, Maclay hoped to obtain the cooperation of "some philanthropically-minded capitalists." On this basis, New Guinea might provide raw materials to Australia, receive manufactured goods in return, and perhaps eventually itself solicit Great Britain to set up a protectorate (Tumarkin 1982b:455–60).

Although Wilson and Gordon were personally sympathetic, Maclay's paternalistic dream of Papuan self-government within the British "empire of free trade" was quickly to be overwhelmed by the cresting wave of European colonial expansion, which in the middle 1880s tumbled over the whole of eastern New Guinea. Ironically, Maclay's own efforts on behalf of independent Papuan development were in the process turned to the advantage of the contending imperial powers.

Early in 1882, Maclay returned to Russia, hoping to persuade the new tsar to support his "Maclay Coast Scheme." While in Europe, he had several portentous meetings. In England, he consulted with Gordon, Wilson, and William MacKinnon, one of the chief movers of British colonial expansion in East Africa, whom Wilson had suggested as a possible supporter. In France, Maclay met the Russian novelist Turgenev, from whom he is said to have sought information about the Communards, some of whom he had visited in 1879 when he inspected a prison in New Caledonia, and whom he apparently thought of as models for his utopian venture (Tumarkin 1982b:43). In Berlin, he met the German anthropologist Otto Finsch, who unbeknownst to Maclay was to become an active agent in the establishment of German colonial power on the Maclay Coast. In Russia, Maclay was presented to the tsar, and became involved himself in a secret Russian plan to establish a naval station in the southwestern Pacific—apparently in the vain hope that this might help to sustain his proposed Papuan Union (Sentinella 1975:307, 345; cf. Webster 1984:271). But when he returned to the southwest Pacific early in 1883, all of these efforts either came to nought or backfired.

Stopping off in Batavia on his return to the Pacific, Maclay transferred— apparently by prearrangement—to a Russian naval ship which he was to accompany on a survey of suitable sites for the proposed naval station. While he was in New Guinea for a last brief visit, in which he brought farm animals and various shoots and seeds for his proposed plantations, his transfer in Batavia became known in Australia. The resulting publicity precipitated an attempt by Queensland to annex New Guinea, in order to forestall the threat of a similar move by the Russians—who in the meantime had decided that the area was unsuitable for a naval station. Opposed by Maclay and Chalmers in various communications to London, the Queensland attempt was overruled by the British government.

In the fall of 1883, when reports circulated that a Scottish adventurer named MacIver planned to colonize the Maclay Coast, Maclay again fired off a telegram to Lord Derby: "Maclay Coast Natives claim political autonomy under European protectorate"—although he privately acknowledged that his efforts "resembled a request to the sharks not to be so voracious" (Tumarkin 1982b: 478; Sentinella 1975:310). But despite London having already intervened to forestall MacIver (Webster 1984:293–94), eastern New Guinea was soon to be partitioned between the British and the then-emerging German overseas empire. Ironically, Maclay himself helped to sate the sharks' voracity: the Germans justified their claim to the northern coast by the fact that Otto Finsch had set up a station on the Maclay Coast in the fall of 1884, after presenting himself to the natives, in their own language, as Maclay's friend (S. G. Firth 1982:22). By the end of that year, the eastern half of New Guinea had been divided between the British and the Germans, with the exploitation of Maclay's coast (now part of Kaiser Wilhelmsland) placed in the hands of the newly founded *Neu Guinea Kompagnie* (Jacobs 1951a, 1951b; Moses 1977).

Even after the fact, Maclay persisted in resisting annexation. A telegram he sent to Bismarck ("Maclay Coast natives reject German annexation") was used by the Iron Chancellor to rally anti-British and procolonial feeling in the Reichstag. Once this move had backfired, Maclay sent a final appeal to London: "Kindly inform the British Government that I maintain my right to the Maclay Coast" (quoted in Webster 1984:307, 309). In 1886, leaving his wife and two sons in Australia, he returned to Russia to seek the tsar's support to form a cooperative colonization venture of his own on an island off the Maclay Coast. During his stay, a great deal of public attention was given to the man who called himself "the white Papuan" and whom the press called "The King of the Papuans." Maclay in fact received applications from hundreds of prospective colonists, who dreamed of a freer life on a warm South Sea island. He had two audiences with the tsar, who appointed a special committee to examine Maclay's detailed "Draft Rules," which combined direct democracy with a great deal of power reserved to him as premier or "elder." Maclay, however, was very vague about just which island he had in mind, and in the end the proposal was rejected, in part because the tsar, embroiled in Balkan controversies, was unwilling to jeopardize relations with Bismarck (Webster 1984:314–25).

Depressed in spirit, long plagued by ill-health and now suddenly grown old, Maclay returned once more to Australia to bring his family back to St. Petersburg. Once there, he devoted himself to getting his diaries and scientific manuscripts in order for publication, dictating when neuralgia and rheumatism made writing impossible. However, the task remained still incomplete at the time of his death in April 1888; it was not until 1923 that his diaries were first published, and not until the early 1950s that a collected edition of his scientific writings was published (Tumarkin 1982b:54).

By that time, Maclay had long since stepped outside of history into the realm of myth. His exploits—enhanced by his obvious talent for self-dramatization—made him something of a legend during his own lifetime. After meeting Maclay in Paris in 1882, the French historian Gabriel Monod described him as "the sincerest man of ideals" he had ever met—"a hero in the noblest and broadest sense of the word" (Webster 1984:274). To Tolstoy, Maclay's work was "epoch-making": he was "the first to prove indubitably by experience that man is the same everywhere" (Butinov 1971:27). From an early point, it was Maclay's experience, rather than his scientific contribution, that formed his heroic reputation. Though he published over a hundred scientific papers, they were mostly nonanthropological or physical anthropological or travel accounts, appearing in what for most readers were obscure publications; the larger anthropological work he planned was never completed. But if his scientific work quickly receded into historical obscurity, Maclay's life experience—compacted by mythical elision—resonated to archetypes old and new. There was the age-old European dream of the Noble Savage, realized in a Papuan Paradise. There was the late-nineteenth-century fantasy of the White Man "who became the ruler and god of a primitive people" (Webster 1984:348). And when faith in Europe's civilizing mission was shaken in the early twentieth century, there was the alternative image of "the lone Ethnographer," and the memory of the nineteenth-century humanist who had fought against slavery and imperialism—most prominently in the Soviet Union, where in 1947 the Institute of Ethnography of the Academy of Sciences was renamed after Miklouho-Maclay. Back in New Guinea, Maclay, promethian bearer of metal axes and knives, had entered local mythology as a vague precursory figure of what later anthropologists were to call the "Cargo Movement" (Lawrence 1964:63–68; cf. Tumarkin 1982b:55).

Paralleling these mythic transformations were a series of elisions that helped to simplify an ambiguous historical complexity. There was the executed Australian Aboriginal criminal whose brain had confirmed the existence of racial differences (and whose body Maclay pickled and sent to Rudolf Virchow in Berlin)—standing in striking contrast to the antiracialist monogenism for which he was to be remembered (Webster 1984:243). There was the Chinese sawyer in the Malayan jungle whom Maclay threatened to shoot for disobedience—a striking instance of the "servitude of others" that was an unmarked but essential ingredient both of Maclay's own freedom and of his utopian visions (157–61). To think of Maclay as Conrad's Kurtz, alone in the jungle, surrounded by adoring natives he had come to uplift, would be to mythicize in a different mode; Maclay's self-empowering impulses were never reduced to Kurtz's horrific exterminating scrawl. But not to hear the Kurtzian resonances in the life of this "nineteenth century scientific humanist" would be tone-deafness to historical complexity.

Herr Kubary:
Lord God of Astrolabe Bay

When Maclay first arrived in New Guinea, Jan Stanislaus Kubary was already doing ethnographic work in the Palau Islands, a thousand miles to the northwest. Although Maclay became aware of Kubary in 1876, when he stopped at Palau on his second voyage to the Maclay Coast, the two men seem never to have met. But in the aftermath of Maclay's final departure for Europe a decade later, their contrapuntal careers were brought into direct relationship, when Kubary arrived on the Maclay Coast, there to play a radically different role in the relations to Papuans and Europeans.

Kubary was born in the same year as Maclay, in Warsaw, Poland. His Hungarian father, butler to an Italian opera producer, died when he was six; his mother, a native of Berlin, remarried the Polish owner of a small footwear factory. As a student in high school, Kubary joined the uprising against Russian rule in 1863; but when his group gathered in the forest with only two rifles, twenty scythes, and some wooden staves, he decided that "to wage war in this manner only invites a beating"—and escaped across the border into Germany. After staying for two months with an uncle in Berlin, he returned to Poland, this time joining the underground civil administration in Cracow. But when he proved unable to carry out an assignment to collect taxes for the rebel government, he "submitted his resignation and was eventually dismissed." Retreating again to Germany, Kubary "broke down morally," confessed his revolutionary activities to the Russian consulate in Dresden, and in return for a promise to serve the Russian government faithfully, was allowed to return to Warsaw. Arrested upon his return, he revealed "the entire organization of the insurgents" in Cracow, after which he was allowed to take up medical studies. Soon, however, he was ordered by the Russian chief of police to go to Paris to persuade an émigré friend to act as agent provocateur to entrap several prominent political refugees—a venture which he then reported to the insurgents, with the result that he was imprisoned by the Russians and marked for deportation to Siberia. However, thanks to the intervention of his mother's family in Germany—and another denunciation of his insurgent friends—he was finally allowed to return to his medical studies (Paszkowski 1969:43–44; cf. R. E. Mitchell 1971).

After four years of this double life, Kubary decided in 1868 to begin anew, and fled again to Berlin. When his uncle refused to aid him this time, he served as an apprentice in a stucco works, stayed for a time with a stonecutter in London, and then returned to Hamburg, the headquarters of the commercial and shipping firm of J.C. Godeffroy and Sons. Since the establishment of their first Pacific factor in Samoa in 1857, Godeffroy had become the dominant traders in central Polynesia, exchanging nails, tools, cotton prints, and other manufactures for copra, bêche-de-mer, and pearl shell; by the late 1860s they were expanding their influence northwestward to the Carolines (S. G. Firth 1973:5). The Godeffroy firm had scientific as well as commercial interests, and when young Kubary visited their museum of the South Seas, he was introduced by the curators to the company patriarch. Impressed by Kubary's multilingual intelligence, Godeffroy offered him a five-year contract to collect specimens in the Pacific (Paszkowski 1969:44; Spoehr 1963:70).

After a year of island-hopping across the Pacific, Kubary arrived in Palau (now Belau) in February 1871, when Maclay was in Rio de Janeiro on his way to New Guinea. Kubary landed on the island of Korror (now Oreor), the center of European influence since Captain Henry Wilson had initiated the modern contact era in 1783. From that time on Korror had taken advantage of its access to firearms to become the wealthiest and most powerful Palauan people, exercising a limited hegemony over the rest. In the early 1860s, an Englishman named Andrew Cheyne tried to establish a trading monopoly by drafting a "Constitution of Pellow" to be signed by the *ibedul* of Korror, who had begun to style himself by the English term "king." When Cheyne later tried to expand his influence by selling guns to Melekeok, the major rival of Korror, he was murdered—to which the British responded by sending military vessels to burn villages, collect indemnities, and execute the *ibedul* (Spoehr 1963:71–72; Parmentier 1987:47, 192–93).

In this context of intergroup rivalry, the then King of Korror tried to en-force on Kubary a position of privileged vassalage, making it difficult for him to travel (lest his trade goods fall into the hands of enemies) and giving him permission to do so only in return for a suitable payment. To maximize his ethnographic mobility, Kubary had "to fight the King with trickery," playing off the factional divisions within Korror, and on a larger scale, the hostilities between Korror and other Palauan groups. Far from standing above Palauan life like a god, Kubary had to struggle to win a degree of freedom of action within a complexly human network of sociopolitical obligations—which he found "a great hindrance" to his activities, "for customs and usage would not permit this and that and the other, and in turn permitted things that I did not want" (Kubary 1873:6).

Seven months after his arrival, Kubary took advantage of the overthrow of the king by an opposing faction to settle three miles away on the small volcanic island of Malakal, where Cheyne had been killed in 1866, and which the natives avoided "because they were afraid of his spirit." Having the advan-tage of linguistic intermediaries, Kubary was by this time sufficiently adept in the Palauan language to say farewell to the assembled chiefs of Korror in the following terms:

> . . . though I am not angry at Korror, your manners and customs have deeply offended me. Your behavior is false throughout, and our good nature you take for stupidity. You call us *Rupak* (chief) to our face, and *Tingeringer* (stupid, crazy) behind our backs. You pretend to be friends and cannot protect us from harm. You want my goods but are too lazy or too poor to give me anything for them. I see through you. At first I did not understand, but now I know your language and will make an end to your doings. I shall be hard as stone. The time of gifts is over. I shall give nothing free. Those who try to force themselves on me I shall treat like enemies. Powder and shot I have enough; war I do not fear. If you wish to treat me like Captain Cheyne whom you murdered, then come. I now forbid every inhabitant to land on Malakal unless he has something use-ful for me, and no canoe may approach safely at night. That part of Malakal where I live is foreign land, and all your laws and customs end there. But I wish to be just, and to him who is friendly to me I shall be friendly also.

Johann Kubary, with Belauans, in the early days of his research for J. C. Godeffroy and Sons. (From Karlheinz Graudenz with Hanns Michael Schindler, *Die deutschen Kolonien: Geschichte der deutschen Schutzgebiete in Wort, Bild und Karte* [Munich: Südwest Verlag, 1982], p. 268.)

Distributing three pounds of tobacco as a parting gift, Kubary sailed off to Malakal, where he hoped to escape further "exploitation by the chiefs" (Spoehr 1963:75; cf. Kubary 1873:6–7).

Despite his withdrawal from Korror, Kubary had still to negotiate relations with the new king, whom he regarded as a puppet of the "reactionary" chiefs, and who in various ways tried to prevent him from travelling among the traditional enemies of Korror on Babeldaob, the largest island in the archipelago. His freedom of action was greatly increased after an influenza epidemic early in 1872, which carried off all but one of the chiefs who supported the new king. Claiming a greater power than any Palauan *kalit* (spirit), Kubary vowed publicly that this man would never die. He took him into his own house, nursed him through a violent fever, and by "bloodletting, morphine, and other means" brought him back to consciousness after ten days (Kubary 1873:12–13). As a result, Kubary became the king's personal physician and took on the care of other patients; when none of them died, his influence was greatly increased, and he was able to carry out his "long cherished plan of visiting the hostile party" on Babeldaob—although not without a watchful retinue.

The next three months in the Molekojok (now Melekeok) area were extremely fruitful. Establishing a "very friendly and intimate" relationship with the *reklai* (the counterpart of the Korror *ibedul*), Kubary was able to use his speaking knowledge of the language to "hear a great deal that has long since

vanished from the memory of the degenerate inhabitants of Korror" (1873:28)
—as well as much about contemporary Palauan life. And because the local
natives were "unspoiled," he was given a great many specimens of material
culture for which he could not bargain—since the Korror people had discouraged him from bringing along trade goods. Kubary felt "more at ease in the
midst of these cannibals and poisoners"—as they had been described to him
by the Korror people—than at any time before (1873:30); he left "deeply
touched" by the tears in the eyes of the *reklai* (43).

Back in Korror the chiefs tried to force Kubary to agree never to mention
his stay among their enemies in his reports, and to destroy all the drawings
he had made among them. He refused, however, placating them with two
of his six European shirts and the promise to photograph them. On this basis,
Kubary was able to work in peace for another year, despite the fact that his
feelings toward the Korror people were extremely negative:

> My relations with the natives have remained unchanged. . . . The advantages
> which I once won from them I have maintained, and my personal safety is
> not endangered, even if the ship should delay in arriving for a long time. My
> stay is not precisely comfortable, according to our ideas, for no one would
> want to live alone in the midst of these savages, whose good behavior was
> achieved only after long struggles. The bond that unites me to the natives is
> fear and the feeling of their own weakness. Unfortunately, I did not find the
> natives of Korror to be as Wilson describes them in 1783. They were no "orna-
> ment of mankind" as far as I was concerned. They had become insolent by vir-
> tue of the murder of Cheyne, and perhaps also because of their treatment by
> greedy white speculators. (Kubary 1873:47)

Despite the various resistances he had to overcome, Kubary was able to
accomplish—in Korror as well as Molekojok—an ethnographic description of
a sort very different than Maclay pursued in New Guinea. His contract with
Godeffroy required him to spend much of his time studying the natural history of the area, and collecting geological, botanical, ornithological, and con-
chological specimens, as well as numerous items of material culture for their
museum; and he also spent time photographing racial "types." But his ethnography was less grounded in contemporary issues of racial anthropology
and more akin to modern sociocultural anthropology than Maclay's. However
inconvenient it may have seemed at the time, Kubary's involvement in the
factional and intervillage struggles of Palauan life gave him an excellent perspective on matters of political and social organization. He also devoted considerable attention to religious matters, and collected a good deal of mythic
material—in contrast to Maclay, who had argued against the missionary Chalmers that mythology could "never have the same significance" for ethnological classification as the "observation of anatomical type" (Tumarkin 1982b:

402). More than a century later, Kubary's work remains a crucial benchmark for any student of the area: at several dozen different points, a recent study of "myth, history and polity in Belau" refers to Kubary's observations, usually in agreement with him, and on a number of occasions, with extensive quotation (Parmentier 1987:61, 77, 80, 161, 163, 172–73, 175, 177, 201, inter alia).

If the bond that tied Kubary to the Palauans was founded on fear—as well as on trade goods and other forms of material and nonmaterial self-interest —it was nonetheless real. On a later trip back to Palau early in 1883, he was made an honorary chief and given "a splendid community house" as a "gesture of gratitude" for his earlier services during the influenza epidemic; and when a British warship appeared in the aftermath of an earlier punitive bombardment, he played a role in negotiating peace between the *ibedul* and the *reklai* (Paszkowski 1969:54–57; Hezel 1983:218–80). However, his bond to the Palauans was not one that impelled Kubary to adopt a systematic policy of native advocacy; on the contrary, in contrast to Maclay, Kubary was to become an aggressive participant in the processes of colonial exploitation.

Although he travelled for Godeffroy for six years after leaving Palau in 1873, Kubary's main base was the island of Ponape, where he married the part-Polynesian daughter of a Methodist missionary, and where he managed his own plantation. When a typhoon devastated Ponape in 1882, Kubary's life entered its last long phase of decline. After working briefly for museums in Tokyo and Yokohama, he returned to Palau to collect for the Leiden Museum. In 1884, he island-hopped on one of the ships of the notorious trader O'Keefe, collecting for the Berlin Ethnographic Museum. Although he had become a British subject in 1875 during a visit to Australia, a decade later he became involved in German imperial ventures under circumstances that suggest the connivance of the German government. A German warship visiting Yap brought notice of the sudden termination of Kubary's contract with the Berlin Museum on the grounds of "fraternization with the natives and extravagance in relation to them" (Paszkowski 1969:57). Stranded without means of livelihood, Kubary was compelled to accept employment as interpreter and guide on the same warship, which was in the Pacific "for the specific purpose of planting the German flag on various islands of the Carolines." When this venture brought Germany and Spain to the brink of war, a settlement mediated by the pope recognized Spain's hitherto tenuous claim (Sentinella 1975: 324; Hezel 1983). By that time, however, Kubary had settled in the territories acquired by Bismarck the previous year.

For a year and a half, Kubary was in charge of a plantation in New Britain belonging to the firm of Hernsheim. Early in 1887, however, his odyssey of decline brought him to the very area where the departing Maclay had warned the natives about men with hair and clothing like his own who might come to exploit them. Entering the employment of the *Neu Guinea Kompanie* as manager of the station at Konstantinhafen on Astrolabe Bay, Kubary became the primary agent of an aggressive policy of land acquisition. Over the next two years, he is reported to have "bought" virtually the entire coast of Astrolabe Bay "in the most cavalier manner, judged even by the standards which the New Guinea Company set itself." Sailing along the coast noting river mouths and prominent features, Kubary would dispense a few trade goods and then post "a sheet of paper on a coconut palm to conclude the 'sale'" —with the full knowledge that "he had not concluded straightforward purchases of land" (Hempenstall 1987:167–68; S. G. Firth 1982:25–27, 83; Sack 1973:138–40).

Land, however, would not work itself, and the labor problem plagued the *Neu Guinea Kompanie* throughout its short, often violent, and unprofitable history—at "a cost of human suffering and death on a scale unknown on the British side of the island" (S. G. Firth 1982:43; cf. 1972 and Moses 1977). Because local native labor disappeared into the bush, the *Kompanie* had to recruit natives from the islands, and eventually turned to Chinese coolies. Even before Kubary arrived, the importation of laborers had provoked charges of "slavery" by an anticolonialist deputy in the Reichstag: "it has been confirmed to me by the well-known explorer, Baron von Miclucho-Maclay, that on German plantations in New Guinea labourers are employed by force" (quoted in Bade 1977:330). Once on the scene, Kubary himself became involved in recruiting, bringing back seventy-one laborers from New Britain in January 1888—twenty-eight of whom must have died during their service, according to overall mortality figures of the period (Paszkowski 1969:59; S. G. Firth 1972:375).

In addition to his land acquisition and labor recruiting, Kubary was a plantation manager. His daughter later recalled him being in charge of "big plantations and hundreds of labourers," to whom he was "severe," but "just" (Paszkowski 1969:58); company reports at the time described "Herr Kubary" as "energetic" (Sack & Clark 1979:6). Glossed in terms of the *Kompanie's* disciplinary regulations, this would have implied the supervision of floggings, which in practice were often much more severe than the statutory limitation of ten strokes a week (S. G. Firth 1982:29). According to one account (Spoehr 1963:95), Kubary took to drink, and led "a harassed vagabond existence." Meanwhile the natives of Astrolabe Bay, experiencing the terrible fulfillment of Maclay's last warning, withdrew (too late) into sullen noncooperation, refusing to work on plantations, rejecting the efforts of missionaries, and organizing several abortive rebellions.

By 1892, Kubary's own health was broken. Advised by a doctor that he must return to Europe or "choose a grave in New Guinea," he took his wife and daughter with him to Germany. He was unable, however, to find employment, and had to sell his collections for a pittance; within months, he was back for another stint in Kaiser Wilhelmsland. After the "dissolution" of his contract in 1895, he negotiated with the Spanish authorities in Manila to reclaim his plantation on Ponape—only to discover when he arrived there the following summer that it had been again devastated, this time by a native revolt. Within a few weeks, he was found lying dead upon the grave of his only son—victim of assassination, heart attack, or suicide in a fit of depression (Spoehr 1963:97; Paszkowski 1969:62).

In 1898, a committee of scientists and men with colonial interests was formed in Berlin to raise money to erect a small monument on Ponape to "the ethnographer who penetrated with deep understanding into the mentality and customs of the native population" (Paszkowski 1969:64). Eight years later, when Kubary's grave was opened, it was empty—the body having apparently been removed by native friends to a sacred graveyard.

It is said that during his New Guinea years Kubary boasted he was "the Lord God of Astrolabe Bay" (Sentinella 1975:327, 329). Recalling his youthful period of moral breakdown and political duplicity—and the moral schizophrenia endemic in so many colonial situations—it is not surprising that he should eventually descend into a Kurtzian darkness unrelieved by utopian visions, or that, having witnessed there "the horror," he might in the end have taken his own life. What cuts across the grain of mythical anthropological expectations is that such a man could also have been a fine ethnographer.

Dr. Malinowski's Less-Civilized Colored Brethren: "Why Does a Boy Sign On?"

Bronislaw Malinowski was born in Cracow in 1884, the year in which eastern New Guinea was partitioned by the Germans and the British, and close to a century since Poland had been partitioned among the Germans, the Austrians, and the Russians. A decade had passed since Maclay and Kubary had accomplished their major ethnographic work; twenty years, since the revolutionary moment in which their careers had taken the turn that led toward exile, exoticism, and ethnography. If Malinowski's career took a similar turn, it had a different starting point, and went on to a very different conclusion. Beginning in the academic situation of Hapsburg Poland, passing through the colonial situation of Australian New Guinea, it ended in the academic situation of late imperial London.[4]

4. In contrast to such largely forgotten figures as Maclay and Kubary (for whom a few paragraphs may offer the illusion of biography), Malinowski occupies a very large space in the history of anthropology; the secondary literature and the primary sources are extensive. Although the treatment accorded him here considerably outweighs that of the two other figures in what was

Malinowski's father exemplified a characteristic career pattern in mid-nineteenth-century Galicia, where—in contrast to the other two occupied areas of Poland—the Austrians had relaxed their earlier Germanizing efforts, and a more liberal administrative policy facilitated a flowering of Polish culture. During the same period, social changes in the countryside impelled the scions of the petty nobility into urban intellectual occupations, often of relatively high status and influence. In this social process, Lucjan Malinowski, after taking a Ph.D. at Leipzig, became Professor of Slavonic Philology at the Jagiellonian University of Cracow, where a new, modernizing nationalism found an outlet in linguistic, historical, philosophical, and scientific studies rather than in revolutionary political activity. A member of the "exclusive clan" of a great "university aristocracy," he was recognized as "the founder of Polish dialectology" (Brooks 1985). Although this "stern and distant" father died when his only son was fourteen, the younger Malinowski was a product of this academic intellectual milieu (Kubica 1988:88). The family lived in an apartment in the Academic Dormitory, which Malinowski's mother apparently had charge of after her husband's death. When ill-health forced her son's withdrawal from the King Jan Sobieski gymnasium, she supervised his education at home and during several recuperative trips to the Mediterranean, Northern Africa, and the Canary Islands. In 1902 he entered his late father's university, where he studied physics and philosophy.

Although there has been some debate as to the relative importance of "the second positivism" and "modernism" (or, in one version, "the second romanticism") in Malinowki's intellectual formation (Flis 1988; Jerschina 1988; Paluch 1981; Strenski 1982), there is no doubt that he was affected by both. His philosophy professors were influenced by Machian positivism, and his doctoral dissertation was a friendly critique of Mach's principle of "economy of thought" (1908). In contrast, his summers were spent at Zakopane in the Tatras mountains, where his circle of intimate friends included several aspiring artists, novelists, and philosophers—one of whom, Staś Witkiewicz, was to become a major Polish cultural figure as a painter, dramatist, and writer (Gerould 1981). Theirs, however, was more a cultural than a political radicalism, oriented beyond the modernism of the Young Poland movement to that of turn-of-the-century Vienna and western Europe generally. When Malinowski broke with Staś in 1914, he marked the rupture by reference to two heroic icons of European modernism: "Nietzsche breaking with Wagner" (1967:34). Malinowski had in fact been profoundly influenced by Nietzsche, whose *Birth of Tragedy*

---

originally conceived as a triptych, it is, in relation to the material available on Malinowski, highly selective—from the particular comparative interpretive perspective of the present essay (cf. Stocking 1983, 1986b, and in process; a recent listing of other relevant materials may be found in Ellen et al. 1988).

was the subject of his first serious philosophical essay in 1904 (Thornton n.d.).

One of two manifestly "anthropological" references in Malinowski's doctoral dissertation was Nietzschean in a more disturbing sense. In arguing for the "objective" validity of scientific laws, Malinowski chose a practical criterion: "even if in the world only one normal man remained, and everyone else lost the ability to give judgments which can be regarded as normal and logical, then even this one man would not have to despair of the values, both material and scientific, of the achievements of mankind," since their "enormous practical importance" would "allow him to destroy his adversaries outright": "the relation of the white man to his less civilized colored brethren illustrates this sadly and emphatically" (1908:56–57). Knowledge and power— the laws of science and the Gatling gun—in the hands of a "normal" individual (male, white, European, and civilized)—thus confirmed and sustained each other, sadly but emphatically.

But this insistence on the objective validity of European science and civilization should not drown out an elegiac undertone of empathic identification. Malinowski may have been more positivist than Staś, but his several preadolescent experiences at the cultural margins of Europe had inspired also a romantic fascination with the culturally exotic. Given his father's interest in Slavic linguistics and folklore, and his own social position in a subjugated nation, which made him sharply aware of the variations of cultural belief and behavior in different social strata, it is not surprising that Malinowski should have turned from physics to anthropology—although he himself later attributed his "enslavement" to anthropology to the reading of Frazer's *Golden Bough* when ill-health enforced a respite from physics (1926a:94; Kubica 1988:95).

Upon completing his university studies in 1906, Malinowski spent two further years in the Canary Islands, where he found social relationships "extremely primitive and Spanish"—"a hundred years behind in respect of culture" (BM/ S. Pawlicki 1/4/07, in Ellen et al. 1988:203). After returning to Poland to receive his doctoral degree, he followed in his father's footsteps to Leipzig, where he studied *Völkerpsychologie* with Wilhelm Wundt; he also attended the lectures of Karl Bücher, an economist who had published a book on the nature of work among civilized and savage peoples. In Leipzig he began an affair with a South African pianist, whom he followed to London in 1910, with fellowship support from the University of Cracow—a venture he justified in terms that Frazer might have appreciated: "for there [i.e., England], it seems to me, culture has reached its highest standard" (BM/ S. Pawlicki 1/5/10, in Ellen et al. 1988:204; Wayne 1985:532).

In England, Malinowski studied sociology and anthropology at the London School of Economics, where formal instruction in ethnology had recently been initiated by members of the new fieldwork-oriented "Cambridge School." Malinowski, in short, entered anthropology when two interrelated transformative processes—academicization and ethnographicization—were already underway. His first several years were spent attending the seminars and lectures of Edward Westermarck and Charles Seligman, and in the British Museum researching a library monograph on the family among Australian Aborigines. But it was from the beginning hoped, if not expected, that he would do what Alfred Haddon called an "intensive study of a restricted area"—following in Seligman's recent footsteps to the Sudan, or among the peasants of the Polish countryside, or, as it was in fact to turn out, along the southern coast of New Guinea, where the Cambridge School had won its reputation with Haddon's Torres Straits Expedition in 1898, and to which Seligman had returned in 1904 (cf. Stocking 1983, 1986b).

But if Malinowski's anthropological situation was from the beginning academic, it was also colonial. When the British Association for the Advancement of Science went to Australia in 1914 for one of its periodic meetings in a white settler colony, Malinowski got free passage as secretary to R. R. Marett, the Recorder of the anthropological section (Mulvaney 1989). Although he carried with him the promise of scholarship support from the London School of Economics and a letter from its Director commending him as an "investigator of exceptional promise and ability," the outbreak of war while he was at sea meant that he disembarked in Australia as a somewhat impecunious "enemy alien," whose personal funds back in Austrian Poland were no longer accessible to him. For the entire period of his fieldwork during the next four years, he was therefore dependent upon the officials in charge of Australian colonial affairs, not only for permission to enter those areas of New Guinea under Australian rule since 1906 or then being taken over from Germany, but also for financial support, and even for his own continued freedom of movement in Australia. This dependency was mediated by members of the Australian scientific community, one of whom intervened to save Malinowski from incarceration in a "Concentration Camp" for enemy aliens when he neglected to get a pass for a trip from Melbourne to Adelaide (Laracy 1976:265). Throughout his fieldwork years, Malinowski's status was the subject of continual negotiations with Atlee Hunt, the Secretary of the Australian Department of External Affairs, and Hubert Murray, the Lieutenant-Governor of Papua from 1908 to 1940 (cf. Young 1984).

Between them, these two men represent a considerable portion of the historical experience that helped to define the colonial situation of Malinowski's ethnography. Educated for the law in Sydney, Hunt became Secretary of the Federal League of Australasia in the late 1890s, and was an insider in the campaign for united commonwealth status within the British empire. As permanent head of the new federal Department of External Affairs, he was closely involved in the final legislative implementation of the "White Australia" policy. He played an important role in drafting both the racialist Immigration

Restriction Bill of 1901 and the Pacific Island Labourers' Act of 1902, which provided for the termination of the importation of "kanaka" laborers by 1904 and for the deportation of any who on December 31, 1906, still remained on Queensland plantations (Parnaby 1964:196–97; Willard 1923; London 1970). When it came to European immigrants into Pacific Islands, however, Hunt was a consistent supporter of the economic interests of white settlers in Papua, of whom there were about twelve hundred in 1914 (Rowley 1958:287–91; Young 1984:3).

As such, Hunt was sometimes at odds with Murray, who as both Lieutenant Governor and Chief Justice of a neglected and underfunded area had a freer reign than the normal colonial governor (Mair 1948:11; Legge 1956: 227–28; West 1968:104–9). Son of a rich Australian pastoralist fallen on hard times, Murray was educated at Oxford (where his younger brother Gilbert became Regius Professor of Greek) and at the Inns of Court. Turning away from white settler society to assimilate the "effortless superiority" of the British ruling class (West 1970:x–xi), Murray was to be known as the archetype of a paternalistic proconsul. Benevolent but authoritarian, he saw "the native problem" as a matter of both "preserving the Papuan" and "raising him eventually to the highest civilisation of which he is capable" (1912:360).

In achieving these ends, Murray opposed the punitive raids associated with the name of Sir William MacGregor, the first British administrator after the annexation in 1884, and with the early-twentieth-century German regime to the north—which had "a reputation for brutality, especially in the unctuous eyes of Papua's Australian administrators." But the protectionist policy of the "Murray System" was in many respects continuous with that of MacGregor, and much more actively interventionist in native life than the Germans, who were "not overly concerned with the indigenes' longterm welfare" (Wolfers 1972:88–89; Joyce 1971b:130). The Australian Papuan administration sought to preserve traditional village life (and to keep it rigidly segregated from that of the few European urban enclaves); but it also intervened to change it in substantial ways. Village constables, selected by the resident magistrates without regard for traditional leadership, were expected not only to keep the peace and to report cases of venereal disease but to help enforce regulations against keeping the dead inside the village, and against lying or using threatening language or engaging in sorcery—or, positively, requiring the cleaning of the village and the planting of coconuts. More active developmentalists may have seen Murray as "pampering" and "coddling" the natives, but he did not discourage Papuans from "signing on"—though the Native Labour Ordinance required local magistrates to supervise the process. The native "chewing betelnut in his village" might be "more picturesque" than the same native "working in a plantation," but it was "to the advantage of the Papuan to learn to work," and the "the best available schools" were the plantation and the mining field (Murray 1912:362; Rowley 1966).

Murray was not without a certain sophistication in both evolutionary and postevolutionary anthropology: he had read Tylor and Maine, and works by members of the Torres Straits Expedition; he was a friend of Seligman's, and later hired F. E. Williams as "government anthropologist." But he was dubious of diffusionist and later of functionalist theory, and attributed to anthropologists a preservationist bias against social change. And though he respected Malinowski's ability, he considered him a German and disliked him personally (West 1968:211–18). Hunt, in contrast, was part of the same gentlemanly community in Melbourne that included Baldwin Spencer and the other Australian scientific men who had hosted the British Association and were now proponents of Malinowski's research plans. Although Murray somewhat ungraciously supported Malinowski's initial request for funds, it was Hunt who became his advocate, writing letters of introduction, securing free travel passes, arranging grants, defending him against charges of pro-German sympathies, facilitating his entry into and helping to extend his stay in the areas of his ethnographic research (Young 1984:5; Laracy 1976).

"Taking leave of civilization," Malinowski arrived in Port Moresby on September 12, 1914 (1967:5). After making the appropriate visit to Government House, he was introduced to Ahuia Ova, an ardent Christian convert (and advocate of "pacifying") who had served so well as Village Constable that he became Central Court Interpreter for Murray—and who a decade previously had served also as Seligman's primary informant (1967:9; Williams 1939; Young 1984:8). Malinowski's project was in fact conceived as an intensive study of a critical ethnological boundary area in Seligman's prior survey work, and for a month he did a kind of linguistic and ethnographic cramming, "borrowing" Ahuia for periods at the Central Court, and for more extended visits to his nearby village—save for a few days of enforced idleness when Ahuia was busy at the trial of a European who had "hung up a native for five hours" (1967:17; Seligman 1910; cf. Stocking 1983:95–96).

On October 13, Malinowski set off on the steam launch *Wakefield*, and headed for the island of Mailu, two hundred miles down the southeast coast, on which the London Missionary Society had maintained a station since 1894. His "travelling companions" included several stereotypical figures of the Melanesian colonial situation: a "brutal" German captain, who was "continually abusing and bullying the Papuans"; the local planter Alfred Greenaway, an English Quaker of working-class background, from whom Malinowski was to get quite useful ethnographic information; and Mailu's resident aristocratic vagabond, "Dirty Dick" De Moleyns, the drunkard son of a Protestant Irish lord. De Moleyns was a "rogue" but a "noble thoroughbred," who though "cultured" lived a "completely uncivilized" life in "extraordinary filth" in a "house without walls," where Malinowski was to find occasional "lubrication" and camaraderie in the weeks to come (1967:25, 37, 40). Also on the *Wakefield*—though unmentioned as a travelling companion—was Igua Pipi, fluent in the

lingua franca Motu, who was to serve as chief factotum in Malinowski's retinue of several native "boys." Once on Mailu, Malinowski became the paying
guest of Reverend W. J. Saville, who with his wife had served on Mailu since
1900, and who in 1912 had published "A Grammar of the Mailu Language"
in the *Journal of the Royal Anthropological Institute*. It was from Saville's mission
house that each day during the next few weeks Malinowski "went to the village"—accompanied on the first occasion by a native policeman.

In retrospect it seems clear that Saville became the negative archetypal focal
point of Malinowski's ambivalent feelings about the "civilizing" mission of colonialism. Initially quite dependent on him, Malinowski was repelled by Saville's
"underhanded dealings" with the Resident Magistrate of the region and by
his "persecution of people unfriendly to the mission." Had he been aware of
Saville's ten commandments for dealing with natives ("5. Never *touch* a native, unless to shake hands or thrash him"; "7. Never let a native see you believe his word right away, he never speaks the truth"), Malinowski might have
been even more "disgusted" than he was by Saville's attitude of white superiority (Young 1988:44). In the beginning, he was willing to make a slight
allowance for the fact that Saville played cricket with the natives and treated
them "with a fair amount of decency and liberality"—were he a German, "he
would doubtless be downright loathsome." But over the first few weeks Malinowski's "hatred for missionaries" rapidly increased, and he began to ponder
"a really effective anti-mission campaign" (1967:16, 25, 31, 37, 41):

> these people destroy the natives' joy in life; they destroy their psychological *raison
> d'être*. And what they give in return is completely beyond the savages. They
> struggle consistently and ruthlessly against everything old and create new needs,
> both material and moral. No question but that they do harm—I want to discuss
> this matter with Armit [the Resident Magistrate] and Murray. If possible also
> with the Royal Commission.

With its empathy for a threatened "savage" life, its ethnocentric presumption
about the limits of "savage" capacity, its implicitly functionalist preservationism, and its ultimate appeal to the good intentions of established colonial
authority, the passage suggests a great deal about Malinowski's characteristic
response to the colonial situation in which his anthropological orientation
matured.

More immediately, Malinowski began to see Saville as a distinct impedi-
ment to effective ethnographic work—and as a kind of antimodel to the emerging archetype of "the Ethnographer" (cf. Stocking 1983; Payne 1981).[5] Still

5. In 1922, Saville in fact attended Malinowski's lectures at the London School of Economics; in 1926, Malinowski wrote an introduction, which has been described as "sincerely com-
plimentary and faintly patronizing" to Saville's *In Unknown New Guinea*. Without referring to
it once, Saville's book closely paralleled the structure and content of Malinowski's monograph—

an ethnographic novice, Malinowski carried into the field the fourth edition of *Notes and Queries on Anthropology*, and his published report on Mailu reflected quite clearly its topically interrogative categories (Young 1988). But *Notes and Queries* also contained Rivers' "General Account of Method," in which a much more "Malinowskian" fieldwork style was clearly enunciated (1912; cf. Stocking 1983:89–93); and there are various passages both in the published Mailu ethnography and in Malinowski's diary and correspondence which indicate that his own ethnographic experience was leading along the same path toward a more participatory observational style. Foreshadowed even before he left Port Moresby ("I have rather little to do with the savages on the spot, do not observe them enough"), this process was linked to his dissociation from Saville. After staying several nights in a *dubu* or men's house during his return from a tour of the southeastern coast of Papua in December, Malinowski clearly sensed the ethnographic potential of more direct involvement, and arrived on Mailu resolved that he "must begin a new existence" (1967:49; cf. Stocking 1983:95–97).

That resolve was facilitated by the fact that Saville was absent from the island for an extended period. In a move presaging his later call for anthropologists to come down from the verandah into the open air (1926a:146–47), Malinowski left the Savilles' house and took up residence in a previously abandoned mission house, where Igua Pipi and several Mailu men were wont to gather in the evening, talking in Motu—which Malinowski had quickly mastered (though not, apparently, the Mailu language itself). On one occasion Malinowski was left for a week with "absolutely nobody" to work with when he refused to pay the £2 the Mailu demanded to allow him to accompany them on a trading expedition (1967:62)—not out of methodological principle (for he systematically used tobacco to purchase cooperation)—but because he thought the price exorbitant. He was able, however, to accompany a second briefer expedition, and on the whole, regarded the weeks of Saville's absence as by far his most productive period (cf. Stocking 1983).

Reflecting on it later, Malinowski suggested that work done "while living quite alone among the natives" was "incomparably more intensive than work done from white men's settlements, or even in any white man's company" (1915:109). Explaining why it was that he had been able to elicit information about sorcery but not about "eschatological beliefs," Malinowski suggested almost incidentally the general principle of a more participant ethnographic

---

although it has been described as "more reliable" on "matters of language," and "richer in quotidian detail" (Young 1988; 49). And just as Saville's attitude to natives seems to have "mellowed" somewhat, so also did Malinowski's toward missionaries: in the later 1920s, he cooperated with the missionary J. H. Oldham in a campaign to win research funds from the Rockefeller Foundation for the International African Institute (see below; cf. Stocking 1985).

method: "My experience is that direct questioning of the natives about a custom or belief never discloses their attitude of mind as thoroughly as the discussion of facts connected with the direct observation of a custom, or with
a concrete occurrence, in which both parties are materially concerned" (275).
Judging from other passages, it is evident that in practice that mutual concern was usually somewhat asymmetrical. In one instance it involved pretending to be worried about protecting himself from ghosts (273); quite often it
involved payment in tobacco, sometimes offered as bribery to test the strength
of native belief in a taboo (185); more generally, it simply involved "witnessing
an occurrence or seeing a thing, and subsequently (or previously) discussing
it with the natives" (109). But if it had in many respects been foreshadowed
programmatically in Rivers' "General Account" (which in turn probably reflected Rivers' prior collaboration with A. M. Hocart), Malinowski's ethnographic experience in Mailu was an important stage in the emergence of the
ethnographic style for which he was later to provide a kind of mythic charter
(cf. Stocking 1983).

The experiential and contextual reality of Malinowski's evolving ethnographic situation was, however, somewhat imperfectly manifest in the
ethnography he wrote after returning to Australia at the end of February 1915.
One must turn to his Mailu diary to find mention of the Kurtzian moment
when his "feelings toward the natives" were "decidedly tending to 'Exterminate
the brutes'," or of "the many instances in which I acted unfairly and stupidly"
(1967:69), or of the pleasure of "having a crowd of boys to serve you"—which
in Igua Pipi's case involved massaging him while telling stories "about mur-
ders of white men, as well as his fears about what he would do if I died in
that way!" (40, 73).

This attitudinal elision—quite understandable in terms of the "scientific"
ethnography Malinowski sought to practice—is paralleled by the very limited
glimpses Malinowski provided of his "colonial situation." That situation is
hinted in his vain attempt to "exert a certain pressure through the village constable" when six sticks of tobacco to each of the actors failed to get them to
perform a ceremony a second time in full daylight so that he could photograph it (1915:300). More positively, from a postcolonial perspective, it is evident in his deliberate omission of certain passages in a magical incantation,
lest they fall into the hands of a white man "eager to put down superstitions"
and "unscrupulous enough to divulge the charm among the natives"—thereby
destroying its efficacy (282). At a more general methodological level, it is evident in his encouraging informants to "compare native social rules with the
introduced European system of administering justice" in order to determine
if there was "any counterpart in native ideas" to the European distinction between civil and criminal law (194).

As that passage suggests, however, Malinowski's ethnographic purpose—

like that of most if not all of his anthropological contemporaries, including anti-evolutionary diffusionists like Franz Boas—was to get behind the circumstances of European contact, in order to reveal the essential ethnic characteristics of the particular native group. Such ethnicity was not presumed to be pristine, and by 1915 not all anthropologists would have generalized it as "savage"—as Malinowski continued to do, if only in the titles of his books, until 1930. But if it was not pristine, it was definitely prior. In Malinowski's case, what was initially at issue were the characteristics that would enable him to solve a particular "ethnological" problem: to clarify ethnic relationships in an area of New Guinea about which Seligman had felt "very little is known" (Seligman 1910:24; cf. Malinowski 1915:106). If his published monograph contained little further reference to what in the introduction was called "the Mailu problem," it is nevertheless the case that it was those underlying precontact ethnic characteristics and relationships that he sought to reconstitute.

Insofar as Malinowski's description departs from the sequence of categories of *Notes and Queries*, it is largely in the total omission of physical anthropological data and the relegation of technology to incidental treatment—both of which might have followed from Rivers' emerging conception of the nature of "intensive study"—as well as in the extensive separate consideration of "Economics." It has been suggested that Malinowski's emphasis on "land tenure and native attitudes to 'work'" reflected the fact that these "were all contentious topics in the colonial situation of 1914"—issues sparking "heated arguments," "ideological obfuscations," and "blatant racial bigotry" in the "after-dinner conversation on the planters' and mission house verandahs" (Young 1988:34). Although most of the conversations mentioned in Malinowski's diary in fact relate to ethnographic topics, some of his comments on Saville do sustain this interpretation. At one point Malinowski specifically discussed "native labor" with the inspector of native affairs in Port Moresby, and he later described himself as "obsessed by the thought of some ethnological government post in N. G."—which might well have pushed him in the same direction (1967:13, 64).

But Malinowski's interest in economic problems is also quite consistent with the prior trajectory of his intellectual interests, which—while no doubt subject to ideological conditioning of a more general sort—had turned to economic issues well before he entered the Melanesian colonial situation, or even into anthropology. Analogically foreshadowed in his doctoral dissertation on "the economy of thought," such concerns would have been a central topic of his study under Bücher. They were explicitly the topic of one of his very first anthropological publications, in which (frequently citing Bücher) Malinowski treated the Australian Intichiuma ceremonies as a first step in the "training of man in economic activity" in a "civilized" style—that is, foresighted, planned, organized, regular, continuous, and repetitive (1912:107).

But however his interest was motivated, Malinowski did make a point of mentioning to Atlee Hunt his emphasis on "the economic and sociological aspects of native life" and (though his ethnography did not show it) on "the process of adaptation of the natives to their new conditions" (Young 1988:12). Hunt was duly impressed with the "class of investigation which he has been conducting," which by emphasizing "the mental attitudes and peculiar customs of the people" rather than "measurements of bodies, etc.," was one "likely to be of much use to the Government in our dealing with natives." He quickly saw to it that Malinowski was funded for a second round of fieldwork in New Guinea (Laracy 1976:265–66).

Although Seligman wanted him to go southeast to Rossel Island to examine another ethnic boundary region (cf. Stocking 1983:97), Malinowski decided instead to go to the Mambare district on the northern coast of Papua, the site of an earlier gold rush, where a series of prophetic cults were now causing government concern (Young 1984:13). In the event, however, Malinowski never arrived at Mambare, and the site of his major fieldwork seems clearly to have been somewhat adventitiously determined, without apparent regard for its administrative relevance. On his way to Mambare in June 1915, Malinowski stopped in the Trobriands, "the leaders of the whole material and artistic culture of this end [of New Guinea]," in order "to get an idea of what is going on among them" and to seek the help of the medical officer and Resident Magistrate, R. L. Bellamy, in securing some museum specimens before Bellamy left to serve in the European war (Young 1984:15–17). Bellamy was an enthusiastically paternalistic administrator, who after ten years in the Trobriands had finally got the natives to line the paths of Kiriwina with 120,000 coconut trees by imposing stiff penalties for failure to do so. With a jail, a hospital, twelve white residents, and a thriving pearl industry in its lagoon, Kiriwina (the largest Trobriand island) was one of the "best governed and most 'civilized' places" in the region (Young 1984:16; cf. Black 1957).

It was also a lushly idyllic tropical island, little touched by the labor trade (Austen 1945:57; Julius 1960:5), whose chiefly aristocracies and erotic dances had already begun to sustain a certain popular image – "part noble savage, part licentious sybarite" (Young 1984:16). Malinowski was clearly captivated, and although for a time he kept assuring Seligman and Hunt that his stay was only temporary, by the end of September he had decided to remain, despite the fact that Seligman had already done some work there: "I am getting such damned good stuff here though, that you will forgive me anything I hope" (BMP: BM/CGS 9/24/15). In the event, Malinowski remained in the Trobriands for eight months; and after a year in Australia, during which he made an initial analysis of his data, he returned for another ten months – Hunt having interceded with the reluctant Murray to extend an original six-month permit (Young 1984:22).

In reassuring Malinowski that territorial "encroachment" was no issue, Seligman pushed him to the study of land tenure, which Malinowski had already told Hunt was one of several topics of "some practical interest" to which he was giving "special attention" (Young 1984:18). Land tenure was of course encompassed in the "whole system of 'ceremonial gardens,'" which Malinowski noted to Seligman as one of several areas of research remaining to be pursued; however, at this point Malinowski approached the system as an "agricultural cult" (in the Frazerian sense). In addition, he planned to focus on the reincarnation "beliefs and ceremonies about the spirits [called] Balóm," the annual harvest feast called Mila Mala, and the "'trading ring' called Kula." With the significant addition of Trobriand sexual practices (which were in fact implicated in the problem of reincarnation), these were to be the topics of his major ethnographic works (BMP: BM/CGS 7/30/15). But while all these topics were certainly matters of current native practice and belief, Malinowski approached them in terms that had little direct relation to problems of present colonial administrative practice. Although he quickly moved beyond the ethnic boundary issues he inherited from Seligman, his ethnographies were still conceived as representations of a specific, precontact cultural system—universalized, for more general audiences, as that of "savages" generally.[6] His magnum opus, *Coral Gardens and Their Magic*—published twenty years later, when the category "savage" had been largely excluded from the discourse of professional anthropology—was still presented as a study of "the essential Trobriander," exemplifying "the ways and manners of Oceania as it flourished for ages, unknown and untouched by Europeans" (1935:I, xix).[7]

According to the long, conventional, mythistoric account of British anthropology, it was Malinowski's Trobriand fieldwork that revolutionized ethnography. Before then, the "standard methods of ethnographic research"—in which the native was a specimen to be measured, photographed, and interviewed—"were such that the social superiority of the investigator was constantly emphasized." But by pitching his tent in the middle of the village, learning the language in its colloquial form, and observing native life directly "throughout the 24 hours of an ordinary working day"—something "no European had ever done"—Malinowski "changed all this." Sustained by the high estimate of his ethnographic work (long after his theoretical contributions had been called into question), this account still served in 1965 as preface to the reprint edition of *Coral Gardens* (Leach 1965:viii–ix).

6. Although Malinowski on one early occasion put this term into quotation marks, he continued to use it in the titles of his books down to the end of the 1920s (1915:311; cf. Malinowski 1929a).

7. By this time Malinowski (in a context that will be noted briefly below) had begun to advocate the study of "culture change" under the influence of European civilization; however, such phenomena were only incidentally mentioned in *Coral Gardens* (cf. I:479–81, in appendix 2, "Confessions of Ignorance and Failure").

Within two years Malinowski's ethnographic heirs were shaken by the striking contrast between the intimate revelations of his field diaries and the methodological injunctions of the first chapter of *Argonauts* (1967; 1922b; cf. R. Firth 1989). But if one makes a certain allowance for the exhortatory and prescriptive character of that mythic charter, it does not now seem that Malinowski grossly misrepresented his ethnographic practice. His "aloneness" among the Trobrianders was relative rather than "absolute": the pearl traders Billy Hancock and Rafael Brudo were never more than a few miles away from Omarakana, where Malinowski pitched his tent in the center of the village. But if his "Capuan days" with fellow Europeans and his bouts of novel reading were rather more frequent than methodological prescription would later imply, there is little doubt that his fieldwork method was in general consistent with that which Rivers (his methodological "patron saint") had called for in 1912, and which Malinowski himself had already begun to implement in Mailu (cf. Stocking 1983).

However, if the methodological contrast is probably more apparent than real, the attitudinal contrast is undeniable: there is nothing in *Argonauts* that prepares us for all those aggressive outbursts against Trobrianders. Nor were the frequent references to "niggers" simply an accident of mistranslation from the Polish "nigrami," as some defensive ethnographic heirs have suggested (Leach 1980); Malinowski also used the word in letters composed entirely in English (Stocking 1983:102). This, too, is at least in part a reflection of his colonial situation; absent from the Mailu diary, the epithet appears only after Malinowski had been in the area long enough to pick up its racialist vocabulary. But without minimizing the psychological and ideological significance of the Kurtzian passages in the diary, it would be a mistake on this basis simply to dismiss Malinowski "as an anthropologist who hates the natives" (Hsu 1979:521).

To begin with, one must keep in mind that the surviving Trobriand diary (which covers only his second trip there) was not so much a chronicle of ethnographic work as an account of the central psychological drama of his life, and an attempt to locate what he called "the mainsprings of my life." That drama was a tale of oedipal conflict, of simultaneous erotic involvement with two women (both the daughters of eminent Australian scientists), and of unresolved national identity, symbolized by his mother back in Poland—the news of whose death in Poland brought the diary to a sudden conclusion, in which his commitment to his future wife was affirmed. Although some of his outbursts against the Trobrianders are manifestly expressions of ethnographic frustration, many of them occur in close relation to this psychological plot of sexual and cultural longing and ambivalence, and may perhaps be interpreted as displaced expressions of the frustrations implicated in it (cf. Stocking 1968, 1983, 1986b).

Insofar as the diary casts light on his ethnographic practice, one must balance these outbursts against less dramatic quotidian passages, as well as the evidence of the ethnographies themselves. Malinowski had a somewhat confrontational fieldwork style, and was perfectly willing to express disbelief in what the Trobrianders took for granted—and in at least one instance when he fixed upon a mistaken interpretation, the natives were unwilling "to contradict the doctor" (Stocking 1977). On the whole, however, it would seem that Malinowski's methodological insistence on the importance of "personal friendships" to "encourage spontaneous confidences and the repetition of intimate gossip" was realized in relationships which, although temporary, differentiated, asymmetrical, and instrumental (like the vast majority of ethnographic relations since then), were nonetheless characterized by a certain degree of positive affect.

As a European, he was set—and set himself—somewhat apart, and took for granted many of the perquisites of colonial power. He had momentary exultations of petty lordship ("delightful feeling that now I alone am the master of this village with my 'boys'" [1967:235]), cast sometimes as a foreshadowing of a later claim to ethnographic authority ("Feeling of ownership: it is I who will describe them or create them" [140]). When "irritated" by the natives, he was several times moved to exercise the ultimate colonial prerogative of direct physical aggression. Repressing that impulse in the case of one of his "boys"—"whom I could willingly beat to death"—he felt he could "understand all the *German and Belgian colonial atrocities*" (279); another time the same servant so "enraged" him that Malinowski in fact "punched him in the jaw once or twice" (250). But if on occasion Malinowski behaved in a manner consistent with Saville's "fifth commandment" of race relations, his status and relation to the natives were quite distinct from those of a missionary or a resident magistrate, and in general he seems to have made it a point to set himself apart from these more direct embodiments of European power. During the month or so he overlapped with Bellamy before the magistrate departed for the European war, they had a falling out—an event Malinowski was later to archetypify, by urging students to "pick a fight" with the district officer as a means of gaining rapport with the groups they were studying. And Bellamy is in fact reported later to have complained that in his absence at the front Malinowski had "undone" much of the work of his ten years in the Trobriands (Black 1957:279). How to gloss that undoing is of course problematic, but it probably referred to the subversion of "progressive" cultural innovations and the violation of the still fairly recently established etiquette of race relations (cf. Nelson 1969).

At a different level from that of everyday ethnographic and race relations, one must take seriously also those passages in the diary which suggest a more systematically sympathetic attitudinal/ideological posture. When in November 1917 Malinowski formulated the "deepest essence" of his ethnographic endeavor, it was in terms similar to those which motivated his own self-analysis. Just as he strove to watch himself "right down to the deepest instincts," so did he seek to discover the native's "main passions, the motives for his conduct, his aims . . . his essential deepest ways of thinking." At that level, "we are confronted with our own problems: What is essential in ourselves?" (1967: 119, 181). At that level, Malinowski clearly felt that the "primitive" Trobriand "savages" who, in particular passional contexts, he berated as "niggers" shared the same "essential" human mental makeup as the ethnographer who would later recreate them.

At this point, however, it is clear that Malinowski still thought of this shared mental makeup in rather traditional evolutionary terms. Between "aims" and "deepest ways of thinking" in the diary passage just cited, there was in fact a starkly disjunctive parenthesis: "(Why does a boy 'sign on'? Is every boy, after some time, ready to 'sign off'?)" (1967:119). Recalling Malinowski's first contribution to anthropological literature, and looking forward to the argument of Sex and Repression, it is possible to integrate the elided passage into the broader themes of Malinowski's anthropology, and of his ethnographic experience. Like the disjunctive parenthesis, the essay on the "economic functions" of the Intichiuma ceremonies had to do with the transition from "savage" to "civilized" labor (1912); in contrast, Sex and Repression makes it clear that the passage from savagery to civilization was also a passage away from a relatively easy and harmonious genital sexuality (1927). For mankind as a whole, the long-run evolutionary consequence of "signing on" might be seen as loss as well as gain — and the loss might be even more sharply felt by a European living on a tropical island, who had vowed to deny himself the sensual pleasures often associated with such exotic realms. Denied the compensating gains of civilization, why, indeed, would the native "boy"— or anyone else —"sign on"? (cf. Stocking 1986b:26–27).

On the other hand, it is obvious that the question also had a pragmatic colonial economic aspect, which Malinowski had previously addressed in a more public context than his diary. In 1915 Australian government leaders, anxious to pick up their "due share of the trade formerly in German hands," established a parliamentary commission on "British and Australian Trade in the South Pacific" (Rowley 1958:47–49). Among the matters considered was the problem of plantation labor, which had recently been exacerbated by the prospect that the Indian and Chinese governments would end the system of indentured service that had helped to supply the needs of plantation owners in many areas of the British empire since the abolition of slavery in the 1830s (Tinker 1974). Despite the earlier termination of the importation of "Kanakas" into Queensland, the issue of Melanesian labor was still a live one, heightened perhaps by the emerging concern that the native races were "dying out"

(Rivers 1922). Along with government agents, traders, planters and missionaries, Malinowski was called upon to testify before the commission in the fall of 1916. Although he had not made it a matter of special study, he felt that his researches might "throw some light on the labour question" (Stocking 1986a).

Generalizing, Malinowski felt that "the native Papuan is not very keen on working for the white man." Left under his own conditions, he had "plenty of work at hand"—work which, though "not of a purely economic description," nevertheless made "life worth living." If he "signed on," it was not out of "deep-seated" motives, but as a response to the "personality and behaviour of the recruiter" and the prospect of something new and different. After a few weeks, "any native would desire to leave if it were not for the penalty"; but after a year "he gets to like life on the plantation"—depending of course on the way "the natives are managed." Although passingly acknowledging the necessity of "firmness," Malinowski emphasized the attempt "to make their lives pleasant." Speaking from "the natives' point of view," he emphasized that they were "very sensitive on the matter of tobacco," and recounted how returning laborers recalled the times when they were allowed to have "corroborees" and to dance. While he was not sure just what the plantation sexual regulations were, he knew that even married natives went to plantations by themselves. And although the Papuan was "not very likely to expressly formulate an emotional state of mind or a defined feeling such as homesickness," he knew that married men "who have got into the habit of domesticity" did not readily "sign on," and when they did "always wanted to get back" (Stocking 1986a).

Malinowski, whose own extended sexual deprivation in the Trobriands was to be the potent experiential archetype of his later psychobiological functionalism, was particularly concerned with the sexual problem (Stocking 1986b: 22–28). Contrasting Papuan sexual customs with those of Indian coolies, he felt that to allow married men to bring their wives would encourage disorder among the unmarried. Even if the Papuans themselves were undisturbed by "immorality," missionaries would object—and in this official testimonial context, Malinowski suggested that their "outcry" would be "quite justified." In a more instrumental mode, however, he went on to suggest that laborers often had access to local women, and "it was almost impossible to think that a young native would spend three years of his life without having sexual intercourse without degenerating into sexual abnormality." Nor would the separation of three or four thousand Papuan men from their wives decrease population, since the reproductive slack would be taken up by adultery—which in the area he knew best was a matter of relatively small social consequence. Although it was "extraordinary" that the Melanesians, who were "relatively high types of men," should share the ignorance Baldwin Spencer had found among

Australian Aboriginals, they did in fact fail to appreciate "the natural con-nexion between intercourse and birth"—one young native, absent for two years, became extremely indignant when a white man suggested to him that his newly delivered wife might have been guilty of infidelity (Stocking 1986a).

Turning finally to the general problem of "development," Malinowski gave a favorable report of Bellamy's enforced coconut planting. He doubted, how-ever, that "it would be possible to induce the natives to engage in any other form of industry." The native Papuan "cannot really see even seven or eight days ahead, though he may be very intelligent in other matters; he has no grasp of a further perspective. . . . there is no incentive to the native except some present desire." After a glancing attack against German colonial re-gimes—which never considered "the welfare of the races they govern" and by transplantation had "decimated" the tribes of Southwest Africa—Malinowski ended with a preservationist appeal. There was "not much likelihood of the native Papuans dying out if left alone, and if they do not come in contact with the white man's civilization." Broadly speaking, he felt that "it would be best to leave them to their own conditions" (Stocking 1986a).

Given the circumstances of presentation (and the exigencies of recording), one hesitates to take every phrase in this somewhat disjointed official testi-mony at interpretive face value—the more so since Malinowski, throughout his life, was quite capable of tailoring argument and rhetoric to instrumental ends. In other contexts he was not so inclined to cater to the sensibilities of missionaries. While portions of the implicit evolutionary argument (includ-ing the crucial matter of sexual ignorance) are quite consistent with his ethnography, it seems clear that evolutionary assumption also served as the medium for expressing Malinowski's ambivalence about colonialism as civiliz-ing process—and about his role as "expert" witness. On the one hand, he offered advice designed to make a system of native labor "work" more effectively; on the other hand, the import of much of his testimony was to suggest that con-tract labor was alien and unsatisfying to the native psyche, and that all things considered, it would be better for them if they were not encouraged to "sign on."

Practical Anthropology and the Tragedy
of the Modern World

In the later pages of his Trobriand diary, Malinowski referred to two essays he hoped to write after he left the field. Among the "main points" of the first, on the "Value of Ethnographic Studies for the Administration," were the stan-dard developmental topics of "land tenure; recruiting; health and change of conditions (such as getting them down from the hilltops)." But Malinowski

Bronislaw Malinowski, with Togugu'a (identified in *The Sexual Life of Savages* as "a sorcerer of some repute and a good informant, who is wearing a full wig") and two other Trobrianders, each holding the limepot used in the preparation of the betel nut stimulant. (Courtesy of Helena Wayne Malinowska and the British Library of Political and Economic Science, London School of Economics.)

insisted that what was important "above all" was "knowledge of a people's customs" that would allow one "to be in sympathy with them and to guide them according to their ideas." Characteristically, colonial government was "a mad and blind force, acting with uncontrollable force in unforeseen directions"—"sometimes as a farce, sometimes as tragedy," but "never to be taken as an integral item of tribal life." And since colonial government was incapable of a more enlightened view, he would cast his "final plea" in terms of "purely scientific value: antiquities [are] more destructible than a papyrus and more exposed than an exposed column, and more valuable for our real knowledge of history than all the excavations in the world" (1967:238).

This preservationist impulse ran even stronger in another essay advancing the idea of a "New Humanism" that might be promoted by a "kind of humanistic R[oyal] S[ociety]." In contrast to the "dead-petrified thinking" of the "'classics,'" it would be inspired by "living man, living language, and living full-blooded facts" (1967:255, 267). Although the "Society of Modern Humanists" was never realized, Malinowski recurred to the "new humanism" in an article drafted during a postwar interlude "far from the trouble and irritation of Europe" in the Canary Islands—the central site of those early ventures with his mother into extra-European otherness (BMP: BM/CGS 10/19/20). It was during this idyllic year with his new wife—whose espousal was the unwritten conclusion of the psychodrama of his diary—that Malinowski crafted *Argonauts of the Western Pacific*, the most literary and the most romantic of his ethnographies (JGFP: BM/JGF 5/8/21; cf. Strenski 1982: Wayne 1985:535). And just as the first chapter of *Argonauts* was the methodological manifesto of the "revolution in social anthropology" he had conceived during that final period in the Trobriands (1967:289), "Ethnology and the Study of Society" was the first programmatic statement of his later psychobiological functionalism (1922a; cf. Stocking 1986b:27–28).

In arguing the theoretical utility of ethnology as the basis of a general science of man, Malinowski saw modern anthropology as the final step in the historical development of humanism. Given its first impulse in the Renaissance by the opening up of a new vista on a forgotten civilization, broadened in the eighteenth and nineteenth century by the discovery of Sanskrit, humanism had now to respond to the challenge of modern (i.e., evolutionary) anthropology, which sought "The broadest basis of comprehensive comparison of all civilization, including those of the savage races" (1922a:217). In contrast to the old, the "New Humanism" would be based on a really scientific, empirical knowledge of human nature, for what "*time* has hidden from us forever, *space* keeps preserved for a while," waiting for the "field ethnologist" (216). He was the only sociologist who could do anything like an experiment, by observing the "differences in human mental constitution and human social behavior under the various forms of physical and mental environment" (217). Avoiding sensationalism, seeking instead a "*comprehensive treatment of all aspects of tribal life and their correlation,*" ethnology could become the "handmaiden" of "a general theory of human society" (218).

Ethnology, however, could claim more than a theoretical usefulness: the first half of Malinowski's essay was an appeal for its direct application in the "scientific management" of native populations—which, until recently, a colonial atmosphere marked by slavery and punitive expeditions had made impossible. Among contemporary colonial problems, the "most sinister" was the gradual dying out of native populations, which Malinowski explained in psychological terms as largely due to "destruction of all vital interest for the native" (1922a:209; cf. Rivers 1922). Berating convention-bound, middle-class "morality mongers" and parochial "petty inquisitors of primitive life" whose "fanatical zeal to prune and uproot" had choked off the natives' "joy of living"

by suppressing the institutions that gave "zest and meaning to life," Malinowski offered one of his earliest published statements on the functional integration of culture:

> every item of culture . . . represents a value, fulfils a social function, has a positive
> biological significance. For tradition is a fabric in which all the strands are so
> closely woven that the destruction of one unmakes the whole. And tradition
> is, biologically speaking, a form of collective adaptation of a community to its
> surroundings. Destroy tradition, and you will deprive the collective organism
> of its protective shell, and give it over to the slow but inevitable process of dying
> out. (214)

The implication was clear enough: while there was much in native life that
must or would "succumb" to processes that Malinowski still thought of in
evolutionary terms, the better part of policy and of humanity was an attempt,
justified in terms of an emerging functionalism, to "preserve the integrity of
tribal life as far as possible" in order to prevent the "complete extinction" of
native peoples (214).

However, more pragmatic developmental pressures, both colonial and personal, strained hard against Malinowski's preservationism. It was not simply
native lives that were at stake; so also were "millions" in European money.
In the South Seas, where white labor was not viable and "Yellow and Hindu"
labor involved a "serious political danger," native survival was essential to the
solution of the labor problem (1922a:209). Despite his reservations about "signing on," Malinowski was quite willing to appeal directly to European economic
interest to strengthen the case for the practical utility of anthropology (cf.
1926b). And it is clear that in the interwar period the advancement of practical anthropology was closely linked with the advancement of his own anthropological career.

During his Australian years, Malinowski's economic position had been as
marginal as his cultural status; visiting his digs in Melbourne, his friend Elton
Mayo found him living in "Slavonic squalor" (EMP:10/1919). But although
at points Malinowski seemed to envision a life of saintly anthropological pov-
erty (1967:282), the motif of professional ambition was closely interwoven with
themes of eroticism and national identity in the Trobriand diary: in the climactic moments of his despair at the news of his mother's death, he complained that "external ambitions" crawled over him "like lice": "F. R. S. [Fellow
of the Royal Society]—C. S. I. [Companion of the Order of the Star of India],
Sir [Bronislaw Malinowski]" (291). Earlier on he had thought of becoming "an
eminent Polish scholar" (160), and in 1922 he still seriously considered the
offer of a newly established chair in ethnology at Cracow. However, because
"money for the new department was scant," and administrative and teaching
burdens would have left him no time to write up his field materials, he de-

clined to accept this direct inheritance of his academic patrimony (Wayne 1985:535). Although he and his Scottish-English wife both obtained Polish citizenship when the nation became independent after the war, the diary suggests that he had for some time felt that his academic anthropological ambitions might better be pursued in Britain—which, given the international stature of the British school, was where a "revolution in social anthropology" would have to be waged (1967:291).

But as a "penniless Pole" approaching forty, with a family under way, Malinowski Kad not yet in 1921 found an economically secure place in what was still a marginally institutionalized academic discipline. His prospects were best at the London School of Economics, where his mentor Seligman was active on his behalf, and it was in the journal of the L.S.E. that his essay on the "new humanism" was published, after he had begun to lecture there in the fall of 1921. When a readership in anthropology was created in 1923, it was with Malinowski specifically in mind; in 1927, when a chair was finally created, he became professor (R. Firth 1963). Malinowski's professorship, however, was at that time the only one at the three major British universities; at Oxford and Cambridge, anthropology still merited only a readership. As a consequence, much of his energy was devoted to the propagation of anthropology and to strengthening its academic base at the L.S.E. (Kuklick n.d.: ch. 2).

The major means to this goal was the International African Institute, an organization of leading Africanist scholars, colonial administrators, and missionaries founded in 1926, largely at the initiative of Dr. J. H. Oldham, the secretary of the recently organized International Missionary Council, and one of a new breed of ecumenical and culturally oriented missionaries (Smith 1934; cf. Stocking 1985:123–24). The titular leader of the Institute was the retired elder statesman of British colonial proconsuls, Lord Frederick Lugard, whose career had taken him from India, where he served in Afghanistan, to East Africa, where he fought Arab slavers and opened up Uganda, to Nigeria, where as High Commissioner and Governor-General between 1900 to 1919 he was known as the architect of "indirect rule" (Perham 1956, 1960). When the British Empire reached its apogee under the "mandate" system established by the Treaty of Versailles (Louis 1967; Beloff 1970), Lugard served for more than a decade as British member of the Permanent Mandates Commission. In 1922 he published what was to be at once a classic defense of the British imperial role in Africa and a justification for the new mandate system: *The Dual Mandate in Tropical Africa.* As "the protectors and trustees of backward races," the "civilised nations" had a responsibility both to develop the "abounding wealth" of the tropics for "the benefit of mankind," and to "safeguard the material rights of the natives, [and] promote their moral and educational progress" (1922:18). Fortunately, there was no necessary contradiction between humanitarianism and economic self-interest: in the very process of bringing "the torch of culture and progress" to "the dark places of the earth, the abode of barbarism and cruelty," mandating nations could at the same time minister "to the material needs of our own civilisation" (618).

At some point early in his involvement with Oldham, Lugard, and the Institute, Malinowski briefed himself by consulting Lugard's *Dual Mandate*, leaving a record of his reactions in some undated notes (BMP). Commenting on Lugard's justification for direct taxation, Malinowski felt that the argument might have been strengthened by an appreciation of the "psychology of the gift," which, if appropriately considered, would make it possible to introduce taxation without hurting native feelings, in fact creating "indigenous ambition" and "esprit de corps." Responding to Lugard's suggestion that "in order to develop a system suited to their [native] needs, the District Officer must study their customs and social organisations," Malinowski felt that this was "rather short shrift for the whole Anthropological point of view"—"he knows nothing of real Anthropology." When Lugard quoted colonial prognosticators on the inevitability of detribalization, Malinowski asked if it was in fact the case, and if it was necessary—suggesting that Lugard did not know how much law, order, and authority there actually was in a primitive tribe. But when Lugard proposed to "evolve from their own institutions, based on their own habits of thought, prejudices, and customs, the form best suited to them, and adapted to meet the new conditions," Malinowski thought this "excellent"—equating it with "the whole antiprogressive conception." Asking "what has been done toward it?" Malinowski dismissed with exclamation marks the previous efforts of Northcote Thomas and C. W. Meek, who had served as government anthropologists in Nigeria. On the crucial issue of land tenure, he noted that "my 'theory' teaches you [the] meaning of [the] words 'communal,' 'tribal', 'ownership': by the time you know that, you know how to collect in a few weeks all the facts necessary to answer the practical questions" —and reminded himself to "make it clear that I worked on *land tenure; economic value; exchange*, etc. long before I knew the practical interest." At points Malinowski was skeptical of Lugard's motives: "he is not free from hypoc[risy] —after all, it is not merely native welfare," but "because *we* are there that we must limit [?] them." But the conclusion was clear enough: "if he had wanted to control scientific Anthropology to fit into his imperial idea—he couldn't have done anything but to create [the] Functional School"; "Indirect Rule is a Complete Surrender to the Functional Point of View."

Joining forces with Oldham, in 1929 Malinowski launched a campaign to win Rockefeller Foundation support for an International African Institute program in "Practical Anthropology" that would study the pressing problems of land tenure and labor as they affected the "changing Native." For the next few years Rockefeller money channelled through the African Institute sup-

ported the fieldwork of a substantial portion of the cohort that was to con-
solidate the "revolution in social anthropology" (Stocking 1985).[8] While the
details of Malinowski's own involvement in African anthropology and the
study of "culture contact" and "culture change" would overleap the bounds
of the present essay, it is clear that he did his best to sell the utility of anthropology to the colonial establishment (cf. James 1973; Kuklick n.d.: ch. 5;
Kuper 1983: ch. 4; Onege 1979; Grillo 1985). In doing so, he seems to have
been motivated largely by his own interest in advancing the academic discipline in which he had finally succeeded in establishing himself. As he noted
privately in 1931, academic anthropologists spent their time breeding young
anthropologists "for the sake of anthropology and so that they in turn may
breed new anthropologists" in a situation where there was "no practical basis
to our science, and there are no funds forthcoming to remunerate it for what
it produces" (BMP: draft memo, "Res. Needs in Soc. & Cult. Anth."). In this
context, Malinowski advertised anthropology in terms that might convince
an ill-informed and reluctant buyer. It was surely he whom his student Au-
drey Richards later had in mind, in evaluating "Practical Anthropology in
the Lifetime of the International African Institute," when she said that "it
looks as though the Anthropologist had been advertising his goods, often
rather clamourously, in a market in which there was little demand for them"
(1944:292).

   In selling anthropology, Malinowski spoke in different voices to different
audiences. In the initial appeal for a "Practical Anthropology," directed to the
Rockefeller Foundation and the colonial establishment, he warned that the
attempt to "subvert an old system of traditions" and "replace it by a ready-
made new morality" would invariably lead to "what might be called 'black
bolshevism'"; in contrast, the anthropologist with no "vested interest" and a
"cold-blooded passion for sheer accuracy" would be able without alarming
them to do a survey of land tenure which would reveal the "'indispensable
minimum'" that must be preserved for the natives, who "would often be not
even aware" of the goal of the study (1929b:28–32). But in defending "practical
anthropology" against criticism by a colonial officer who felt that anthropologists should stay in their academic laboratories and leave colonial administration to "practical men," Malinowski struck a somewhat different chord.
Citing "the history of 'black-birding' in the South Seas," he argued that practical men, by their ignorance of native customs, had provoked punitive expeditions in which "the 'practical man' himself would act as the murderer"

---

   8. The "revolution in social anthropology" was of course to be at least as much the work
of A. R. Radcliffe-Brown, to whom a number of Malinowski's students shifted their allegiance
in the 1930s, and who upon Malinowski's departure for America succeeded him as the dominant
figure in the British sphere (Stocking 1984, 1985).

(1930a:411; cf. P. E. Mitchell 1930). In appealing to a "community of interests" among "practical men of goodwill" in the colonies, his critic had failed
to recognize the "profound, indeed irreconcilable, differences" among them
—the "greed and ruthless rapacity" of the white employer, the "mawkish senti-
mentalism, wrong-headed dogma or false humanitarianism" of the missionary—and had failed even to consider "the native African, 'savage' and detribalized alike" (1930a:424).

Malinowski's own approach to the native African evolved somewhat in
the early 1930s, with slightly variant messages being offered around a common theme at each moment along the way (cf. Rossetti 1985; James 1973). In
1930 he warned against the dangers of a caste society such as was developing
in South Africa and the American South—"where neither race displaces the
other," and "the social disabilities weigh heavily on the lower and demoralize
the higher stratum" (1930b, as quoted in 1943:663). The following year, in a
symposium on "The Colour Bar," he in fact described segregation as "at present a necessity"—identifying himself with the positions taken by Lugard and
the American racialist Lothrop Stoddard, as opposed to four others who had
"merely belittl[ed] the importance of race prejudice" as "superstitious." But in
taking a stand on the "bedrock of reality," Malinowski insisted (against Stoddard) also on the "bedrock of justice and wisdom." Arguing that the color
bar should work both ways, he advocated not only the restriction of white
immigration into East Africa—"at present the danger spot of the whole world's
racial situation"—but the deportation of whites already there, in order to give
the colored races "some elbow room" (1931:999–1001; cf. 1929c).

Three years later, when he made a two-month inspection tour of fieldwork-
ers of the International African Institute, Malinowski had first-hand experience of the color bar in South Africa. While there, he gave several lectures,
two of which, directed to audiences of white educationalists, were later published as "Native Education and Culture Contact" (1936). Malinowski insisted
on the "difficulties and the dangers" of the "schooling of unblushingly European type" that was being "mechanically thrust" on "peoples living in the
simple tribal conditions of Africa" (481). Depriving the native child of his
"cultural birthright" to "his own tradition and his own place in his tribal life,"
such schooling did not offer him in exchange "the charter of citizenship in
our own civilization and society." The "white community of South Africa,"
moved "not by any malice or racial viciousness" but by "the sheer force of
economic necessity," was "not prepared to give a Native, however educated
and intelligent, that place to which he is entitled by his training" (484). Unable "for political reasons" to recognize that more land and economic opportunities should be given to natives, the "friends of the African" within the
European community instead offered "more and better education," as if it were
"a panacea which can work by itself" (491). But those who "talk about 'segre-

gation' and want to attach a positive meaning to that term must realize that unless some sort of political scope is given to the African he will not be satisfied with anything less than equal political rights with the white settlers" (498). In this context, Malinowski favored an education—carried on in the English language by speakers of the vernacular—that would not "estrange the African from his tribal culture" or "develop in him claims and desires which his future salary and status will never satisfy" (501). Now that the development of "modern anthropological technique in fieldwork" had enabled us "fairly easily to learn all there is to be learnt about Natives and their culture," there was no further excuse for "committing blunders or continuing in them" (507).

While he was in South Africa, Malinowski also gave a talk to an audience of blacks on "African (Negro) Patriotism." In it, he contrasted anthropologists with two groups of "pseudo-friends": sentimental "Negrophiles" like Norman Leys, and Christian friends of "Sable coloured brethren" who had in fact done little to prevent slavery, labor exploitation, and land grabbing. Acknowledging the existence of a racial school among anthropologists (and the "reality" of race as a topic of inquiry), as well as the tendency of all anthropologists to ignore or despise detribalized Africans, he insisted that anthropology was changing. Referring to his own articles of 1922 and 1929 to document the move, he argued that the focus of anthropology was shifting from the "naked African" toward the African "in trousers." For the former, functional anthropology had and still offered a "moderate but effective championship": recognizing the value of African culture (even to the point of defending such traditional practices as witchcraft and cannibalism), it resisted the taking of tribal lands, the perversion of tribal laws, or the imposition of an alien Christian morality, favoring political autonomy and economic development along "natural" lines. But it was now time for functional anthropology to face also the problems of the modern Negro—equality of status, freedom of competition in the labor market, and the protection of racial self-esteem; it was time, in short, to "recognize the reality of the detribalized African and fight for his place in the world." While there was clearly a level of substantive consistency between this talk and those to the white educationalists, the differences of emphasis and rhetoric were apparently quite dramatic. One African woman in the audience was "emotionally swept away," proclaiming that in an atmosphere of hypocrisy and humbug, Malinowski's "sympathetic understanding of an oppressed people" amounted "to sheer heroism" (BMP: Zamunissa Cool/ BM, 7/7/34, 8/28/34).

Not then inclined to play the same heroic role before audiences of fellow Europeans, Malinowski filed the talk away in a folder with the annotation "Nig Lec." (BMP: "African [Negro] Patriotism"). But behind a sometimes obscuring cloud of instrumental rhetoric, spoken in different voices to different audiences, his views on the future of native peoples and the responsibilities of the anthropologist continued to evolve. In 1936, when he appealed to Lord Lugard to support the work of Jomo Kenyatta, who had become interested in anthropology while earning money as a linguistic informant during the early part of his long stay in England (Murray-Brown 1972:180), Malinowski put the case in crassly instrumental political terms:

> Mr. Kenyatta proposes to devote himself to anthropological field-work from the practical point of view on his return to his native country. . . . Mr. Kenyatta started his work in my Department about two years ago. At that time he had a definitely political bias in all his approach. This, I think, has been almost completely eradicated by the constant impact of detached scientific method on his mental processes. The highly depoliticising influence of scientific anthropology has worked a remarkable change. Another two years of systematic study and the hall-mark on his type of approach provided by a Diploma in Anthropology; also the obligation under which he will feel himself towards the [International African] Institute, will, I am certain, complete the change. Since Mr. Kenyatta has considerable influence on African students, and also on the educated Africans in Kenya, the contribution will not only be towards the advancement of theoretical studies, but also towards the practical influence of anthropology. (BMP: BM/LL 12/7/36)

Unswayed by the brainwashing power of social anthropology, Lugard was the lone dissenter when the matter came to a vote in the Institute's governing bureau (BMP: [unsigned]/BM 12/21/36); Kenyatta, his mental processes still politicized, went on to become the leader of the independence movement and the first president of the Kenyan nation. But in 1938, he did publish his doctoral dissertation, to which Malinowski wrote an introduction wherein by implication he called into question the historical realization of Lugard's whole project, by commending Kenyatta for "help[ing] us to understand how Africans see through our pretences, and how they assess the realities of the Dual Mandate" (1938a:x). The year before, in the preface to a volume entitled *The Savage Hits Back*, he hailed the author as one who was "frankly the native's spokesman, not only of the native point of view, but also of native interests and grievances."

> It has always appeared to me remarkable how little the trained anthropologist, with his highly perfected technique of field-work and his theoretical knowledge, has so far worked and fought side by side with those who are usually described as pro-native. Was it because science makes people too cautious and pedantry too timid? Or was it because the anthropologist, enamoured of the unspoiled primitive, lost interest in the native enslaved, oppressed, or detribalized? However that might be, I for one believe in the anthropologist's being not only the interpreter of the native but also his champion. (1937:viii)

Although offered rather casually in a brief occasional piece, as an opinion he had "always" held, the passage may perhaps be taken as self-reflective commentary on Malinowski's evolving awareness of what it was to be "the native's spokesman." Enamored of "the unspoiled primitive" even before he came to anthropology, but taking for granted the overwhelming knowledge/power of European civilization, he had for much of his career been a spokesman of "the native point of view" of the precontact "savage"—preserved insofar as possible from enslavement, oppression, and detribalization. In the later 1920s, seeking the means to propagate his science, he greeted "indirect rule" as a policy compatible with this underlying preservationism, and offered in return a "practical anthropology" as the means by which the interests of natives, colonizers, administrators, and anthropologists could all be advanced. As he gained more systematic and direct experience with the processes of culture contact in the African colonial situation in the early 1930s, the "savage"—now often "so-called" or called into question by quotation marks—was pushed into the wings of "practical anthropology." The "detribalized native" was given center stage, at first as the object of administrative policy, then with a greater appreciation of native "interests and grievances," and finally with an incipient awareness of the emergence of Africans as a world historical political force (cf. Rossetti 1985; James 1973).

In the preface to Kenyatta's book, Malinowski found it "amazing" how Mussolini's Abyssinian venture had "organised public opinion in places and among natives whom one would never have suspected of having any complicated views on the League of Nations, on the Dual Mandate, on the Dignity of Labour, and on the Brotherhood of Man," and how the "Chinese incident" was "uniting the world of coloured peoples against Western influence" (1938a:x). That same year, in the introductory essay to the Institute's memorandum on *Methods of Study of Culture Contact*, he noted the emergence of a "new African type of nationalism, of racial feeling, and of collective opposition to Western culture" which had been aroused by the systematic denial of certain essential "elements of our culture": the "instruments of physical power," the "instruments of political mastery" ("even when they are given Indirect Rule, this is done under our control"); "the substance of economic wealth"; and admission "as equals to Church Assembly, school, or drawing-room" (1938b:xxii–xxiii).

The last essay Malinowski prepared for publication before his death, written after he had left England for the United States and was no longer directly involved in the colonial propagation of British anthropology, provides a final marker of the change. For the most part a reprinting of the earlier essay on "Native Education," it was substantially modified in the concluding sections, where he attacked segregation as amounting to "a complete political and legal control of Africans by whites" (1943:661). Malinowski suggested that "a complete transition of the whole of Africa to European standards" would require not only "the complete withdrawal of Europeans from Africa so as to restore the land, the political power, and opportunities which are now usurped at the African's expense," but also an infusion of capital from Europe "and the whole Western world," the fruits of which would not be "garnered, as now, by European capitalists," but "presented to Africans" (660). However, Malinowski still did not foresee emergent African nationalism as leading to the end of the colonial system. On the contrary, what was "actually occurring" was "the formation of a rigid caste system" in which "one of the two component cultures" was systematically deprived of the "fundamental necessities of a civilized human being" (662–63). And though he offered once again proposals for appropriate native education, he did so with the caveat that raising their level of aspiration without "any wherewithal to satisfy the resulting claims is the royal road to social catastrophe" (664). In the end, he could do no more than fall back on an analogy to his own early experience as a Pole within the Hapsburg Empire:

> Speaking as a European, and a Pole at that, I should like to place here as a parallel and paradigm the aspirations of European nationality, though not of nationalism. In Europe we members of oppressed or subject minorities . . . do not desire anything like fusion with our conquerors or masters. Our strongest claim is for segregation in terms of full cultural autonomy which does not even need to imply political independence. We claim only to have the same scale of possibilities, the same right of decision as regards our destiny, our civilization, and our mode of enjoying life. (665)

The appeal to his Polish identity was a characteristic Malinowskian trope: "speaking as a Pole, on behalf of the African, I again can put my own experience as a 'savage' from Eastern Europe side by side with the Kikuyu, Chagga or Bechwana" (1936:502). But if this experience did not provide a very satisfactory model for the future of race relations in the colonial world, it may have helped him to understand what it was to have "a two-fold social personality"—as in the case of several students of "African extraction" who had been in his classes. One of these, of course, was Jomo Kenyatta, who had served as spokesman of the Kikuyu "before more than one Royal Commission on land matters" (Kenyatta 1938:xx); and it seems reasonable to suggest that Malinowski's changing consciousness of the changing aspirations of Africans may in part have reflected their relationship—that his own mental processes were, to some extent, remolded by the politicizing influence of African nationalism.

Malinowski, however, had no more been transformed by African nationalism than Kenyatta had been by social anthropology. The two men continued to move from different starting points, along different trajectories; their visions of the present world were as different as their visions of the future.

There was a brief historical moment when the author of *Facing Mount Kenya* and his "friend and teacher, Professor Malinowski," could meet on common ground (Kenyatta 1938:xvii). In many respects, Kenyatta's book could have stood as documentation for Malinowski's views on traditional African education. Its central chapter was devoted to showing that cliteroidectomy, or female circumcision, which was attacked by missionaries as "something savage and barbaric, worthy only of heathens who live in perpetual sin under the influence of the Devil," was not simply a "mere bodily mutilation," but "the *conditio sine qua non* of the whole teaching of tribal law, religion, and morality" (128, 147). The book's conclusion opened with a resoundingly functionalist affirmation "that the various sides of Gikuyu life here described are parts of an integrated culture," of which "no single part is detachable: each has its context and is fully understandable only in relation to the whole" (296).

However, the ground on which the two men met was not that of the "detribalized native" but that of precontact Kikuyu culture: the "system of education" Kenyatta described was that existing "prior to the advent of the European" (Kenyatta 1938:95). If years in mission schools and British academic life had given him, like Malinowski, a "two-fold social personality," the two felt their psychic dualism rather differently. Thus when Kenyatta spoke of having to keep "under very considerable restraint the sense of political grievances which no progressive African can fail to experience" (xvii), Malinowski glossed the comment a bit patronizingly in terms of his own civilizational angst:

> In fairness to Mr. Kenyatta, and as a matter of wisdom in any co-operation between Europeans of goodwill and Africans who have suffered the injury of higher education, we have to recognize the fact that an African who looks at things from the tribal point of view and at the same time from that of Western civilisation, experiences the tragedy of the modern world in an especially acute manner. (1938a:ix)

And in stark contrast to Malinowski's backward-looking Hapsburg paradigm of cultural autonomy without political independence, Kenyatta's book ended with a ringing call for "unceasing" struggle toward "complete emancipation" (1938:306).

Malinowski never ceased to trumpet the virtues of "scientific anthropology" and its applicability to the solution of practical problems. But if his rhetoric was often a reflection of mood and moment, there is also evidence to suggest that he became increasingly disillusioned in the interwar period with the civilization that science had produced. Born "into a world of peace and order," to a generation that "cherished legitimate hopes of stability and gradual development," he had lived through a profound "historical demoralisation" (1938a:ix). By 1930, he had come to see "the aimless drive of modern mechanization" as "a menace to all real spiritual and artistic values" (1930a:405). In the middle 1930s, he spoke of our "ultra-efficient modern culture" as a "Frankenstein monster with which we are as yet unable to cope" (1934:406); in 1938, quoting the words of William James, of progress as "a terrible thing" (1938a:ix).

In 1908, Malinowski had defended the objective validity of scientific knowledge by an appeal to colonial power, and he continued to think of both forces in terms of a virtually irresistible inevitability. But by the 1930s, his attitude toward science had clearly changed: it was now "the worst calamity of our days" (1930a:405). What was needed was "not an acceleration of 'progress,' which we neither understand, nor master, nor even approve of, but, rather, the greatest possible slowing down." Rather than speaking of "the benefits of Western civilization as the ultimate goal of all humanity," we should be thinking of how "to prevent the spread of our own troubles and cultural diseases to those who are not yet affected by them" (1934:406). The pathos of the primitive — which since Rousseau had been a projection of self-pity — was now again strongly reinforced by the pathos of the civilized. Once problematic primarily for the Melanesians, "signing on" had become problematic for all mankind.

Ethnographic Archetypes, Motivating Myths, Colonial Power, and the Ironies of Ethnographic Knowledge

To compare the anecdotally recounted ethnographic experiences of three different anthropologists among three different groups in three different colonial situations is a risky enterprise at best. But since we began this essay by placing Malinowski in a kind of archetypal relation to the other two, let us treat the three in similar fashion. Without pretending to pursue the comparison systematically, we may see them as representing different moments in the more general colonial situation of ethnography, different phases in the development and institutionalization of anthropology, and different responses to its political and ethical dilemmas.

Maclay's arrival on the northern coast of New Guinea comes close to realizing the imagined primal scene of the anthropological encounter. Far from working under Rivers' umbrella of established colonial power, Maclay was, once the corvette sailed away, effectively alone in a lush tropic jungle among a previously "untouched" people. Although they were soon to be entangled in a rapidly developing colonial situation, it was still fluid enough that a man of Maclay's richly romantic temperament could imagine resisting or reshaping it. His ethnographic interests were largely sacrificed to this foredoomed effort, and there were ambiguities as well in his ethnographic enterprise. Despite his unusual sensitivity to certain ethical and political implications of anthropological fieldwork, a darker Kurtzian impulse to power was clearly evident in Maclay's paternalistic protectionism; and the ethnographic knowledge produced in this context of power relationships was, by present standards, of a somewhat limited sort.

In contrast to the precolonial situation of Maclay on the northern New Guinea coast, the people Kubary dealt with on Palau had been contacted for a century. Although European power was still somewhat tenuously manifest through buccaneering traders and occasional punitive gunboats, Kubary's ethnography was from the beginning enmeshed in a complex network of local politics and trade. Temperamentally pragmatic to the point of duplicity, he seems to have adapted in an eminently practical way to inequalities of power and influence. Far from imagining a resistance to the further encroachment of colonialism, when he found himself stranded in the Pacific without institutional support he became an active agent in its implementation. And yet the ethnographic knowledge he produced is surely more recognizable to us today than that of Maclay.

When Malinowski began his ethnographic career, both the colonial situation and the institutional development of the anthropology of the southwest Pacific were in a very different phase. At the time he first landed on Mailu, an Australian expeditionary force was already occupying German New Guinea, where Maclay had done his fieldwork and Kubary had served as plantation manager (Mackenzie 1927:xv). The establishment of European power was no longer problematic; what was at issue was rather the transfer of colonial power in spheres where administrative and economic structures were already in place—though any given area, like the Trobriands, might still be within Rivers' window of optimum ethnographic opportunity. Although the institutionalization of anthropology was still precarious, the lineaments of its modern academic framework were already visible. If Malinowski, too, was an Eastern European émigré dependent on makeshift arrangements for his continued research, he had nonetheless come to the southwest Pacific with money channelled through an academic department, and could realistically aspire to a university career back in Europe—which was where his "revolution in anthropology" would have to be consolidated. And despite the shock of his diaries, his ethnographic work remains a landmark in the history of anthropology—one of the relatively few rich lodes of ethnographic material that have been and will long be the foci of continuing theoretical discussion, one of the relatively few anthropological oeuvres that had a substantial impact on the intellectual and cultural movements of their era.

Against this brief summary sketch, we may consider Malinowski's own mythic view of his two predecessors. Assuming that they were not somehow reversed in transcription or translation, one wonders how much he really knew of the two "types" of the ethnographic proportion which by implication he established in 1917. As precursors in his ethnographic realm, and fellow émigrés from east of the Oder, they were certainly known to him by reputation. But his implicitly negative characterization of Kubary as a "concrete methodologist" suggests that he was not closely familiar with Kubary's Palauan work. It seems also unlikely that he would have had much direct familiarity with the published writings of Maclay, which had appeared in relatively inaccessible Russian journals, and in a Dutch publication in Batavia. Had he read them, he would scarcely have described Maclay as an ethnographer of a "new type," since his work was in fact "concrete" in a pre-Riversian sense, inasmuch as it focussed largely on physical anthropology, material culture, demography, and linguistics of the word-list variety (Webster 1984:346).

But if it seems unlikely that Malinowski had a close familiarity with either archetype's contribution to ethnographic knowledge, he must have had an idea of their current reputation in the local arena of colonial power. And just as Maclay's influence was "always primarily a moral one" (Webster 1984:348), so would Kubary during World War I have been perceived in moral terms. Maclay—the Kurtzian resonances of his own unpublished diary hidden from view—could be romanticized as the European ethnographer venturing alone to live among uncontacted natives, who not only brought back the grail of scientific knowledge, but became their defender from the destructive impact of European power. Kubary—who ended his career in the active service of German colonialism in a nearby area recently occupied by Australian troops—could scarcely have avoided being touched by the responsibility for German "colonial atrocities." To a man who knew his Conrad (cf. Clifford 1988), the image of Kubary as Kurtz might easily have suggested itself; and if the Kurtz in Malinowski could at moments "understand" such atrocities, those recurring Kurtzian impulses had no place in the mythic charter he would write for the "revolution in anthropology." Like the ethnography it introduced, that charter was very much a product of the romantic primitivist side of Malinowski's persona.

In identifying himself archetypically with Maclay against Kubary, Malinowski may be said, metaphorically, to have gone behind the moral and methodological complexities and ambiguities of his colonial situation to return to an imagined primal Garden of prelapsarian anthropological innocence. Having left behind the cultural baggage of civilization (though not of scientific anthropology), the lone Ethnographer there encountered the precontact Primitive, distilled the essence of a particular cultural Otherness, and brought back to civilization an exotic, esoteric knowledge of universal human import. In such a context, the colonial situation of ethnographic fieldwork finds a place in Malinowski's mythic charter only as a series of stock characters from whom the Ethnographer is encouraged to dissociate himself. In such a context, the Ethnographer could forestall a choice between Maclay's quixotic resistance to European power or Kubary's Kurtzian complicity in it: going be-

hind the European presence to recapture a primitive precontact essence ethnographically, he could in a sense preserve it from the demoralizing and destructive impact of European contact without coming to terms with that process
in the real world.

There was, however, another Malinowskian voice besides that of the romantic primitivist. There was also the Malinowski whose doctoral dissertation insisted on the power that scientific knowledge gave the European over
his "less civilized colored brethren," who read Machiavelli while in the field,
whose interest in the advancement of ethnographic knowledge was inseparable
from the advancement of his own career, and who, despite his suspicion that
natives might be happier if they did not "sign on," was not unwilling to offer
advice as to how to make them work more efficiently once they had. Unlike
his romantic primitivist alter ego, this other more real-politikal Malinowski
chose, after his fashion, to come to terms with the colonial system.

In the real historical world, the Garden in which the Ethnographer encountered the Primitive had long since been violated (Wolf 1982). Expropriat-
ing the Garden, European power had imposed upon its inhabitants the labor
demanded of all fallen humankind—the fruits of which were also subjected
to expropriation. And in the real world, the Ethnographer, too, was subject
to the demands of labor—not only to earn his own bread, but to nurture the
marginally institutionalized discipline by which he earned it. He might carry
back to Europe the knowledge of a prelapsarian ethnographic Garden, but
the market for that rather exotic fruit was limited. A more utilitarian product
seemed to be required, and this Malinowski sought to provide. He did not
himself "sign on" for the "dirty work of Empire at close quarters"—as Kubary
had perhaps felt forced to do at an earlier moment in the institutional development of anthropology; but neither would he tilt at the windmills of a colonial
power now much more substantial than in the era of Maclay. Between these
two archetypes, somewhere "within the limits of truth and *realpolitik*" (1931:
999), he sought a middle course: to offer to the colonial establishment a new
kind of anthropological knowledge—academic, but practical—that would facilitate a more effective, a more economical, a more harmonious, and a more
humane administration of colonial populations, simultaneously promoting
both European interests and native welfare (cf. James 1972; Rossetti 1985; Le
Clerc 1972; cf. Onege 1979). In a market of few buyers, such a product could
perhaps provide the resources to pursue ethnographic research and to further
the institutional development of anthropology—as indeed it did do (cf. Stocking 1985).

Malinowski himself saw the move to "practical anthropology" as "de-roman-
ticizing": "romance is fleeing anthropology as it has fled many human concerns, [and] we functional anthropologists have to rely upon the other attraction which science presents, the feeling of power given by the sense of control

of human reality through the establishment of general laws" (1930a:408). But while the power of scientific knowledge never lost its attraction to Malinowski, his somewhat opportunistic attempt to make it more "practical" did not by any means represent a complete transformation of his anthropology. Moving toward the historical world, Malinowski's anthropology remained imperfectly historical. Trumpeting its utility for colonial establishment, it nevertheless distanced itself from the exercise of colonial power. Proclaiming its "deromanticization," it left plenty of room for the romantic impulse to operate in the space it created for ethnographic research.

In advocating the study of cultural contact as "one of the most significant events in human history" (1939:881), Malinowski urged the anthropologist to "train his vision forward rather than backward" (1938:xxvi). But although he was critical of the idea of a precontact "zero point," his proposed study of contact situations as "integral wholes" had a somewhat statically ahistorical character. In the posthumously published columnar analyses of *The Dynamics of Culture Change*, active historical agency was firmly lodged in the first column of "white influences, interests and intentions" (1945:73). As he suggested in a paper forwarded to a conference on colonialism in Africa held in Rome in the aftermath of the conquest of Ethiopia, colonization depended on "the effective demonstration of force," which made Africans both individually and collectively "completely malleable"; furthermore, it was the "duty" of the administrator "to initiate and control change" (1939:883). Thus the second column of Malinowski's contact chart, "the processes of culture contact and change," was a "translation" of white intentions "into practical action," which, despite the "vitality of African tribalism," was "sooner or later bound gradually to engulf and supersede" the "surviving forms of tradition" catalogued in the third column (1945:81). Although Malinowski acknowledged "new forces of spontaneous African reintegration or reaction," this category was incorporated analytically only as a fifth righthand column, after that of the "reconstructed past"—and even then, it was actually utilized only "in some cases": in analyzing warfare, but not witchcraft, native diet, land tenure, or chieftainship (1945:73–76).

Despite Malinowski's move toward the study of change, the new space created for ethnography remained still in a certain sense outside the processes of world history. Though he had come to recognize and even identify with the stirrings of African nationalism, Malinowski did not envision the end of the colonial system, except perhaps in some "ultimate" (a)historical moment—and the same can probably be said for most if not all of his anthropological contemporaries (cf. R. Firth 1977:26). In the historical present, he sought to maintain a certain distance between anthropology and the actual processes of colonial policy and practice, both on the ground and in the metropole. For although Malinowski felt free to criticize the failures of existing colonial policy, and in a general way to suggest alternatives, he made a point of disavowing "academic men meddling in colonial politics" (1930a: 419). Limiting itself to "the study of the facts and processes which bear upon the practical problems," and leaving to statesmen "the final decision of how to apply the results," practical anthropology offered to the colonial establishment a putatively utilitarian cargo of unbiassed scientific understanding—but without being involved either in the determination or the implementation of colonial policy (1929b:23).

In the event, Malinowski's incipient move toward the study of social change in the colonial world was to a great extent forestalled by the shift, under the aegis of Radcliffe-Brown, back toward a more static analysis of social structures in the ethnographic present (Kuper 1983:34, 107, 112). And in the event, the position of the "practical anthropologist" proved more than a bit problematic. Commenting on "Applied Anthropology" several years after Malinowski's death, Evans-Pritchard emphasized the tension between practical and scientific concerns, arguing that the anthropologist would best employ his knowledge and his time in the solution of scientific problems, which might have no practical value whatsoever. Although allowing a role for the anthropologist as "advisor" to colonial governments, Evans-Pritchard was concerned that he be given full access to all documents that affected the interests of natives, in order to assure that they got a "square deal" within the limits of "administrative requirements and imperial policy." But his main point was that the future of anthropology lay in its academic development: what was needed was "more and bigger university departments" (Evans-Pritchard 1946; cf. Grillo 1985).

The role of colonial research grants and colonial research institutes in the postwar period is beyond the scope of this essay; so also the much mooted issue of whether or not the work of Malinowski and his students actually provided information that facilitated colonial rule.[9] More to the present point is the nature of the discursive space created by the "revolution in anthropology." At a pragmatic methodological level, we may regard Malinowski's mythic charter as a critical move in the constitution of the privileged moment in the characteristically atemporal structure of much of twentieth-century anthropological discourse. In nineteenth-century evolutionism, the objects of ethnography existed as a series of static moments along a diachronic scale extending upward from the privileged moment of cultural origins at the beginning of human time (cf. Stocking 1987). With the dehistoricization of anthropology—of which Malinowski's *Argonauts* was a major marker—that tem-

9. On these issues see, among others, Asad 1973; LeClerc 1972; Huizer & Mannheim 1979; Hymes 1973; Kuklick 1978; Kuklick n.d.; Kuper 1983; and Loizos 1977, as well as other sources mentioned in this volume.

poral scale was compressed into a single moment ambiguously situated outside the flow of time. Insofar as it was the product of the ethnographer's own
participant observation, it was a "present" moment; but insofar as its constitution erased a present colonial situation in order to recapture a presumed
precontact cultural essence or structural form, it existed in the "past"—and
doubly so since there was always a substantial interval between observation
and publication. By a convention that was not named until 1942, this privileged moment of modern ethnography came to be called the "ethnographic
present" (Burton 1988; Fabian 1983; cf. Stocking 1989a). Although closer perhaps to the real world than the "primal scene" of the archetypal anthropological encounter, it was an imagined space in which that encounter could,
after the fashion of Malinowski's mythic charter, be reenacted again and again.

To suggest this is not to imply that Malinowski was "a fraud" or that those
who followed in his footsteps did not make substantial contributions to ethnographic knowledge. At the very least, the present consideration of three
ethnographic archetypes should hint at certain ironic complexities in the relationship of motivating myths, colonial power, and ethnographic knowledge.
As the instances of Maclay and Kubary suggest, purity of motive and pris-
tinity of situation have never been guarantors of the quality of ethnographic
knowledge. Such knowledge has always been implicated in (i.e., both facilitated and constrained by) asymmetries of power.[10] There never was a moment
of ethnographic innocence; all of anthropology is postlapsarian. But so long
as it was possible simultaneously to operate under an umbrella of colonial
power and to maintain a certain distance from the forces upholding it, vari-
ants of the myth of the primal encounter could serve as a powerful motivating agency in the production of ethnographic knowledge, helping several
generations of anthropologists to "get on with the work" without too much
worry about ultimate questions of knowledge and power.

That the Malinowskian archetype had some such mythic potency is suggested by the intensity of the reaction to the publication of his Trobriand
diary in 1967; dismay, deprecation, denial all evidenced the depth of disen-
chantment (cf. Firth 1989). By that time, of course, the charmed colonial circle of the ethnographic present had been broken, and the real world power
relations that make ethnographic knowledge possible were being permanently
altered (Holland 1985; Huizer & Mannheim 1979). As native nationalisms
intent on defining the terms of their own development won a place in the
equation of knowledge and power, the primitivist visions that long inspired

10. Lest the scope of the present essay be misunderstood it is perhaps worth making explicit
that it does not pretend to offer an exhaustive consideration of the effect of such constraints
and facilitations on the ethnography of any one of its three archetypical figures; for an example
of a more systematic analysis, see the essay by Ira Bashkow in this volume.

European anthropology became increasingly an ideological burden. But if they may no longer be seen as enabling ethnography, primitivist impulses will no doubt continue to motivate anthropologists for as long as contrasts of culture allow a space for the play of alienated imaginations—and for the shadowy dance of archetypes from the dreamtime of anthropology (cf. Torgovnick 1990).

Acknowledgments

My interest in Maclay was first stimulated in the spring of 1984, when, during an interview with Academician Y. Bromley, then Director of the Institute of Ethnography in Moscow, I was presented with a copy of Tumarkin's English-language edition of Maclay's diaries. Upon my return, I was able, thanks to David Koester's facility with the Russian language, to get a sense of Maclay's overall anthropological oeuvre as contained in *Sobranie Sochineii* (1950–54). Richard Parmentier kindly made available his copy of an English translation of Kubary's "Die Palau-Inseln in der Südsee," and gave me the benefit of his specialist appreciation of Kubary's ethnographic work. Suzanne Falgout, Nancy Munn, and Ira Bashkow also offered helpful references and information. Bill Young, my research assistant during a year at the Getty Center for the History of Art and the Humanities in Santa Monica, provided me with extensive notes on Kubary's *Ethnographische Beiträge zur Kenntniss der Karolinischen Inselgruppe und Nachbarschaft* (1885). Ralph Austen, Barney Cohn, and John Comaroff made useful bibliographical suggestions, and Laura Albert and Andrea Lee-Harshbarger were helpful in tracking down sources during the final reworking. Along with several of those just mentioned, Raymond Fogelson provided helpful comments on an earlier, much shorter version of this paper, which was presented at the Fourth Meeting of the Federación de Asociaciones de Antropología de España in 1987, at the University of Virginia in that same year, and at the University of Colorado in 1989, and subsequently published in Spanish translation (cf. Stocking 1989c). A draft slightly shorter than the present version was presented to the Fishbein Center Workshop in the History of the Human Sciences at the University of Chicago on March 2, 1990, and was the beneficiary of that group's characteristically sharp and stimulating criticism. I am grateful also to Helena Wayne Malinowska and to the archivists at the London School of Economics and Yale University for access to Malinowski manuscripts at earlier stages of the longer-term research project to which this manuscript relates, as well as to the archivists of the several other manuscript sources noted.

References Cited

ACHP. See under Manuscript Sources.
Asad, T., ed. 1973. *Anthropology and the colonial encounter.* London.
Austen, L. 1945. Cultural changes in Kiriwina. *Oceania* 16:14–60.

Bade, K.-J. 1977. Colonial missions and imperialism: The background to the fiasco of the Rhenish mission in New Guinea. In *Germany in the Pacific and Far East, 1870–1914*, ed. J. Moses & P. Kennedy, 312–46. St. Lucas, Queensland.

Balandier, G. 1951. The colonial situation: A theoretical approach. In *The sociology of black Africa: Social dynamics in central Africa*, trans. D. Garman, 34–61. New York (1970).

Baudet, H. 1965. *Paradise on earth: Some thoughts on European images of non-European man.* New Haven.

Beloff, M. 1970. *Imperial sunset: Britain's liberal empire, 1897–1921.* New York.

Bensaude-Vincent, B. 1983. A founder myth in the history of sciences? The Lavoisier case. In *Functions and uses of disciplinary histories*, ed. L. Graham et al., 53–78. Dordrecht, The Netherlands.

Biskup, P., B. Jinks, & H. Nelson. 1968. *A short history of New Guinea.* Sydney.

Black, R. H. 1957. Dr. Bellamy of Papua. *Med. J. Aust.* 2:189–97, 232–38, 279–84.

BMP. See under Manuscript Sources.

Brooks, M. Z. 1985. Lucjan Malinowski and Polish dialectology. *Polish Rev.* 30:167–70.

Burton, J. W. 1988. Shadows at twilight: A note on history and the ethnographic present. *Proc. Am. Philos. Soc.* 132:420–33.

Butinov, N. A. 1971. A nineteenth century champion of anti-racism in New Guinea. *Unesco Cour.* (Nov.): 24–27.

Clifford, J. 1988. On ethnographic self-fashioning: Conrad and Malinowski. In *The predicament of culture: Twentieth-century ethnography, literature and art*, 92–113. Cambridge, Mass.

Docker, E. W. 1970. *The blackbirders: The recruiting of South Seas labour for Queensland, 1863–1907.* Sydney.

Ellen, R., et al., eds. 1988. *Malinowski between two worlds: The Polish roots of an anthropological tradition.* Cambridge.

EMP. See under Manuscript Sources.

Evans-Pritchard, E. E. 1946. Applied anthropology. *Africa* 16:92–98.

Fabian, J. 1983. *Time and the other: How anthropology makes its object.* New York.

Firth, R. 1963. A brief history (1913–63). In *Department of anthropology programme of courses, 1963–64* (London School of Economics), 1–9.

———. 1977. Whose frame of reference? One anthropologist's experience. In Loizos 1977:9–31.

———. 1989. Second introduction: 1988. In repr. ed. of Malinowski 1967:xxi–xxxi. Stanford.

Firth, R., ed. 1957. *Man and culture: An evaluation of the work of Bronislaw Malinowski.* New York (1964).

Firth, S. G. 1972. The New Guinea Company, 1885–1899: A case of unprofitable imperialism. *Hist. Stud.* 15:361–77.

———. 1973. German firms in the Pacific Islands, 1857–1914. In *Germany in the Pacific and Far East, 1870–1914*, ed. J. Moses & P. Kennedy, 1–25. St. Lucas, Queensland.

———. 1982. *New Guinea under the Germans.* Melbourne.

Flis, A. 1988. Cracow philosophy of the beginning of the twentieth century and the rise of Malinowski's scientific ideas. In Ellen et al. 1988:105–27.

Frye, N. 1957. *The anatomy of criticism.* Princeton.

Gerould, D. 1981. *Witkacy: Stanislaw Ignacy Witkiewicz as an imaginative writer.* Seattle.

Gould, E. 1981. *Mythical intentions in modern literature.* Princeton.

Greenop, F. S. 1944. *Who travels alone.* Sydney.

Grillo, R. 1985. Applied anthropology in the 1980s: Retrospect and prospect. In *Social anthropology and development policy,* ed., R. Grillo & A. Rew, 1–36.

Halpern, S. A. 1989. Historical myth and institutional history. MS.

Hempenstall, P. J. 1987. *Pacific islands under German rule: A study in the meaning of colonial resistance.* Canberra.

Hezel, F. 1983. *The first taint of civilization: A history of the Caroline and Marshall Islands in pre-colonial days, 1521–1885.* Honolulu.

Holland, R. F. 1985. *European decolonization, 1918–1981: An introductory survey.* New York.

Hsu, F. 1979. The cultural problem of the cultural anthropologist. *Am. Anth.* 81:517–32.

Huizer, G., & B. Mannheim, eds. 1979. *The politics of anthropology: From colonialism and sexism toward a view from below.* The Hague.

Hymes, D., ed. 1972. *Reinventing anthropology.* New York.

Jacobs, M. C. 1951a. Bismarck and the annexation of New Guinea. *Hist. Stud., Aust. & N.Z.* 5:14–26.

———. 1951b. The Colonial Office and New Guinea, 1874–84. *Hist. Stud., Aust. & N.Z.* 5:106–18.

James, W. 1973. The anthropologist as reluctant imperialist. In Asad 1973:41–70.

Jerschina, J. 1988. Polish culture of modernism and Malinowski's personality. In Ellen et al. 1988:128–48.

JGFP. See under Manuscript Sources.

Joyce, R. B. 1971a. Australian interests in New Guinea before 1906. In *Australia and Papua New Guinea,* ed. W. J. Hudson, 8–31. Sydney.

———. 1971b. *Sir William MacGregor.* Melbourne.

Julius, C. 1960. Malinowski's Trobriand Islands. *J. Public Serv.* (Territory of Papua and New Guinea) 2:5–13, 57–64.

Kenyatta, J. 1938. *Facing Mount Kenya: The tribal life of the Gikuyu.* London.

Kubary, J. 1873. Die Palau-Inseln in der Südsee. *J. Mus. Godeffroy* 1:177–238 (page numbers refer to the manuscript English translation in the Human Relations Area Files in New Haven).

———. 1885. *Ethnographische Beiträge zur Kenntniss der Karolinischen Inselgruppe und Nachbarschaft.* Vol. 1, *Die sozialen Einrichtungen der Pelauer.* Berlin.

Kubica, G. 1988. Malinowski's years in Poland. In Ellen et al. 1988:89–104.

Kuklick, H. 1978. The sins of the fathers: British anthropology and African colonial administration. *Res. Soc. Knowl., Sci. & Art* 1:93–119.

———. n.d. The savage within: The social meaning of British anthropology, 1885–1945. MS.

Kuper, A. 1983. *Anthropology and anthropologists: The modern British school.* London.

Laracy, H. 1976. Malinowski at war, 1914–1918. *Mankind* 10:264–68.

Lawrence, P. 1964. *Road belong cargo: A study of the cargo movement in the southern Madang district of New Guinea.* Atlantic Highlands, N.J. (1979).

Leach, E. 1965. Introduction to repr. ed. of Malinowski 1935:I, vii–xvii.

———. 1980. On reading *A diary in the strict sense of the term*: Or the self-mutilation of Professor Hsu. *RAIN* 36:2–3.

———. 1990. Masquerade: The presentation of self in holi-day life. *Cambridge Anth.* 13(3): 47–69.

LeClerc, G. 1972. *Anthropologie et colonialism: Essai sur l'histoire de l'africanisme.* Paris.

Legge, J. D. 1956. *Australian colonial policy: A survey of native administration and European development in Papua.* Sydney.

Loizos, P., ed. 1977. Special number on colonialism and anthropology. *Anth. Forum* 4(2).

London, H. I. 1970. *Non-White immigration and the "White Australia" policy.* New York.

Louis, W. R. 1967. *Great Britain and Germany's lost colonies, 1914–1919.* Oxford.

Lovejoy, A. O., & G. Boas. 1935. *Primitivism and related ideas in antiquity.* Baltimore.

Lugard, F. D. 1922. *The dual mandate in British tropical Africa.* London (1965).

Mackenzie, S. S. 1927. *The Australians at Rabaul: The capture and administration of the German possessions in the southern Pacific.* Sydney.

McNeill, W. H. 1986. *Mythistory and other essays.* Chicago.

Mair, L. P. 1948. *Australia in New Guinea.* London.

Malinowski, B. 1908. O zasadzie ekonomii myslenia [On the principle of the economy of thought]. Trans. E. C. Martinek. M.A. thesis, Univ. Chicago (1985).

———. 1912. The economic aspect of the Intichiuma ceremonies. In *Festkrift tillegnad Edvard Westermarck i Anledning av hans femtidrosdag den 10 November 1912*, 81–108. Helsingfors.

———. 1915. The natives of Mailu: Preliminary results of the Robert Mond research work in British New Guinea. In Young 1988:77–331.

———. 1922a. Ethnology and the study of society. *Economica* 2:208–19.

———. 1922b. *Argonauts of the western Pacific: An account of native enterprise and adventure in the archipelagoes of Melanesian New Guinea.* London.

———. 1926a. Myth in primitive psychology. In *Magic, science and religion and other essays*, 93–148. Garden City, N.Y. (1954).

———. 1926b. Anthropology and administration. *Nature* 118:768.

———. 1927. *Sex and repression in savage society.* London.

———. 1929a. *The sexual life of savages in northwestern Melanesia.* London.

———. 1929b. Practical anthropology. *Africa* 2:22–38.

———. 1929c. Review of *Report of the commission on closer union of the dependencies in Eastern and Central Africa. Africa* 2:317–20.

———. 1930a. The rationalization of anthropology and administration. *Africa* 3: 405–29.

———. 1930b. Race and labour. *Listener* 4: suppl. 8.

———. 1931. A plea for an effective colour bar. *Spectator* 146:999–1001.

———. 1934. Whither Africa? *Intnl. Rev. Missions* 25:401–7.

———. 1935. *Coral gardens and their magic.* 2 vols. Bloomington, Ind. (1965).

———. 1936. Native education and culture contact. *Intnl. Rev. Missions* 25:480–515.

———. 1937. Introduction to J. Lips, *The savage hits back*, vii–ix. New Haven.

———. 1938a. Introduction to Kenyatta 1938:vii–xiii.

———. 1938b. The anthropology of changing cultures. In *Methods of study of culture contact in Africa*, Memorandum 15 of the International African Institute, vii–xxxv. London (1939).

―――. 1939. Modern anthropology and European rule in Africa. *Convegno di Scienze morali e storiche, 4–11 Ottobre 1938–XVI. Tema: L'Africa*, 2:880–901. Reale Accademia d'Italia. Rome.

―――. 1943. The Pan-African problem of culture contact. *Am. J. Soc.* 48:649–65.

―――. 1945. *The dynamics of culture change: An inquiry into race relations in Africa*. New Haven (1965).

―――. 1967. *A diary in the strict sense of the term*. New York.

Miklouho-Maclay, N. 1950–54. *Sobranie Sochineii*. 5 vols. Moscow.

―――. See also Sentinella; Tumarkin.

Mitchell, P. E. 1930. The anthropologist and the practical man: A reply and a question. *Africa* 3:217–23.

Mitchell, R. E. 1971. Kubary: The first Micronesian reporter. *Micronesian Rep.* 3:43–45.

Moses, I. 1977. The extension of colonial rule in Kaiser Wilhelmsland. In *Germany in the Pacific and Far East, 1870–1914*, ed. John Moses & Paul Kennedy, 288–312. St. Lucas, Queensland.

Mulvaney, D. J. 1989. Australian Anthropology and ANZAAS: "Strictly scientific and critical." In *The commonwealth of science: ANZAAS and the scientific enterprise in Australia, 1888–1988*, ed. R. MacLeod, 196–221. Melbourne.

Murray, J. H. P. 1912. *Papua or British New Guinea*. London.

Murray-Brown, J. 1972. *Kenyatta*. London.

Nelson, H. H. 1969. European attitudes in Papua, 1906–1914. In *The history of Melanesia*. 2d Waigani Seminar. Canberra and Port Moresby.

Pagden, A. 1982. *The fall of natural man: The American Indian and the origins of comparative ethnology*. Cambridge.

Onege, O. F. 1979. The counterrevolutionary tradition in African studies: The case of applied anthropology. In Huizer & Mannheim 1979:45–66.

Paluch, A. K. 1981. The Polish background of Malinowski's work. *Man* 16:276–85.

Parmentier, R. 1987. *The sacred remains: Myth, history and polity in Belau*. Chicago.

Parnaby, O. W. 1964. *Britain and the labor trade in the southwest Pacific*. Durham, N.C.

Payne, H. C. 1981. Malinowski's style. *Proc. Am. Philos. Soc.* 125:416–40.

Paszkowski, L. 1969. John Stanislaw Kubary—Naturalist and ethnographer of the Pacific islands. *Aust. Zool.* 16(2): 43–70.

Perham, M. 1956. *Lugard: The years of adventure, 1858–1898*. London.

―――. 1960. *Lugard: The years of authority, 1898–1945*. London.

Richards, A. 1944. Practical anthropology in the lifetime of the International African Institute. *Africa* 14:289–300.

Rivers, W. H. R. 1912. General account of method. In *Notes and queries on anthropology*, ed. C. H. Read et al., pp. 108–27. London.

―――. 1913. Report on anthropological research outside America. In *Reports upon the present condition and future needs of the science of anthropology*, by W. H. R. Rivers, A. E. Jenks, & S. G. Morley, pp. 5–28. Washington, D.C.

―――, ed. 1922. *Essays in the depopulation of Melanesia*. Cambridge.

Rossetti, C. 1985. Malinowski, the sociology of modern problems in Africa, and the colonial situation. *Cah. Etud. Afr.* 25:477–503.

Rowley, C. D. 1958. *The Australians in German New Guinea, 1914–1921*. Melbourne.
———. 1966. *The New Guinea villager: The impact of colonial rule on primitive society and economy*. New York.
Sack, P. G. 1973. *Land between two laws: Early European land acquisitions in New Guinea*. Canberra.
Sack, P. & D. Clark, eds. 1979. *German New Guinea: The annual reports*. Canberra.
Saville, W. J. 1912. A grammar of the Mailu language. *J. Roy. Anth. Inst.* 42:397–436.
Scarr, D. 1969. Recruits and recruiters: A portrait of the labour trade. In *Pacific island portraits*, ed. J. W. Davidson & D. Scarr, 95–126. Canberra.
Seligman, C. G. 1910. *The Melanesians of British New Guinea*. Cambridge.
Sentinella, C. L., ed. 1975. *Mikloucho-Maclay: New Guinea diaries, 1871–1883*. Madang.
Smith, E. W. 1934. The story of the Institute: The first seven years. *Africa* 7:1–27.
Smith, E. 1973. *Some versions of the fall: The myth of the fall of man in English literature*. London.
Sontag, S. 1966. The anthropologist as hero. In *Against interpretation*, 69–81. New York.
Spoehr, F. M. 1963. *White falcon: The house of Godeffroy and its commercial and scientific role in the Pacific*. Palo Alto, Calif.
Stocking, G. W., Jr. 1968. Empathy and antipathy in the heart of darkness. *J. Hist. Behav. Sci.* 4:189–94.
———. 1977. Contradicting the doctor: Billy Hancock and the problem of Baloma. *Hist. Anth. News.* 4(1): 4–7.
———. 1983. The ethnographer's magic: Fieldwork in British anthropology from Tylor to Malinowski. *HOA* 1:70–120.
———. 1985. Philanthropoids and vanishing cultures: Rockefeller funding and the end of the museum era in Anglo-American anthropology. *HOA* 3:112–45.
———. 1986a. Why does a boy "sign on"?—Malinowski's first statement on practical anthropology. *Hist. Anth. Newsl.* 13(2): 6–9.
———. 1986b. Anthropology and the science of the irrational: Malinowski's encounter with Freudian psychoanalysis. *HOA* 4:13–49.
———. 1987. *Victorian anthropology*. New York.
———. 1989a. Paradigmatic traditions in the history of anthropology. In *Companion to the history of modern science*, ed. G. N. Cantor et al., 712–27. London.
———. 1989b. The ethnographic sensibility of the 1920s and the dualism of the anthropological tradition. *HOA* 6:208–75.
———. 1989c. Los modelos de Malinowski: Kubary, Maclay y Conrad como arquetipos etnográficos. Trans. F. Estévez. *Eres* 1:9–24.
———. In process. *After Tylor: The reformation of anthropology in post-Victorian Britain, 1888–1938*.
Strenski, I. 1982. Malinowski: Second positivism, second romanticism. *Man* 17:266–71.
Thorton, R. 1985. "Imagine yourself set down . . .": Mach, Frazer, Conrad, Malinowski and the role of imagination in ethnography. *Anth. Today* 1(5): 7–14.
———. n.d. Malinowski's reading, writing, 1904–1914. MS.
Tinker, H. 1974. *A new system of slavery: The export of Indian labour overseas, 1830–1920*. London.
Todorov, T. 1982. *The conquest of America: The question of the other*. New York (1984).
Torgovnick, M. 1990. *Gone primitive: Savage intellects, modern lives*. Chicago.

Tumarkin, D. 1982a. Mikluoho-Maclay: Nineteenth century Russian anthropologist and humanist. *RAIN* 51:4–7.

———. 1988. Miklouho-Maclay: A great Russian scholar and humanist. *Social Sciences* (U.S.S.R. Academy of Sciences) 19:175–89.

———, ed. 1982b. *N. Miklouho-Maclay's travels to New Guinea: Diaries, letters, documents.* Moscow.

Wayne (Malinowska), H. 1985. Bronislaw Malinowski: The influence of various women on his life and works. *Am. Ethnol.* 12:529–40.

Webster, E. M. 1984. *The moon man: A biography of Nikolai Miklouho-Maclay.* Berkeley.

Weiner, A. 1976. *Women of value, men of renown: New perspectives in Trobriand exchange.* Austin, Tex.

West, F. 1968. *Hubert Murray: The Australian proconsul.* Melbourne.

———, ed. 1970. *Selected letters of Hubert Murray.* Melbourne.

Willard, M. 1923. *History of the White Australia policy to 1920.* London (1967).

Williams, F. E., ed. 1939. The reminiscences of Ahuia Ova. *J. Roy. Anth. Inst.* 69:11–44.

Wolf, E. 1982. *Europe and the people without history.* Berkeley.

Wolfers, E. P. 1972. Trusteeship without trust: A short history of interracial relations and the law in Papua and New Guinea. In *Racism: The Australian experience,* ed. F. S. Stevens. Vol. 3, *Colonialism,* 61–147. Sydney.

Young, M. W. 1984. The intensive study of a restricted area; or, Why did Malinowski go to the Trobriand Islands. *Oceania* 55:1–26.

———. 1988. Editor's introduction. *Malinowski among the Magi: "The natives of Mailu,"* 1–76. London.

Manuscript Sources

ACHP   A. C. Haddon Papers, University Library, Cambridge.

BMP   Bronislaw Malinowski Papers, British Library of Political and Economic Science, London School of Economics.

EMP   Elton Mayo Papers. Baker Library, Harvard University.

JGFP   J. G. Frazer Papers. Trinity College, Cambridge.

TOOLS OF THE TRADE

*The Production of Ethnographic Observations
on the Andaman Islands, 1858–1922*

DAVID TOMAS

A Cambridge contemporary once described Radcliffe-Brown's life on the Andaman Islands as that of a "primitive autocrat" who exercised "a beneficent but completely authoritarian sway over the simple Andamanese, who had not been in a position to criticise his grand gestures" (Watson 1946:83). Although this stereotypical image of European colonial relations with the Other cannot be directly confirmed in the sparse surviving record of his fieldwork, what is possible—and what has thus far been lacking in the literature—is a historical account of the colonial situation of his ethnographic activity. Such an account will enable us to see his fieldwork and its literary product not simply as a revolutionary innovation in the development of a profession but in relation to a flourishing ethnographic tradition that developed over half a century in one of the more obscure corners of Britain's Imperium.

That these remote islands in the Bay of Bengal should have nurtured the type and quality of anthropological activity they did reflects a nineteenth-century obsession with instances of presumed racial "purity." In the words of William Henry Flower, "we have here the rare case of a population, confined to a very limited space, and isolated for hundreds, perhaps thousands, of years from all contact with external influence, their physical characters unmixed by crossing, and their culture, their beliefs, their language, entirely their own" (1888:295). Isolation produced a perfect "natural history museum" in which the indigenous population, treated "as living fossils" (304), was the medium

---

David Tomas is Assistant Professor in the Department of Visual Arts, University of Ottawa. His doctoral dissertation (McGill University, 1987) explored the relationship between authority, observation, and photography in nineteenth-century British anthropology. He is currently working on a book on the history of representation on the Andaman Islands.

for a series of important anthropological representations (Flower 1879; Man 1883; Brown 1922). These moved in a trajectory from readily observable and collectible material and physical aspects of Andaman life—curios and skeletal material—through a more problematic communicative arena linked to their incarcerated bodies, in which language was both object and medium, toward the increasingly elusive and equivocal realms of cultural practices and beliefs, moving finally toward a theoretically constituted sphere of cultural psychology and social organization. These images were produced by a succession of tools of observation beginning with maritime surveys, then progressing through craniometric measurement, linguistic queries, ethnographic questionnaires, photography, and culminating in a functional analysis that articulated theory and ethnographic observation. Once adopted, most of these tools remained active components of the anthropologist's "toolbox" throughout the period, but their foregrounding at particular moments reflected the intellectual movement of British anthropology during the nineteenth and early twentieth centuries, a period in which the Andamanese were to remain a privileged ethnographic case.

Whether conceived as living human fossils, pure race, or the archetype of a pretotemic society, the Andamanese were one of a relatively small number of peoples who offered "living proof" of some fundamental anthropological "truth." At every step, that proof depended not only on dominant tendencies in anthropological theory back at the intellectual center, but on the type of investigative methodology that could be marshalled at different stages of an evolving colonial situation. At each point, a dominant form of investigation was correlated with a characteristic mode of communication and an articulated relationship of power and authority. In the beginning, when the hostile Andamanese were still resisting colonization, artifacts, skulls, and bones were collected in the absence of direct verbal communication. Once the Andamanese were finally enmeshed in a process of acculturation, centered on a colonial settlement and rapidly expanding penal colony, discrete items of cultural information were collected by way of ethnographic questionnaires or photographic procedures governed by an observational methodology propagated in questionnaire form. In the end, when the Andamanese in the vicinity of the colonial settlement had been almost wiped out or assimilated into the everyday life of a penal colony, the meaning of Andamanese cultural practices and beliefs within a now increasingly inaccessible Andamanese culture could be authoritatively reconstituted, even in the aftermath of a relatively unsuccessful fieldwork sojourn, by a university-trained anthropologist attuned to the latest developments in French social theory. We may even say that while the image of Radcliffe-Brown's "benevolent autocracy" over "the simple Andamanese" remains problematic, there are perhaps grounds for attributing to Radcliffe-Brown—and to the functionalist method he helped to promulgate – an epistemological and interpretive authoritarianism, the culmination of a richer and more extensive interrelationship between colonial and ethnographic practices on the Andaman Islands.[1]

The "Andaman Homes":
Creating a Site for Ethnographic Observation

Dangerous coastlines and the implacable hostility of the Andamanese, coupled with a widespread belief that they were cannibals, ensured the Andaman Islands' virtual isolation until the late eighteenth century (Ritchie 1771:61; Colebrooke 1807:385; Earl 1850:9; Anon. 1859:v). There is evidence to suggest that they were frequented, before European colonization, by Malay pirates and others engaged in the slave trade (Topping 1791:44; Anon. 1908: 13–14), as well as by Burmese and Chinese traders seeking trepang (bêche-de-mer) and edible birds nests (Anon. 1859:60; Mouat 1863:21–22; Portman 1899:I, 11–12, 19, 51, 116). However, it was the British, whose military and commercial interests in the Bay of Bengal were directly connected to their activities in India, who first began to take a systematic interest in the islands. Following a series of survey expeditions by the British East India Company, there was an abortive attempt at colonization in 1789, which was abandoned in 1796. After a lapse of sixty years, a "scheme" to found "a penal settlement and harbour of refuge" was hastened to fruition by the need to create a major penal colony for the Sepoy mutineers of 1857. Established at Port Blair on South Andaman Island, the colony was used until 1945 to incarcerate Indian revolutionaries and nationalists, as well as a variety of common criminals (Majumda 1975).

The foundation of the Settlement in 1858 inaugurated a series of "serious difficulties . . . in consequence of the harassing attacks on . . . working parties by the aborigines, whose cupidity was excited by the iron tools and other implements which in their eyes presented an appearance of adaptability as weapons of the chase." The "Government Gardens" were "likewise freely robbed, until at length stern repressive measures had to be adopted whereby they were instructed for the first time in the laws of private property" (Man 1885a:262). Accordingly, the Andamanese were "duly instilled" with "a wholesome dread of [British] power" and subjected to "efforts" directed "to the civilization of the race and the establishment of a better understanding between [settlers] and the original possessors of the soil." This sequence of pacification was offi-

---

1. Since the time span of this essay is confined to the period in which he had not yet assumed his hyphenated name, Radcliffe-Brown will be referred to by the name to which he was born, and under which his early work was published (and will herein be cited).

cially inaugurated in 1861 by the capture and detention of individuals in special encampments known as "Andaman Homes." The strategy "effected a marked improvement in . . . relations with the tribes in South Andaman by affording them convincing proof of . . . friendly intentions towards them"; it also furthered "one of the objects which had prompted the re-establishment of the colony—*i.e.*, of reclaiming the savages from their barbarous custom of murdering all strangers who approached their shores" (262).

The capture of six Andamanese in January 1861 after a series of altercations prompted an administrative crisis for the Superintendent of Port Blair. Captain J. C. Haughton thought it would be "impossible" to detain the captives "without an amount of restraint which would defeat entirely our object in keeping them," for he noted that "the temptation to escape is too great, and they are as slippery as eels." He nevertheless ordered that they be detained "with a view to their being made, if possible, the means of intercourse with their countrymen hereafter" (Haughton 1861:255). A touristic itinerary was organized around prominent symbols of military and technological power, notably iron in its various forms, for "every thing like metal they admire and want" (Hellard 1861:259). The prisoners were clothed the day after their capture; the next day attempts were made to learn something of their language; and on the following day they were taken on a tour of a gunboat and a blacksmith's shop. After a short detention, three were released with a range of presents (yams, plantains, old iron hoops, etc.). The others—named Jumbo, Friday, and Crusoe, with the collective surname "Blair"—were sent to Rangoon on a steamer, the object being "to impart to them some idea of the power and resources of their captors" (Fytche 1861:263). Unfortunately, the trip was marred by Jumbo's death from pulmonary disease aggravated by exposure sustained during an escape attempt. The immediate conversion of Jumbo's body into an osteological specimen forestalled a more careful observation of Andamanese death rituals: "his comrades . . . performed some singular ceremonies over the body, which I wished to have witnessed repeated the next morning: but owing to some rather precipitate measures, taken without the slightest reference to myself, to prepare a skeleton of the deceased for presentation to the Asiatic Society's Museum, I was unable to do so" (Tickell 1864:164; Anon. 1862:345). The fragile health of the remaining captives and the failure to breach linguistic barriers hastened the repatriation of the two survivors.

Although the experiment of sending captives to Rangoon and Moulmein was considered a failure (Fytche 1861:266; Tickell 1864:169), the pacification strategy was not abandoned. Writing at the turn of the century after he had discussed the events with the Andamanese, a prominent settlement administrator and Andaman ethnographer retrospectively endorsed Haughton's experiment: "he took the only step which is of any use in taming the Andamanese; *i.e.*, he sent them away from their own country for a considerable period to a land where they saw something of civilization, realized somewhat the extent and greatness of our power and their own insignificance and weakness, and, though well and kindly treated, were kept under a certain amount of discipline" (Portman 1899:I, 306). The difficulty was simply that "sufficient time had not been allowed for the results of the visit to Moulmein to impress the others," and "the story of the Moulmein captives only influenced, (and that slowly), one Sept of the Áka-Béa-da tribe." As a result, "considerable time would have to elapse before the Andamanese of the whole tribe were convinced of our friendly disposition" (1899:I, 332, 359). In the interim, however, colonial discipline had effectively been cast in a visual mold: to see and experience material configurations of power was to become aware of their possibilities.

There is, however, another dimension to this story. As blatant incarceration and overt violence were acknowledged to be counterproductive practices in the long run, another method had to be used to "wean" the itinerant Andamanese from their "wild habits" and create "artificial wants, to supply which should involve the necessity of frequent visits to the settlement, and thus form as it were the nucleus of increasing intercourse with a superior race" (Tickell 1864:169). The principal method adopted was the distribution of free food (often of dubious quality), tobacco, and iron, which coupled with the policy of detention, paved the way for the foundation of special encampments specifically designed to mediate between British colonial interests and Andamanese economic and social activities (Haughton 1861:258; Portman 1899:I, 410–14, 443, 462, 465; cf. Fytche 1861:264; Man 1885a:263). Eventually, "a trade was established for them, weapons, curiosities, etc., being brought in and sold, the proceeds being used to defray the cost of tobacco and other luxuries, by which their hearts were won" (Portman 1881:470). Although the strategy proved successful, its long-term effects were devastating, for it altered the economic and social landscape of Andaman interpersonal relations and hastened the collapse of a decentralized and pluralistic hunting and gathering economy (Man 1885a:263). However, from the British point of view, it achieved its short-term aim. When language barriers were finally bridged in the Andaman Islands, it was in the context of the specially constructed encampments known as Andaman Homes.

Although detention and linguistic communication were two of the principal motivating factors that prompted the foundation of the first Andaman Home at Ross Island, Port Blair, in 1863 (Portman 1899:I, 377), the directives of the Superintendent of Port Blair, Lieutenant Colonel R. C. Tytler, indicate that it was also considered to be a "master" environment for the acculturation and management of indigenous activities. From its inception, the first Home functioned as the center of "a system of entire pacification" and "foundation stone for civilizing a people hitherto living in a perfectly barbarous state, re-

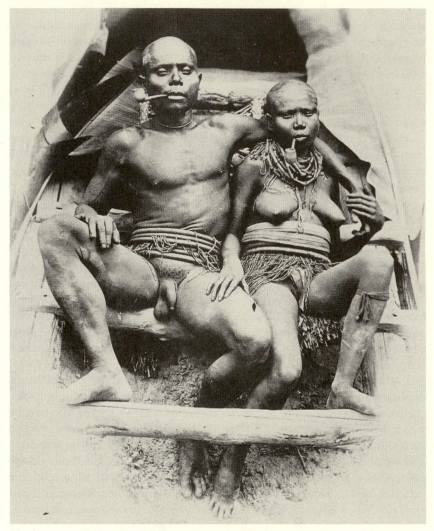

Chief and his wife, seated on the steps of the Andaman Home near Port Blair, in a photograph taken by G. E. Dobson in May 1872. (Courtesy of the Royal Anthropological Institute of Great Britain and Ireland.)

plete with treachery, murder, and every other savageness." There the Andamanese would "see the superior comforts of civilization compared to their miserable savage condition," and would "learn to appreciate their now comfortable home and mode of living." But they were also held in "custody as hostages, for it undoubtedly secures the better behaviour of these inhospitable people towards our Settlement; whereas their leaving us might injure and abolish all the good that has already been established, and might take years again to regain and recover were we to lose the great advantage we now hold and possess." In order simultaneously to make these hostages an acculturative example and to protect them from cultural recontamination, access by Andamanese still "in their fresh and ungovernable state of wildness" was limited: "occasionally, about once a fortnight, a few might with advantage be induced to come over for a very short visit, so as to satisfy their tribes on their return of the care we take of their people living under our charge, and after feeding and otherwise kindly treating them to return them to their woods" (Tytler quoted in Portman 1899:I, 376–78).

The homes were successful, both from an administrative and ethnographic point of view. By the early 1880s they contained, "besides the large number of sick and convalescents . . . a certain quantity of people belonging to different tribes" who were kept "for six months at a time, in order that by their labour in selling the produce of the gardens, diving for lost articles, rowing boats, etc., they may keep up the funds of the department," as well as serving as "hostages for the good behaviour of the tribe to which they belong" (Portman 1881:476). By 1894, the tally of Andamanese in the South Andaman Homes was 127 Haddo, 33 Táracháng, 7 Duratáng, and 3 Góp-láka-bàng. On the eve of the new century, Portman noted that "many of these, in fact a large majority, were people from the North and Middle Andamans," and that outside the Homes there were no aborigines on the South Andaman, except the notoriously hostile Jarawas (Portman 1899:II, 692): "Twenty years ago the Andamanese resented living in the Homes for long, and preferred the free sporting life in their jungle encampments. Now the only encampments of the Andamanese in the South Andaman are the Homes, which contain nearly 250 Andamanese, against under 100 of 20 years ago" (II, 700).

During the same period, the Homes were functioning to homogenize and transform the indigenous population. They became the generative locale for hybrid intertribal identities, simply because they provided the only stable context for communication and marriage (Anon. 1908:26; Man 1885a:261, 263). By the end of the century their effect on the precolonial hunting and gathering life of the Andamanese was disastrous. Tribal autonomy disintegrated following outbreaks of pneumonia (1868), syphilis (1876), ophthalmia (1876), measles (1877), mumps (1886), influenza (1890), and gonorrhea (1892). Although attempts were sometimes made, as in the case of the 1876 syphilis outbreak, to displace responsibility onto the convict guards (Man 1883:83, n. 2; Anon. 1908:116), the connection between the Homes and the spread of infectious disease was acknowledged by administrators.

The surviving Andamanese assimilated a variety of European roles, in addition to their roles as cultural brokers, interpreters, and jungle police. Some became navigators (Portman 1899:II, 670–71), others domestic servants, gardeners, waiters, Jinricksha drivers, and photographic assistants (Portman 1899:II, 864). They were also running dynamos and engines, and were used to collect natural produce such as edible bird nests and trepang. By 1908, the Homes were officially portrayed as "a free asylum to which every Andamanese that likes is admitted":

> he may stay as long as he pleases and go when it suits him. While there he is housed, fed and taken care of, and for the sick there is a good and properly maintained hospital. From the Home, too, are taken such little necessaries and luxuries as the people desire to friends at a distance and during each of the many tours taken around the coasts by the officials (Anon. 1908:55).

By the late 1880s the South Andamanese were almost completely assimilated in the Settlement's operations and could serve as intermediaries in British attempts to establish friendly relations with the Önges of Little Andaman Island (Ball 1874:172; Portman 1881:485, 1888:569ff., 1899:II, chs. 19–20; Cadell 1889:67–68).

Just as the individuals and groups who passed through the Homes transmitted knowledge of colonial power and resources to the far reaches of the islands, so also they became the center of an efficient system of ethnographic knowledge gathering, because one did not need to go into the field to generate a considerable body of information about the customs, habits, and language of the Andamanese. There was even a connection between disease and information: bodies found their way in skeletal form back to museums and craniological collections in England; administrators, while tending to the sick in a measles epidemic, devoted spare time "to an attempt to learn what proved to be a very difficult tongue" (Temple 1930:11). However, the process of collecting a vocabulary of the principal southern group of tribes in the vicinity of Port Blair was slow (Ball 1874:173; Ellis 1882:45–48), and conversations were eventually conducted in a mixture of Hindustani and the South Andaman "Áka-Béa-da" dialect (Portman 1899:II, 622; cf. TP: Portman/Tylor 1/24/1899). Even so, a large enough vocabulary was amassed by the mid to late 1870s to ensure the successful pursuit of further ethnographic inquiries (Ellis 1882: 45–47; Prain 1932:15). It soon became evident, for example, that the Andamanese were not a homogeneous linguistic and social unit, but were in fact nine (later, eleven) linguistically distinct tribes whose distribution could be shown on a map of known tribal encampments (Man 1878a:106–7; Man and Temple 1880; Anon. 1908:26).

Between 1863 and 1908 and Andaman Homes thus functioned as a principal site for acculturation and ethnographic observation—a profoundly contradictory situation, inasmuch as they were designed to facilitate a transition to a state of civilization, whereas the strategy behind ethnographic observation, at this period, was to reconstruct essential precontact representations of an isolated island people. Although the Homes created the necessary contextual stability needed for long-term observation, they also continuously undermined the object of study. What was needed, therefore, in addition to a stable context, was a series of observational tools designed to frame and filter the object so as to restore it to a pristine precontact condition.

Skulls and Artifacts as Indicators of Racial Affinity and Evolutionary Status

The first such tools were skulls, bones, and artifacts. These were of course particularly appropriate in a situation where direct verbal communication was difficult and interpersonal relations limited. But they were also assumed to be helpful in solving the "important scientific questions" suggested by this isolated Negrito population of strikingly diminutive stature. In an anthropological milieu still heavily influenced by what has been called the "ethnological paradigm," these were initially matters of racial derivation and affinity: "who are the natives of the Andaman Islands, and where among the other races of the human species, shall we look for their nearest relations?" (Flower 1888:300, 1881a:239; cf. Stocking 1987:74–75). Osteological material and skulls in particular were important tools used by physical anthropologists to construct a comparative "scientific" history of the human races at a time when the debate between monogenists and polygenists on the origin of man appeared exhausted, and the whole spatially conceived question of origins was being temporally recast in Darwinian evolutionary terms (Stocking 1987:76). As "perhaps the most primitive, or lowest in the scale of civilization, of the human race" (Owen 1862:248), the Andamanese were an important case for those who sought to subordinate speculative questions of origins to scientific methodology and observational rigor.

The Andaman Islands first attracted the attention of anthropologists in England when Richard Owen, anti-Darwinian doyen of British comparative anatomy and paleontology, published data and cautious conclusions in 1861 based on an examination of an "imperfect" Andamanese skeleton which was finally presented to the British Museum (Owen 1862:244, 1863:34; Mouat 1863:331). Owen's paper remained inconclusive on the older question of diffusion vs. independent origin: while there were no "anatomical grounds for deriving the Andaman people from any existing continent," he could "offer no encouragement to the belief that they originated in the locality to which they are now limited" (1862:247–48). But Owen was less indecisive in regard to potential evolutionary connections to "Darwinian" ancestors: "The Andamaners resemble the orangs and chimpanzeee [sic] only in their diminutive stature;

but this is associated with the well-balanced human proportions of trunk to limbs: they are, indeed, surpassed by the great orangs and gorillas in the size of trunk and in the length and strength of the arms, in a greater degree than are the more advanced and taller races of mankind" (249).

When Owen's paper was presented to the Ethnological Society of London in 1862, the prominent Darwinian physical anthropologist, George Busk, cautioned against hasty conclusions based on the analysis of a single specimen, drawing attention to the need for a collection of Andaman crania (Owen 1863:49). Busk later attempted to shed a comparative light on Andamanese origins by measuring two additional skulls and comparing the results with Owen's original data and with eight lower-caste Hindu male and female skulls, as well as thirteen so-called Veddah skulls from Sri Lanka chosen "partly on account of their geographical relations . . . and partly because, in the small size of the cranium, they appear to approach perhaps the nearest of all mankind to the Andamanese" (1866:208). However, the comparison was inconclusive, producing no more than a vague reference to "the great proportionate development of the more animal part of the face" (209). But if Busk's procedures were later discredited (Sullivan 1921:186), the paper marks the beginning of comparative statistical studies of Andaman osteological material.

While physical anthropologists at the center of the Imperium were beginning to engage in intricate craniometric exercises and speculating on the position of the Andaman Islander in an evolutionary schema, on the periphery the story occasionally took a somewhat skeptical turn: "It is stated at the Andamans, that many skulls of convicts have been sent away as those of the aborigines, whilst *a tame monkey, received from India* and given to the crew of a passing man-of-war, has lately received a new specific name in London as being indigenous on these islands!" (Day 1870:153n.). As this observation suggests, gathering trustworthy and authentic ethnographic evidence depended on a complex and often fragile thread of authority that linked periphery with center. The tenuousness of this thread is also evident in the occasional necessity of subterfuge. Having been promised a skeleton for the Hunterian Museum, a local medical man reported that "both the Commissioner and the officer in charge of the Aborigines have the greatest possible objection to the natives being interferred with in any way—and especially with any meddling with their remains. But in a few months they are going on tour to the Nicobar islands, and while they are away my friend will secure the skeleton and I will send it on to you" (ML: Dr. A. J. Wall/Sir J. Fayrer 10/31/1877). A letter written four months later acknowledged problems due to Andamanese burial procedures: "Mr Man . . . knows of one body being now exposed on a tree and if he can get the tribe to remove to a distance he will get me the skull" (ML: Dougall/Fayrer 8/2/1878). Man "succeeded with some difficulty in procuring and forwarding to Europe and Calcutta no fewer than 29 or 30 skeletons (most of them perfect) of Andamanese adults of both sexes" (Man 1882:275).

During the same period, there was a continuing flow of artifacts back to England. In 1878, Colonel Lane Fox (later, Pitt Rivers), the leading champion of the diffusionist approach to material culture, studied Man's collection of Andaman "arts and implements" with a view to establishing "any social connection with other races of mankind" (1878:440). Fox argued that artifacts were "more reliable data with which to trace out the early history of mankind" than belief systems and rites, which were "as little understood for the most part by the people who practise them, as those by whom they are recorded," since "words are subject to variations arising from defects of hearing, memory, and other causes, from which the arts are exempt." Because language changed more rapidly in a "low condition of culture" than the material arts (which began to develop more rapidly only as "civilization progresses"), it made more sense to focus on the "simple arts" of a "primitive" people than on their language. The proof of these observations was given by Man's collection of Andamanese artifacts, "where it is seen that many of the forms of implements are said to be the same throughout the Andaman tribes, whilst the language has changed so greatly that men of different tribes are unable to converse with one another" (Fox 1878:451). Notwithstanding such claims, material artifacts were to play only a minor instrumental role in the methodological development of Andaman ethnography at a time when race was still the prime object of "scientific" inquiry. By 1885 there was such a glut of artifacts in England that H. N. Mosely, working at the Pitt Rivers Museum in Oxford and faced with another shipment of artifacts from Man, complained of having "already far too much Andaman & Nicobar things"; in his opinion, Man "was the sort . . . who might send four or five entire Nicobar villages with all the inhabitants beside" (TP: Mosely/Tylor 1/2/1885).

In the meantime, the flow of skeletal material continued. The most systematic interpreter was William Flower, Curator of the Hunterian Museum of the Royal College of Surgeons (and, after 1884, Director of the British Museum), who studied the relations of the Andamanese to the "other black races" (1879:132). By 1879, Flower was able to examine nineteen "more or less complete" adult skeletons and thirty skulls (1879:110). He later confirmed the accuracy of his estimates of the average height of the Andamanese by comparing them to the average height of thirty live individuals published by E. S. Brander (Brander 1880; Flower 1881b:124). By 1885, Flower had refined the accuracy of earlier measurements with measurements made on an additional ten adult skeletons—"obtained through the kindness of Mr. E. H. Man" (1885: 115). As Flower pointed out, "the study of such a race as the Andamanese would throw much light not only on their own affinities, but also upon the general value of anatomical characters in the classification of man, if it could be thoroughly carried out by comparison with an equal number of individuals of more or less related races, treated in the same manner." He cautioned, however, that "at present this cannot be" because of the inadequacy of the comparative material: "Of how few groups of the human species do we possess even a fair approximation to the average proportions of the limb bones, of the pelvis, even of the better-studied bones of the face and cranium?" (Flower 1879:128–29). But since the supply of osteological material for the most relevant groups did not substantially improve, craniological investigations soon suffered the same marginal fate as the study of material artifacts.

It might be argued, however, that at this early phase of the development of Andaman ethnography skulls had a certain paradoxical advantage as an ethnographic tool. To observe a living indigenous population one had to be *in contact*, to communicate, examine, handle, and measure. But in the case of osteological "observation," one did not have to be directly "in the field." The field could supply the raw material for observation and analysis in England. Furthermore, osteological and craniological studies provided, albeit in somewhat oblique fashion, a simple solution to the problem of intercultural communication. If one could not communicate directly with living informants, one could still engage in a kind of dialogue with their bones, the most permanent components of their bodies: "After having had twenty-four skulls in my room for a few days, repeatedly examining, handling and measuring them, the special characters of each became so distinctly revealed, that I could in a moment recognize each one from the other; as no doubt would be the case with the living individuals of the race" (Flower 1879:112).

There was, however, a distinction to be made between the generically tactile and statistical handling of skulls and their particular functions in an Andamanese system of customs and beliefs. Although Flower handled skulls in his quest to classify the Andamanese within an overall evolutionary picture of the races, he ignored the usages that skulls may have had in the Andaman Islands, uses that had already prompted curiosity and commentary (Owen 1863:37; Ball 1874:171; Brander 1880:423). Skulls and bones were, in fact, important ritual items carried around and constantly exchanged by the Andamanese (Man 1883:146; Thomson 1882; Brown 1922:112–13). In 1902, W. L. Duckworth, a Cambridge physical anthropologist, examined an obvious cultural artifact (a skull still retaining traces of red and white paint that was accompanied by its carrying sling) from a purely physical point of view. He acknowledged that he was not interested in the "ethnological significance of such a method of preparation of the skull" (1902:33), but the distinction between the painted object and its "physical" description is striking; especially when compared to Brown's later description of social healing and mnemonic functions of disinterred skulls and bones in the reaggregation sequence of a rite of passage (Brown 1922:285–94; cf. Van Gennep 1960). In the hands of researchers such as Owen, Flower, and Duckworth, skulls were stripped of cultural significance and circulated in a craniometric system of observation, as a means to reflect on racial types and evolutionary theories. But in the process it was easy to forget that skulls and bones when covered with skin were home to unique social and cultural consciousnesses. It was these that began to attract the attention of advanced anthropologists in the last quarter of the nineteenth century.

Notes and Queries:
The Meta-tool of Evolutionary Anthropology

Conceived as an objective vehicle "to promote accurate anthropological observation on the part of travellers, and to enable those who are not anthropologists . . . to supply the information . . . for the scientific study of anthropology at home (Anon. 1874:iv), *Notes and Queries on Anthropology* was the primary theoretical and methodological link between British anthropologists at home and observers in the field in the closing decades of the nineteenth century (Anon. 1874, 1892). Drawn up by a committee of the British Association for the Advancement of Science in 1874, this manual of questions and advice was heavily influenced by E. B. Tylor, who had recently published his magnum opus, *Primitive Culture* (1871). Of its 146 pages, 112 were devoted to that category, leaving a meager twenty-six for the physical "Constitution of Man." Compact enough to be carried "in the carpet bag of every traveller" (Busk 1875:498), its concentrated cognitive structure allowed a fledgling discipline desperately short of manpower to create instant observers whose activities could be rationalized in terms of a unified system of "scientific" categories (Fox 1875:484–85).

Notes and Queries on Anthropology had a definitive influence on two major Andaman ethnographies. The first was a series of articles published by E. H. Man in the 1880s, the second a monumental fifteen-volume study of the Andamanese produced by M. V. Portman and W. S. Molesworth in the 1890s — unique in that twelve of the volumes consisted of a photographic record of various facets of Andamanese social activity and manufacture (Anon. 1908:39).

Foremost of the nineteenth-century "self-taught students" of Andaman ethnography (ACHP: Temple/Haddon 3/16/06), Edward Horace Man was the son of the founder of the Penal Settlement at Port Blair and was himself in charge of the Andaman Homes from 1875 to 1879. In 1880, Man returned to England for a two-year leave of absence, was elected a member of the Anthropological Institute a year later for his contributions to British anthropology, and presented detailed ethnographic observations before its members in 1882 (Prain 1932:17). Subsequently published in three installments in the Institute's *Journal*, these were quickly acclaimed as an example of the most advanced ethnographic writing of the day (Evans 1883:563; Anon. 1883:251), and they were reprinted in monograph form in 1885 and again in 1932.

On the Aboriginal Inhabitants of the Andaman Islands was regarded as "a model for ethnologists," because it followed throughout "the lines laid down in the British Association volume of 'Notes and Queries on Anthropology'" (Anon. 1883:251). In contrast to the conventional form of narrative or anecdotal accounts, its systematic layout, coupled with Man's extended period of study in the Homes, produced a formidable claim to scientific veracity. The monograph's authority was predicated on its ability to answer the series of "leading questions" posed in the British Association handbook; as one reviewer of *Notes and Queries* observed in regard to its questionnaire form: "Well asked is half answered" (Anon. 1875:226). Man's candid introductory acknowledgment of the manual's formative role in the production of his ethnography clearly signalled his allegiance to the most progressive tendencies in British anthropological circles (1883:69, 1885:v–vi; Prain 1932:13).

The monograph's success derived from its power to salvage an authentic image of the "primitive" from the intense contradictions that existed in an observed reality. Man noted in his introduction that his remarks were "restricted to those communities who have been found living in their primitive state, and who may therefore be fairly considered as representatives of the race, being unaffected by the virtues or vices of so-called civilisation" (1885:xxiv). Acknowledging his debt to the handbook and to Lane Fox for having sent him the first edition soon after it was published—"which fortunately was coincident with my first experiencing the need of such a work"—Man went on to discuss observational truth. This, he realized, was a key issue for any "self-taught" observer aspiring to professional standards of scientific accuracy:

> I think it is due to the reader as well as to myself to explain that on all points where there appeared the least risk of falling into error, by directing inquiries among those long resident in our midst, I took the precaution of substantiating my observations by seeking information on such matters from natives of distant villages who from time to time happened to visit our Settlement; but in every instance, whatever the nature of the communication or the character of my informant, I recognised the necessity and importance of testing through other channels the truth and accuracy of every detail before finally accepting it. (Man 1885b:x)

Although he implicitly acknowledged the role of the Settlement and Homes in his observational practices, their actual colonial presence was effectively eclipsed by these "methodological" statements which framed his already filtered observations so as to bring them closer in line with the governing "scientific" ethos of *Notes and Queries on Anthropology*.

Man did discuss geographic features, theories of Andamanese racial origin, and the historical background to British occupation, including the Homes, Orphanage, and Penal Settlement in the monograph's introduction. However, that discussion did not successfully negotiate the disjuncture between colonial reality and the ethnographic dictates of a discipline centered in England. The success of a colonial system of acculturation was openly acknowledged through statements to the effect that the Andamanese were "instilled" with "a wholesome dread of our power," civilized through the medium of Homes and station steamer, so as to promulgate "knowledge of our power, resources, and kindly intentions" (Man 1885b:xiii). But the reality on the ground was contradictory:

> It cannot, however, be contended that our attempts to reclaim the Andamanese from their savage state have produced unmixed beneficial results, for it is found that in proportion as they gain in intelligence and tractability, the more fat and indolent do they become, and having no incentive towards exertion frequently lose in great measure their quondam skill in hunting;—availing themselves of the privileges of free board and quarters, they spend their time for days together in singing, dancing, and feasting; the spirit of independence becomes thus less conspicuous, as they learn to depend upon others for the supply of their daily requirements, instead of being compelled to make such provision for themselves. (xxiii)

This situation was compounded by the destructive effects of jungle clearance, tobacco-smoking "among members of both sexes," and "the deterioration which has taken place in their morals through their unavoidable contact with the alien convict population"—a reference to an epidemic of measles in 1877 and the spread of syphilis (xxiii–xxiv). Since the erosion of incentive and integrity were the direct result of pacification strategies inherited and actively pursued by administrators, including Man, such statements clearly illustrate the blurring of pacification, acculturation, and ethnographic systems in the minds of "self-taught students" of Man's caliber.

According to one observer, there were no Andamanese to be seen around Port Blair by 1872; he had to visit a Home in order to see any of the local population at all (Dobson 1874:463–64). It is not surprising that Man should therefore have conducted most of his observations in and around the Homes and substantiated them by questioning other natives who happened to pass through the settlement (Man 1883:69, 103–4, 1885b:ix; Portman 1899:II, 621–22; Prain 1932:11–16). There is an abundance of evidence to confirm the subtle mesh of alien material culture and physiological habits that was beginning to subvert indigenous patterns of behavior by this time. Thus, in connection with a visit to an Andaman Home, the observer, G. E. Dobson, recalled: "We were received by the wife of the chief, who had hastily donned a frock provided by the Government to receive visitors in, but very soon after-

wards, perceiving that no ladies were in our boat, she got rid of that unneces-
sary encumbrance, and presented herself in nature's garb, adorned by a single
leaf, a garter tied below one knee, and a necklace composed of the finger-
and toe-bones of her ancestors" (Dobson 1874:463–64). Other paraphernalia
of civilization made more insidious inroads on Andamanese life styles and
often penetrated the ethnographer's filter to register their effects in the midst
of anthropology's salvaged representations. Thus tobacco often prompted contradictory ethical and moral observations. Man openly acknowledged its widespread use, including its dissemination in the form of gifts to denote, among
other things, goodwill (cf. Man 1878b:452), and subsequently lamented its
destructive physiological effects (1883:112–13, 1885a:263). Such comments were
clearly the products of over two decades of colonial nurturing in which European artifacts made significant inroads into Andamanese life styles where
European morality still had tenuous influence.

If the Settlement and Homes provided the context for framing Andamanese
activities in the midst of considerable inroads by an alien culture, questionnaires functioned as a more refined filter to eliminate colonial residues during
the production of authentic ethnographic representations. The more or less
successful reconstruction of a significantly eroded indigenous culture through
the observational optic provided by *Notes and Queries* is testimony to its central role in sustaining the successful illusion of anthropology's quest for the
unadulterated representation of the Andaman Other in the late nineteenth
century. The manual's authority, augmented by its filtering function, forestalled a critical approach to the actual observational methodology underlying Man's ethnographic reconstructions, even when it was freely admitted
that most of these observations were conducted around the Homes. It was
only later, at the turn of the century, that limited criticisms of Man's arms-
length "survey" of Andaman culture were advanced by Man's colleague, M. V.
Portman. Noting that Man "had no facilities for living in the jungles and studying the Andamanese in their own haunts," he argued that "the work, which
is an answer to 'Notes and Queries on Anthropology,' deals almost entirely
with the South Andaman Group of Tribes, and often with single Tribes of
that Group." Furthermore, "Mr. Man's medium of communication with the
aborigines was either Hindustani, or the Áka-*Béa*-da dialect of Andamanese,
and as many of his advisers were members of other Tribes, some of the mistakes . . . may have been due to their imperfect knowledge of the languages
mentioned, or to their having failed to understand the questions put to them"
(Portman 1899:II, 622). Portman summed up his reservations in a personal
communication to E. B. Tylor:

> After nearly 20 years experience with the Andamanese, I adhere to my opinion
> that much of the Notes on their Anthropology published by Man is incorrect,
> and the language he knew was a hotch-potch of three or four dialects. His work

is chiefly written on the information of a few boys of different tribes, and two convict Jemadars. This is not my idea of accurate scientific research, and the results, though good for 1881, will not do for 1899. (TP: Portman/Tylor 1/24/99).

Although such criticisms highlight the severe limitations of Man's observational practices, his monograph was considered definitive in British anthropological circles until the publication of Brown's seminal study in 1922. During the interim there was another powerful addition to the Andaman ethnographic toolbox.

An Ultimate Note Pad?
Photography and the Andamanese

The presumed anthropological value of photography resided in its descriptive permanence and its ability to reproduce the kind of "tedious minuteness" of factual detail required by science (Tylor 1883:243). An observer could almost "automatically" produce "facts about which there can be no question" (Read 1892:87). The process also allowed one to salvage and chemically fix the pure visual presence of a people and culture faced with extinction, transubstantiating individuals of flesh and blood into visual specimens as permanent as the ancestral bones reposing in Museums and collections at the center of the Empire. Perhaps the most radical and distant of these specimens was a life-size composite or generic photograph of eight male Andamanese skulls exhibited by Francis Galton in 1881. Produced "under the instruction of Mr. Flower," it was presented as an example of the power of Galton's pet project, composite photography, to produce synthetic images of "true anthropological averages" to "test whether any given series is generic or not." Although Galton's method for the "pictorial definition of races" (Galton 1882:691) was not widely adopted, for a time photography did seem to be a potentially powerful addition to the anthropologist's toolbox.

Man took a considerable number of photographs during his residence on the Andaman Islands, probably beginning as early as the mid-1870s and continuing until he retired in 1901. The majority of the dozen or so published photographs transmit an obvious fiction designed to illustrate and summarize points made in the main body of the text: "What is the habitual posture in sleep?" "How do friends and relations meet after long absence or danger—with shouting, weeping, &c.?" (Anon. 1874:11, 66; cf. Edwards 1989). They concretize in diorama form the particular "ethnographic space" schematized and propagated through *Notes and Queries on Anthropology*. In contrast to these representations of a pseudopristine Andamanese material culture and social activity, Man took many photographs that document the range and penetration of European activity on the Andaman Islands in the closing decades of

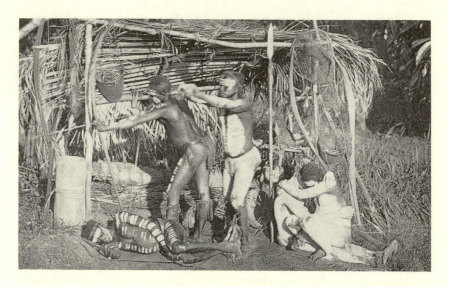

"Andamanese shooting, dancing, sleeping, and greeting." (From Man 1883: facing p. 174.)

the century, including one of the large cellular jail constructed at Aberdeen between 1896 and 1910. But these representations of the colonial situation of his ethnography were never published.

With the exception of one short note by Portman, there is little or no published commentary on the use of photography in the Andamans. Portman's note is, however, of particular interest because it describes how photography could be absorbed into anthropology's toolkit. Portman seems to have become interested in photography in the early 1890s during his third tour of duty as officer in charge of the Andaman Homes. At that time he was producing, in collaboration with W. S. Molesworth, a monumental, twelve-volume photographic study of the Andaman tribes. Following the thematic guidelines of *Notes and Queries on Anthropology* (Portman 1896a:366), the study was regarded in anthropological circles as a visual complement to Man's classic monograph (Read 1893:402) and stands as a testimony to the manual's ability to orchestrate the production of representations by other media according to its encoded system of observation. In Portman's estimation "the Physiognomy and Motions of the Andamanese, as given by Mr. Man, can only be intelligibly rendered by photography" (1899:II, 624).

Although Man used photography as a complement to *Notes and Queries on Anthropology* (Edwards 1989:73–74), Portman's programmatic proposal to conjoin the two in a major visual project marked an unusual departure from the common textual practices of the period, insofar as it inverted the hitherto dominant relationship between written word and scientific illustration. In contrast to the earlier consensus as to what one should *look* for, Portman's definition of "scientific photographs" placed emphasis on how one should *see* the things one should look for (1896b:86). A scientifically inspired anthropological photography, under the governing influence of *Notes and Queries on Anthropology*, could forestall an aesthetically impregnated subjective vision. Portman drew attention to the camera's focussing screen as *the* crucial interface in the production of ethnographic photographs: "A good *focussing glass* . . . should always be used as our object is to get great and accurate detail, not to make pictures. 'Fuzzygraphs' are quite out of place in anthropological work" (81). Sharp focus would be the primary anti-aesthetic procedure for the scientific representation of other peoples. In contrast to Galton's earlier proposal for a generic composite solution to the "pictorial definition of races," Portman sought to preserve a way of life through sequences of "properly taken photographs, with the additional explanatory letter-press." Following the observational logic of *Notes and Queries* in documenting the "Constitution of Man," Portman advised that the "external characters could be illustrated, and large photographs of the face, in full face and profile, should be taken," and that "in posing the subject for these, the body must be upright, and the face so held that the eyes looking straight before the subject are fixed on an object on a level with them. . . ." Turning to "Culture," he noted: "photography will be found of the greatest use in answering the questions accurately. The manufacture of different implements, weapons, &c. . . . indeed almost every act of the life of a primitive people may be photographed" (76).

Presented as a crowning addition to an already powerful system of ethnographic observation, photography was also part of an interlocking colonial system—illustrated in exemplary fashion in a drawing (circa 1885) produced during one of Man's periodic visits to the Nicobar Islands. Depicting Man's photographic activity, his interest in collecting vocabularies, the prominence of transportation, and the protective presence of the police in these enterprises, the drawing is a microcosm of the production of ethnographic observations in the Bay of Bengal. That its subjects intuitively recognized the peculiar powers of photography is suggested by the fact that there was a North Andaman word whose etymology directly connected the photograph with the spirit world: *ot-jumulo*: a reflection, shadow, or photograph (Brown 1922:166). However, it was not long before this crowning nonverbal addition to the nineteenth-century anthropologist's toolkit was eclipsed, along with the governing observational logic ensconced in *Notes and Queries on Anthropology*, by a more formidable methodology that effectively and permanently redefined the relationship between an observer and theorist.

Drawing produced during one of E. H. Man's periodic visits to the Nicobar Islands. (Courtesy of the Royal Anthropological Institute of Great Britain and Ireland.)

Exhausting the Nineteenth-Century Toolkit:
A. R. Brown's Andaman Sojourn

In 1906, Sir Richard Temple, recently retired from a military and administrative career in South Asia that included ten years as Chief Commissioner of the Andaman and Nicobar Islands, wrote a letter to A. C. Haddon, a leader of the move to establish anthropology at Temple's alma mater, the University of Cambridge. Having given the welcoming address to the new Board of Anthropological Studies a year previously (Temple 1905), Temple now offered his old ethnographic haunt as an appropriate area for research: "Man has left for good. Portman no good at all now. All the work done has been amateur or at best that of self-taught students. There is practically a clear field for the trained scientific student." As Temple saw it, however, the new group of university-trained anthropologists would dedicate themselves to the old question of racial origins: "the idea is that the whole S. E. Asiatic Continent was populated aboriginally by the Negritos whose relics are in the Andamans and Malay Peninsula and Archipelago—the purest by far in the Andamans." Above this lowest stratum were three others: the Mon-Khmer (whose "purest ancient relics" were the Nicobarese), the Indo-Chinese, and the Tibeto-Burmese— each of the "upper strata driving out the lower in succession towards the east & the coasts & leaving relics everywhere." By August of that year, A. R. Brown (unhyphenated until the mid-1920s) was in Calcutta; as the first Anthony Wilkin Student in Ethnology, he was ready to begin fieldwork among these "high and dry relics of *very* ancient times," in order, as his later monograph suggests, to accomplish a "hypothetical reconstruction of the history of the Andamans and of the Negritos in general" (Brown 1932:vii; ACHP: Temple/ Haddon 3/16/06).

By the time he arrived in India, Brown had undergone one year of anthropological and archeological training under Haddon, W. H. R. Rivers, Duckworth, and William Ridgeway at Cambridge, and had presumably prepared by reading the work of his predecessors (Langham 1981:244; Stocking 1984b:143–44). That there was little change in the colonial situation which greeted him in 1906 is apparent from a passage in his 1922 Andaman ethnography on the "diminution of population," the "merging" of various "formerly distinct and often hostile communities," the corruption of their languages, the abandonment or adoption of customs, and the use of Andamanese in gathering natural produce or tracking escaped convicts. He concluded: "The result of this system is . . . a free circulation of natives in all parts of the Great Andaman" (1922:19–20). Outlining his plans to Haddon shortly before his departure from Calcutta, he said that "everyone is agreed that the Nicobars will afford much more invaluable material than the Andamans where all the natives except the Önges and Jawara have become mere hangers-on to the

settlement." He therefore planned to spend the first month or two on Great
Andaman: "This should give me time to see all the natives individually and
talk to them, measure them, and experiment on them, since there are not
more than 450 all told, men, women & children." After doing "as much as
is possible" on Little Andaman, he would proceed to the Nicobars for the
remainder of his trip (ACHP: Brown/Haddon 10/8/06).

Brown's sojourn represented more than just another application of traditional tools to a particular fieldwork situation, for he was the first of a new
type of post–Torres Straits Cambridge "field-anthropologist"–university trained
to experience the indigenous subject at first hand according to a more "intensive" model of ethnographic fieldwork (Stocking 1983:83). The apprentice Had-
donesque observer appears, however, to have been initially trumped by the
difficulties that greeted him (Langham 1981:248; Stocking 1984a:109). In an
undated "first report" to Haddon, we find that, owing to stormy weather and
constant rain, he was limited to the study of "such Andamanese as were in
the neighbourhood" of the Settlement, who had "so far left their own mode
of life (having lived for years in the Settlement) that they do not remember
'the things of the old time.'" Because most of his apparatus had been delayed,
he was unable to pursue physical and psychological researches, and his early
attempts to collect genealogies were abandoned in favor of acquiring a working knowledge of Hindustani—an indispensable tool, since the Andamanese
had little knowledge of English. Meanwhile, he was looking for an interpreter
(ACHP: Brown/Haddon n.d.).

More positively, he reported that he was spending most of his time with
a party of Önges from Little Andaman—"the only ones who retain something
of their old customs," and who "do not know a single word of any language
but their own," save for the Hindustani for such "lately introduced" items
as sugar and rice. Lacking any intermediary, Brown labored to learn their
language, but his progress was "slow and tedious." Travelling to Little Andaman itself was difficult at that time of year, and the possibility of a hostile
reception required "a strong escort of police." He hoped still to spend the month
of December there, "but if I have to overcome the difficulties (1) of language
(2) of a population scattered in small groups over a large area, a month will
not give me a great deal of time in which to obtain much information." Echo-
ing Temple's race strata hypothesis, Brown felt that his time might be better
spent in the Nicobars (ACHP: Brown/Haddon n.d.).

Judging from their absence from his published work, Brown seems never
to have reached the Nicobars (although he did collect some Nicobarese artifacts [Anon. 1915:11–12]), and the duration of his research on Little Andaman is problematic; in 1922 he commented on the linguistic difficulties he
encountered in a three-month visit, but in 1914 he alluded to a visit of only
"several weeks" (1922:viii, 1914:41). The preface also records a less ambitious

plan for fieldwork: a "study of the tribes of the Great Andaman, particularly those of the North Andaman among whom Mr Man had not worked" (1922: viii). It was among these groups that he made his most notable coup—the observation of a North Andaman peace-making ceremony, an event not previously recorded—although it is unclear whether he travelled north to see this ceremony or arranged to see it performed in the relative comfort of the Settlement (Brown 1922:134–35; Temple 1922c:371). He seems never to have mastered the local dialects and had to depend, as his first report indicates, on Hindustani and interpreters (1922:vii–viii), which perhaps contributed to his admitted "failure" in the study of Andaman social relations by Rivers' genealogical method (69n, 72n, 82n). Other problems appeared later, when he returned to England and, owing to technical incompetence, was unable to analyze the osteological material he had brought back with him (viii).

Given the range and magnitude of this litany of failures, it is not surprising that his eventual Andaman monograph was self-acknowledged as an "apprentice work," from the point of view of fieldwork technique (Brown 1922:ix). In retrospect it seems clear that Brown's difficulties should be considered as a symptomatic episode marking an important transitional phase in the observational practices of British anthropology. From this standpoint, one notes the absence of any clear reference in *The Andaman Islanders* to *Notes and Queries on Anthropology*—save by implication in the organization of the appendix on "The Technical Culture of the Andaman Islanders," which was Brown's attempt, shortly after his return from the field, to deal with the issues of Temple's Negrito hypothesis (Stocking 1984b:144). Between 1910 and 1922, however, there were developments in Brown's theoretical orientation that made it possible for him to salvage his fieldwork experience in the name of modern ethnography's first encounter with the Andamanese.

Dispensing with the Toolbox: Radcliffe-Brown on Observation, Description, and Method

Heralded even before its appearance as "probably . . . the final word on the subject" (ACHP: Haddon/Smuts 4/16/20), *The Andaman Islanders: A Study in Social Anthropology* was greeted by Temple as "a revolutionary book," a "sample of approved work by the modern type of Cambridge-trained student" (Temple 1922a:125, 1922b:106). It has since been acknowledged as a classic transitional functionalist text and forerunner of a new synthetic approach to religious phenomena, ritual customs, and social institutions (Fortes 1955:29). Its final intellectual form was engendered by Durkheimian thought, tempered by a series of exchanges with Rivers, and nurtured over a long gestation period. It is known that Brown seriously began to engage Durkheimian thought sometime in 1909–10, and that he had begun to reconsider his Andaman material under its influence as early as 1910, when he presented a series of lectures on Comparative Sociology at Cambridge University (Stocking 1984a). Another French influence that has escaped notice is Arnold Van Gennep's seminal study *Les rites de passage*, which was published in 1909 and reviewed by E. Sidney Hartland in December of the same year (cf. Brown 1922:285–305, esp. 292–93). If Brown did read this review, which appeared in the same number as Andrew Lang's response to his own paper on Andaman religion (Lang 1909, Brown 1909), he would probably have been struck by a passage in which Hartland argued that "what is wanted now is to make a thorough ethnographical study, –not a description merely,– of a people typical of its race and culture, examining its institutions, arts, customs, ideas, tales, and so forth in relation to its habitat and probable provenience, the totality of its culture, and the influences which have produced or modified that culture, comparing moreover the various items examined with similar items elsewhere, and discussing the interpretations put upon them." Such a work, Hartland continued, "would really yield us something like a true picture,–at all events, the best picture obtainable,–of one definite type of culture; and a series of such works would effect a revolution in our knowledge of the history of human ideas and civilization" (1909: 510). Having been regarded for fifty years as a privileged ethnographic case, the Andamanese provided just the sort of material by which "mere" ethnographic description could be challenged in the name of comparative and scientifically "true" interpretation.

In pursuing that challenge, Brown had first to mount a sustained barrage of criticism against his ethnographic predecessors, and especially "Mr. Man"– this, despite the fact that his own analysis depended heavily on their accumulated knowledge. But by criticizing Man's interpretations, Brown in fact cleared the way for the use of earlier ethnographic observations as data for his own interpretive method. In an early statement on the relationship between method and interpretation he argued that "the interpretation of the beliefs of savages is always a matter of enormous difficulty. Such interpretations are therefore valueless unless a very strict method is followed. They are indeed worse than valueless, since they falsify observation" (1909:258). While he was in substantial agreement with Man's observations, he suggested that "our differences are almost entirely differences of interpretation, and as between two different interpretations of one phenomenon there is only one test by which we can choose, and that test is strictness of method" (1910:271). Clearly, observational practice was to be subordinated to rigorous interpretative methodology–albeit only retrospectively, since the distinctions Brown now proposed would have been constantly subverted by the scramble to extract information from informants under difficult local conditions. Given his recent experience in the Andamans, it is not surprising that he was unable to "enter into the question of these methods" in 1909, although he asserted the value of a comparative approach in order "to discover what beliefs are essential and what are secondary" (1909:258).

During the same year, Brown engaged in sharp controversy, involving accusations of religious bias and scientific and methodological ineptitude, with Father Wilhelm Schmidt, over the nature of Puluga, whom Man had described as a "Supreme Being." Brown's comments summarize his understanding of "strict methods" at this early point in his career. They implied "a mind free of preconceived opinions"; "an intimate knowledge" of indigenous "life and thought"; a geographically circumscribed "comparative" approach to "beliefs and customs"; and a strict adherence to "evidence of observation" (1910:33). These points, however, hardly represented a revolution in anthropological methodology, and in fact resonate of the points discussed by Man in the introduction to his classic monograph—a convergence that seems to have prompted Andrew Lang to comment, "We are likely to understand the subject better when we have Mr. Brown's book in our hands and can compare it with that of Mr. Man. In the meantime, between monsoons and moons in mythology, and arguments drawn from conchology and conjectural etymology, a wise passiveness seems an appropriate mental attitude" (1910:53).

In the absence of systematic interpretation, there was at this point little to differentiate Brown's claims to have adhered to a strict "method" from similar claims by earlier Andaman ethnographers to have judiciously followed the rigorous "method" of leading questions disseminated in nineteenth-century editions of *Notes and Queries*—except perhaps that in the latter case one could judge such claims against the interpretative grid manifest in a clear graphic structure of presentation. The implicit basis of Brown's claim to methodological authority at this time had less to do perhaps with his actual fieldwork than with his academic status. *Notes and Queries* was specifically designed to guide the nonspecialist, to legitimate the knowledge-gathering activities of "self-taught" students like Man. In contrast, Brown was, as Temple had suggested, a new type: the "trained scientific student" of anthropology. Although supported by fieldwork experience, his authority was in a sense prior to it. Inscribed on his ethnographic "body" through initiatory university training, it even enabled him to construct a new order of anthropological fact, after the fact of fieldwork, and even in the face of its failure.

Brown's ability to accomplish this depended on the reorientation of his theoretical position that began in 1910 under the influence of Durkheim. Elaborated in correspondence with his mentor Rivers between 1912 and 1914, Brown's distinction between "static" and "dynamic" interpretations "in the study of social institutions" was used to undercut the argument from survivals, which had been central to evolutionary theory, and which had been preserved in

Rivers' diffusionism. Rejecting survivals, Brown looked instead for the "function" of every item of culture in terms of its role in the maintenance of the present sociocultural system—knowledge that was inaccessible to the native, as it was to the observer intent on hypothetical historical reconstruction (Stocking 1984b:146–56). It was this theoretical reorientation that set the stage for the synthetic tour de force of the two central interpretive chapters of *The Andaman Islanders*. Attacking the "intellectualist" hypothesis of the British evolutionists, as well as explanations based on the "emotions" of terror, awe, and wonder, Brown explained the "meaning" of Andaman myths and rituals in terms of their "social function": "to maintain and to transmit from one generation to another the emotional dispositions on which the society (as it is constituted) depends for its existence" (234).

In contrast to *Notes and Queries*, which took for granted the separation of fact gathering and theory, Brown's ethnographic tour de force was presented in 1922 as the product of a fusion of the "armchair worker" and the "labourer in the field":

> It is often urged that in ethnology description and interpretation should be most carefully separated. So far as this means that the facts observed by the ethnologist should be recorded free from all bias of interpretation, the necessity cannot be too often or too strongly urged. If, however, it is meant to imply that efforts at interpretation are to be excluded from works of descriptive ethnology, there is much to be said against such an opinion. In trying to interpret the institutions of a primitive society the field ethnologist has a great advantage over those who know the facts only at second hand. However exact and detailed the description of a primitive people may be, there remains much that cannot be put into such a description. Living, as he must, in daily contact with the people he is studying, the field ethnologist comes gradually to "understand" them, if we may use the term. He acquires a series of multitudinous impressions, each slight and often vague, that guide him in his dealings with them. The better the observer the more accurate will be his general impression of the mental peculiarities of the race. This general impression it is impossible to analyse, and so to record and convey to others. Yet it may be of the greatest service when it comes to interpreting the beliefs and practices of a primitive society. If it does not give any positive aid towards a correct interpretation, it at least prevents errors into which it is only too easy for those to fall who have not the same immediate knowledge of the people and their ways. Indeed it may be urged, with some reason, that attempts to interpret the beliefs of savages without any first-hand knowledge of the people whose beliefs are in question, are at the best unsatisfactory and open to many possibilities of error. (1922:230–31)

He went on to argue, "in this science, as in others, if progress is to be made, the elaboration of hypotheses and the observation and classification of facts must be carried on as interdependent parts of one process, and no advantage, but rather great disadvantage, results from the false division of labour whereby theorists and observers work independently and without systematic cooperation" (231–32). Having linked interpretative processes and observational practice under the authority of a (university-) trained or cultured intuition, he went on the emphasize the governing role of "a scientific and carefully elaborated method": "The most urgent need of ethnology at the present time is a series of investigations of the kind here attempted, in which the observation and the analysis and interpretation of the institutions of some one primitive people are carried on together by the ethnologist working in the field" (232).

Insofar as we can judge from the surviving record of his actual fieldwork, the differences between Brown's ethnographic work and that of earlier "labourers in the field" who functioned under the authority of *Notes and Queries* were not so great as his retrospective account would seem to imply. He and they both functioned within the colonial situation which he called the Andaman "system." Although the genealogical method and the introduction of psychological testing were relatively recent innovations, his attempt to apply them was by his own admission unsuccessful. An obvious point of comparison is the length of study: Man was in the Andamans for almost thirty years; and although Brown's stay has customarily been dated "1906–8," he was probably in the Andamans for little more than a year, if that. By his own account, it would have taken "two or three years to learn to speak the language sufficiently well" to pursue the successful questioning of natives from Little Andaman—but this did not deter him from writing a paper on Andaman languages (1914). In the emergent disciplinary market of modern anthropology, however, the currency of time could be converted into that of academic training, at rates very favorable to the latter. Although Brown would later suggest that "it is only by actually living with and working amongst a primitive people that the social anthropologist can acquire his real training" (1922:vii, ix, x), it is clear that he had, even before landing in Port Blair, the status of "trained scientific student"—which, as Temple had suggested, Man could never be.

This difference was consolidated, in retrospect, by a conjuring act: a revised preface for the second edition of *The Andaman Islanders*. There the fading memory of the struggling neophyte ethnographer was eclipsed by the authoritative presence of a functionalist theoretician who by implication recast his fledgling fieldwork in a hypothetico-deductive mode: "In this work I sought to formulate some hypotheses and test them by the simple culture of the Andamans"—a mature theoretical orientation that enabled him to distinguish between data and interpretation: "I did not question [Man's] records of what the natives told him but only the meanings that he attached to their statements. It therefore seemed to me necessary for ethnology to provide itself with a method of determining meanings as effective and free from 'personal equation' as the methods by which a linguist determines the meanings of words

Unidentified ethnographer with a group of Önges, from A. R. Brown's Andaman album, c. 1906. (Courtesy of the Pitt-Rivers Museum, University of Oxford.)

or morphemes in a newly studied language" (Brown 1932:ix). The method he found for "determining as accurately as can be what meanings [myths and rituals] have for the people to whose culture they belong" was condensed in "the notion of function" (ix). And while it required that the ethnologist "take into account the explanation given by the natives themselves," such explanations were not "scientific explanations" (1922:234–35). They were merely "data," and like that of "Mr. Man," simply grist for the functionalist mill.

Man's earlier contributions to Andaman ethnography were marked by the contradiction between a vague survey of colonial space and a fictional ethnographic space governed by *Notes and Queries*. Brown's book effectively resolved such contradictions by the simple gesture of wishing away a colonial situation and replacing it with a coherent and therefore powerful synchronic reconstruction of the major categories of Andaman social life. This gesture was accompanied by a subtle transformation in his method from an ostensibly context-sensitive inductive process into an authoritarian deductive methodology: not only was his ethnography reconstructed *post factum* but he never returned to the Andaman Islands in order to open the inductive loop and again observe. In fact his method precluded this possibility, for it presented as its final reconstituted product a closed timeless picture of the integrated organic life of Andamanese culture. It might be said that he had in fact transformed the nature of ethnography: from the privileged domain of practice, it became the site for the authoritative work of theory.[2]

The Twilight of Andaman Studies

As former chief administrator of the Andamans and collaborator on Man's linguistic researches, Sir Richard Temple was an obvious candidate to assess Brown's magnum opus, and in fact discussed it in a series of reviews during the 1920s (1922a, 1922b, 1922c, 1923, 1925, 1929). Acknowledging the work as "a revolutionary theory of social anthropology," he nevertheless felt that it placed "too much stress on the value of the author's observations and too little on that of his predecessors" (1922a:121). Temple's passive acceptance of a potential revolution in anthropological method and his response to the summary treatment of Man's observations reveal a complex and often contradictory reaction to a rapidly changing anthropological landscape. He was prepared to abandon archaic tools, but he still felt it necessary to defend the integrity of an earlier "witness" (Temple 1922b:107). While acutely aware of the lethargy and resistance to be found in "vested interests" and obsolete "knowledge" (1922a:126), he nevertheless felt that the production of anthropological knowledge was a social process that necessarily implied the role of prior investigations in the generation of new knowledge (1922b:107).

What Temple failed to note was that most of the earlier generation of observers had also been engaged in contradicting, correcting, and rewriting — "in the interests of truth and science" (Man 1883:69) — an ongoing anthropological portrait of the Andamanese. Nor did he appreciate that in Brown's case the implicit basis of the claim to methodological authority had less to do with his actual fieldwork than with his "revolutionary theory of social anthropology." Temple failed, in short, to recognize the full significance of the new authority he himself had hailed in 1906. As the first university-trained student of anthropology in Britain, Brown adopted an overtly self-conscious scientific ideology and identity, and he cultivated this identity in terms of the most advanced sociological theories of his day. He not only promoted the image of an autonomous observer capable of operating according to his own "intimate knowledge" and personal authority (Brown 1910:34); he assumed

2. Although it might be argued that such a transformation has been widely diffused in twentieth-century anthropology, a more wide-ranging account of this period would have to take into consideration the work of Malinowski, who in these years worked his own transformation of ethnography, along quite different lines — signalled, perhaps, by his pencilled comment in the margin of *The Andaman Islanders:* "Why don't you quote them?" (BMSC: Brown 1922:49; cf. Stocking 1983, and in this volume).

the role of an "inductive" theorist. By forging a methodological loop between hypothesis, observation and interpretation, he was in a position to claim a founding authority in what he later described as a new "theoretical natural science of human society" (Brown 1952:189).

In putting aside the traditional observational toolbox for the mega-tool of theory, Brown was able to exorcise the colonial "system" that had been the context, and contributing cause, of his initiatory failure in the field. He did so in part by a binary rhetorical strategy not dissimilar to that of Man, who had confined his remarks on the "contact with civilized races" (topic number XCV of *Notes and Queries*) to a supplementary paper that later served as an introduction to his monograph (Man 1885a). For Brown, the domain of observation – and the colonial situation in which it had been carried on – was largely confined to first chapters of his book; thereafter, the book was scripted according to his "revolutionary theory of social anthropology." The Andamanese were no longer the representational products of a particular domain of ethnographic practice so much as ciphers in a new theoretical project whose power resided in its ability to construct a coherent vision of aboriginal Andamanese religious life and thought out of the data provided by survivors of the Andaman "system" which by 1906 had been in existence for half a century. Given a local "political situation" that rendered "further serious research" among the Andamanese "difficult" (Temple 1922a:288), the book marked at once an anthropological beginning and an ethnographic closure.

Acknowledgments

I would like to thank Lee Drummond, Elizabeth Edwards, John Galaty, Ken Little, and George W. Stocking for comments on various drafts of this paper. For their help in tracing material and other services, I would like to thank Ms. E. Allen of the Hunterian Museum, The Royal College of Surgeons of England; Ms. Elizabeth Edwards of the Pitt-Rivers Museum, University of Oxford; Dr. David W. Phillipson, University Museum of Archaeology and Anthropology, University of Cambridge; Dr. Christopher Pinney, formerly Photographic Librarian, Royal Anthropological Institute, London; and the staffs of Special Collections and Photographic Services, University of California, Santa Cruz.

Research for this paper was funded by Social Sciences and Humanities Research Council of Canada Predoctoral and Postdoctoral Fellowships.

References Cited

ACHP. See under Manuscript Sources.
Anon. 1859. *Selections from the records of the Government of India (Home Department)*. Vol. 25. Calcutta.

———. 1862. *J. Asiat. Soc. Bengal* 31:345.

———. 1874. *Notes and queries on anthropology.* 1st ed. London.

———. 1875. Anthropological notes and queries. *Nature* 11:226.

———. 1883. Anthropological notes. *Athenaeum* 2887:251.

———. 1892. *Notes and queries on anthropology.* 2d ed. London.

———. 1908. Local gazetteer: The Andaman and Nicobar Islands. Calcutta.

———. 1912. *Notes and queries on anthropology.* 4th ed. London.

———. 1915. University of Cambridge, Museum of Archaeology and of Ethnology. Thirtieth annual report of the Antiquarian Committee to the Senate with list of accessions for the year 1914. Museum issue with one plate.

Ball, V. 1874. Visit to the Andamanese "Home," Port Blair, Andaman Islands. *Indian Antiq.* 3:171–73.

BMSC. See under Manuscript Sources.

Brander, E. S. 1880. Remarks on the aborigines of the Andaman Islands. *Proc. Roy. Soc. Edinburgh* 10:415–24.

Brown, A. R. 1909. The religion of the Andaman Islanders. *Folk-Lore* 20:257–71.

———. 1910. Puluga: A reply to Father Schmidt. *Man* 10:33–37.

———. 1914. Notes on the languages of the Andaman Islanders. *Anthropos* 9:36–52.

———. 1922. *The Andaman Islanders: A study in social anthropology.* Cambridge.

———. 1923. The methods of ethnology and social anthropology. *S. Afr. J. Sci.* 20:124–47.

———. 1932. *The Andaman Islanders.* 2d ed. Cambridge.

———. 1952. On social structure. In *Structure and function in primitive society,* 188–204. London.

Busk, G. 1866. Description of two Andamanese skulls. *Trans. Ethnol. Soc.* 4:205–11.

———. 1875. The president's address. *J. Anth. Inst.* 4:476–501.

Cadell, T. 1889. The Andamans and Andamanese. *Scott. Geogr. Mag.* 5:57–73.

Colebrooke, R. H. 1807. On the Andaman Islands. *Asiat. Res.* 4:385–94.

Day. F. 1870. Observations on the Andamanese. *Proc. Asiat. Soc.* 1:153–77.

Dobson, G. E. 1874. On the Andamans and Andamanese. *J. Anth. Inst.* 4:457–67.

Duckworth, W. L. 1902. Note on the skull of an Andaman Islander. *Man* 2:33–34.

Earl, G. W. 1850. On the leading characteristics of the Papuan, Australian, and Malayo-Polynesian Nations. *J. Indian Archipelago* 4:1–10.

Edwards, E. 1989. Images of the Andamans: The photography of E. H. Man. *J. Mus. Ethnog.* 1:71–78.

Ellis, A. J. 1885. Report of researches into the language of the South Andaman Island. In Man 1885b.

Evans, J. 1883. Address. *J. Anth. Inst.* 12:563–66.

FGP. See under Manuscript Sources.

Flower, W. H. 1879. On the osteology and affinities of the natives of the Andaman Islands. *J. Anth. Inst.* 9:108–35.

———. 1881a. Presidential address to the Department of Anthropology. In Flower 1898:235–48.

———. 1881b. Stature of the Andamanese. *J. Anth. Inst.* 10:124.

———. 1885. Additional observations on the osteology of the natives of the Andaman Islands. *J. Anth. Inst.* 14:115–20.

————. 1888. The pygmy races of men. In Flower 1898:290–314.

————. 1898. *Essays on museums and other subjects connected with natural history*. London.

Fortes, M. 1955. Radcliffe-Brown's contributions to the study of social organization. *Brit. J. Sociol.* 6:16–30.

Fox, A. L. 1875. The president's address. *J. Anth. Inst.* 5:468–88.

————. 1878. Observations on Mr Man's collection of Andamanese and Nicobarese objects. *J. Anth. Inst.* 7:434–51.

Fytche, A. 1861. A note on certain aborigines of the Andaman Islands. *J. Asiat. Soc. Bengal.* 30:263–67.

Galton, F. 1882. On the application of composite portraiture to anthropological purposes. *Report of the fifty-first meeting of the British Association for the Advancement of Science, York.* London.

Hartland, E. S. 1909. Les rites de passage. *Folk-Lore* 20(4): 509–11.

Haughton, J. C. 1861. Papers relating to the aborigines of the Andaman Islands. *J. Asiat. Soc. Bengal* 30:251–67.

Hellard, S. 1861. Notes on the Andamanese captured at Port Blair. *J. Asiat. Soc. Bengal* 30:258–63.

Lang, A. 1909. The religion of the Andaman Islanders. *Folk-Lore* 20(4): 492–97.

————. 1910. Puluga. *Man* 10:51–53.

Langham, I. 1981. *The building of British social anthropology: W. H. R. Rivers and his Cambridge disciples in the development of kinship studies, 1898–1931.* Dordrecht, Holland.

Majumdar, R. C. 1975. *Penal settlement in Andamans.* Delhi.

Man, E. H. 1878a. The Andaman Islands. *J. Anth. Inst.* 7:105–9.

————. 1878b. On the arts of the Andamanese and Nicobarese. *J. Anth. Inst.* 7:451–67. Includes (a) Extract of letter from E. H. Man, Esq., to his father, Col. Man and (b) List of Andamanese and Nicobarese implements, ornaments, & c., etc.

————. 1882. On the Andamanese and Nicobarese objects presented to Maj.-Gen. Pitt Rivers, F.R.S., by E.H. Man, Esq., F.R.G.S., M.R.A.S., M.A.I. *J. Anth. Inst.* 11:268–94.

————. 1883. On the aboriginal inhabitants of the Andaman Islands. *J. Anth. Inst.* 12:69–116 (pt. 1), 117–75 (pt. 2), 327–434 (pt. 3).

————. 1885a. On the Andaman Islands, and their inhabitants. *J. Anth. Inst.* 14:253–72.

————. 1885b. *On the Aboriginal inhabitants of the Andaman Islands.* London.

————. 1932. *On the Aboriginal inhabitants of the Andaman Islands.* London.

Man, E. H., R. C. Temple. 1880. Note on two maps of the Andaman Islands. *J. Roy. Geogr. Soc.* 50:255–59.

Mathur, L. P. 1985. *Kala Pani: History of Andaman and Nicobar Islands, with a study of India's freedom struggle.* Delhi.

ML. See under Manuscript Sources.

Mouat, F. J. 1863. *Adventures and researches among the Andaman Islands.* London.

Owen, R. 1862. On the psychical and physical characters of the Mincopies or natives of the Andaman Islands, and on the relations thereby indicated to other races of mankind. *Report of the thirty-first meeting of the British Association for the Advancement of Science,* 241–49. London.

————. 1863. On the osteology and dentation of the aborigines of the Andaman

Islands, and the relations thereby indicated to other races of mankind. *Trans. Ethnol. Soc.* n.s. 2:34–49.

Portman, M. V. 1881. On the Andaman Islands and the Andamanese. *J. Roy. Asiat. Soc.* n.s. 13:469–89.

————. 1888. The exploration and survey of the Little Andamans. *Proc. Roy. Geogr. Soc.* 10:567–76.

————. 1896a. Notes on the Andamanese. *J. Anth. Inst.* 25:361–71.

————. 1896b. Photography for anthropologists. *J. Anth. Inst.* 25:75–87.

————. 1899. *A history of our relations with the Andamanese.* 2 vols. Calcutta.

Prain, D. 1932. Memoir: Edward Horace Man C.I.E. 1846–1929. In E. H. Man, *The Nicobar Islands and their people.* London.

Radcliffe-Brown, A. R. See under Brown.

Read, C. H. 1892. Prefatory notes (ethnography). In *Notes and queries on anthropology,* 2d ed., 87–88.

————. 1893. Mr. Portman's photographs of Andamanese. *J. Anth. Inst.* 22:401–3.

Ritchie, J. 1771. *An hydrographical journal of a curfory survey of the coasts and islands in the Bay of Bengal.* London (1787).

Schmidt, W. 1910. Puluga, the supreme being of the Andamanese. *Man* 10:2–7.

Stocking, G. W. 1983. The ethnographer's magic: Fieldwork in British anthropology from Tylor to Malinowski. *HOA* 1:70–120.

————. 1984a. Dr. Durkheim and Mr. Brown: Comparative sociology at Cambridge in 1910. *HOA* 2:106–30.

————. 1984b. Radcliffe-Brown and British social anthropology. *HOA* 2:131–91.

————. 1987. *Victorian Anthropology.* New York.

Sullivan, L. R. 1921. A few Andamanese skulls with comparative notes on Negrito craniometry. *Anth. Papers Am. Mus. Nat. Hist.* 23(4): 174–201.

Temple, R. C. 1905. The practical value of anthropology. *Indian Antiq.* 34:132–44.

————. 1922a. A revolutionary theory of social anthropology. *Man* 22:121–27.

————. 1922b. A new book on the Andamans. *Nature* 110:106–8.

————. 1922c. The Andaman Islands: A study in social anthropology. *Geogr. J.* 60: 371–72.

————. 1923. Remarks on the Andaman Islanders and their country (I & II). *Indian Antiq.* 52:151–57, 216–24.

————. 1925. Remarks on the Andaman Islanders and their country (III & IV). *Indian Antiq.* 54:21–29, 46–55, 81–94.

————. 1929. Remarks on the Andaman Islanders and their country. *Indian Antiq.* 58:1–48.

————. 1930. Edward Horace Man. *Man* 30:11–12.

Tickell, S. R. 1864. Memoranda relative to three Andamanese in the charge of Major Tickell, when Deputy Commissioner of Amherst, Tenasserim, in 1861. *J. Asiat. Soc. Bengal* 33:162–73.

Thomson, A. 1882. Description of Andamanese bone necklaces. *J. Anth. Inst.* 11:295–309.

Topping, M. 1791. Extract from the log of the cutter 'Mary' from Pulo Pinang to the Great Andaman, 1791. In *Selections from the records of the Madras Government,* no. 19, 42–45. Madras (1855).

TP. See under Manuscript Sources.

Tylor, E. B. 1871. *Primitive culture.* 2 vols. London.

Van Gennep. A. 1909. *The rites of passage.* Chicago (1960).

Watson, E. G. 1946. *But to what purpose: The autobiography of a contemporary.* London.

Manuscript Sources

ACHP   A. C. Haddon Papers, University Library, Cambridge.

BMSC   Bronislaw Malinowski Collection, Special Collections, University of California, Santa Cruz.

FGP   Francis Galton Papers, University College London.

ML   Museum Letters, Hunterian Museum, Royal College of Surgeons of England, London.

TP   Tylor Papers. Pitt-Rivers Museum, University of Oxford.

THE CONSTRUCTION OF ALGONQUIAN HUNTING TERRITORIES

Private Property as Moral Lesson,
Policy Advocacy, and Ethnographic Error

HARVEY A. FEIT

The ownership of land has been a major point of conflict in colonial contexts around the world, and a subject of recurrent debate in anthropology. Within Americanist anthropology, the major dispute has been about the kinds of property rights that constitute Algonquian family hunting territories, and about how they came to be. Since Frank G. Speck first provided a professional account of Algonquian family hunting territories as a form of private property in 1915, there have been two opposing views on the central issues in dispute.

The dominant view in recent decades, often closely tied to evolutionary issues going back to Lewis Henry Morgan, is that private property forms were not found in Native American hunting societies before contact with Europeans. Best exemplified by the late Eleanor Burke Leacock (1954), scholars on this side of the debate argue that Algonquian family hunting territories were the result of postcontact changes brought about by the fur trade, or by the trade in combination with other factors, such as ecological changes and consequent shifts in wildlife harvesting patterns or the more recent availability of cash incomes and commoditized food supplies. Although such hunting territories were relevant to the study of the impact of European colonization

––––––––––––

Harvey A. Feit is Professor of Anthropology at McMaster University, Ontario, Canada, and is currently president of the Canadian Anthropology Society. He has carried out fieldwork and applied research among James Bay Cree (Quebec), and is working on a book entitled *Hunting with the North Wind*.

on land ownership, and the commoditization of locally produced marketable goods (Murphy & Steward 1956), they were irrelevant to questions of the social evolution of property ideas and institutions in hunting and gathering societies not influenced by European colonial relations.

The other side of the debate was part of the Boasian critique of evolutionism and was based on Robert Lowie's use of Speck's material in *Primitive Society* (1920), which was Lowie's rejoinder to Morgan's *Ancient Society* (1877). According to this view, Algonquian family hunting territories were forms of private land ownership by individuals or families, which were either characteristic of hunting and gathering peoples in general or were developed by some hunting and gathering societies under specific ecological and demographic conditions before European contact. Developed over the three decades following Lowie's presentation (Speck 1928a, 1939; Cooper 1938, 1939; Speck & Eiseley 1939, 1942; Hallowell 1949), this view has largely been rejected since Eleanor Leacock's ethnohistorical and ethnographic study of Montagnais hunting territories was published in 1954 (Bishop & Morantz 1986; Feit 1986).

Despite the fact that earlier anthropologists on both sides of the debate assumed that Algonquian family hunting territories are an existing, or developing, form of private property, more recent fieldwork has shown that—even after more than three hundred years of fur trading and seventy-five or more years of government administration and cash incomes—the territorial practices and concepts of northern Algonquians are not adequately described as such. Recurrent research has shown (1) that individual rights to hunting territories are part of systems in which "rights" and "duties" are predominantly attached to distinctive social forms in the larger communities, including multifamilial hunting groups, and to distinctive forms of egalitarian leadership (Feit 1991); (2) that the system reflects a concept of spiritual and social reciprocity that conflicts with a concept of private property and is reproduced in ways that derive in significant part from non-European sources (Scott 1988); (3) that despite continuing transformation, reciprocal practices relating to land and resource use are still manifest (Tanner 1979); (4) that these transformations derive from the interactions of a complex array of external and internal processes (Feit 1982; Bishop & Morantz 1986). In short, there are now strong reasons to think that it was erroneous to claim that Algonquian territoriality ever was, or was becoming, a kind of private property system.

The central question then is, why did Speck construct his accounts of Algonquian hunting territories as if they conformed to notions of private property? It has been argued that Speck's ethnographic constructions were ideologically motivated, that he "tried to do by fiat what the Jesuits had tried and failed to do in the seventeenth century: transform the Montagnais from a people who honoured collective rights to lands into individualized property-holding families" (Leacock 1986:143; cf. 1972:19). It is in fact commonly assumed that Speck was driven by a desire to disprove Morgan's thesis and to discredit its use by Friedrich Engels in what was to become the foundation document of Marxist anthropology (Engels 1884; cf. Hickerson 1967: 316–18). But such claims do not constitute a historical account of the development of the ethnography of Algonquian family hunting territories.[1] Such an account must take into consideration the "colonial situation" of land ownership issues in North America at the turn of the century, the development of government policies and ideologies in that period, and the links between the development of Americanist ethnography and wider social science advocacy.

The Stages of Progress and the Allotment of Indian Lands

Morgan's interest in Iroquoian ethnography, and his early ethnological theories, developed in the context of his involvement in disputes over land ownership on the colonial frontiers of the preceding period (Resek 1960; Trautman 1987; Leacock 1963:lv–lvi). In 1844, when Morgan was twenty-six, he met Ely Parker, son of a chief of the Tonawanda Seneca, who had been selected by his community to be educated in American schools so he might help his people to resist the loss of their lands in upper New York State and their removal west of the Mississippi (Resek 1960:27–30). It was in the context of providing political and legal services, which shaped Senecan responses to his initial ethnographic interests, that Morgan developed the impetus for intensive research on the Tonawanda. The result, in 1851, was the monograph that John Wesley Powell, founder of the Bureau of American Ethnology, later called "the first scientific account of an Indian tribe given in the world" (quoted in Resek 1960:41). Although Morgan was unsuccessful when he sought appointment as United States Indian Commissioner so that he might directly shape policy, as the leading authority on American Indians he periodically made policy recommendations to government officials. In 1876 and 1877, for example, in the context of the continuing "conquest" of the West he wrote publicly, as well as advising President Rutherford B. Hayes by letter, that culture change could not occur quickly and that large lands needed to be set aside for Indians, lands which might later become Indian states. He also defended Indian resistance at Little Big Horn, although acknowledging that evolutionary change was inevitable (43, 145).

Morgan's career as a lawyer for railway and mining corporations, which

---

1. For an informative recent analysis of the structure of Speck's anthropological production, see Deschênes 1979, 1981.

focussed on acquiring public lands for their operations in the Midwest, had given him personal experience of "the transformation of communal into private property," and its consequences, including the destruction of Indian ways of life (Resek 1960:104). His activities and experiences with land transfers and their consequences were linked to the primary role property came to play in his explanations of the transformations in forms of family, economy, and society (140–41), and in the development of his evolutionary schema. In turn, that schema was used by others to support public policy decisions insofar as the allotment of Indian land in severalty was defended in evolutionary terms as a transition from a nomadic communistic hunting life to an individualistic agricultural state (Schurz 1881:14–15).

By the time Morgan published *Ancient Society* (1877), Indians in the United States—their powers weakened by the virtual extermination of the buffalo and the population losses brought on by disease—had effectively ceased armed resistance to the invasion and colonization of their lands. By the 1870s Indians on reserves were put under the total bureaucratic control of Indian Agents, who superseded or bypassed tribal authorities. The transition was marked by the decision in 1871 to end treaty making with Indians, after some 370 treaties. The logic of the decision was in fact reflected in Morgan's thought by the demotion of the component groups of the *League of the Iroquois* from "nations" to "tribes"—the latter, by customary usage, having no fixed relation to the land, but merely "wandering" over the face of the earth (Berkhofer 1979:169–71; cf. Morgan 1851, 1877).

In the 1880s an alliance of government officials and reformers intensified the process of subordination by a program of detribalization aiming at rapid assimilation. The reservation system was to be terminated as it was claimed that it provided a land base on which communal economic and governance practices could be continued; in contrast, the allotment of reservation lands into individual holdings would aid the transformation of "communalistic" Indians into "individualistic" Americans. The General Allotment Act of 1887, known as the Dawes Act, provided for the allotment to each native family of 160 acres of reserve lands, with the Secretary of Interior selecting lands for those who refused or failed to do so themselves. The land was to be held in trust for twenty-five years before being fully transferred, after which the native owner was subject to the laws which governed all citizens, and the lands could be bought, sold, and taxed. In the meantime, reservation lands remaining after allotment were to be purchased by the government, with Indian consent, and could then be sold or otherwise disposed of, with the funds received held in trust and used for the education and civilization of former tribal members. This legislation and policy was in force until the mid-1930s, by which time 80 percent of Indian lands of 1887 had been lost through the sale of "surplus" lands and disposals of allotments (Berkhofer 1979:166–75).

In the later nineteenth century, this policy continued to be buttressed by evolutionary anthropologists, including Powell in the Bureau of American Ethnology, who distributed copies of *Ancient Society* to his staff, so that Bureau ethnologists "went into the field with Morgan's book and with his kinship charts" (Resek 1960:150). Powell's two-decade-long program for identifying and classifying American Indian languages was closely linked to the needs of the newly expanded government Indian bureaucracy (Kehoe 1985:46; Hinsley 1981). Powell directly brought evolutionary ideas into the debates over Indian policy, arguing before Congress that for allotment to be successful it would be necessary for Indians to adopt the form of the civilized family, to accept individual property and lineal inheritance (Dippie 1982:167). Powell's widely read exploration reports on the western country had called public attention to its resource potentials; and he addressed land and resource policies as well as Indian policy, arguing for government action and regulated use of natural resources, a view consistent with his evolutionary models of the final stages of social progress (Hinsley 1981:136).

Despite expectations, by the turn of the century the effectiveness of allotment-driven assimilation policies was being widely questioned, as progress in dispossession of lands was not accompanied by systematic acculturative change. However, the doubts did not result in major reversals of the policies, partly because of the growing influence of westerners in Congress as new states were formed and the continuation of pressures for public access to Indian lands and resources (Hoxie 1984:106–13, 156–62). In the first decade of the twentieth century, progressive conservationism was made a national policy by President Theodore Roosevelt; it was used to promote increased exploitation of the nation's natural resources under government control, on a scale which encouraged allocating rights to public lands for large corporate development of resources (Hays 1959:69–90, 263–66; Hoxie 1984:167–73). The discussions of the Indian policy thus continued in the context of the ongoing rapid dispossession of Indian lands.

In his first annual message to Congress, President Theodore Roosevelt characterized the General Allotment Act as "a mighty pulverizing engine to break up the tribal mass"; Merrill E. Gates, President of both Amherst College and of the Lake Mohonk Conference of the Friends of the Indian, defended allotment, arguing that "there is an immense moral learning that comes from the use of property" (quoted in Berkhofer 1979:175, 173). And the discussion was reflected in scholarly journals as well. Thus in 1907, George Bird Grinnell, a personal friend and adviser to President Roosevelt, and a popular writer on Indian topics whose extended western experience included service as naturalist with General Custer in 1874, published an article on "Tenure of Land among the Indians" in the *American Anthropologist* in which he argued that "there is nothing in an Indian's traditions or experience that enables him even to imagine the ownership of land by persons" (1907:1). Because the earth was "regarded as sacred" and owned by the tribe as a whole, Grinnell maintained that "in the case of every land cession the Indian has been made to seem to agree to something which the mind of the primitive Indian could by no means grasp" (3, 11). Grinnell felt that the gap between people at this evolutionary level and that of contemporary American society was too great for rapid change, and he was concerned with the rapidity of Congressional dispossession. However, he did not *per se* oppose allotment, because it "may be futile to attempt to stem this tide," and in any case he felt it was the only way to settle peoples who were "wanderers and beggars like the Cree of northern Montana" (10, 11).

Less sympathetic views than Grinnell's were advanced by government staff directly involved in Indian administration and in conservationism. Writing in the *Annals of the American Academy of Political and Social Science* in 1909, Francis E. Leupp, the Commissioner of Indian Affairs, argued that goverment policy was "designed to change the wandering, improvident and semi-civilized hunter to a domestic, industrious and enlightened citizen" by "giving to each Indian a home," which should in the first instance be "agricultural" (1909: 622–23). Such a policy would take "cognizance not only of the interests of the Indians, but also of those of the whites, and gives proper weight to the justifiable selfishness which insists upon such method of administering the lands of the Indian wards as will have due regard for the rights of their trustees" (620).

Ethnographic Fieldwork and Indian Welfare in Oklahoma and Quebec

By the time Frank Speck began to write on Algonquian hunting territories, he had already had some experience with the consequences of the allotment policy. Born in Brooklyn in 1881 to a family recently moved from a community in the lower Hudson Valley, he suffered from precarious health, which led to his being placed in the care of a family friend at Mohegan, Conn., Mrs. Fidelia A. Fielding, a "conservative Indian widow." In her charge from about the age of seven to fourteen, Speck not only learned Mohegan, but "nonconformity and social rebellion." John Witthoft, a close friend and colleague of Speck, called her "the most important formative influence of his life" (1974:761).

When Speck entered Columbia in 1900 he had already considerable knowledge of several Indian languages that were "not generally known to be still spoken" (Hallowell 1951:69). Before his graduation in 1904, he had co-authored with his professor of comparative philology, J. D. Prince, several articles in the *American Anthropologist*. Encouraged by Prince to contact Franz Boas, Speck in 1904 began fieldwork under Boas' supervision in the Indian Territory and Oklahoma—where allotment had been going on for fifteen years. He completed his doctoral dissertation on the Yuchi in 1908—by which time he had already begun what proved to be a lifetime connection with the institution from which his degree was formally granted, the University of Pennsylvania (Speck 1909c). In 1907, he began the fieldwork among Algonquians that was to be the major interest of his anthropological career (Hallowell 1951, 1968; Siebert 1982; Wallace 1949, 1951; Witthoft 1974).

From the time he was an undergraduate, Speck had published articles in nonprofessional journals. Among these was the magazine of the Hampton Institute in Virginia, a philanthropic venture serving Indian as well as black youth. Starting in 1907, the *Southern Workman* published pieces by Speck, including several on conditions in Oklahoma and the Indian Territory (1907a, 1907b; see also 1908, 1909a, 1909b, 1912a, 1912b); in 1912, it was the venue of his first general article on Indian policy: "Conservation for the Indians." Speck argued that "those who have interested themselves in the problems of the Indians" had been mostly concerned with "how to induce the Indian to absorb the modern form of civilization" and had not considered "how much of this it is good for him to absorb." Alluding to the recent experience of blacks and Eastern European immigrants, Speck emphasized what he called "the conservative aspect" of the Indian problem, offering some rather general proposals against detribalization and deculturation. On the one hand, he proposed that Indians should be left in their "ideal homes" in the "vast tracts of uninhabited wilderness on this continent." On the other, he suggested that the newly founded Society of American Indians should "realize the importance to themselves" of a policy of conservatism—a proposal that involved him in further exchange with the Society's leading figure, Arthur C. Parker (1912b: 328–30; Parker 1912; Speck 1913a, 1914b).[2]

During this period Speck was also clearly concerned with the welfare of the particular Indian groups among whom he was doing fieldwork. His work among the Montagnais began in July 1908 (Deschênes 1981:218), and in his first account of his Montagnais findings—published in the *Southern Workman* —Speck compared their situation to that of colonial peoples elsewhere: "In some respects their condition is comparable to that of the Indians of the upper Amazon River who spend their lives in a hunt for rubber, and to that of the Negroes in certain parts of Africa who labor under life contracts." While

2. Grandnephew of Morgan's friend Ely Parker, Arthur Parker entitled his response to Speck "Progress for the Indian." Speck's reference to immigrant populations suggests perhaps an influence of Franz Boas, who in the years of Speck's studentship was himself turning to public policy issues (Stocking 1979).

"nominally free men," they were practically the "slaves" of the Hudson's Bay Company: "although he does not realize it [the Montagnais] is always slaving at his killing job in the woods to catch up with his credit" (1909b:148).

Speck also made policy recommendations for the specific situations he encountered. In a newspaper clipping covering his trip in 1912, and in a letter to Edward Sapir, his former classmate and close friend, then chief ethnologist of the anthropological division of the Geological Survey of Canada, Speck reported that there was "great suffering" among the Montagnais of the St. Lawrence River. Attributing it in part to bans on fishing for salmon (because the rights were leased by the government to "multi-millionaire sportsmen"), he appealed to Sapir to help with relief and medical aid. Sapir did forward the matter to the Canadian Department of Indian Affairs, which assured him that relief supplies had been provided. Speck did not expect that much would be done to remedy the situation permanently, because the leasing practice was well established and "a powerful opposition still remains to be fought down" (FGSP box 11; ESC: FGS/ES 7/7/12; D. C. Scott/ES 7/18; ES/FGS 7/12/12).

During Speck's continuing fieldwork among the Montagnais at Lac St. Jean, he made friends with Armand Tessier, the regional Indian Agent. In December 1912, Tessier wrote a long letter to all the large French language newspapers in Quebec opposing the provincial government restrictions on all killing of beaver and the sale of beaver pelts, which deprived the Indians of needed food and cash incomes, and which must have also placed a drain on his welfare funds as an Indian Agent. His letter, which was translated into English in Ottawa for the federal civil servants, spoke in favor of an exemption for Indians to the law banning the killer of beaver.

> The Indian is reputed to be careless and improvident. I contend on the contrary that so far as concerns fur-hunting he is endowed with a fineness of perception and a prudence that a white man has not. . . . Accompanied by his family, the Indian carries on his operations over a tract of land along a river or in the neighbourhood of a lake, and that is what he calls his "hunting ground." That is his patrimony. It has been bequeathed him by his father, who himself got it from his ancestors. From father to son these hunters have at the same place followed the fur animals, killed the beaver each year, and each year they have found it again and there always are some. There is nothing astonishing in that to anyone who knows how the Indian acts. . . . Instinctively the hunter understands that Providence by a wise law that man has no right to amend or change has placed the beaver there for his subsistence; but he understands also that he must not abuse it. It is for that reason that, guided by his instinct, and with the object of conservation, the Indian, obedient to a natural law that is worth more to him than all written laws, "never kills all the members of a beaver family." He knows enough always to spare a sufficient number for the continuation of the family, for the propagation of the race. He takes care of the beavers that live in his tract of land as the farmer takes care of his flock. He can tell at any

time the number that he can dispose of each year without ruining his hunting ground. (DIAC: vol. 6750, file 420-10, 1/13/13; cf. Tessier 1912)

In addition to publishing this tract, Tessier organized and circulated a petition among Lac St. Jean whites asking the Quebec government to comply with an exemption, and he expected three thousand signatures, including those of the leading political figures and clergy in the region (DIAC: Tessier 1/6/13). Tessier's program was successful; in 1914 he reported to his superiors in Ottawa that Quebec had granted permission to sell two thousand beaver pelts, worth ten thousand dollars (DIAC: Dufault/Tessier, 6/9/14; Tessier/D. C. Scott, 7/10/14).

How much Speck contributed to the resolution of this problem is unclear. It is likely that Tessier first raised the issue of restrictions on Indian hunting and trapping, for it was new in this region, although it had been a long-standing problem in parts of Quebec (DIAC: Tessier 1/6/13; J. D. McLean/Meredith et al. 11/6/11). Speck, on the other hand, had encountered some hunting territory material in his fieldwork among northeastern Algonquians over the previous four years, and he appears to have mapped Penobscot family hunting territories as early as 1910 (1931:573, 1940:203). Both Speck and Tessier had access to the published sources, in exploration reports from northern Quebec, on hunting territories among the peoples north and west of Lac St. Jean. Speck himself cited A. P. Low, the geological explorer of the Labrador peninsula, who had observed that "each family is supposed to own a portion of territory, with the exclusive rights to it" (Speck 1918a:90; Low 1896:50; see also O'Sullivan 1895:106; but cf. David 1907:207, who denied that the system was still in use at Lac St. Jean). Tessier and Speck were thus entering into an existing dialogue on hunting territories, not creating one.

But if neither of them "discovered" the family hunting territory, they did develop this evidence in a new way, in the context of Indian policy and conservation debates, initially in Canada and later in the United States. And the positions they developed were extraordinarily similar. Speck had a copy of Tessier's published letter in his files (FGSP: box 3, file 2296, 1912), and he briefly quoted Tessier's views comparing Indian and white hunters in an article he wrote in 1913 (Speck 1913b:25). In that same article Speck presented his findings on hunting territories for the first time, using much of the same material and often the same language that Tessier had used:

The Indians are commonly accused of being improvident as regards the killing of game because they depend upon it for their living. This, I maintain, is grossly incorrect, the Indians being, on the contrary, the best protectors of the game. . . . Accompanied by his family, the Montagnais operates through a certain territory, known as his "hunting ground," the boundaries determined by a certain river, the drainage of some lake or the alignment of some ridge. This is his fam-

ily inheritance, handed down from his ancestors. Here in the same district his
father hunted before him and here also his children will gain their living. Despite the continued killing in the tract each year the supply is always replen-
ished by the animals allowed to breed there. There is nothing astonishing in
this to the mind of the Indian because the killing is definitely regulated so that
the increase only is consumed, enough stock being left each season to insure
a supply the succeeding year. In this manner the game is "farmed" so to speak,
and the continued killing through centuries does not affect the stock fundamentally. . . . Instinctively, the hunter understands how Providence, by a wise
law, which no man or government or game commission can improve on, has
placed the beaver there for his subsistence. He understands, moreover, that he
cannot abuse this providence. Thus it is that the Indian, obeying a natural law
of conservation, which is worth more than any written law to him, "never destroys
all the members of a beaver family." He knows enough to spare a sufficient number for the continuation of the family and the propagation of the colony. He
takes care of the beaver and other animals as well that live in his territory, the
same as a farmer does his breeders. He can, indeed, tell at any time the number
of animals which he can dispose of each year in his district without damaging
his supply. (1913b:21–22)

Although the hunting territory system was described in Tessier's letter of
1912 and Speck's article of 1913, neither then made a claim about the legal
status of hunting territories as property, nor offered any specific assertion about
Indian rights. This may have reflected the fact that land rights were not an
issue at the time at Lac St. Jean, because there had been no treaties made
in this area. Neither was there any parallel in Canadian Indian policy to the
United States allotment program; the pattern was rather one of sporadic assimilationist attempts offset by government efforts "to keep the Indians con-
tented and satisfied with their lot as *Indians*" (Sniffen 1911:165–66). In this
context, both Tessier and Speck argued in terms of the social consequences
of the ban on killing beaver, and the lack of need for such a ban because
Indians themselves were conservationists.

"You Can Write This Down for Me"

After returning to Lac St. Jean in the spring of 1913, Speck reported that
he was having a map of the hunting territories made on birch bark (ESC:
FGS/ES 4/9/13); that summer he conducted a survey in the Ottawa valley
with continuing support from Sapir and the Geological Survey of Canada,
and with a specific mandate to study hunting territoriality (Speck 1915b:2).
He gathered data from several bands, one of which was not only experiencing
the effects of white intrusions but vocally protesting and resisting the colonization of their lands. The Temagami Indians had less accessible hinter-

Frank Speck with Chief Aleck Paul (partly cut out by photographer) and an Ojibwa woman, probably Paul's wife, at Temagami, Ontario, in 1913. (Courtesy of the National Museums of Canada, Ottawa, neg. no. CMC 23944.)

land to which to retreat than did the Montagnais of Lac St. John, and they were in a province where treaties had been and were continuing to be signed and implemented. Among them Speck found what he called his "best opportunity for investigating the social and economic organization" of the family hunting territories (Speck 1915c:297).

It was here that Speck recorded the speech of Aleck Paul, second Chief of the Temagami Band of Ojibways, and an English speaker, which he later published in several places, (Potts & Morrison 1988). The speech makes it is clear that the linkage between hunting territoriality and Indian land rights was actively argued by Indian leaders, and that Speck was more agent than author in the discourse on Indian rights and claims. Part of Chief Paul's speech was quoted by Speck in the *American Anthropologist*:

> In the early times the Indians owned this land, where they lived, bounded by the lakes, rivers, and hills, or determined by a certain number of days' journey in this direction or that. Those tracts formed the hunting grounds owned and used by the different families. Wherever they went the Indians took care of the game animals, especially the beaver, just as the Government takes care of the land today. . . . We Indian families used to hunt in a certain section for beaver. We would only kill the small beaver and leave the old ones to keep breeding. Then when they got too old, they too would be killed, just as a farmer kills his pigs, preserving the stock for his supply of young. The beaver was the Indians' pork; the moose, his beef; the partridge, his chicken; and there was the caribou or red deer, that was his sheep. All these formed the stock on his family hunting ground, which would be parceled out among the sons when the owner died. He said to his sons, "You take this part; take care of this tract; see that it always produces enough." That was what my grandfather told us. . . . We were to own this land so no other Indians could hunt on it. Other Indians could go there and travel through it, but could not go there to kill the beaver. Each family had its own district where it belonged, and owned the game. That was each one's stock for food and clothes. If another Indian hunted on our territory, we, the owners, could shoot him. This division of the land started in the beginning of time, and always remained unchanged. I remember about twenty years ago some Nipissing Indians came north to hunt on my father's land. He told them not to hunt beaver. "This is our land," he told them; "you can fish but must not touch the fur, as that is all we have to live on." Sometimes an owner would give permission for strangers to hunt for a certain time in a certain tract. This was often done for friends or when neighbors had a poor season. Later the favor might be returned. (1915c:294–95)

Several phrases in this text echo parts of Tessier's and Speck's writings, and Speck referred to it as a "translation" (1915c:294), which suggests that he had a role in its final English form. Chief Paul, however, clearly went beyond what Tessier and Speck had previously written.

In other articles Speck quoted Chief Paul at greater length, with specific reference to the political issue of the recognition of land rights:

Chief Aleck Paul of the Temagami band, in his chiefly regalia, 1913. (Courtesy of the National Museums of Canada, Ottawa, neg. no. CMC 23985.)

You can write this down for me: . . . What we Indians want is for the Government to stop the white people killing our game, as they do it only for sport and not for support. We Indians do not need to be watched about protecting the game, we must protect the game or starve. We can take care of the game just as well as the Game Wardens and better, because we are going to live here all the time. . . . When the treaty was made, about sixty years ago, the Government said: "You Indians own the game. . . . These Indians need to have their rights in the land and the game recognized and protected as much as the new settlers." (1913b:24; cf. 1914a:37)

The treaty mentioned by Chief Paul was the Robinson-Huron Treaty of 1850, the first of the major land rights concession treaties in Canada. The Temagami, who had been seeking inclusion in the treaty for nearly thirty years, were again petitioning the goverment for land at the time of Speck's visit. When the Government of Ontario in 1911 banned shooting and fishing within the Forest Reserve it had established around Lake Temagami, Chief Aleck Paul wrote a letter of protest; and just over a week before Speck arrived, a meeting was held with federal government representatives (without provincial representatives present) to try to select the site of a possible reserve (Potts & Morrison 1988:15–16). The event has recently been recounted by Chief Gary Potts of the Teme-augama First Nation:

> Speck arrived under the auspices of the Canadian government, his research financed by the Geological Survey. Since the land claim had started, the only officials our people had ever met were local Indian Agents and provincial fire rangers. Suddenly, here was a government man who was interested in our past and present life, our land tenure system, our political organization, our myths and stories. This couldn't be a coincidence. The people must have assumed Speck had been sent to gather information to help settle our claim. They welcomed him and openly told him just about anything he wanted to know. (Potts & Morrison 1988:16)

Chief Paul's speech, and the Temagami political position it expressed, incorporated nearly all the elements that have been taken by anthropologists as characterizing the classical model of the Algonquian family hunting territory system. The Temagami were certainly arguing for traditional, indeed aboriginal, territorial rights. The focus on legal rights required that the territory system be aboriginal in origin. The Temagami clearly saw territoriality as having both a family or kin-group basis and a "tribal" component; they were arguing for personalized family property rights, but not to the exclusion of "tribal" rights. Chief Paul was making a collective claim to rights; the Temagami sought recognition under the treaty as a group with collective rights, and they wanted a block of land put aside for a reserve for the community. As none of this was done in 1914, much of their subsequent legal claims up to the present day have reasserted these rights.[3]

Speck's ethnographic account was thus organized around a prior social policy position that already was being asserted by Indians themselves, as well as by non-Native activists, including Speck. The broad outline of that ethnography is drawn from and paralleled by the Indians' own policy arguments. But the ethnography was also structured by Speck's own involvement in the process, for he took the arguments of the Temagami and set them in the very

---

3. The Temagami claims are still being fought in the courts and in political arenas, and the data recorded by Speck are still cited. It is ironic that in a major legal ruling Mr. Justice Steele found that Speck's memoir was "not tainted with the partisanship shown by many witnesses at this trial" (1984).

different context of United States colonization policies, and thereby reshaped the ethnography of the Algonquian family hunting territories.

From Policy Advocacy to Ethnological Theory

Convinced that he had a mandate "to make public to the white people encroachments upon Indian rights to the land" (1914a:36), Speck published his Temagami findings almost immediately upon his return to the United States. In the September 1913 issue of the *Red Man* he quoted Chief Aleck Paul at length, and Armand Tessier more briefly, arguing that his data revealed "one among a number of fallacies current among historical writers which do injustice to the Indians by putting them on a lower cultural scale than they deserve" (1913b:21). The contrast with Speck's 1909 portrayal of the Montagnais is striking: the impoverished dependents of the Hudson's Bay Company had become active owners and managers of land and resources, requiring only to be left to continue their own practices.

While Speck at this point made no assertions of his own concerning property rights or land claims, these connections were clearly on his mind. On November 13, 1913, the magazine section of the Philadelphia *Public Ledger* published an article on his findings under the headline "Penn Professor's Discovery Confounds Indian 'History'—Doctor Speck Establishes that the American Redskin Hunts on His Own Family Ground, is a Protector of Game, and is no Mere Rover Through the Forests":

> [Speck] is known to the red men as their friend and protector. Many times he has interceded for them at Quebec and Ottawa, and the Indians know this and appreciate it, and it was therefore to him that they have given the proof of their ownership of the forests, not as tribes merely, but as individuals, thus upsetting all established data.

By this account, the "discovery" of individual hunting territories was "Dr. Speck's"; the Temagami had simply convinced him of its "truth" and provided "ample proofs to establish his claim" (Lovell 1913).

Two months later, in an article in the *Southern Workman*, Speck directly addressed "The Basis of Indian Ownership of Land and Game." Taking as his target the most prominent public proponent of Indian nomadism, he opened with a quotation from Theodore Roosevelt's *Winning of the West* (1889):

> To recognize Indian ownership of the limitless prairies and forests of this continent (that is, to consider the dozen squalid savages who hunted at long intervals over a territory of a thousand square miles, as owning it outright) necessarily implies a similar recognition of the claims of every white hunter, squatter, horse thief, or wandering cattleman. In fact, the mere statement of the case

is enough to show the absurdity of asserting that the land really belonged to the Indians. The different tribes have always been utterly unable to define their own boundaries.

Speck began by simply asserting that "Mr. Roosevelt is quite in error as regards most, if not all, of the hunting tribes of the northern part of this continent." Noting that this "attack upon the fundamental claims to their domains is a matter of considerable importance to the Indians, both in the United States and Canada," Speck argued that while "perhaps excusable through ignorance," the dissemination of "misconceptions resulting disadvantageously to a weaker race" was nevertheless "an injustice" (1914a:35). After quoting Chief Aleck Paul, Speck went on to claim "these conditions formed the primary social insititution" of the Indians: "the whole territory claimed by each tribe was subdivided into tracts, owned from time immemorial by the same families and handed down from generation to generation" (37–38).

Speck's argument was further refined in lectures and papers that variously summarized the work he had completed to date. His public talk in the Houston Club at the University in January 1915 formed the basis for these:

> I should like at least to show that the Indian tribes of eastern and northern North America did have quite definite claims to their habitat. Moreover, as we shall see, these claims existed even within the family groups composing the tribal communities. . . . It would seem, then, that such features characterize actual ownership of territory.

Again confronting Roosevelt, Speck offered a list of places from which he had data among the Algonquian (including Newfoundland, Labrador, Nova Scotia, Maine, Quebec, and Ontario), a brief general description of the territorial system, two paragraphs from Chief Paul's speech in a footnote, and more detailed data from Timiskaming, Temagami, Penobscot, and MicMac (1915a; cf. 1915d).

Although Speck was to remain active in the policy arena despite the limited impact of his initiatives,[4] by 1915 the primary locus of his hunting territory argument had shifted to the arena of professional discourse. From later

4. In 1926, the *General Magazine and Historical Chronicle* at the University of Pennsylvania carried three articles on the theme of "Assimilating the Red Man" (Vaux 1926; Welsh 1926; Work 1926). George Vaux, from the Indian Bureau, denied that Indian claims to ownership of areas was "land-tenure of the kind we Anglo-Saxons have developed." In a response entitled "Annihilating the Indian," Speck suggested that such plans were discussed in the absence or "exclusion of possible native points of view." Quoting most of the published version of his 1915 talk at the University of Pennsylvania, he noted that he had "emphasized the application of this information, hoping that it would reach the attention of those in authority in Indian affairs, for whom it was intended as an aid in their handling of the situation—an expectation not realized in the case of Mr. Vaux, who illustrates the indifference in [sic] the part of the administrators toward ethnological facts" (1926:262, 267–69).

evidence, it seems likely that Speck was stimulated by Robert Lowie's recent attack on Morgan's social evolution scheme, on the grounds that matrilineal descent groups did not precede patrilineal descent, and that unilineal descent was not universal among North American Indians and was absent in the least complex societies (Speck 1918a:82, citing Lowie 1914). But it is important to emphasize that it was not Morgan but Roosevelt (and those he stood for) against whom Speck had originally been speaking. His anti-evolutionism was not simply a Boasian inheritance; it was embedded in his policy concerns. The evolutionists he was arguing against were powerful mainstream spokesmen, active in Republican and Democratic party politics, in the government bureaucracy, and in advising the government. Although Speck's subsequent development of the argument reformulated his anti-evolutionism, it was never entirely separated from policy issues.

The transition from writing about hunting territories for a broad but informed audience to writing about them primarily for other anthropologists took place in an article in the *American Anthropologist* in 1915. Its title—"The Family Hunting Band as the Basis of Algonkian Social Organization"—indicated that for a professional audience the emphasis was to be not primarily on the claims to land rights but on the family group as the fundamental social unit in hunting societies, in evident contrast to social evolutionary models. But after an opening sentence vaguely suggesting its general ethnological relevance, Speck followed his University of Pennsylvania talk with only minor editorial modifications. Deleting the references to Roosevelt, but retaining his arguments for Indian conservation and Indian land ownership, he thus introduced into the anthropological literature an argument that had germinated in the realm of policy issues.

But the transition into the professional literature was not an easy one, first because it highlighted the problem of the generality and reliability of his data. Speck's policy experience and inclination led him to emphasize that the authority of his materials flowed in part from having some material from several communities, and in part from his being able to present a "Native voice" on the issues, as Chief Paul's mandate had indeed authorized. But the extent of the Native voice he could claim to represent remained problematic in his texts, and for Speck himself. In his *American Anthropologist* paper, Speck quoted a short edited translation from Tessier's letter, with a footnote referring to it as "a statement prepared *by* the Montagnais of Lake St. John" (1915c:294; emphasis mine). The fact that the text is written in the third person, and Speck refers to its having been "prepared," make it unlikely that it was written by Montagnais. Speck himself acknowledges the ambiguity of the provenance of the Montagnais text when he goes on to note that the following Ojibway text, from Chief Paul, "is interesting because it gives us a first-hand translation of the *actual statements* of an Indian authority himself" (1915c:294; emphasis mine). Thus Speck, somewhat self-consciously, stretches the authority of the "Native voice," probably both to acknowledge Indian participation in the process of describing hunting territories, as well as to legitimate his more generalized scholarly assertions. Speck converted a Temagami voice, or Temagami and Montagnais voices, into a general Algonquian voice, for which he had considerably less authority and evidence.

Speck's *American Anthropologist* paper (1915c), and the longer monograph on the Ottawa valley bands published by the Geological Survey of Canada (1915b), were initially met with a certain caution and criticism. Some of his closest colleagues were concerned whether other researchers would confirm Speck's findings. In the summer of 1915 Edward Sapir had at least two researchers probing for evidence of Algonquian family hunting territories (RHLP: ES/R. H. Lowie 9/27/16). Both confirmed their existence, and these confirmations were reported to Speck, who mentioned the data in a later publication (1918a:88–89; see also Davidson 1928).

Others, however, expressed early doubts in print. Criticizing Speck's data as superficial, William Mechling argued that the development of family hunting groups as a result of contact with Europeans would be consistent with "Morgan's statement" (1916a, 1916b). Even a fellow Boasian, Alexander Goldenweiser, who found Speck's arguments convincing and his conclusions "epochmaking," nevertheless felt that the monographs were "in part vague, almost fragmentary" (1916:278; FGSP: AG/FGS 3/20/16; cf. P. Goddard/FGS 3/13/16). It was in replying to these criticisms that Speck for the first time explicitly mentioned Morgan and McLennan, addressing their assumption that "the matrilineally organized tribes represented the primitive, at least the earlier, condition from which others had emerged" (1918a:82; cf. 1917, 1918b, 1920). Against this, he claimed to show that "the looser stage"—the family grouping with patrilineal tendencies—was a "relatively older, more primitive phase of culture" (1918a:100)—thus finally spelling out clearly the argument he had introduced into the professional literature in 1915.

The most widely known case for the relevance of the northeastern Algonquian for evolutionary social theories was developed not by Speck but by Robert Lowie: "thanks to Professor Speck's capital investigation," the assumption "that when peoples support themselves by the chase there is of necessity communal ownership of hunting-grounds" should be abandoned because "it must now be regarded as an established fact that in parts of North America . . . the hunting-grounds themselves were the property of individual families" (1920:211; Murphy 1972). Two years later Speck noted Lowie's argument with approval, going on, however, to claim that the social organizational implications of his studies were "of still more importance" to the evaluation of theories of social evolution (1922:83–85). Twenty years further on, Speck himself joined in asserting that his findings "must inevitably be troubling to those who, like Morgan, and many present-day Russians" would claim that hunters represent "a stage prior to the development of the institution of individualized property" (Speck & Eiseley 1942:238). Thus, although his initial formulations did not have their origins in theoretical or ideological issues, by 1942 Speck himself was prepared to make the argument in these terms.

The Colonial Situation of an Ethnographic Error

Although eventually incorporated into an anti-Morganian ethnological argument, it was Speck's policy arguments that shaped the most criticized features of his research into Algonquian family hunting territories. The ethnographic data are decidedly sketchy, general, and characterized more by ideal norms than by specific instances and their variations. This may arise in part from the culture trait assumptions common during the period, but culture trait studies were often extraordinarily detailed. Part of the cause is no doubt Speck's fieldwork practice (cf. Deschênes 1979:39–46). Although reportedly a good fieldworker, his trips were often a cross between museum specimen collecting trips and fieldwork. Eventually he made sixteen trips to Lac St. Jean and a total of twenty-seven to the Montagnais between 1908 and 1935, but in 1915 he had spent only about fifty-five days at Lac St. Jean (Deschênes 1981:218). In the Ottawa valley his stay at Temagami lasted two weeks, and he never returned (Potts & Morrison 1988:19; cf. Speck 1915e).

The constraints and possibilities inherent in the political situation of Indians and anthropologists on the active frontier of colonization shaped what happened during those brief field trips. Where the process of land colonization and acquisition by whites was far advanced, the ethnographic record tended to be weak, and distorted by the fact that most of these groups were reporting on a system of practice that was in various degrees disrupted or abandoned (e.g., Penobscot). Four of the groups Speck reported on in 1915 appear to have been carrying on family hunting territory practices at the time of his research, but only one was not experiencing immediate threats. Thus there was limited material to draw on from contemporary practice among many of the groups Speck studied. It is significant that Speck's central, legitimizing, and defining cases developed not from these more long-settled and disrupted areas, nor from the more northerly and isolated peoples in northern Quebec, where conflicts were more sporadic and not yet fundamentally threatening, and therefore relatively unarticulated. The two key cases, Lac St. Jean and Temagami, were from areas in which colonization was several decades old and was intensifying, and in which there was an active political response or resistance to at least some aspects of the process.

Where colonization of lands had not proceeded to near completion, and where there was active political response to the colonization of Indian lands, this context led politically active interviewees and interviewers to present a rather formalized and ideal model of family hunting territory practices, rather than an ethnographically rich account of everyday examples and of everyday problems and variations. Such simplification was expedient in public presentations, and it made the political case less vulnerable to criticism in the political arena, although it did the reverse in academic settings. Political activism made short, intensive fieldwork highly productive (Potts & Morrison 1988), but it also shaped the kind of data which was collected.

The policy context affected not only the data collection but also the specific content and organization of the ethnographies. The specific ethnographic features emphasized in Speck's generalized accounts of family hunting territoriality were those essential to identify them as legally recognizable forms of private property. The linkage was made explicit when Speck reviewed his data in the light of authoritative conceptions of "property" and "private property." In a paper delivered in 1926, Speck quoted L. T. Hobhouse (1922) to the effect that for things temporarily controlled or possessed to become property there were three requirements: (1) possession must be recognized by others, that is, it must be a right; (2) with regard to things of a permanent nature, the right must be respected in the absence of the possessor; and (3) control must be exclusive, not universal. Speck added that Hobhouse also distinguished property as private, joint, or common depending on who exercises the rights (1928a:324). In the course of a review of the evidence from various parts of the world, Speck incorporated (with only minor changes) two long passages from his 1915 *American Anthropologist* articles that he felt defined Algonquian hunting territoriality in a form consistent with Hobhouse's requirements for establishing the presence of private property. Social recognition was established by the fact that territories generally had known and recognized boundaries, as indicated by Speck's ability to get informants to agree on maps of the territories. Permanence of the right to use land was indicated by the established procedure of inheritance, and also by the conservation of resources over generations, as well as by his claim that the family units that constituted the social order were themselves united by land rights as well as by their kinship ties. The exclusiveness of the rights was established by the prohibition against trespass for purposes of killing beaver and by the procedures for granting permissions for access. The ownership by individuals or families was established by documenting the family hunting groups who had rights to each territory and by inheritance practices. In contrast to his other more "classically" organized ethnographic survey reports (e.g., 1909c, 1935, 1940), Speck's ethnographies of hunting territories generally consist of reporting these traits repeatedly, for diverse Montagnais and Algonquian groups (1922, 1923, 1927, 1928b, 1931, 1939).

That the initial ethnology of Algonquian family hunting territories was so closely tied to processes of ongoing colonization of Indian lands and so-cieties is ironic. The social policy focus of Speck's ethnography was so thor-oughly lost from view in the debates of the succeeding years, and in their histories, that even the anthropologists who later insisted that the develop-ment of family hunting territories could only be comprehended within a his-tory of colonization, colonialism, and economic change still tended to see the anthropological debates as a frozen ideological dispute outside of a dy-namic, historical, sociopolitical context. This was possible because the critics' defense of evolutionism associated it with Morgan, but not with Roosevelt, Grinnell, or others outside anthropology but key to government policy mak-ing. The political and economic context of Speck's policy critiques faded from sight, as did the web of linkages between advocacy and ethnology.

Speck himself argued for Indian rights in numerous political contexts throughout the rest of his career. Not least of these political activities was his work, beginning in the 1920s, for and with the Cayuga Iroquois of the Six Nations in Canada (1941). Lewis Henry Morgan had worked with an-other nation of the Iroquois Confederacy nearly a century before. Both Speck and Morgan were disturbed by the processes of colonization of Indian lands going on around them. They differed, however, in their visions of what might be possible for Indians in the future. Speck held out a more "romantic" fu-ture, one more authentically linked to what was distinctive in the Indians' past; Morgan argued for time and space to moderate the "progressive" changes he saw as inevitable. While recognizing the differences between both men's models, explanations, and visions, it is important to note the similarity of the processes by which they each constructed ethnographies and developed ethnological theories in the context of their social praxis and political advo-cacy for Indians.

Acknowledgments

This paper presents the results of research funded by the Social Sciences and Humani-ties Research Council of Canada (grant 410-85-1325), and by the Arts Research Board of McMaster University. It has gone through a number of versions, and I have bene-fitted in the process from the comments and suggestions of Matthew Cooper, James Morrison, Colin Scott, George W. Stocking, Jr., Bruce Trigger, and two anonymous reviewers.

References Cited

Berkhofer, R. F. 1979. *The white man's Indian: Images of the American Indian from Colum-bus to the present.* New York.
Bishop, C., & T. Morantz, eds. 1986. Who owns the beaver? Northern Algonquian land tenure reconsidered. *Anthropologica* 28 (1–2).

Cooper, J. M. 1938. Land tenure among the Indians of eastern and northern North America. *Pennsylvania Archaeol.* 8:55–60.

———. 1939. Is the Algonquian family hunting ground system pre-Columbian? *Am. Anth.* 41:66–90.

David, P. C.-E. 1907. Les Montagnais du Labrador et du Lac St-Jean. *15th Congrès international des Américanistes,* 1:205–11. Quebec.

Davidson, D. S. 1928. Family hunting territories of the Waswanipi Indians of Quebec. *Indian notes* (Museum of the American Indian, Heye Foundation) 5:42–59.

Deschênes, J.-G. 1979. *Epistémologie de la production anthropologique de Frank G. Speck.* Master's thesis, Laval University.

———. 1981. La contribution de Frank G. Speck à l'anthropologie des Amérindiens du Québec. *Rech. amérindiennes au Québec* 9:205–20.

DIAC. See under Manuscript Sources.

Dippie, B. W. 1982. *The vanishing American: White attitudes and U.S. Indian policy.* Middletown, Conn.

Engels, F. 1884. *The origin of the family, private property and the state.* Ed. E. B. Leacock. London (1972).

ESC. See under Manuscript Sources.

Feit, H. A. 1982. The future of hunters within nation-states: Anthropology and the James Bay Cree. In *Politics and history in band societies,* ed. E. Leacock and R. Lee, 373–411. Cambridge.

———. 1986. Anthropologists and the state: The relationship between social policy advocacy and academic practice in the history of the Algonquian hunting territory debate, 1920–50. Paper at Fourth International Conference on Hunting and Gathering Societies, London, September 8–13.

———1991. Gifts of the land: Hunting territories, guaranteed incomes and the construction of social relations in James Bay Cree society. In *Cash, commoditisation and changing foragers,* ed. N. Peterson and T. Matsuyama, 223–68. Senri Ethnological Studies. Osaka.

FGSP. See under Manuscript Sources.

Goldenweiser, A. A. 1916. Review of Speck 1915b, 1915c. *Am. Anth.* 18:278–80.

Grinnell, G. B. 1907. Tenure of land among the Indians. *Am. Anth.* 9:1–11.

Hallowell, A. I. 1949. The size of Algonkian hunting territories: A function of ecological adjustment. *Am. Anth.* 51:35–45.

———. 1951. Frank Gouldsmith Speck, 1881–1950. *Am. Anth.* 53:67–75.

———. 1968. Speck, Frank G. In *International Encyclopedia of the Social Sciences* 15: 115–17.

Hays, S. P. 1959. *Conservation and the gospel of efficiency: The progressive conservation movement, 1890–1920.* New York (1969).

Hickerson, H. 1967. Some implications of the theory of the particularity or "atomism" of northern Algonkians. *Curr. Anth.* 8:313–43.

Hinsley, C. M. 1981. *Savages and scientists: The Smithsonian Institution and the development of American anthropology, 1846–1910.* Washington, D.C.

Hobhouse, L. T. 1922. The historical evolution of property, in fact and in idea. In *Property, Its Duties and Rights, Historically, Philosophically and Religiously Regarded. Essays by Various Writers,* 1–31. New York.

Hoxie, F. E. 1984. *A final promise: The campaign to assimilate the Indians, 1880–1920.* Cambridge.

Kehoe, A. B. 1985. The ideological paradigm in traditional American ethnology. In *Social contexts of American ethnology, 1840–1984,* ed. J. Helm, 41–49. Washington, D.C.

Leacock, E. B. 1954. *The Montagnais hunting territory and the fur trade.* American Anthropological Association, memoir 78. Washington, D.C.

————. 1963. Introduction to Morgan 1877:Ii–Ixx, IIi–IIxx, IIIi–IIIviii, IVi–IViii.

————. 1972. Introduction to Engels 1884:7–67.

————. 1986. The Montagnais-Naskapi of the Labrador peninsula. In *Native peoples: The Canadian experience,* ed. R. B. Morrison & C. R. Wilson, 140–71. Toronto.

Leupp, F. E. 1909. Indian lands: Their administration with reference to present and future use. *Annals of the Am. Acad. Polit. & Soc. Sci.* 33(3):620–30.

Lovell, M. R. 1913. Penn professor's discovery confounds Indian "history"—Doctor Speck establishes that the American Redskin hunts on his own family ground, is a protector of game, and is no mere rover through the forests." *Public Ledger* (Philadelphia), November 23, 1913 (mag. sec.).

Low, A. P. 1896. *Reports on explorations in the Labrador Peninsula along the Eastmain, Koksoak, Hamilton, Manicouagan and portions of other rivers in 1892–93–94–95.* Annual report, Geological Survey of Canada, vol. 8, report L. Ottawa.

Lowie, R. H. 1914. Social organization. *Am. J. Sociol.* 20:68–97.

————. 1920. *Primitive society.* New York.

Mechling, W. H. 1916a. Review of Speck 1915b, 1915e. *Am. Anth.* 18:281–82.

————. 1916b. Dr. Speck's "The family hunting band." *Am. Anth.* 18:299–302.

Morgan, L. H. 1851. *League of the Ho-de-no-sau-nee, or Iroquois.* New Haven (1954).

————. 1877. *Ancient society.* Ed. E. B. Leacock. Cleveland (1963).

Murphy, R. F. 1972. *Robert H. Lowie.* New York.

Murphy, R. F., & J. H. Steward. 1956. Tappers and trappers: Parallel process in acculturation. *Econ. Dev. & Cult. Change* 4:335–55.

O'Sullivan, H. 1895. Report of an exploration of part of the Hudson Bay Slope performed by Mr. Henry O'Sullivan, Inspector of Surveys. *Report of the Commissioner of Crown Lands for the Province of Quebec for the twelve months ending 30th June 1895,* appendix 41, 100–118. Quebec.

Parker, A. C. 1912. Progress for the Indian. *South. Workman* 41:628–35.

Potts, Chief G., & J. Morrison. 1988. The Temagami Ojibwa, Frank Speck and family hunting territories. Paper presented at the American Society for Ethnohistory Conference, Williamsburg, Va., November 11.

Resek, C. 1960. *Lewis Henry Morgan, American scholar.* Chicago.

RHLP. See under Manuscript Sources.

Roosevelt, T. 1889. *The Winning of the West.* St. Clair Shores, Mich. (1977).

Schurz, C. 1881. Present aspects of the Indian problem. In *Americanizing the American Indians: Writings by the "Friends of the Indian," 1880–1900,* ed. F. P. Prucha, 13–26. Cambridge (1973).

Scott, C. 1988. Property, practice and aboriginal rights among Quebec Cree hunters. In *Hunters and gatherers 2: Property, power and ideology,* ed. T. Ingold, D. Riches, & J. Woodburn, 35–51. Oxford.

Siebert, F. T. 1982. Frank G. Speck, Personal reminiscences. In *Papers of the Thirteenth Algonquian Conference*, ed. W. Cowan, 91–136. Ottawa.

Sniffen, M. K. 1911. Canada and her Indians. *South. Workman* 40:165–68.

Speck, F. G. 1907a. Observations in Oklahoma and Indian Territory. *South. Workman* 36:23–37.

———. 1907b. Negro and white exclusion towns in Indian Territory. *South. Workman* 36:430–32.

———. 1908. The Negroes and the Creek nation. *South. Workman* 37:106–10.

———. 1909a. Notes on Creek mythology. *South. Workman* 38:9–11.

———. 1909b. The Montagnais Indians. *South. Workman* 38:148–54.

———. 1909c. Ethnology of the Yuchi. *Univ. Pennsylvania, Anth. Pub. Univ. Mus.* 1:1–154.

———. 1912a. An ethnological visit to the Montagnais Indians. *South. Workman* 41:85–90.

———. 1912b. Conservation for the Indians. *South. Workman* 41:328–32.

———. 1913a. Conserving and developing the good in the Indian. *Red Man* 5:463–65.

———. 1913b. The Indians and game preservation. *Red Man* 6:21–25.

———. 1914a. The basis of Indian ownership of land and game. *South. Workman* 43:35–38.

———. 1914b. Educating the white man up to the Indian. *Quart. J., Soc. Am. Indians* 2:64–68.

———. 1915a. Basis of American Indian ownership of the land. *Old Penn Wkly. Rev.* 13:491–95.

———. 1915b. *Family hunting territories and social life of various Algonkian bands of the Ottawa Valley.* Ottawa.

———. 1915c. The family hunting band as the basis of Algonkian social organization. *Am. Anth.* 17:289–305.

———. 1915d. Basis of American Indian ownership of the land. In *University of Pennsylvania, University Lectures delivered by members of the faculty in the Free Public Lecture Course, 1914–1915*, 181–96.

———. 1915e. *Myths and folk-lore of the Timiskaming Algonquin and Timagami Ojibwa.* Ottawa.

———. 1917. Game totems among the Northeastern Algonkians. *Am. Anth.* 19:9–18.

———. 1918a. The social structure of the Northern Algonkian. *Am. Sociol. Soc. Pub.* 12:82–100.

———. 1918b. Kinship terms and the family band among the Northeastern Algonkian. *Am. Anth.* 20:143–61.

———. 1920. Correction to kinship terms of the Northeastern Algonkian. *Am. Anth.* 22(1):85.

———. 1922. *Beothuk and Micmac.* Indian Notes and Monographs, Museum of the American Indian, Heye Foundation, ser. 2, no. 22.

———. 1923. Mistassini hunting territories of the Labrador Peninsula. *Am. Anth.* 25:452–71.

———. 1926. Annihilating the Indian. *Gen. Mag. & Hist. Chron.* 28:262–70.

———. 1927. Family hunting territories of the Lake St. John Montagnais and neighboring bands. *Anthropos* 22:387–403.

————. 1928a. Land ownership among hunting peoples in primitive America and the world's marginal areas. *Proc. 22nd Intl. Congr. Americanists* (Rome) 2:323–32.

————. 1928b. *Territorial subdivisions and boundaries of the Wampanoag, Massachusetts, and Nauset Indians.* Indian Notes and Monographs, Museum of the American Indian, Heye Foundation, ser. 2, no. 44.

————. 1931. Montagnais bands and early Eskimo distribution in the Labrador Peninsula. *Am. Anth.* 33:557–600.

————. 1935. *Naskapi: Savage hunters of the Labrador Peninsula.* Norman, Okla.

————. 1939. More Algonkian scapulimancy from the north and the hunting territory question. *Ethnos* 4:21–28.

————. 1940. *Penobscot Man.* Philadelphia.

————. 1941. An ethnologist speaks for the pagan Indians. *Crozier Quart.* 18:213–18.

Speck, F. G. & L. C. Eiseley. 1939. The significance of hunting territory systems of the Algonkian in social theory. *Am. Anth.* 41:269–80.

————. 1942. Montagnais-Naskapi bands and family hunting districts of central and southeastern Labrador peninsula. *Proc. Am. Philos. Soc.* 85:215–42.

Steele, [Judge]. 1984. Reasons for judgment, in the Supreme Court of Ontario, between the Attorney General for the Province of Ontario and the Bear Island Foundation and Gary Potts *et al.*

Stocking, G. W. 1979. Anthropology as *Kulturkampf:* Science and politics in the career of Franz Boas. In *The uses of anthropoology,* ed. W. Goldschmidt, 33–50. Washington, D.C.

Tanner, A. 1979. *Bringing home animals: Religious ideology and mode of production of Mistassini Cree hunters.* London.

Tessier, A. 1912. Communication: Les lois de chasse et les sauvages. *L'Action sociale* 12/27/1912.

Trautman, T. R. 1987. *Lewis Henry Morgan and the invention of kinship.* Berkeley.

Vaux, G. 1926. Some activities of the federal Indian bureau. *Gen. Mag. & Hist. Chron.* 28:100–106.

Wallace, A. F. C. 1949. In memoriam of Frank G. Speck. *Pennsylvania Archaeol.* 19: 51–53.

————. 1951. The Frank G. Speck collection. *Am. Philos. Soc. Proc.* 95:286–89.

Welsh, H. 1926. The Indian question of 1882 and 1925. *Gen. Mag. & Hist. Chron.* 28:106–11.

Witthoft, J. 1974. Frank Gouldsmith Speck. In *Dictionary of American Biography, Supplement Four, 1946–1950,* 761–63. New York.

Work, H. 1926. Assimilating the Red Man. *Gen. Mag. & Hist. Chron.* 28:97–100.

Manuscript Sources

In writing this paper I have drawn on research materials collected from the following manuscript sources, cited as abbreviated below:

DIAC   Department of Indian Affairs Records, Public Archives of Canada, Ottawa (RG-10).

ESC   Edward Sapir Correspondence, Canadian Ethnology Service, National Museums of Canada, Ottawa.

FGSP   Frank G. Speck Papers, American Philosophical Society Library, Philadelphia.

RHLP   Robert H. Lowie Correspondence and Papers, Bancroft Library, University of California, Berkeley.

CONTESTED MONUMENTS

The Politics of Archeology in Southern Africa

HENRIKA KUKLICK

Cecil Rhodes, the singularly powerful promoter of the economic and territorial expansion of Britain's southern African empire, was obsessed with one item in his large collection of African artifacts—a carved soapstone bird, resembling a bird of prey with human limbs, which has been sold to him in Cape Town by a travelling hunter in 1889. Rhodes gave it the place of honor in the library of Groote Schuur, his house outside Cape Town, and five wooden replicas decorated the banister of the stairway linking the entrance hall to the upper rooms. His friends were recipients of castings, and treble-sized versions of the bird guarded the gates of his English house near Cambridge (Rotberg 1988:387; Summers 1963:1, 1971:xvi; Walton 1955:79).

The bird was one of eight such carvings, each standing roughly five feet tall on its original pillar, that had once graced an impressive group of stone ruins in Mashonaland, part of the territory that was to become a colony named for Rhodes. Spread over some sixty acres, the ruins included "by far the largest single prehistoric structure in sub-Saharan Africa" (Garlake 1973:27). They were called "Great Zimbabwe" to distinguish them from the two-hundred-odd similar and less impressive ruins that once dotted the area, which the Shona called "zimbabwe"—their word for a court, house, or grave of a chief, and the name now carried by the African state installed in the former colony.

In the same year Rhodes acquired his Zimbabwe bird, he also gained a Royal Charter for his British South Africa Company. The Company sent its "Pioneer Column" from South Africa to occupy Mashonaland in 1890, and in 1895 its territory south of the Zambezi was named Rhodesia. In 1914 the

---

Henrika Kuklick is an Associate Professor in the Department of History and Sociology of Science at the University of Pennsylvania. Her most recent work is *The Savage Within: The Social History of British Anthropology, 1885–1945* (New York: Cambridge University Press, 1991).

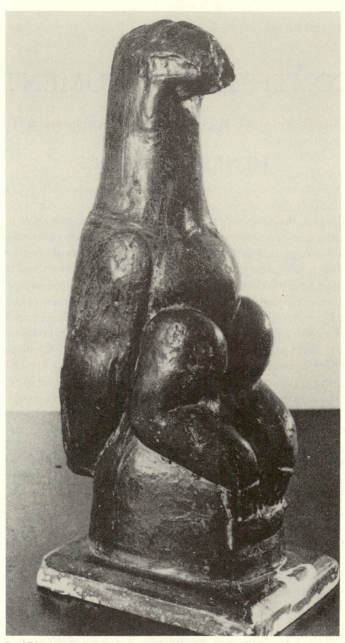

Cecil Rhodes's Zimbabwe bird. (From Roger Summers, *Ancient Ruins and Vanished Civilizations of Southern Africa* (Cape Town: T. V. Bulpin, 1971.)

British government renewed the Company's charter on condition that white settlers be granted self-government in ten years. In 1923 the whites and a very few eligible African voters narrowly rejected the option of a merger with the Union of South Africa. Instead the country became a British colony in which income qualifications excluded almost all Africans from the electoral rolls and the government enjoyed virtual autonomy. Although Britain retained the right to veto legislation that discriminated against Africans, it never exercised that right. Between 1953 and 1964, Southern Rhodesia became part of the Central African Federation, which also included Nyasaland (now Malawi) and Northern Rhodesia (now Zambia); the Federation dissolved when Malawi and Zambia became independent African-ruled states. In 1965 a white supremacist regime in Southern Rhodesia proclaimed their country's Unilateral Declaration of Independence from Britain, changing the country's name to Rhodesia. Brought down by international economic sanctions and guerilla warfare, the Rhodesian regime ended in 1979. In 1980 the new country of Zimbabwe inaugurated as its first Prime Minister the leader of the African freedom fighters, Robert Mugabe.

Through all of these changes, the images of Great Zimbabwe and of the Zimbabwe bird in particular remained constant features of state iconography. In 1924, when Southern Rhodesia was granted its Arms (based on those of Cecil Rhodes), a Zimbabwe bird was represented on its crest. Zimbabwe birds came to be found everywhere, from government buildings to trademarks, symbolizing Southern Rhodesia. During the period of the Central African Federation, birds appeared on the paper money and coins issued by the Bank of Rhodesia and Nyasaland. When the Federation dissolved, the new flag contrived for the country of Southern Rhodesia contained the arms; so, too, did the flag of the white supremacist regime of Rhodesia. Today, a representation of the same Zimbabwe bird presides over Zimbabwe's flag, and a bird is found on all manner of government artifacts, from postage stamps to the logo of the television system. Moreover, when the new state Zimbabwe assumed management of the museum at Great Zimbabwe, birds retrieved from foreign collections were reunited there. The Zimbabwe birds are now "widely affirmed to be the most precious symbols of the new state" (Garlake 1982:16; Frederikse 1982:349; Summers 1963:2).

To every group that has made an icon of the ruins, they have been material evidence of a prosperous and powerful state that once held sway in the land. There, however, the resemblance between different groups' received histories of Great Zimbabwe ends. Seeking to legitimate their rule, British settlers and African nationalists subscribed to very different accounts of the building of the ruins, placing their construction alternatively in ancient times and the relatively recent past, and identifying the builders—or, at least the architects—either as representatives of some non-African civilization or

members of the indigenous population. The stories of Great Zimbabwe have
served to rationalize either colonial rule or African autonomy. An account
of the images of the ruins promulgated by the state and accepted by diverse
sectors of the population reveals changing power relationships in the country. But Zimbabwe's story is not unique. As we will see, in other colonial re-
gimes archeological exegesis has been similarly employed to legitimate political authority.

Alien Traces of a "Former Civilised Race"

The territory occupied by the British South Africa Company was the only
British colonial preserve acquired for the explicit purpose of exploiting its
mineral resources. Rhodes's Company received its charter on the strength of
an agreement, negotiated in 1888 with Lobengula, the ruler of the powerful
Ndebele kingdom, giving it the right to mine gold in Mashonaland. The two-
hundred-odd force of Rhodes's Pioneer Column—raised when Rhodes was
the Prime Minister of the Cape Colony and at the height of his political power
in South Africa—were described to the British government as "miners," the
peaceable vanguard of European settlement in the new colony. The Pioneers
(among them the hunter who sold Rhodes his Zimbabwe bird) evidently joined
Rhodes's venture expecting to become rich through prospecting. Each was
promised fifteen claims of gold in Mashonaland and given rights to a vast
tract of land advertised as extremely fertile—though many sold their land rights
back to the Company before beginning their march north. Accompanied by
five hundred of the Company's Police, the Pioneers reached the site of the
colony's new capital without military incident, having been led on a circuitous route by the famous hunter-naturalist F. C. Selous—said to be the model
for Allen Quartermain, the hero of H. Rider Haggard's *King Solomon's Mines*
(Chanaiwa 1973:84; Keppel-Jones 1983:158; Paver 1950:159–61, 179).

The British settlers' occupation of Southern Rhodesia could be rationalized in a number of ways. Selous himself offered a naturalist's justification:
the country was a natural habitat for them, "the fairest and most fertile of
the regions now for the first time since the dawn of history attracting the
attention of a civilised and energetic race of men." In it "European children
would grow up strong and healthy, and our English fruits retain their flavour"
(1889:661–62). Because Lobengula, acting under the misapprehension that his
agreement effected recognition of his sovereignty, had been brought to agree
formally that his country lay within the British sphere of influence, they could
also argue that they had secured permission to colonize from the local authority. But Rhodes and his kind in southern Africa were accustomed to invoking their version of the history of the area to demonstrate that African poli-

ties had no stronger claim to the land than they did (Rotberg 1988:251). The story they told about Great Zimbabwe was of a piece with this supposed history.

Indeed, historical legend had inspired the colonization of Zimbabwe. Before Rhodes sent his agents north, he and his fellow South Africans knew the stories circulated from the beginning of the sixteenth century by the Portuguese colonists of East Africa about their trading partner, the fabulously wealthy and powerful kingdom of Monomotapa (Mwene Mutapa), reputedly based at Great Zimbabwe. Many believed this empire was truly ancient, perhaps even the location of King Solomon's mines, and the biblical city of Ophir. Their speculations were encouraged by the reports of Carl Mauch, a German explorer who had in 1871 become the first European to visit Great Zimbabwe and publish his impressions, who believed the architecture of the ruins to be that of the Israelites of King Solomon's time, reminiscent of Solomon's Temple and the palace visited by the Queen of Sheba. Following Mauch's report, prospectors descended upon Lobengula, requesting permission to mine; their disappointing yields did not deter Rhodes from pursuing the quest with added vigor. When he paid his first visit to Great Zimbabwe, in 1891, the local chiefs were told that the "ancient temple" the "Great Master" was visiting had once belonged to white men (Garlake 1973:65; Bent 1896:33; Rotberg 1988:176, 243; Summers 1952).

Rhodes began financing research projects on Great Zimbabwe almost immediately after his men occupied Mashonaland. A relentless collector of artifacts and a passionate reader (and rereader) of the classics, he himself looked in Egypt for ancient birds that resembled his Zimbabwe treasure, postulating a common source for their design. Believing that history taught valuable practical lessons, he commissioned complete translations of all the ancient sources of Gibbon's *Decline and Fall of the Roman Empire*, as well as of the (mostly Portuguese) records of southeastern Africa in the early modern period (Bent 1896:xiv; Garlake 1973:65, 69; Rotberg 1988:95, 383–87). When we consider the work on Great Zimbabwe which Rhodes financed, we must therefore ask what cautionary lessons it was intended to convey. Of the projects he sponsored, two are of special interest: an archeological expedition mounted in 1891 by J. Theodore Bent, an English author and explorer; and an archival search for descriptions of Zimbabwe in European libraries undertaken shortly thereafter by Alexander Wilmot, a Scottish-born South African ex–civil servant and politician who was then the leading history textbook writer for South African schools (Thompson 1985:92).

Bent's expedition, financed by the Royal Geographical Society and the British Association for the Advancement of Science as well as the British South Africa Company, brought him to Zimbabwe for two months' work, accompanied by Mrs. Bent and R. W. M. Swan, the team's cartographer and surveyor. His published report, which raised most of the points later debated, dismissed the possibility that the Shona in the area could have built Great Zimbabwe. To be sure, their peaceful and industrious character was superior to that of other Africans, and their appearance suggested that their ancestors included non-Africans. The Shona were actually descended from the Makalanga (Karanga), whose name the Portuguese translated as "Children of the Sun," the dominant tribe of Monomotapa. And it was "a well accepted fact that the negroid brain could never be capable of taking the initiative in work of such intricate nature" as building the ruins. Africans were congenitally incapable of the social organization required for such a task because they were both natural wanderers and essential anarchists. Monomotapa had "split up, like all Kaffir combinations do after a generation or so, into a hopeless state of disintegration." And the present population of Rhodesia was incapable of uniting to fight their common enemy, the Zulu (of whom the Matabele were an offshoot), who had migrated from the south in waves, mounting assaults that nearly depopulated Mashonaland. If Africans had built Great Zimbabwe, they would have had to have done so "as the slaves of a race of higher cultivation" (Bent 1896:xiv, 33, xiv, and passim).

Bent argued that the ruins' builders were migrants from somewhere in south Arabia, of Semitic stock, with the commercial instincts characteristic of their race. Unable to specify their nationality, he frequently referred to them simply as the "ancients"—a name that persisted in popular discussions of the creators of Great Zimbabwe. The present local culture in fact provided evidence of a "former civilised race who dwelt here," for the Africans grew foodstuffs and played a complicated game they could only have acquired from foreigners. That the departed race was from the ancient Middle East was evident from the architecture and decoration of the ruins: the orientation of the structures denoted sun worship, and the stylized statues of birds and phalli indicated reverence of the female and male elements in creation—characteristic religious practices of the Assyrians, Egyptians, and Phoenicians. The ancients' worship of stone monoliths proved Phoenician influence, if not identity. The Sabeans—the Queen of Sheba's people—were also possible ancient colonists (Bent 1896:85–86, 105, 118, 175–76, 180–86, 218–19).

The character of the structures revealed the colonial purposes of the ancients. Standing as "a garrison in the midst of an enemy's country," the monuments protected an alien people who "never considered the country their own." They had come to extract the vast quantities of gold that the ancient world imported from Mashonaland, using mining technology identical to the Phoenicians' and Egyptians'. The inferior construction of more recent walls revealed the ancient race's phased withdrawal from the area. In its migrations elsewhere, the alien race progressed, "eventually developing into the more civilised races of the ancient world." Bent was vague as to the precise cause of the ancients' departure and the relation of their colony to the kingdom of Monomotapa,

The largest structure at Great Zimbabwe — the largest prehistoric structure in sub-Saharan Africa — as photographed for Gertrude Caton Thompson. This structure has been variously known as the "Elliptical Building," the "Temple," the "Circular Ruin," and the "Great Enclosure." (From Gertrude Caton Thompson, *The Zimbabwe Culture* [Oxford, 1931].)

but he suggested that the ancients had suffered at the hand of wild invaders and that Portuguese reports of Monomotapa's grandeur were highly exaggerated (Bent 1896:42, 176, 70, 139, 218–22, 228, 231–37).

Wilmot's archival research led him to make only a few modifications in the story Bent had told, and these were generally to turn Bent's tentative speculations into positive assertions. Most important, he made the story of the decline of the Great Zimbabwe civilization a cautionary tale for southern Africa's white settlers: the ancients had not withdrawn, but had weakened the quality of the kindgom's ruling stock by interbreeding with local Africans. The early Portuguese had accurately described a still degenerating society: a kingdom that had lost many ancient technological skills, although it still exploited its mineral resources sufficiently to sustain a thriving gold trade; an elite still of sufficiently high moral character to be susceptible to conversion by the bearers of superior religions — Christianity and Islam. By the middle of the seventeenth century, however, Monomotapa was so degraded that it fell to "great bands of marauding savages," dropping precipitously on the scale of civilization—although its descendants still managed to work feebly the mineral deposits that served "the most recent 'diggings' of the British South Africa Company" (Wilmot 1896:216, 118, 119, 143–46, 152–82).

As for the mines, they were "very probably the mines of Ophir one thousand years before Christ." Great Zimbabwe was settled when the ancient kingdoms of Israel and Phoenicia were both at the height of their powers, and had formed an alliance for colonial purposes. They had the capacity to exploit the land's resources effectively, and the British were their successors: "In all history there is no greater analogy than that between the Empire of Britain and that of Phoenicia at its culminating point of glory, six hundred years before the birth of our Savior" (1896:118).

In an introduction to Wilmot's book, H. Rider Haggard stressed this analogy, describing the Phoenicians as "this crafty, heartless and adventurous race, who were the English of the ancient world without the English honour." Although the comparison was a commonplace in Britain and the Continent throughout the nineteenth century, the analogy had particular force in reference to the supposed historical experiences of both peoples in a specific place, confirming Wilmot's assertion that southern Africa was "eminently a white man's country" in which the African population was providentially placed as a source of "cheap labour" (1896:55–58, xvii, 68–69, 83, 77–83, 86–90; Wilmot quoted in L. Thompson 1985:93; cf. Bernal 1987:338).

Even before 1900, Rhodesian ruins had attracted the destructive attentions of treasure hunters, particularly those of the Ancient Ruins Company, Limited, authorized in 1895 by the British South Africa Company to plunder for profit in all of the ruins save Great Zimbabwe—with the stipulation that the company receive 20 percent of the prospectors' finds and that Cecil Rhodes be offered the first chance to purchase any treasure excavated. The Ancient Ruins Company did not survive beyond 1900, and its wanton destruction of ruins inspired passage of the Ancient Monuments Protection Ordinance in 1902. Nevertheless, one of its founders, W. G. Neal, a prospector from South Africa who turned to archeological treasure hunting after meeting Bent, soon reemerged disguised as a bona fide archeologist (Garlake 1973:70, 1978:34; Schofield 1935).

At the end of the century, southern Africa's empire builders had little time for archeology, however. Between 1893 and 1897, the indigenous peoples of the British South Africa Company's domain mounted a variety of resistance movements, which were suppressed by military means. One group of the Company's soldiers, in particular, became Rhodesian heroes, the thirty-two members of Allan Wilson's Shangani patrol, all of whom died in 1893 in an unsuccessful attempt to capture Lobengula; a crypt was immediately erected for their remains at Great Zimbabwe. In 1895 the Company's Administrator in Southern Rhodesia, L. Starr Jameson, led the unsuccessful raid against the Afrikaner regime in the Transvaal that is known by his name, resulting in the uproar that forced Rhodes to resign the Cape Colony premiership and removed Jameson to a British prison. And between 1899 and 1901 Rhodes and other South Africa–based colonists were preoccupied with the Anglo-Boer War. All of these events were to be reflected in the popular articulation of the Great Zimbabwe legend (Huffman 1976:47).

Shortly after the cessation of hostilities, Richard N. Hall burst upon the popular archeology scene. An Englishmen settled in Southern Rhodesia and making his living as a journalist, Hall began working with W. G. Neal, who provided the records of the Ancient Ruins Company. First presented by Hall at a meeting of the Rhodesia Scientific Association in 1901, their work provoked considerable discussion—not all of it favorable—and in the following year resulted in *The Ancient Ruins of Rhodesia*. Hall was able to extract an archeological appointment from Cecil Rhodes, then on his deathbed, and between 1902 and 1904, he was employed by the British South Africa Company to undertake at Great Zimbabwe "not scientific research but the preservation of the building," in order to make the ruins more attractive to tourists (Garlake 1973:72). Hall exceeded his charge, recovering a goodly number of relics—and disturbing the site so as to make the stratigraphical reading of the archeological record even more difficult. He also wrote another book, *Great Zimbabwe*, published in 1905 (Chanaiwa 1973:120; R. N. Hall 1909:9; Summers 1971:xvii).

Dedicating their book to Wilmot, Hall and Neal told much the same tale as their predecessors had done. But their history was far more violent. Wilmot had represented the early aboriginal population of the Great Zimbabwe region as "comparatively mild, intelligent, and docile," posing the ancient colonists "no great difficulty in forming a settlement" (1896:69). Mindful perhaps of the recent African resistance, Hall and Neal conjured up a new scenario in which Great Zimbabwe was built by a vast population of unwilling laborers. To control them during the long period of the ruins' construction, a far greater number of ancients than previously assumed had to have taken up protracted residence in the area. When the ancients departed—probably unwillingly—they left behind the legacy of their long stay, their mixed-blood descendants, the superior Makalanga who ruled Monomotapa. In appearance and behavior, the Makalanga's then-contemporary progeny were still exhibiting traces of Semitic blood, but they had lately become a "timid race of slaves." The once proud race of Monomotapa had been thoroughly broken by wave upon wave of savage attackers, of whom the Matabele were just the most recent (Hall & Neal 1902:123, 99–100, 122–33).

Amateurs and Professionals in Archeological Debate

In 1905, the locally grown saga of Great Zimbabwe was challenged by an invasion of outsiders, brought by the British Association for the Advancement of Science for its first meeting in South Africa. At the suggestion of Sir Lewis Michell, a Director of the British South Africa Company (and Rhodes's banker and biographer), an archeological expedition to Great Zimbabwe was mounted to provide a paper for the South African meetings. Financed by the Association and the Rhodes Trustees, the six-month expedition was led by David Randall-MacIver, a promising young student of the famed Egyptologist Flinders Petrie.

As Randall-MacIver dryly reported at the Association's Johannesburg sessions, his findings were "not of the nature which the general public expected." Far from being ancient, the ruins had been built no earlier than the fourteenth or fifteenth century. Moreover, they had not been constructed over a protracted period but during a single epoch, in the course of which the builders' skills improved somewhat. But they were not architectural marvels. Although many were visually attractive, and some quite spectacular, they had been built with fairly rudimentary techniques. Nor was there any evidence that an alien race had ever occupied the country. True, there had been foreign culture contact and trade from the eleventh century, bringing artifacts that had been mistakenly construed as evidence that non-Africans were responsible for the stone structures in which they were found. But there was no reason to believe that the ruler of the kingdom of Monomotapa was of a different race from his subjects; Portugese sources stated explicitly that the kingdom was "peopled by heathens whom the Moors call Kaffirs." Unquestionably, this powerful kingdom had once controlled much of the area that became Southern Rhodesia, and it seemed "extremely probable that the builders of the Rhodesian ruins may have succumbed to . . . such invasions" as had plagued the country's peoples in recent times. Great Zimbabwe had not been the site of fabulous gold mines, but a distribution point for minerals mined elsewhere—by Africans. In sum, the ruins had been built by Africans, in entirely African style, to serve African purposes. The structures were elaborated versions of designs still seen in African huts everywhere in the country; even the famous birds resembled the tribal emblem of a contemporary people. Because the culture of the monuments' architects was evidently continuous with that of contemporary Africans, ethnographic observation would definitively determine which of Rhodesia's peoples had built Great Zimbabwe (Randall-MacIver 1906b:vii; 102, 103; cf. 59–68, 75, 78, 83–86, 96–103; cf. 1905, 1906a).

As the first trained archeologist to investigate the ruins, Randall-MacIver came to southern Africa prepared to ridicule the amateur methods of his predecessors, and to lament the damage they and others had done in ignorance.

In his analysis, he was able to turn evidence used by local investigators against them, making extensive use of Portuguese documents compiled by G. M. Theal and reinterpreting previous archeological findings. When he presented his conclusions, first in Southern Rhodesia, then in South Africa, and later at a meeting of the Royal Geographical Society in London, his audience saw him as the champion of professional British archeologists, fighting southern African amateurs. Indeed, his Rhodesian venture was an important step in his career. When he was commissioned for the job, he was a very junior archeologist—the Laycock student of Egyptology at Worcester College, Oxford; two years later, he was the head of a significant expedition in Egypt and the Sudan. And when the *Encyclopaedia Britannica* looked for an author for the entry on "Zimbabwe" in the eleventh edition (1910–11), Randall-MacIver was the obvious choice as the recognized authority.

There were some white settlers in southern Africa, such as F. C. Selous, who regarded Randall-MacIver's work favorably, for reasons that will shortly become clear. But most shared the opinion of the explorer and colonial official Sir Harry Johnston that the opinion of a supposed expert who came from abroad to pronounce on local matters could never be more reliable than that of someone "intimately acquainted with the Bantu negroes of Africa" (1909: 564). There were also some scholarly critics who judged Randall-MacIver wrong from academic positions back in Britain: men such as J. W. Gregory, Professor of Geology at Glasgow, and A. W. Keane, Professor of Hindustani at University College, London—upon whose work Hall and Neal had relied (Randall-MacIver, 1906a:336–37, 340). They, however, were not archeologists. The leading members of his professional community arrayed themselves behind Randall-MacIver. And they were formidable figures indeed: Henry Balfour, Curator of the Pitt Rivers Museum and Fellow of Exeter College, Oxford; Arthur Evans, Extraordinary Professor of Prehistoric Archaeology at Oxford—an authority on Phoenician culture well qualified to reject assertions that it had touched southern Africa; J. L. Myres, Lecturer in Classical Archaeology at Oxford; A. C. Haddon, Lecturer in Ethnology at Cambridge; and C. H. Read, Keeper of British and Medieval Antiquities and Ethnography at the British Museum—under whose auspices Frank Shrubsall, a physical anthropologist, examined the British Museum's collection of skeletal remains from Great Zimbabwe and determined them to be of the same race type as the Africans then living around the ruins (Randall-MacIver 1906a: 336–47; Shrubsall 1906).

For some of Randall-MacIver's British supporters, endorsement of his work entailed an appraisal of African potential that was anathema to white settlers. In his presidential address to the anthropology section of the British Association at the South Africa meeting, Haddon spoke of Bantu social organization as lending itself to discipline, giving African peoples the capacity

for great achievements when they were led by those of their own who possessed great "executive ability"—men such as Lobengula and the Zulu warriors
Shaka and Cetshwayo (1905). In his review of Randall-MacIver's book, Myres
argued that "the modern Kaffir, with his peculiarly autocratic chieftaincy,"
could easily be seen as the descendant of the ruin builders, for his culture
made him "competent to organize both the building of a Zimbabwe and the
working of 'King Solomon's Mines.'" Myres even chastised Randall-MacIver
for conceding a point of his predecessors' arguments, suggesting that Randall-
MacIver had meant to say not that the kingdom of Monomotapa fell to a
barbarous *race*, but to invaders of different *culture* (1906:68, 70).

When Hall undertook to refute Randall-MacIver's argument, he had therefore to appeal primarily to white settlers for support. His *Pre-Historic Rhodesia*,
published in 1909, was produced with the aid of over three hundred subscrib-
ers, including a host of southern Africa's educators, amateur scientists, Native Commissioners, and political figures (1909:ix–xviii). Hall's counter-attack
was a brief for the superiority of local knowledge. If Randall-MacIver had
discussed Great Zimbabwe with local Africans, he would have found that
they themselves disclaimed all connection with it, variously saying that they
knew nothing of its builders, that it was the work of the devil, or that the
ancients had built it. If he had been apprised of the degree to which the ruins
had been disturbed by previous archeologists and prospectors (who, of course,
included Hall), he would have known that the professional archeologist's
stratigraphic method could not be strictly applied there. Most important,
Randall-MacIver had misinterpreted the archeological record as material evidence of cultural progress, whereas the ruins attested to cultural degeneration: the older the building, the higher was its technical standard. As an outsider, he had failed to recognize the significant differences between African
peoples. The waves of invasion that had buffeted the area for centuries immemorial had brought peoples of increasingly inferior stocks, higher in belli-
cosity and lower in virtue. So rude was the culture of the most recent people
that their leavings had made Hall physically sick; the great German bacteriolo-
gist Robert Koch had inspected the spot and confirmed that his affliction was
caused by the Africans' unsanitary habits (1909:13–14, 149–51, 246–47, 250,
273, 395–420).

With Hall's final effort, the story of Great Zimbabwe was fully articulated
as a moral tale justifying the establishment of white settler society in southern Africa. It was a tale consistent with the settler belief that Africans had
no clear title to the land either by virtue of long occupation or capacity to
use natural resources productively. Wave upon wave of migrants had descended
not only upon Zimbabwe, but had coursed throughout Africa, making population displacements a routine feature of the continent's history. One historian
of southern Africa concluded in 1897 that "the ownership which the Bantu

tribes could claim [to the land] had no deep roots in the past. It was won by force, and as it was won and as it was upheld, so it could with no glaring injustice be swept away" (quoted in Thompson 1985:95). Moreover, the tide of population movements and conflict had actually swelled around the beginning of the nineteenth century, as the last vestiges of Monomotapa were being obliterated. The product of African societies' own internal dynamics rather than a response to European colonialism, the strife between Africans had then intensified, causing a depopulation that left vast tracts of land vacant for white settlement. African political-economic orders were destroyed, reducing the peoples of the region to the pathetic state that the first settlers reported. Great Zimbabwe stood as a testament to a high point of civilization reached in ancient times, from which the region had since been in decline. Most important, that civilization was non-African, for Africans were incapable of great achievements unless forcefully supervised by a superior race. Africans might be productive members of civilized societies if they were properly led, but they could do nothing of great consequence by themselves (Cell 1989:485–86; Cobbing 1988; Kgoale 1986:322).

It is important to note that much of this narrative could be reconciled with orthodox academic opinion. No one would deny, even today, that Africa has been repeatedly swept by waves of migrants, and that in the early nineteenth century the strife accompanying the consolidation of the southern African Zulu nation brought phenomenal devastation—known in the Zulu language as the *Mfecane* or "time of troubles"—although there is still argument about the relative importance of the African and colonial elements in its cause. Moreover, the idea that culture was a function of race, once characteristic of anthropology generally, persisted in archeology; until the mid-twentieth century, archeologists were wont to assume that material evidence of cultural change in a given area indicated change in the ethnic composition of the population, brought about through migration (Balfour 1929; Burkitt 1928:174; G. Clark 1966; J. Clark 1953; Thompson 1990:80–87).

It was thus possible for white settlers in Southern Rhodesia who claimed particular expertise in African matters to contrive a new story of the building of Great Zimbabwe that still justified their occupation of the country, but did not seem ridiculous to academics abroad. Selous indicated the direction this argument might take in a favorable comment at the London meeting at which Randall-MacIver presented his work to the Royal Geographical Society. It was easier to accept that Great Zimbabwe had been built by Africans if, as Randall-MacIver had suggested, its construction was rudimentary. Selous recalled that "nothing could have been more rude" than the decorations and walls of the monument; "there was not a single straight line in them." To accept that the ruins had been built fairly recently to designs still recognizable in African material culture, it was only necessary to reappraise the results of

The Conical Tower located in the Elliptical Building, which was the focus of much of the speculation about Great Zimbabwe's alien architects. (Photograph courtesy of Anthony Hart Fisher.)

the Zulu and Matabele invasions of Mashonaland. In his years of exploring Mashonaland before the British came, Selous had learned from its inhabitants that they had lived in stone walled towns and extracted gold from quartz until the Zulu came in the eighteenth century, and he believed that they still had the skills necessary to build Great Zimbabwe, given the leadership Africans themselves were clearly capable of providing in viable social structures (quoted in Randall-MacIver 1906a:341; cf. 340, 343).

As the African population of Southern Rhodesia became quiescent—or adopted protest strategies suited to the framework of colonial rule—such views became easier to accept, and various white students of African culture began to endorse Randall-MacIver's argument. The most notable among them were the Reverend Samuel S. Dorman, a missionary-ethnographer; J. F. Schofield, an accomplished amateur archeologist employed as an architect by the Public Works Department of the British South Africa Company; and Charles W. Bullock, a Native Commissioner whose ethnographic work on the Shona was widely respected by anthropologists, who became the country's Chief Native Commissioner. By 1928, when the journal of Rhodesia's Native Affairs Department published an article claiming that Great Zimbabwe was built by ancient colonists from the Middle East, the editor inserted footnotes and appended an extended comment indicating that no knowledgeable person should believe it (Beek 1928; Bullock 1927:38; Chanaiwa 1973:118–19).

Nevertheless, the image of Zimbabwe as ancient and exotic persisted in the popular mind. And in 1923 there arrived at the University of the Witwatersrand in Johannesburg an apostle of a new anthropological school that promised to impart a gloss of academic respectability to the popular theory—Raymond Dart, the newly appointed Professor of Anatomy. An Australian, Dart had worked at University College, London, under the distinguished paleoanthropologist (and fellow Australian) Grafton Elliot Smith, the Professor of Anatomy. At University College, Smith and his colleague W. J. Perry, Reader in Cultural Anthropology, presided over a graduate program in "Human Studies," using an extreme diffusionist model to synthesize all of anthropology's parts—physical anthropology, cultural analysis, and archeology. Although their program had been generally rejected by the early 1930s, the battle for theoretical supremacy waged in Britain during the 1920s between Smith and Perry and functionalist anthropologists was seen by its participants and spectators as a contest of equals. The diffusionists represented the course of human history as a series of episodes of progress and degeneration, and they identified the Great Zimbabwe ruins as a case in point for their theory (Massingham 1928; *Nature* 1925; Perry 1923:161). Central to their narrative was the invention of a culture complex that fortuitously emerged in ancient Egypt. Distinguished by clearly defined social hierarchy and an obsession with death —denoted by mummification and the worship of stone monoliths—this "Archaic Civilization" was spread because its carriers migrated everywhere that precious minerals were to be found, imagining them to be "Givers of Life." Perry and Smith called these wanderers "The Children of the Sun," which as it happened, was the phrase by which the Portuguese had translated the name of the Karanga, whose kingdom they had seen as based on mining (Kuklick 1991).

Shortly after he arrived in South Africa, Dart achieved a scientific celebrity that gave him an audience for pronouncements made outside his area of expertise. Analyzing the "Taungs skull," a fossil found in 1924 in Botswana, he interpreted it as the missing link between man and the lower primates, arguing that it placed the origin of the human species in Africa, rather than in Asia as most paleontologists (including Elliot Smith) believed. Although Dart was not to be professionally vindicated for decades, he successfully prosecuted his case in the South African newspapers, becoming in consequence the kind of local hero Hall had been. His fame established, Dart began expounding the diffusionist creed. He infuriated serious Southern Rhodesia archeologists by reanimating the ancient-exotic theory of Great Zimbabwe's origins, pointing to such evidence as rock paintings in Cape Province, which he interpreted as eyewitness accounts by Bushmen of the very people who built the ruins—men with white or light brown skins, wearing ancient Babylonian, Phoenician, and even Egyptian garb, standing next to considerably smaller figures who were supposedly naked Bushmen (Dart 1925; Lewin 1987: 50–60; Schofield 1926; *Times* 1988).

Professionalism Triumphant

The stage was thus set for a new confrontation when the British Association was scheduled to hold its second South African meeting in late July and early August of 1929, again in Cape Town and Johannesburg. In 1928 the Association appointed a young archeologist, Gertrude Caton-Thompson, to head an expedition to examine "the ruins of Zimbabwe or any other monument or monuments of the same kind in Rhodesia which seem likely to reveal the character, dates, and source of culture of the builders." It seemed a repeat performance of the earlier one: again, the costs were borne by the Association and the Rhodes Trustees; again, the investigator was a student of Flinders Petrie. Moreover, Caton-Thompson was expected to reach the same conclusions Randall-MacIver had, albeit with more thorough documentation (Caton-Thompson 1983:111).

There were, however, significant differences. By 1928 the organizing force of Caton-Thompson's expedition, J. L. Myres, had become a very powerful figure. As General Secretary of the British Association, he was in a position to bring scientific enlightenment not only to southern Africa but also to the British public, by arranging a British Museum exhibition of Rhodesian artifacts, for which he wrote the catalogue. Caton-Thompson herself, although only thirty and without formal credentials, was at a more advanced stage of her career than Randall-MacIver had been. She had worked with Flinders Petrie in London and the field, and she had studied at London and at Cambridge with a range of specialists including Haddon and Miles Burkitt (who after visiting Great Zimbabwe in 1927 had dated it between A.D. 1000 and 1200). She had served as the field director for the Royal Anthropological Institute, was the author of a book, and was already recognized as one of the outstanding archeologists of her generation (Burkitt 1928:160–66; Caton-Thompson 1983:82–86; Fallaize 1929).

Unlike Randall-MacIver, however, Caton-Thompson faced an organized opposition in the form of a rival expedition funded by the South African government and led by Professor Leo Frobenius, President of the Frankfurt Research Institute for Cultural Morphology. Frobenius had proven himself ready to find exotic origins for notable African achievements by arguing that sculptures found in Ife, Nigeria, were of classical Greek derivation—probably the last vestiges of the lost culture of Atlantis. But because the Southern Rhodesian government felt that the British Association's expedition had priority, it denied Frobenius permission to excavate, and the work on the Zimbabwe question he presented at the Association meetings was based on research he had conducted in India (Caton-Thompson 1983:132–33; Garlake 1978:38–40).

Caton-Thompson carried on her investigations between April and September of 1929, accompanied by two women assistants, one of whom, Kathleen Kenyon, was herself to become an eminent archeologist. The all-female composition of the team, who supervised their African laborers without the help of male intermediaries, delighted the popular press, and they enjoyed cooperation from both the South African and Southern Rhodesian governments. The South African Defense Force provided an airplane, a pilot, and a photographer, who took the first aerial pictures of the ruins. Help and advice was provided by various Southern Rhodesian government departments, particularly by the members of the Native Department. The Colonial Secretary of Southern Rhodesia paid all the wages of the expedition's workmen, all the living expenses incurred by Caton-Thompson's party, and all the running costs of a car lent by the Transport Department. And because Great Zimbabwe was by 1929 becoming a tourist attraction, it was served by a simple hotel, which provided a comfortable base (Caton-Thompson 1931:v–viii, 1983:117).

Anticipation of Caton-Thompson's performance, and the event itself, provided the South African press with sensational material. Hers was not the only notable story provided by the British Association meetings, which re-

ceived extensive media coverage: all the important talks were broadcast on
the radio, as well as described in the newspapers. The most thoroughly reported address was probably that on "Holism" delivered by General J. C. Smuts,
the once and future Prime Minister of South Africa, who was a distinguished
naturalist. But Caton-Thompson and Frobenius, her appointed antagonist,
also received considerable attention. Two days before Caton-Thompson spoke,
Frobenius addressed a packed house, which was disappointed when he evaded
the issues that she was expected to raise. Hundreds of people were turned
away from Caton-Thompson's lecture, and she was obliged to deliver it again
at Johannesburg's Town Hall two days later. Her effective lecture style was
much remarked, as was her quick response to questions from the audience—
which Raymond Dart tested to the limit (*Cape Times* 1929a, 1929b, 1929c;
D. Hall 1929; Caton-Thompson 1983:130, 136; *Times* 1929).

Dart delighted the press by indulging in an "outburst of curiously unsci-
entific indignation," delivering his remarks "in tones of awe-inspiring violence" (*Cape Times* 1929d). He insisted that Caton-Thompson had not refuted
the hypothesis that Zimbabwe was built in ancient times by exotic visitors,
claimed that her work served to inhibit the growth of archeological research
conducted by southern Africa's own residents, and at the conclusion of his
outburst stormed from the room. Frobenius, however, brought himself to con-
gratulate her on behalf of German science; L. S. B. Leakey endorsed her judgment (having confided to her in private that she had persuaded him to abandon his earlier belief that the ruins dated from before the Christian era); and
the response was generally adulatory (*Cape Times* 1929c; Caton-Thompson
1983:129, 132).

While Caton-Thompson was conducting her research, she kept a large file
labelled "Insane," into which she put the many archeological suggestions she
received from local enthusiasts—evidently supporters of the interpretation she
was charged with refuting (Bullock 1949:51). Incredulous that anyone could
ever have believed the ruins of exotic origin, when "every detail in plan,
building, and contents seems African Bantu," she praised them as material
evidence of considerable indigenous achievement. "Instead of a degenerate
off-shoot of a higher Oriental civilisation, we have, unsuspected by all but
a few students, a vigorous native civilisation, showing national organisation
of a high kind, originality, and amazing industry" (Caton-Thompson 1929b:
621; *Cape Times* 1929b).

Caton-Thompson's praise was highly qualified, however, and her analysis
in fact incorporated many historical points that had appealed to white settlers. It therefore proved persuasive to a larger local audience than had Randall-
MacIver's. She judged the technical standard of the building low, arguing that
it bespoke the recent construction of the ruins: they could not have survived
for millennia. Moreover, she traced a saga of degeneration after the fashion
of Bent and Hall, found traces of foreign influence, and dated the oldest parts

of the monuments six centuries earlier than Randall-MacIver (*Cape Times* 1929c, 1929e; Caton-Thompson 1929a:432–33).

Because Caton-Thompson came to Rhodesia from Greece and Egypt, it was perhaps inevitable that she would compare the Zimbabwe ruins unfavorably to classical ones. But she went so far as to declare that the "architecture at Zimbabwe . . . strikes me as essentially the product of an infantile mind, a pre-logical mind." Though certain design features reflected Persian, Arabic, and Saracenic sources, this connection was only a remote one effected by the trade on which the Zimbabwe civilization was based. Had the peoples who originated the designs been directly involved in constructing the ruins, they would have employed more sophisticated techniques. Most important, Hall was right, and Randall-MacIver was wrong, in dating the buildings of inferior technical quality: "The time-scale in Rhodesia's case leads, I believe, away from the best towards deterioration, and not from immaturity to maturity" (Caton-Thompson 1931a:103, 57).

Caton-Thompson's account of the social organization and history of the Zimbabwe culture was a compromise between the views of Hall and Randall-MacIver. The mixture of artifacts she found in the ruins proved to her that Hall had been right to see the structures as the work of slave laborers. But the kingdom they served was an African one, an absolute monarchy devoted to a "divine king." Citing the work of local authorities, she speculated that the kingdom might be equated with the one the Portuguese called Monomotapa, and that its rulers might have been the Rozwi, one of the peoples incorporated into the Shona, whose marriage customs blurred whatever racial distinction once obtained among them. Although this kingdom had reached its zenith in the tenth or eleventh century, when its culture began to be devastated by "migratory Bantu hordes," the Zimbabwe culture did not finally fall until the beginning of the eighteenth century, when the inhabitants of the area were still "capable of erecting excellent stone walling with elaborate decoration." Traces of the culture were even visible in the twentieth century: as Randall-MacIver had observed, the general architectural and design motifs were evident in contemporary African workmanship. But Caton-Thompson conceded to Hall that the bearers of the Zimbabwe culture no longer resided in the area, although they were African; the closest approximation of the Zimbabwe culture was that of the Venda of the Transvaal, who had been pushed south from Zimbabwe by the migratory hordes (1931a:192, 182; 34–37, 53, 60–64, 99–104, 119, 160, 175–82, 194–95, 1983:119).

In Britain, as in southern Africa, Caton-Thompson's work won the attention of a wide public beyond her professional peers. Though British imperial enthusiasm was no longer so high, there were still many citizens who, encouraged by the popular press, reveled in the colonial fantasy of King Solomon's mines. The broadcast of Caton-Thompson's findings and the publicity attendant upon the British Museum exhibition brought forth expressions of disbelief that Great Zimbabwe was a recent African achievement—some of them from people such as J. W. Gregory, who rehearsed the protests they had made earlier to Randall-MacIver's work. In such venues as the letters column of the *Times*, professional archeologists battled amateur enthusiasts (Boggis 1930; Cope 1929; Gregory 1929, 1930; *Illustrated London News* 1929; Maugham 1930a, 1930b; Rickard 1930). Caton-Thompson defended herself, but her honor was guarded most vehemently by J. L. Myres—who not only prosecuted the case of professional archeology but also railed against colonial adventurism, pointing out that the mineral wealth of Rhodesia had been far less than anticipated (Myres 1930a, 1930b, 1930c, 1930d; Caton-Thompson 1930).

In intellectual circles, however, Caton-Thompson's work was treated as a definitive triumph for professional archeology. Little was made of the differences between her account and Randall-MacIver's; indeed, to her professional audience, the conclusions of her study were entirely expected. As one reviewer commented, if the point of her expedition was "exploding what was to archeologists a moribund theory of the exotic origin of the ruins it was probably not worth the trouble involved" (Hobley 1931:161; Braunholtz 1932). But by employing such a rigorous method, her investigation raised many problems for future archeologists to investigate (as, in fact, they did). It was the virtually unanimous judgment of all of the reviewers who considered Caton-Thompson's work for serious journals, as well as of writers for responsible publications such as the *Times*, that her work was definitive proof of the superiority of professional work over that of amateurs (C. W. H. 1931; N. M. 1931; Schebesta 1931; *Times* 1930; *Times Literary Supplement* 1931). It was surely no coincidence that the anthropological section of the British Association elected David Randall-MacIver to serve as its President in 1931—and that he made the triumph of scientific archeology the subject of his presidential address (1933).

What were the theoretical issues Caton-Thompson's professional audience agreed that she had raised? In introducing her book with a quotation from Elliot Smith ("Theories must be founded on facts, not possibilities") she must have had diffusionism in mind; she certainly took seriously the threat to her interpretation posed by that of Frobenius, which had a family resemblance to diffusionist argument, as well as to white settler ideology. Frobenius saw the Zimbabwe culture as but one manifestation of a great prehistoric civilization that joined Egypt, Crete, the Near East, Mesopotamia, Arabia, and East Africa, the Zimbabwean offshoot of which was inspired by the drive for mineral wealth and sustained between roughly 4000 B.C. and 900 B.C.[1] Although

---

1. Frobenius's assertions were sufficiently vague to admit of various interpretations. For W. E. B. Du Bois, for example, Frobenius was the "greatest student of Africa" because he had described the ancient African civilizations that so inspired Pan-African nationalism (1947:79n.).

Frobenius's work received respectful attention in Britain, his analysis was seen as broadly speculative and incompletely documented—and therefore no real challenge to Caton-Thompson's (Caton-Thompson 1931a, 1931b, 1983:133; *Times Literary Supplement* 1931). Diffusionist hypotheses as such were not discussed in the reviews of Caton-Thompson's interpretation, but the frequent suggestion that it showed the need for more research into the causes and processes of cultural degeneration indicated the effect the diffusionists had in fact made on the British anthropological community (*Discovery* 1936:181; C. W. H. 1931:886; Hobley 1931:167; N. M. 1931:436; *Nature* 1929b:607; Westermann 1931).

The overwhelming endorsement that Caton-Thompson received from her professional peers made it impossible for students of African culture among the whites of southern Africa to dismiss her work. The British professional acceptance of her analysis of cultural degeneration may have smoothed the way for its acceptance, since white southern Africans had their own reasons to establish a degenerative trend in African culture. Caton-Thompson's account could in fact be reconciled with a version of African history that legitimated colonial rule. A reviewer in the journal of Southern Rhodesia's Native Affairs Department, for example, was pleased to note that she had found evidence of non-African influence on the builders of the ruins—a minor point in her argument that she later qualified—and that she attributed the final decline of the Zimbabwe culture to the devastating African wars that began in the eighteenth century and reduced the indigenous population to the pathetic state that virtually mandated colonialists' rule and cleared the land for their settlement (Schofield 1937:69; Caton-Thompson 1983:129; H. B. M. 1931).

Caton-Thompson's account further commended itself to Rhodesia's apologists because her praise for the achievement of Great Zimbabwe's creators was so qualified. When Charles Bullock, for example, ridiculed those who persisted in believing that the monuments had been built by exotic visitors, he drew heavily on Caton-Thompson's description of their defects.

> [N]o other race but our happy-go-lucky Bantu could be accused of erecting them. Who else could build a place as big as the "Temple" without working from a plan? Who else would just make encircling walls come together by a little deviation from the symmetrical when they were not going to meet? What other race would build walls 30 feet high without using a plumb line? (Bullock 1949:52)

The structures were a lesson writ in stone for Africans and colonialists alike. To Africans, they were "material evidence that the Bantu had once capable and forceful leadership able to facilitate what is lacking to-day, that is continuity of purpose and effect," leadership that contemporary Africans should obviously try to imitate (53). To colonialists, they were a reminder of the mission that justified their rule—the uplift of the country's indigenous peoples.

To be sure, there were still scholars in southern Africa who refused to believe the Great Zimbabwe ruins were of recent vintage and African design. Raymond Dart and his colleague M. D. W. Jeffreys churned out articles purporting to show that southern African peoples indulged in forms of nature worship characteristic of the ancient Near East; that the rock paintings of southern Africa employed ancient Egyptian decorative motifs and portrayed features of the aquatic culture of ancient Egypt; that the language now used in the area of Zimbabwe contained imported words, some of which referred to places in Arabia in biblical times; that the blood groups of those African peoples supposedly in residence from the early Christian era had a pattern characteristic of the peoples who lived in (and migrated from) Asia at that time. When in 1952 the radiocarbon dating technique was applied to wood extracted from the inner wall of one of Zimbabwe's structures and indicated that building began in the eighth century, Dart hastened to point out that the technique admitted of the possibility that construction dated from the fourth century. He triumphantly proclaimed that science had effected a compromise between the ancient and medieval dates advanced for the ruins—and proved that they could not have been built by Bantu peoples, since none were in southern Africa during the construction period (Dart 1948, 1955, 1957, 1962, 1963; Jeffreys 1954, 1967).

Nor were Dart and Jeffreys the only persons writing about Great Zimbabwe in southern Africa. In the decades that followed the publication of Caton-Thompson's book, it was scarcely possible to pick up a number of the *South African Archaeological Bulletin* or of *NADA*, the Southern Rhodesia Native Affairs Department Annual Report, and not find some item related to the ruins. A study of the Zimbabwe controversy in 1950 noted that a comprehensive bibliography of works on the ruins would surely number over a thousand, and it "would offer all things to all men" (Paver 1950:38). The list has continued to grow, and it has continued to include work done by unrepentant amateur proponents of the ancient-exotic theory. Archeologists have in fact laid themselves open to attacks from amateurs by lamenting the damage done by previous workers and suggesting that no reading of the remains can be definitive because the evidence itself is unclear; even the introduction of the radiocarbon dating method was accompanied by an enumeration of the reasons its results were imprecise (Bruwer 1965; Caton-Thompson 1958:200; Chanaiwa 1978: 185; Hromnik 1981:8–19; Mallows 1984).

The development of Great Zimbabwe as one of Rhodesia's main tourist attractions further encouraged amateur speculations. To the Southern Rhodesian Publicity Bureau, the story of the Great Zimbabwe's ancient origins was an effective advertisement for tourism, advanced in booklet and poster form through the 1930s. When this story could no longer be proclaimed un-

Southern Rhodesia Publicity Bureau Poster, 1938. (National Archives of Zimbabwe.)

abashedly, the ruins were instead promoted as "Rhodesia's Mystery". By the 1960s, when the National Park around the ruins housed every sort of tourist facility, roughly a hundred thousand people visited Great Zimbabwe each year. Tourists contributed so much to Rhodesia's economy that when the country was subjected to economic sanctions after it proclaimed its Unilateral Declaration of Independence there was considerable anxiety about the decline of tourism at Great Zimbabwe (Berlyn 1969; Nazaroff 1931:767–68; Summers 1968:1).

But if fantasies about King Solomon, the Queen of Sheba, and the building of Zimbabwe promoted Rhodesian tourism, they did not affect archeological research conducted under state auspices. If tourists read the guidebooks put out by the archeological museums at Zimbabwe and elsewhere, they found descriptions provided by state employees working along lines suggested by Gertrude Caton-Thompson, not Richard Hall. The most notable state researchers were Neville Jones, employed by the National Museum of Southern Rhodesia between 1936 and 1948; Keith Robinson, Inspector of Monuments for Rhodesia from 1947 to 1970; Roger Summers, employed by the National Museum from 1947 to 1970; J. Anthony Whitty, Surveyor for the Rhodesian Historical Monuments Commission from 1955 to 1961; Peter Garlake, Inspector of Monuments for Rhodesia between 1964 and 1970; and Thomas Huffman, Inspector of Monuments and Senior Curator of Archaeology at the Queen Victoria Museum in the 1970s. Their work was, and remains, respected in international archeological circles. Southern Rhodesian officials recognized the fables that activated the tourist trade as fables. Thus a government booklet evidently intended to encourage Britons to settle in the country after World War II described the ancient saga of Zimbabwe as but a "pretty legend," which some might find appealing. And when the journal of Southern Rhodesia's Native Department published Dart's article claiming vindication through the scientific miracle of radiocarbon dating, it took care to run with it an article on the implications of the new technique reprinted from the South African *Sunday Mail*, in which it was reported that the conclusions of Randall-MacIver and Caton-Thompson stood with only slight modification (Government of Rhodesia 1945:89; *Sunday Mail*, 1955; Summers 1971:229–34).

The Controversy Revived

In 1970, five years after Rhodesia's Unilateral Declaration of Independence, Summers and Garlake left Rhodesia, because they could no longer work under the Rhodesian regime and sustain their intellectual integrity. Archeology had become thoroughly politicized, and the controversy over the building of Great Zimbabwe had been reactivated. The proximate cause was quite possibly the discovery of a new group of ruins at Bindura in 1968, whose excavation Garlake supervised as the Senior Inspector of the Historical Monuments commission. As he pointed out, the Bindura ruins were important evidence for interpreting Zimbabwe, since radiocarbon dating showed them to be of an age with the major ruins, but they had not been despoiled by previous predators. This new discovery was bound to provoke argument (Whatmore 1969; *Antiquity* 1971; *Rhodesian Herald* 1969a, 1969d).

Hard on the heels of the announcement of the findings at Bindura came a discussion in the Rhodesian parliament, in which Col. George Hartley, the M.P. from the Fort Victoria District, where the ruins were located, rose to demand that the guidebook be censored by the Minister of Internal Affairs, because it promoted the view that Rhodesia's stone ruins were erected by the indigenous people of the country. This notion was "nothing but pure conjecture"; there were many theories about the builders of the ruins, and the theory that Great Zimbabwe was the work of "light-skinned" people deserved serious consideration. The Minister responded that he agreed with Hartley and that he had told the personnel of the country's archeological institutions that it would be "more correct" to convey to the public that there was no incontrovertible evidence about the origin of Great Zimbabwe (*Rhodesian Herald* 1969b).

The Minister acted quickly, with the evident approval of many white residents of Rhodesia. State employees at Zimbabwe were told that they would lose their jobs if they credited "black people" with the monuments (although "yellow people" were acceptable putative builders), that they must not discuss the radiocarbon dates of the ruins, and that they were to give out guidebooks that had been "physically censored" by order of the Minister (Frederikse 1982: 10–11). The internationally regarded Professor of Archaeology at Cape Town, Raymond Inskeep, who was visiting Rhodesia at this time, protested in vain that no reputable archeologist doubted that the ruins were of relatively recent African construction, and that government efforts to suggest otherwise were "sinister." Inskeep's comments were front page news; as the Rhodesian magazine *Property and Finance* contended, the implication of this view was clear: if "for centuries Rhodesia was the center of a sophisticated Negroid 'civilisation' . . . there should be no legitimate opposition to a Black take-over of the country" (quoted in *Antiquity* 1971). If the letters column of the *Rhodesian Herald* is a reliable indicator of white settler opinion, this view was widespread (*Rhodesian Herald* 1969c; Clarke 1969a, 1969b; Harris 1969; Layland 1969a, 1969b; Lee 1969; Richards 1969; Ridler 1969; Ure-White 1969; Wright 1969).

The pages of the *Rhodesian Herald* also bear witness to the descending hand of official censorship, which rested heavily on Rhodesian society in the Unilateral Declaration of Independence period, during which a State of Emergency was consistently maintained. When in 1969 one Edmund Layland characterized as "monstrous imposture" the hypothesis that Zimbabwe was built by Africans, his letter was printed with a rejoinder from *Herald* writer John Whatmore: no reputable archeologist had denied the African origin of the ruins since 1914, and the authorities cited by Layland were not professionally qualified to render judgment. But later that year, when the *Herald* reported the radiocarbon dating of the Bindura ruins, the story included a disclaimer at its end: "Critics of the archaeologists' findings attribute the Zimbabwe buildings to Arab or Phoenician civilizations" (1969d). In this official climate, *Property and Finance* was able to proclaim blandly in 1972 that to portray Zimbabwe as a "Bantu achievement" was to argue "against all objective evidence" (quoted in Frederikse 1982:12).

As an editorial in the *Rhodesian Herald* pointed out in 1969, Zimbabwe had become a contested symbol for Rhodesian whites because African nationalists had made it their own. From 1961, the parties agitating for African rights effectively renamed their country, anticipating the day when they would assume power, by incorporating the name Zimbabwe into their titles.[2] Indeed, so charged did the word Zimbabwe become that the Rhodesia Broadcasting corporation banned any mention of all of the political groups operating under the banner of Zimbabwe. The meaning of the ruins, however, had not always been the same for African nationalists. In the 1930s, there were Shona partisans who accepted the ancient-exotic interpretation of Great Zimbabwe's origins, and described the early use of their ancestors as forced laborers by non-Africans as emblematic of the indignities since suffered by their people under colonialism. But in the Pan-African political argument that captured the nationalist imagination all over sub-Saharan Africa after World War II, Zimbabwe was one of the powerful African states that had been suppressed by colonialism, the vanished glories of which would return when the descendants of their citizens created new states with the old names. White supremacists and African nationalists thus revived the debate over the building of Great Zimbabwe because they were contesting the ownership of the entire country (DuBois 1947:172–74; Fagan 1970; Frederikse 1982:266; Summers 1963:29).

For roughly a decade before the Universal Declaration of Independence, archeological research sustained a history of the kingdom of Great Zimbabwe

2. The name "Zimbabwe" was attached to the country's African political parties as a by-product of the repeated banning of parties known by other names. The party formed in 1957 as the Southern Rhodesian African National Congress from a fusion of the African National Council (founded in 1934) and the African National Youth League (founded in 1955) became the Zimbabwe African Peoples Union in 1961. Later, members dissatisfied with the leadership provided by Joshua Nkomo formed the Zimbabwe African National Union, the party that became (and remains) the governing party of Zimbabwe under Robert Mugabe.

that African nationalists could embrace with some enthusiasm. Garlake, Hoffman, Robinson, Summers, Whitty, and others reconceptualized the Zimbabwe problem, following up a point made by both Randall-MacIver and Caton-Thompson, seeing the stone walls of the ruins as enclosures for housing a small elite fraction of the state's population. Although they agreed that the Great Zimbabwe complex was distinguished from other African stone structures by its size and complexity, they shifted their attention from analysis of the construction of the ruins per se to the social structure they embodied. In this context the complex was significant as the capital of a large state subordinate to a divine king, with a hierarchy of classes, occupational differentiation, and a formal political structure. With a population of roughly 18,000 at its height, it dominated an area extending into present day Mozambique, Botswana, Lesotho, and South Africa. Built between roughly 1250 and 1450 by descendants of the Shona people who had occupied the area since at least the end of the first millennium, the walls of the ruins testified to an internally generated evolution and to technical progress. The Zimbabwe state's rise and fall had an economic basis: although established in an environmentally blessed area, its expanding population depleted the natural resources; dependent on East Coast African markets for the gold it mined, the state's surplus-generating trade collapsed when world gold prices fell and the coastal cities declined. By the end of the fifteenth century, Great Zimbabwe was already a ruin; the Mwena Mutapa kingdom that succeeded Zimbabwe as the dominant power in the region had a different center. But there had been no break in the continuity of the culture of the area's people; the various sub-groups of the Shona moved about, but they maintained residence in the general area. It was thus possible from later Shona culture to interpret the significance of the monuments, including the social organization they embodied and the religious meaning of such decorations as the famous birds (Connah 1987:183–213; Huffman 1981, 1987:1–3).

Recent archeological analyses of Great Zimbabwe have thus agreed with Caton-Thompson's original formulation in many particulars. But there have been critical changes in interpretation: full acknowledgment of extraordinary African enterprise in mining, trade, construction, and state organization; recognition of a progressive historical trend, rather than degeneration from an early cultural height; elimination of the marauding African hordes from the story of Great Zimbabwe's decline, and with it recognition of the continuity of Shona culture and occupation. Thus white supremacists could not tolerate recent archeological opinion, for it could not be reconciled with a justification of colonialism—as Caton-Thompson's clearly could be. When Thomas Huffman wrote a new guidebook for the ruins late in the U.D.I. period, he was obliged to introduce it with a statement that visitors might choose to believe that ancient colonists built Great Zimbabwe—though cognoscenti could easily recognize his understated endorsement of recent archeological research in the notes he wrote on the various parts of the monument. Recent research, however, readily served African aspirations. In the museum display at Great Zimbabwe mounted since the nation assumed its new identity as Zimbabwe, the ruins are presented as the center of a city-state created by the Shona people, who are the dominant ethnic group of the country (Frederikse 1982:349; Huffman 1976).

The Genre of Colonial Archeology

A cursory look at an archeological dispute that once flourished in the United States suggests that this colonial people approached its aboriginal population with many of the same attitudes that prevailed in colonial Zimbabwe. For many decades after independence, controversy raged over the Native American earthworks known as the "mounds"—heaps of earth ranging in size from small piles to an immense hill extending over sixteen acres and a hundred feet in elevation, which covered human remains and material artifacts. Contemplating the mounds in ignorance of the observations of earlier colonists (who had witnessed mound construction by Native Americans as late as the early eighteenth century), an extraordinary array of settler observers concluded that they were very ancient and that the present aboriginals could not have built them. There were a few dissenters from this consensus, Thomas Jefferson among them, but in gross outline it prevailed among self-appointed experts ranging from rustic clerics to the national intelligentsia—who named as putative earth workers such candidates as the Phoenicians, the Vikings, the Lost Tribes of Israel, the Polynesians, and the (white) builders of ancient Mexican civilization whose migrations took them through the country (Silverberg 1968: esp. 2–7, 19–24, 32, 44, 48, 51, 56–59, 79, 92–94, 98, 136–37, 154–70).

Committed to the view that they were morally entitled to settle North America because they were capable of using the land to its fullest potential, white settlers represented aboriginals as irredeemable savages. This characterization affected American anthropology as the discipline emerged through the nineteenth century. If American Indians were "unwilling to change and perhaps incapable of it," it followed that they had no history; they could not have had an earlier, mound-building culture (Trigger 1978:93, 87–95). When the American Ethnological Society was founded in 1842, it saw the issue of the mounds as one of the crucial problems for the new discipline, and commissioned E. G. Squier to synthesize the accumulated evidence about them. Generating many publications with his colleague E. H. Davis, Squier concluded that the mounds "far exceed anything of which the existing tribes of

Indians are known to have been capable" (quoted in Silverberg 1968:127).

As the century drew to a close, however, Native American resistance to colonial expansion became less threatening. By 1871 an Act of Congress could proclaim that "hereafter no Indian nation or tribe within the territory of the United States shall be acknowledged or recognized as an independent nation," and the colonization of the remaining frontier zones was accomplished with relative ease (quoted in Officer 1971:30). Anthropologists then reinterpreted the mounds. Led by John Wesley Powell and his colleagues at the Bureau of American Ethnology, as well as by Frederic Ward Putnam at Harvard's Peabody Museum, researchers determined that the mounds had been recently built by Native Americans still resident in the country and—most important—that they expressed a culture of a considerably lower level than had previously been thought (Silverberg 1968:80–81, 110–35, 168–84, 197–221; Thompson & Lamar 1981:9). As had been the case in southern Africa, North American colonists were reluctant to credit aboriginals for the building they did on the land and, by implication, thereby to acknowledge that they were in established residence rather than transients. They would do so only when colonial title to the land seemed no longer in dispute, and when they could preserve their moral rights to the land, even though aboriginals had built on it, by representing those achievements as relatively inconsequential.

As another comparative case, we may consider the relatively recent phenomenon of Israeli archeology, which developed as a distinctive variant of the long-established field of biblical archeology (the effort to find documentation for religious tradition). Israeli archeology has its antecedents in the work done by Jewish settlers of Palestine under the British Mandate after World War I, and has been used to further the Zionist cause. Since Israel was created in 1948, archeology has become a grass-roots movement, enrolling myriad amateur enthusiasts in projects great and small all over the country. For the largest excavations, the Israeli Defense Forces' personnel and equipment have been placed in service, and some projects have been treated as national emergencies, worthy of "archeological offensives" mounted to preserve sites from the depredations of wandering Bedouins, who could easily take valuable treasures over the border for sale. Archeologists have been routinely summoned by the country's prime ministers to report on their activities, and their more sensational findings have been announced in flash bulletins by the broadcast media and accorded banner headlines in the newspapers (Yadin 1971:32, 13; Albright 1970:57–58; Silberman 1982:199–200; Yeivin 1955:3–5).

Archeologists have worked to establish the special qualities of their land as a nurturing environment, and to demonstrate that the current occupants of Israel have moral title to it by virtue of their priority of settlement. They have argued that the peculiar conditions in Palestine made it "the cradle of man's cultural development in his first advance beyond the end of the Middle

Stone Age," the source of "the impulse to cultural development, both technical and agricultural," which was the basis of "rich and highly-advanced civilizations" elsewhere (Yeivin 1955:3–5). They have identified a continuous Jewish presence in the territory of Israel from biblical times to the present, and
have reached the (somewhat problematic) conclusion that this presence was
maintained from the start by populations who had fixed ties to the land; the
tribes who moved into the area to form ancient Israel were settlers rather than
true nomads (Albright 1970:61).

Israeli archeologists have done more than this, however. They have found
in the archeological record evidence that their ancient forebears were para-
gons of contemporary virtues. No one has produced archeological findings
with greater national appeal than Yigael Yadin—surely the only professor of
archeology who has ever served as Chief of Staff of the military forces of his
country. Yadin directed two major excavations of ancient military sites—that
of the fortress of Masada, where in the beginning of the Christian era Jewish
zealots made a heroic stand against the Romans; and that of the site of the
Second Revolt of the Jews against the Romans in the second century, led by
the heretofore purely legendary Bar-Kokhba. In each instance, Yadin found
in the written and material records evidence that Jews were both extremely
disciplined fighters and dedicated to the practices of their faith, even under
the most difficult of conditions. The zealots at Masada were especially exemplary because they chose to commit suicide en masse rather than live as
Roman captives (a conclusion from which there is some scholarly dissent).
Masada, in particular, has become a national symbol. A major tourist attraction, it is commemorated on Israeli stamps and coins, and is the site of an
annual ceremony staged by the Israeli tank corps—whose new recruits swear
that "Masada shall not fall again." As then-President Golda Meir observed
in 1971, the country has a "Masada Complex." The implication of the archeologists' findings is that in the special environment of Israel the Jewish people
take on a distinctive character; the land is their natural habitat—an inspiring
(and consoling) message in an embattled state created after the Holocaust (Yadin 1966:54, passim; cf. 1971:23–26, 124–26, passim; Silberman 1989:99, 100;
cf. 88).

What is at issue is not the rigor of Israeli archeology, which is obviously
work of very high quality. So, too, was the research done by Gertrude Caton-
Thompson and the analysis it prompted. But sound archeological evidence
can document the legitimacy of political regimes as effectively as can fanciful
accounts. No matter by whom or to what scholarly standard the archeological research discussed in this paper has been done, it has dealt with the same
fundamental questions, and it has been used to legitimate the occupation of
a particular land by pointing to the history of that land's tenants.

By the criteria of what passes for international law, the rights of ownership are established by long use. If the land's claimants—be they Zulu, Indians, or Arabs—can be seen as wanderers with no truly fixed ties to the land, colonists will insist that they have as much right to territory as aboriginals. They will even insist that *ceteris paribus* their claims have greater weight, since they have greater virtue, an argument that can be made either by denigrating the qualities and accomplishments of aboriginal peoples or by celebrating those of the colonists. There is no novelty in the observation that history often serves to rationalize national purpose, and that archeology is a form of historical inquiry. But the history espoused by officialdom conventionally serves to sanction present practices by arguing that they have always been thus. Colonial ventures are ruptures of what has always, or at least has previously, been. In this context, archeology has been a vehicle for explaining away the obvious, for transforming a decisive break with the past into an inconsequential moment, and it can do this because its esoteric practices uncover a past invisible to the naïve observer. Absent approval from the deity (which, of course, many have claimed), colonialists may not be able to find a better means to justify actions illegal by any people's customary standards.

References Cited

Albright, W. F. 1970. The phenomenon of Israeli archaeology. In *Near eastern archaeology in the twentieth century*, ed. J. A. Sanders, 57–63. New York.

Antiquity. Editorial. 45:1.

Balfour, H. 1929. South Africa's contribution to prehistoric archaeology. Presidential address—Section H (Anthropology). *Rep. Brit. Assn. Adv. Sci.* 97:153–63.

Beek, J. L. R. W. 1928. The Bushmen and Zimbabwe. *NADA* 6:104–9.

Bent, J. T., 1896. *The ruined cities of Mashonaland*. 3d ed. London.

Berlyn, P. 1969. Attention to detail is essential if we want tourists to return. *Rhodesian Her.*, September 9:6.

Bernal, M. 1987. *Black Athena*. New Brunswick, N.J.

Boggis, R. J. E. 1930. Letter to the *Times*, April 12:8.

Braunholtz, H. J. 1932. Zimbabwe. Review of *The Zimbabwe culture* by G. Caton-Thompson. *Geogr. J.* 79:323–25.

Bruwer, A. J. 1965. *Zimbabwe: Rhodesia's ancient greatness*. Johannesburg.

Bullock, C. 1927. *The Mashona*. Cape Town.

————. 1949. Bushman paintings, Zimbabwe and romanticism. *NADA* 26:50–53.

Burkitt, M. 1928. *South Africa's past in stone and paint*. Cambridge.

C. W. H. 1931. The Great Zimbabwe problem. Review of *The Zimbabwe culture* by G. Caton-Thompson. *Nature* 127:884–86.

Cape Times. 1929a. Holism, mechanism, vitalism. July 27:15, 22, 23.

————. 1929b. Rock paintings in Africa: Dr. Frobenius avoids speculations. August 1:23.

————. 1929c. The Zimbabwe mystery. August 3:13.

————. 1929d. Professor Dart not satisfied. What African people want to know. August 3:13, 14.

————. 1929e. Zimbabwe of Bantu origin. August 3:21, 22.

Caton-Thompson, G. 1929a. Zimbabwe. *Antiquity* 3:424–33.

————. 1929b. The southern Rhodesian ruins. *Nature* 124:619–21.

————. 1930. Early Rhodesian gold. Letter to *Nature* 125:163.

————. 1931a. *The Zimbabwe culture: ruins and reactions.* Oxford.

————. 1931b. The Zimbabwe culture: Guesses and facts. Letter to *Man* 31:235.

————. 1958. Review of *Zimbabwe cavalcade* by B. G. Paver. *Antiquity* 32:199–201.

————. 1983. *Mixed memoirs,* Gateshead, Eng.

Cell, J. W. 1989. Lord Hailey and the making of the African Survey. *Afr. Aff.* 88:481–505.

Chanaiwa, D. 1973. *The Zimbabwe controversy.* Syracuse.

————. 1978. Historiographical traditions of Southern Africa. *J. South. Afr. Aff.* 3: 176–93.

Clark, G. 1966. The invasion hypothesis in British archaeology. *Antiquity* 11:172–89.

Clark, J. D. 1953. Environment and culture-contact in prehistoric Africa south of the Sahara. In *Proceedings of the Second Pan-African Congress on Prehistory,* ed. L. Balout, 359–65, Paris.

Clarke, G. 1969a. Letter to the *Rhodesian Herald.* September 22:7.

————. 1969b. Letter to the *Rhodesian Herald.* October 15:7.

Cobbing, J. 1988. The Mfecane as Albi: Thoughts on Dithakong and Mbolompo. *J. Afr. Hist.* 29:487–519.

Connah, G. 1987. *African civilizations.* Cambridge.

Cope, J. P. 1929. The riddle of the Zimbabwe ruins. *Illus. London News* 84:1136.

Dart, R. 1925. The historical succession of cultural impacts upon South Africa. *Nature* 115:425–29.

————. 1948. The ritual employment of bored stones by Transvaal Banto tribes. *S. Afr. Archaeol. Bull.* 3:61–66.

————. 1955. Foreign influences of the Zimbabwe and Pre-Zimbabwe eras. *NADA* 32:19–30.

————. 1957. The earlier stages of the Indian transoceanic traffic. *NADA* 34:95–115.

————. 1962. Death ships in South West Africa and South-East Asia. *S. Afr. Archaeol. Bull.* 17:231–34.

————. 1963. Paintings that link South with North Africa. *S. Afr. Archaeol. Bull.* 18:29–30.

Discovery. 1936. Zimbabwe. 17:180–81.

Du Bois, W. E. B. 1947. *The world and Africa.* New York.

Fagan, B. W. 1970. Review of *Zimbabwe: Rhodesia's ancient greatness* by A. J. Bruwer. *Antiquity* 44:320–22.

Fallaize, E. N. 1929. The ancient ruins of Rhodesia. *Discovery* 10:45–48.

Frederikse, J. 1982. *None but ourselves.* New York.

Garlake, P. S. 1973. *Great Zimbabwe.* New York.

————. 1978. *The kingdoms of Africa.* Oxford.

————. 1982. Prehistory and ideology in Zimbabwe. In *Past and present in Zimbabwe,* ed. J. D. Y. Peel & T. O. Ranger, 3–19. Manchester (1983).

Government of Southern Rhodesia. 1945. *Southern Rhodesia: past and present.* N.p.

Gregory, J. W. 1929. "Early Rhodesian mining and Zimbabwe." Letter to *Nature* 124: 723.

————. 1930. Early Rhodesian gold. Letter to *Nature* 125:47–48.

H. B. M. 1931. Zimbabwe culture: ruins and reactions. Review of *The Zimbabwe culture* by G. Caton-Thomson. *NADA* 9:110–11.

Haddon, A. C. 1905. Presidental address. Section H–Anthropology. *Rep. Brit. Assn. Adv. Sci.* 75:511–26.

Hall, D. 1929. Scientists in South Africa. After 25 Years. *Times*, September 6:11.

Hall, R. N. 1909. *Pre-historic Rhodesia.* London.

Hall, R. N., & W. G. Neal, 1904. *The ancient ruins of Rhodesia*, 2d ed. London.

Harris, J. R. 1969. Letter to the *Rhodesian Herald.* October 1:5.

Hobley, C. W. 1931. Rhodesia. Review of *The Zimbabwe Culture* by G. Caton-Thompson. *Man* 31:166–68.

Huffman, T. N. 1976. *A guide to the Great Zimbabwe ruins.* Salisbury.

————. 1981. Snakes and birds. *Afr. Stud.* 40:131–50.

————. 1987. *Symbols in stone.* Johannesburg.

Illus. London News. 1929. A secret of South Africa's past: The mysterious ruins of Zimbabwe and Ophir; or, A medieval "Rand"? Zimbabwe–Home of unknown gold diggers. 84:1134–35.

Jeffreys, M. D. W. 1954. Zimbabwe and Galla culture. *S. Afr. Archaeol. Bull.* 9:152.

————. 1967. Manga-Mecca. *NADA* 9:21–24.

Johnston, H. H. 1909. Pre-historic Rhodesia. Review of R. N. Hall, *Pre-historic Rhodesia. Geogr. J.* 34:562–64.

Keppel-Jones, A. 1983. *Rhodes and Rhodesia.* Kingston/Montreal.

Kgoale, M. 1986. Apartheid, education and history. *J. South. Afr. Stud.* 12:319–23.

Kuklick, H. 1991. *The savage within.* New York.

Layland, E. 1969a. Letter to the *Rhodesian Herald.* September 10:7.

————. 1969b. Letter to the *Rhodesian Herald.* September 19:13.

Lee, M. E. 1969. Letter to the *Rhodesian Herald.* September 16:5.

Lewin, R. 1987. *Bones of contention.* New York.

Mallows, W. 1984. *The mystery of the Great Zimbabwe.* London (1985).

Massingham, H. J. 1928. The mystery of Zimbabwe. *Saturday Rev.* 146:868–69.

Maugham, R. C. F. 1930a. Letter to the *Times.* April 9:12.

————. 1930b. Letter to the *Times.* May 3:8.

Meredith, M. 1979. *The past is another country,* London.

Myres, J. L. 1906. The Rhodesian ruins. Review of *Medieval Rhodesia* by David Randall-MacIver. *Geogr. J.* 28:68–70.

————. 1930a. Zimbabwe the riddle of the ruins. Evidence from the site. *Times*, April 7:15, 16.

————. 1930b. Letter to the *Times.* April 10:10.

————. 1930c. Letter to the *Times.* April 24:8.

————. 1930d. Letter to the *Times.* May 9:12.

N. M. 1931. Review of *The Zimbabwe culture* by G. Caton-Thompson. *J. Afr. Soc.* 30: 435–36.

Nature. 1925. Current topics and events. 115:432.

———. 1929a. The Zimbabwe ruins. 124:390–91.

———. 1929b. Zimbabwe. 124:605–7.

Nazaroff, P. S. 1931. What are the Zimbabwe ruins? *Blackwood's Mag.* 229:765–92.

Officer, J. E. 1971. The American Indian in federal policy. In *The American Indian in urban society,* ed. J. O. Waddell & O. M. Watson, 8–65. Boston.

Paver, B. G. 1950. *Zimbabwe cavalcade.* London (1957).

Perry, W. J. 1923. *The children of the sun.* 2d ed. London (1927).

Randall-MacIver, D. 1905. Report on ruins in Rhodesia. *Rep. Brit. Assn. Adv. Sci.* 75: 301–4.

———. 1906a. The Rhodesia ruins: Their probable origin and significance. *Geogr. J.* 27:325–47.

———. 1906b. *Medieval Rhodesia.* London (1971).

———. 1933. Archaeology as a Science. *Antiquity* 7:5–20.

Rhodesian Herald. 1969a. Discovery of gaming counters of old pottery at Bindura. September 5:11.

———. 1969b. In parliament yesterday: Zimbabwe's origin questioned. September 6:4.

———. 1969c. Archaeologist's verdict on Zimbabwe. September 11:1.

———. 1969d. Carbon test on Zimbabwe type site. November 4:4.

Richards, H. A. 1969. Letter to the *Rhodesian Herald.* October 10:11.

Rickard, T. A. 1930. Early Rhodesian gold. *Nature* 125:47.

Riddler, P. F. 1969. Letter to the *Rhodesian Herald.* November 13:7.

Rotberg, R. I., with the collaboration of M. F. Shore. 1988. *The founder: Cecil Rhodes and the pursuit of power.* New York.

Schebesta, P. P. 1931. Review of *The Zimbabwe culture* by G. Caton-Thompson. *Africa* 4:512–15.

Schofield, J. F. 1926. Ancient coins from Pondoland. *Nature* 117:953.

———. 1935. Zimbabwe: The Ancient Ruins Company, Limited. *Man* 35:19–20.

———. 1937. The builders of Zimbabwe. *Discovery* 18:67–71.

Selous, F. C. 1989. Mashonaland and the Mashonas. *Fortn. Rev.* 51:661–76.

Shrubsall, F. 1909. Letter to the editor. *Geogr. J.* 34:691.

Silberman, N. A. 1982. *Digging for God and country.* New York.

———. 1989. *Between past and present,* New York.

Silverberg, R. 1968. *Mound builders of ancient America.* New York.

Summers, R. 1952. Carl Mauch on the Zimbabwe ruins. *NADA* 29:9–17.

———. 1963. *Zimbabwe: A Rhodesian mystery.* Johannesburg.

———. 1971. *Ancient ruins and vanished civilizations of Southern Africa.* Cape Town.

Sunday Mail. 1955. New tests date occupation of Zimbabwe. Reprinted in *NADA* 32: 112–13.

Thompson, L. 1985. *The political ideology of apartheid.* New Haven.

———. 1990. *A history of South Africa.* New Haven.

Thompson, L., & H. Lamar. 1981. Comparative frontier history. In *The frontier in history,* ed. H. Lamar & L. Thompson, 3–13. New Haven.

Times. 1929. The Zimbabwe ruins: Vigorous native civilization. August 3:9.

———. 1930. The Zimbabwe exhibition: Mystery of soapstone carvings. April 7:16, 18.

———. 1988. Obituary, Raymond Dart. November 24:18.

Times Literary Supplement. 1931. The meaning of Zimbabwe. June 4:440.

Trigger, B. G. 1978. *Time and traditions.* New York.

Ure-White, P. 1969. Letter to the *Rhodesian Herald.* September 16:5.

Watermann, D. 1931. Review of *Erythaa* by Leo Frobenius. *Africa* 4:515–16.

Watson, J. 1955. The soapstone birds of Zimbabwe. *S. Afr. Archaeol. Bull.* 10:78–84.

Whatmore, J. 1969. Bindura ruins: Another Zimbabwe. *Rhodesian Her.*, September 4:7.

Wilmot, A. 1986. *Monomotapa (Rhodesia).* With a preface by H. R. Haggard. London.

Wright, A. 1969. Letter to the *Rhodesian Herald.* October 15:7.

Yadin, Y. 1966. *Masada.* New York.

———. 1971. *Bar-Kokhba.* New York.

Yeivin, S. 1955. *Archaeological activities in Israel (1948–55).* Jerusalem.

THE DYNAMICS OF RAPPORT IN A COLONIAL SITUATION

David Schneider's Fieldwork on the Islands of Yap

IRA BASHKOW

After reading the first seven hundred pages of the field notes of his student David Schneider, Clyde Kluckhohn confessed to "a feeling of embarrassment— as if I had stolen a peek into a friend's private diary"; the notes were "frankly, almost as (perhaps more than!) revealing of you as of Yap people and culture" (HYE: CK/DS 3/3/48). Two weeks later, Schneider wrote back from the field that "the value of all that material" on his own "concerns and emotions" was that it might allow his evidence on Yapese culture and personality to be "'corrected'" later for "'observer's bias.'" Concerned, like Kluckhohn, with the ethnographic equivalent of psychoanalytic transference, Schneider said that although he would hesitate to "publish the sort of notes I have been writing," at least "I will know later, when the materials are written up, to what extent I *pulled* paranoid material and to what extent my behavior impelled it" (HKP: DS/CK 3/16/48; cf. Kluckhohn 1944b:505, 1945:139).

Inasmuch as Schneider never wrote about Yapese culture and personality, his concern proved superfluous. Already by late June, when he returned to the United States, he had decided "to throw that overboard" and "report" instead on "kinship" (SPR: DS/Gorer 7/7/48). Later, however, in the 1960s, Schneider came to regard the kinship studies project to which he had turned in his post-Yap scholarship as itself an insidious mode of perpetuating a more general "observer's bias"—the "ethnocentric bias" that was integral to the very aims of kinship study (Schneider 1984:177, 197). In this context, it may be appropriate to draw upon "all that material" in Schneider's field notes in or-

---

Ira Bashkow is a graduate student in the Department of Anthropology at the University of Chicago. He is currently studying the relationship between cargo movements and development programs in colonial and contemporary Papua New Guinea.

der to illuminate his turn to kinship study (cf. Schneider 1965a, 1965b, 1969b, 1972, 1989).

That material appears differently now than when it was written. In 1947, another Harvard reader felt that Schneider was oversensitive to the "situation created by [his] own presence" (HPM: Oliver/Scott 12/1/47). Today, we may discern in this same sensitivity a potent reflexivist concern not then yet respectable in the discipline. For unlike Malinowski's *Diary in the Strict Sense of the Term*, where intimacy is manifest primarily in Malinowski's reflections on his romantic relationships, the intimacy of Schneider's field notes is manifest when Schneider reflects on the dynamics of his rapport with Yapese informants—the ways in which his own identity was construed by them, in relation to their experience of colonial domination, and in the context of his own identification with victims of oppression.[1]

Immigrant Radicalism, Ivy League Anthropology, and the Study of Subjectivity

Born in Brooklyn on the last day of World War I, Schneider was the first child of Eastern European Jewish Bolsheviks. His childhood, as he later re-

---

1. An extremely heterogeneous document of some 1,650 pages, the field notes contain a wealth of ethnographic and contextualizing material far in excess of the portion digested in Schneider's published writings. Typed up in triplicate (with carbons) while Schneider was in the field, they served at once as a personal diary and as a record of interviews and observations; thus they tend to collate a varied ethnographic reportage with politically and psychologically vivid accounts of relationships with informants, as well as analyses of these again in relation to Schneider's reactions, intellectual interests, and psychological fluctuations. Coupling often profound and sometimes brutal introspection with a record of his movements, queries, and recording activities, Schneider's field notes are a document of rare immediacy for the history of anthropology, specifying evolving interpersonal and intellectual dimensions of a field encounter in almost daily detail and with reflexive attention to its own perspective. I am greatly indebted to David Schneider for the field notes themselves and for his willingness to let me use them—without requesting any measure of editorial control. I am also grateful for his graciousness in consenting to be interviewed; our conversations took place on August 17, 18, 22, and 23, 1989, at Schneider's home in Santa Cruz.

The ribbon copy of the notes is held by Regenstein Library at the University of Chicago (SFN); one carbon is kept in the archives of the Harvard Peabody Museum (HYE). Each copy is interleaved with a small measure of unique material—correspondence or handwritten notes—and both include some thirty pages of notes by Schneider's colleagues. Although the copies follow the same page order, they use different methods of pagination until page 550; the page numbers on the Regenstein copy being sequential from start to finish, I have used them in citations throughout. In editing the notes, I have sought to preserve the flavor of material that was composed impromptu under field circumstances; I have thus corrected Schneider's spelling and in a few cases clarified punctuation, but refrained from imposing an arbitrary consistency on Schneider's attractively idiosyncratic and irregular style of punctuation and capitalization.

membered it, was partitioned between two spheres. One was the immigrant world of his parents, a world of militant Stalinist politics and fervent hopes for a new and more egalitarian America. In this world, Schneider's father ran a leather business that went bankrupt in the Depression, when he took a job as a travelling salesman of ladies' dresses. The other and more attractive world was that of Cherry Lawn, an "extremely progressive" rural boarding school in Connecticut to which Schneider was sent at age nine following the birth of his only brother. He had been doing so poorly in public school that his parents, worried that he had a congenital deficiency, had sent him to a counselor, who recommended the change. At Cherry Lawn, Schneider's resistance vanished and his performance improved; but his family's privations in the Depression tugged at his conscience along the tether of tuition, and when the time came he chose a college subsidized by the state (DSI).

Following a common poor man's route to premedical training, Schneider studied industrial bacteriology at the New York State College of Agriculture at Cornell, on the same campus as the sister private school. There he was classed with a group of opportunistic "city folk," who were resented by fellow students more genuinely committed to the soil as a vocation. His efforts to pay his way reinforced his perception as an outsider. In the familiar rituals of college life, he participated almost exclusively in the close-but-distant role of a service employee, observing the football fanfare behind an Indian head-dress and tray of novelties and the fraternity mysteries from behind an apron in the kitchen. Although his extracurricular attentions were focussed on class injustice, he did not see himself as following in the footsteps of his parents, with whom he in fact broke ties after Stalin's pact with Hitler. But he "tried on" the labor activism of the American Student Union, and in his sophomore year this considerable distraction from his studies elicited threats of expulsion from the bacteriology program, where he was earning mostly D's. Schneider thought of following two friends to Spain to fight against fascism, but he decided instead to transfer to the study of anthropology (DSI).

In the state college the program was officially Rural Sociology, but it benefited from "strong informal links" to the liberal arts faculty at the university, where the young Harvard-trained anthropologist R. Lauriston Sharp had been hired one year before, and was soon to join the social psychologist Leonard Cottrell in setting up a combined Department of Sociology and Anthropology (Smith 1974:11). During this period Sharp was interested in the neo-Freudian currents of "culture and personality" anthropology, highlighting in his classes the work of Ruth Benedict and Margaret Mead. In 1939, Mead herself lectured at Cornell on the relevance of anthropology to contemporary problems—which in that season between *Kristallnacht* and the invasion of Poland meant, above all, the terrifying success of Hitler's movement in magnetizing some common element in the personalities of millions. Anthropology, optimistically, might help to arrest these dark impulses; at the very least it celebrated the social value of the diversity that Nazi fascism attacked (Yans-McLaughlin 1984, 1986). And in America culture and personality anthropologists sought to expand the boundaries of social "tolerance," by demonstrating, ethnographically, "the relativity of normality," and showing how the "apparent weakness" of many "less usual types" was "illusory" from the perspective of "potentialities" honored in other cultures (Benedict 1934:277–78; Mead 1928; cf. Caffrey 1989). Although culture and personality anthropology championed the "deviant" and emotionally "tortured" more than the economically oppressed (Benedict 1934:278–79), a leftism circumscribed by nonconformism was not uncongenial to Schneider. He thought he had found his calling, and he stayed in Ithaca for another year after graduation, earning the first advanced degree conferred by Sharp's department (Smith 1974:11; DSI).

His master's thesis was an exploration of "the relationship between dreams and culture," based on 148 dreams of Yir-Yoront aborigines collected by Sharp some years before in northeastern Australia (Schneider & Sharp 1969:13). Although Schneider found a methodological guidepost in Freud's discussion of "typical" dream motifs (Freud 1900:274–310), his paper pointed toward a relativization of the "dream work," utilizing Sharp's Yir-Yoront materials to interrogate the cultural patterning of motivation and the cultural relativity of the internal symbology of the psyche. Given that Schneider was back at work refining this essay on the eve of his departure for the Yap Islands, it is notable, too, that the paper considered in detail Yir-Yoront dream "symbols" associated with white Australians "and their culture"–prefiguring the reflexive impulses manifest in his fieldwork (Schneider & Sharp 1969:44).

In the fall of 1941, with Sharp's encouragement, Schneider transferred to the Department of Anthropology at Yale, where the ultra-positivist behavioralist George Murdock had succeeded to the chairmanship upon the death of Edward Sapir two years before. Sapir was in many ways a poignant archetype for Schneider, who was soon initiated into a vivid oral tradition linking Sapir's death with "nasty anti-semitic treatment," including the denial of Sapir's application for admission to Yale's Graduate Club (HKP: DS/CK 9/12/50; cf. Darnell 1990:401–2). In the "sons of light" versus "sons of darkness" structure of the legends, the sons of light were sympathetic to the theories of the Viennese Jewish psychoanalyst; and broader resonances had been noted by Sapir himself, who suggested that the "discovery of the world of personality" was "apparently dependent upon the ability of the individual to become aware of and to attach value to his resistance to authority." Freud was the flag of "temperamental radicals," whereas "naturally conservative people" found it "difficult to take personality valuations seriously" (Sapir 1934:592). As this mythic structure was played out in Yale's social science community, the establishmentarian majority at the Yale Institute of Human Relations tended to acknowledge Freud's "genius," but questioned his "scientificity"; less in need of an emancipatory vision, they felt that the necessary "first step" was to formalize Freud's unruly theories into general and mostly mechanistic "hypotheses," which could then be related to the behavioristic principles of Clark Hull (Murdock 1949:xvii; May 1971:160–63; 1950; Dollard et al. 1939; Morawski 1986; Darnell 1984, 1990). Dissatisfied with Yale's behavioralization of Freud, and put off by the community's more general resistance to nonconformity, Schneider left within six months, profoundly disillusioned, and thinking to "quit anthropology forever" (DSI; cf. Oren 1985).

This brief Yale period, however, was of some consequence in setting the direction of over a decade of Schneider's research. Paradoxically, it was Murdock, whom he regarded as a general intellectual "enemy" (Darnell 1990:347; DSI), who proved to be greatly influential. Son of a Connecticut Yankee farmer of substantial means, Murdock had followed "half the males of our Murdock lineage" to Yale, where he joined a Greek letter fraternity, engaged in intramural sports, and worked on the college newspaper (Murdock 1965:351–59). Swept by "patriotic fervor" in his freshman year, he joined the Connecticut National Guard, but after four months in camp decided that the "life of a rear-rank private" was not for him; later he enrolled for officer training, emerging as second lieutenant, though World War I ended just before his embarkation. After a year at Harvard Law School, he took advantage of his father's legacy to travel in the Orient, returning with the determination to "devote a year to graduate work in anthropology." When Franz Boas "flatly refused" to admit him at Columbia, calling him "nothing but a dilletante" (358), Murdock returned to Yale, where he completed a doctorate in sociology with the social evolutionist Albert Keller. Remaining at Yale until 1960, he was to become one of the most powerful academic opponents of Boasian anthropology in the United States.

When Schneider encountered him in 1941, Murdock was at the peak of his intellectual energies. His massive Cross-Cultural Survey had by then successfully negotiated its initial pilot period and was being funded by the Institute of Human Relations (Ford 1970:7). That very season, too, Murdock was completing the first draft of his major theoretical statement, *Social Structure* (1949). Together these two projects embodied Murdock's vision of a "scientific anthropology," based on the "formulation and verification, on a large scale and by quantitative methods, of scientific generalizations of a universally human or cross-cultural character" (Murdock 1949:xv, 1940a:364). Physically, the Survey was a cross-indexed set of files, in which Murdock aspired to contain "all" of the available "cultural information" on a "representative sample" of "the various societies of the world" (1940a:362). Its scheme of classification incorporated the suggestions of nearly one hundred "leading specialists in many fields" to render the materials of the Survey responsive to as broad as possible a range of interests (Murdock et al. 1938:xiii). But although in general it was intended to be theoretically agnostic, "an exception" was the section on "social and kin groupings and organization," where "a series of analytic distinctions" was incorporated in the interests of "consistent usage" (Ford 1971:182). The particular distinctions were derived from Murdock's own theory, which might be described broadly as a compound of structural-functionalism and updated social evolutionism. Accepting the Boasian critique of evolutionism in the narrow sense of its application to "unilinear" theories, Murdock did not postulate a set of "stages" so much as hypothesize a set of likely (though "in some instances" predetermined) "transitions," whose motivational logic was provided by Hull's behaviorist psychology and Keller's formulation of "cultural change" as an adaptive process "accomplished through the blind trial-and-error behavior of the masses of a society" (1949:xii–xiv, xvi–xvii, 184, 197). The transitions were between "types" and "sub-types" of "social organization" (xii, 197–99), and the analytic discriminations used in founding this typology were concisely defined in the companion "working manual" of the Survey's *Outline of Cultural Materials* (Murdock 1949:15, 202–26; Murdock et al. 1945).

Schneider took a lecture course in which Murdock read directly from the manuscript of *Social Structure*, and worked for Murdock on the Cross-Cultural Survey. Although he could not presume to contest Murdock's command of the comparative ethnographic literature, and had as yet no developed sense of his theory's limitations, Schneider had a rather powerful sense that evolutionism was not "his kind" of anthropology—a sense born of his distrust of the notion of civilizational "progress," and confirmed by his personal relationship with Murdock, who seemed "prejudiced against anyone who wasn't Old New England WASP" (DSI). The closest approximation to a moment of sympathetic personal contact in the long history of their relationship came with Schneider's decision to leave Yale and end his studies: getting up from behind his desk and placing a hand somewhat awkwardly on Schneider's shoulder, Murdock assured him, "I know you'll be a success in something, Dave—but it wasn't anthropology" (DSI).

Immediately after leaving Yale, and again after the war, Schneider worked in Washington for the Division of Program Surveys, an agency of the Department of Agriculture, which was then pioneering "open-ended" interview techniques for public opinion polling. But his main anthropological "connection" during this period was the English anthropologist Geoffrey Gorer. An eclectic Freudian close to Mead and Benedict, Gorer had been a maverick on the faculty at Yale, where he was the only one to encourage Schneider's interests in personality psychology. After the attack on Pearl Harbor, Gorer began a program of research on "Japanese National Character" at the Office of War Information in Washington (Mead 1959:352), where he contacted Schneider at the Division of Program Surveys. When Schneider was drafted late in 1942,

Gorer advised him to "take copious notes" on his process of "acculturation" in the army, in which he served as a psychiatric social worker. Out of Schneider's army experience came a report published in the bulletin of Mead and Gregory Bateson's Institute for Intercultural Studies, as well as two papers in *Psychiatry*—one of which analyzed the "sick role" in army basic training as a culturally "patterned kind of behavior" (1947:326-27, 1946; DSI). When the Social Science Research Council turned down Schneider's application for a demobilization grant under the "G.I. Bill," he went to see Gorer and then Mead, saying that he was not willing to try a second time to work his way through graduate school. Mead told him to go to Harvard "and see Clyde Kluckhohn and tell him that he owes me academic favors and that you are one of them" (DSI).

Mead's intuition in dispatching Schneider to Kluckhohn proved sound; the two were to develop a psychological intimacy comparable in intensity to psychoanalytic exploration. Kluckhohn was known for encouraging students "to go ahead on their own" to discover their creative potential by exploring novel ideas and unorthodox approaches (Parsons 1962:143; DSI; Taylor et al. 1973; cf. Kluckhohn 1939a:341). In contrast to Murdock, Kluckhohn, too, was an outsider, although in a different way than Schneider. To judge from an autobiographical statement he contributed (anonymously but recognizably) to a psychological study of social scientists, Kluckhohn was acutely conscious of ambiguities in his upbringing and position (Roe 1953). Five years after his mother had died giving him birth, he was adopted into the family of her well-to-do brother, whose wife was not accepted by the "more snooty" residents of their Iowa home town. Although money from his foster father enabled him to attend Princeton, "rather involved dificulties" (vaguely referred to as "ill health" in two posthumous sources, but perhaps related to his homosexuality) led to Kluckhohn's departure in his freshman year (Roe 1953:18; cf. Parsons 1962:141; Fischer & Vogt 1973:1; FSI; DSI). There followed an extended visit to a ranch near Ramah, New Mexico, owned by relatives of Kluckhohn's adopted mother: intellectuals with "a good library" who became his second adopted family (Roe 1953:18). Their "nearest neighbors" were the Navajo, among whom Kluckhohn visited frequently in the remaining thirty-eight years of his life (Fischer & Vogt 1973:1-2).

Kluckhohn's aspirations were at first literary, and in 1927 he published a romantic travelogue of a summer horseback adventure through the Navajo reservation. But at his second college, the University of Wisconsin, Kluckhohn was convinced by his teachers that his ornamental prose "was not likely to set the world on fire" (Roe 1953:18). With Lauriston Sharp, later Schneider's teacher, Kluckhohn formed a "Sanskrit letter" club for weekly "intellectual discussion," as a "counterweight" to the Greek-letter fraternities (Smith 1974:8). Graduating in 1928, he returned to the southwest for several years and then went off to Vienna, where the royalties from his novel paid for a ten-month psychoanalysis (HKP; FSI), and to Oxford, where he studied as a Rhodes Scholar under the anthropologist R. R. Marett. After two years teaching in New Mexico, Kluckhohn finally entered Harvard for his doctorate, and when Lloyd Warner left for Chicago in 1935, Kluckhohn (although still a student) was appointed as instructor (Fischer & Vogt 1972:2; Eggan 1968:139). His intellectual affinities, however, were strongly Boasian (Kluckhohn 1944b; Caffrey 1989:265; Parsons 1962:146); in 1936–37 he commuted to Yale in order to study linguistics with Sapir, staying over in Sapir's home (HKP: CK/DS 9/27/50). Although Kluckhohn's advisor, Alfred Tozzer, had been linked to Boas since before the infamous censure episode of 1919 (Stocking 1968:295), the dominant tradition at Harvard was anti-Boasian, and Kluckhohn was not made full professor until 1946, when he was offered a position at Chicago. He was prevailed upon to stay by Talcott Parsons, then organizing the Department of Social Relations, to which Kluckhohn moved his office that autumn (HKP: Parsons/CK 3/11, 3/18, 3/21/46).

Parsons' new department aimed to gather under a single institutional umbrella sociologists, anthropologists, and clinical and experimental psychologists, toward the promotion of a theoretical "convergence" of interdisciplinary scope (Parsons 1956). It was, however, a very different place from the Institute of Human Relations at Yale, where "behavioral scientists" sought to eradicate "subjectivity" and "individual idiosyncracies," in order to foster rigorous "hypothetico-deductive" research (Morawski 1986:237, 239). At Social Relations, the four central founding members—Parsons, Kluckhohn, the psychoanalytic psychologist Henry Murray, and the social psychologist Gordon Allport—were all self-consciously idiosyncratic scholars, outsiders in their own departments, who were strongly committed to revaluing "subjectivity" in more positive theoretical and methodological terms. Later, Social Relations unorthodoxies became orthodox, but in these first years, when it was nicknamed by undergraduates the "Department of Residual Relations," it was a place of exciting unconventionality; Schneider later remembered it as "just what I had wanted" (DSI). He was there when its doors opened, enrolled on a special fellowship for his tuition, arranged by Kluckhohn, with a research assistantship in the Laboratory of Social Relations as well. There, although his field of "concentration" was Social Anthropology, under Parsons' program for encouraging interdisciplinary contact he was "distributed" to Murray's Psychology Clinic at 64 Plympton Street, and on working days was sometimes invited to Murray's nearby home for elegant set lunches (DSI). Moreover, at Social Relations, Freud was prized. Parsons had just entered into formal psychoanalytic training at the Boston Psychoanalytic Institute (Parsons 1970:840), which led him to highlight problems of unconventional predispositions (Parsons et al. 1951) within the general framework of his attempt to "construct a theory of the subjective" (Bierstedt 1981:395). Although Parsons' prose was notoriously leaden, Schneider found his lectures "simply beautiful, and clear as bells" (DSI). Kluckhohn was then urging students to gain "firsthand familiarity" with psychoanalysis, preferably, if possible, before conducting fieldwork (Kluckhohn 1944b:501, 503, 1945:124; DSI). In Schneider's case, however, the sudden possibility of fieldwork forestalled any further training in the study of subjectivity, when, after less than six months at Harvard, he was asked to participate in an anthropological expedition to the Caroline Islands in western Micronesia.

The Beginnings of American Anthropology in Micronesia

The Harvard Yap Expedition was one of twenty-one expeditions launched that season in the region, under a "cooperative" arrangement with Micronesia's colonial administration (HPM: "Notice to all Participants," 5/13/47; Murdock 1948b:423–24). The program was initiated and organized by Schneider's erstwhile teacher, Murdock, and its story was interwoven with colonial developments in Micronesia.

Stretching eastward from the Philippines, Micronesia was a vast island territory which included three island groups: the Marshalls, which came under German rule in the late nineteenth century, the Marianas (including Guam), and the Carolines (including Yap), both of which were ruled by Spain until 1899. Then, as part of the treaty ending the Spanish-American war, the United States received the large island of Guam, but was rebuffed in an attempt to purchase the Carolines, which were sold instead to Germany, along with the remaining Marianas (Brown 1976:237; Hezel 1983).

In October 1914, the Japanese Navy took advantage of the outbreak of World War I to quickly and quietly conquer the German islands. By 1919, Japan had secretly negotiated British support for its claims in Micronesia, in exchange for Japanese recognition of the annexations by Australia and New Zealand of German Samoa, Nauru, and Kaiser Wilhelmsland in New Guinea. Although these arrangements were opposed by the United States, they were ultimately confirmed under the League of Nations "Class C" Mandates, sanctioning their administration "as integral portions" of the colonial power (Peattie 1988:44–47, 55). The decision offended both those, like President Wilson, who were opposed to the legitimacy of simple military annexation, and also those who pleaded United States' interests in the region (Rattan 1972). After the Japanese attack on Pearl Harbor in December 1941, a similar pair of American constituencies proposed future policies for the region.

The first, favoring Micronesia's "internationalization," was headquartered

in the State Department and in the Department of the Interior. Guided by
the firm anticolonialist "pledges" that were announced in the 1941 Atlantic
Charter, State Department planners sought to make Micronesia the "seed" of
a system of international "trusteeships," under which colonies "released" during the war would be "prepared" for "independence." The system was to be administered by the newly contemplated United Nations Organization, and take
the place of the old League of Nations Mandates (Hull 1948:1234–37, 1596;
U.S. Dept. of State 1947:9). Its model for "trusteeship" was the United States'
administration of the Philippines, which was scheduled to receive its independence shortly after the war's end (Hull 1948:1491; Hitch 1946; Kennedy
1945:332). In the Department of the Interior, which administered the Philippines, early plans for Micronesia translated that precedent into liberal, assimilative policies, emphasizing the opening of Micronesia to economic "development," and the prompt organization of self-government on a Western,
democratic model (Richard 1957:II, 60–62; Ickes 1946).

The constituency favoring Micronesia's annexation was slower getting organized, for within the Navy—its historic and eventual home—its advocates
had their hands full, during the first year of the war, with mobilization, recon-
naissance, and the planning of invasion (Richard 1957:II, 55). Instead, the
annexation forces were set in motion by scholars at East Coast universities,
and particularly Columbia, where an "emergency meeting" of sixteen faculty
members, including the anthropologist Ralph Linton, was convened in March
1942 by Professor of Government Schuyler Wallace (I, 9; Connor 1950; Linton & Wagley 1971:61). Anticipating enlarged postwar requirements for administrators overseas, the meeting planned an "Emergency Program of Training in International Administration," and was later regarded as the founding
moment of the postwar "area studies" concept (Connor 1950:12; Wallace 1944:
32). That it became significant for the history of Micronesia was a circumstan-
tial matter. After failing to sell the program to other government agencies,
Wallace gained an *ad hoc* appropriation of $60,000 from the Navy, as a favor
from the prewar dean of Columbia's School of Engineering, who was then
serving as an assistant to the Secretary of the Navy. In August 1942, a new
"school" opened at Columbia (Connor 1950:8–15; Richard 1957:I, 9–12).

For the first two months of the school's existence, no one in the Navy
was charged with "cognizance" over occupation planning, or even for over-
sight of the school, its students, or its curriculum. The school's curriculum,
designed by Wallace to be a showpiece to other agencies, emphasized problems of long-term administration (Richard 1957:I, 46–49, 63–65; Wallace 1944;
Hessler 1943), and at first seemed useless to naval officials, who then envisioned transferring control of captured Micronesian islands promptly to a
civilian agency (Connor 1950). But in September 1942, when the Navy planned
to terminate its association with the program, Wallace fought back politically

to keep the school afloat, bringing the school to the attention of President Roosevelt and Under Secretary of the Navy James Forrestal, and arranging a series of visits by high-ranking officials (Connor 1950:12–17). These secured "top recognition" for the school, and led to the creation of a two-man naval office to "advise" on "naval participation in the administration of occupied areas" (Richard 1957:I, 13–14). Once established, the office quickly mushroomed into a seven-officer "section" (35), and became a platform for advocating a naval role in the postwar administration of Micronesia. Murdock joined in the spring of 1943, bringing along with him the Yale Cross-Cultural Survey (50).

Urging its "practical value" as ethnographic intelligence on indigenous peoples in the war zones, Murdock shortly after Pearl Harbor had displayed the Marshall Islands file to Army and Navy intelligence officials. They advised a concentration of future efforts on regions of strategic importance, and a grant from the Carnegie Corporation enabled Murdock to hire a team of translators and assistants, in a rush to complete the Survey's files on Micronesia (Ford 1970:7; NAS2:1942–43; NAS1: "Cross-Cultural Survey File . . ." [1944]; Richard 1957:I, 50). Meanwhile, Murdock's outline was distributed to other agencies, which collected "information of practical value on the peoples" of other regions. From Murdock's perspective, there was "no conflict between theoretical aims and practical utility such as is inherent in most scientific research" (NAS1: "Strategic Bulletins . . ." 1/2/43). Just as the scientific objectives of the Survey proved readily convertible to applied aims, these applied involvements furthered the program of gathering "a large number of cases" (Murdock 1940a:369).

Murdock's earlier army experience had acquainted him with the forms of military organization, and the no-nonsense, cultural self-assurance of his scientistic progressivism impressed Navy officers inclined to suspect the university man of impracticality and abstract-mindedness (Useem 1945:4). Murdock quickly became a Navy insider, with access to top officials in the Pacific Ocean Areas Command and in the Office of the Chief of Naval Operations. In April 1943, two months after arranging a Navy takeover of Cross-Cultural Survey research on Micronesia, he accepted a commission as a Navy lieutenant commander, persuading his Yale colleagues, John Whiting and Clelland Ford, to enlist as Navy lieutenants (junior grade) (IHR: Murdock/Chief of Naval Personnel 8/14/45; Whiting 1986:684). The three entered active duty in the Naval Office of Occupied Areas as "Research Unit Number One" for the Japanese Mandated Islands of Micronesia (Richard 1957:I, 50).

It would not be an exaggeration to say that the memorandum sent from the Office two days after their arrival established the postwar framework of colonial rule in Micronesia. Travelling over the signature of the Office's Officer-in-Charge, the memorandum percolated up the echelons to the Secretary of the Navy and Joint Chiefs of Staff. In reaction to planning for Micronesia

then in process at the Department of Interior, and to the news that President
Roosevelt had provisionally endorsed the Hull proposal, it urged the Navy
to resist these internationalist developments, in language that leaves little doubt
of Murdock's primary authorship:

> For years to come, the chief significance of these islands will remain their actual
> or potential use as sea and air bases. Most of the islands consist of small vol-
> canic or coral island atolls with little economic importance, with a scanty na-
> tive population possessed of a very primitive social organization, and with only
> a primitive political tradition. Autogenous government has always been limited
> to feudalistic family, clan and village systems. . . . Attempts to impose govern-
> ment systems based on representations which cut family and village lines are,
> for the time being, doomed to failure.

For these "strong reasons" the memorandum argued, "it would be extremely
unwise" to establish "prematurely" in Micronesia a "civilian government which
attempted to rule the inhabitants along a Western cultural pattern."

> All in all, the interest of the inhabitants (and incidentally, the best interests
> of the United States) would best be served by establishing in most of these is-
> lands a strong but benevolent government – a government paternalistic in char-
> acter, but one which ruled as indirectly as possible (i.e., one which made mini-
> mum interference with local family and organization and custom).

The memo called upon its powerful recipients to insist upon "full and un-
divided" naval control "until the final peace treaty is signed," and, if possible,
"on a permanent or at least a semi-permanent basis" (quoted in Richard 1957:I,
18–19).

In May, the three-man "Research Unit" was transferred to Columbia University, where Wallace's program had at last received an official designation
as the Naval School of Military Government and Administration (Wallace
1944:30). There Murdock and his colleagues pressed on toward the completion of the Survey's files on Micronesia, synthesizing the collected materials
in a series of eight *Civil Affairs Handbooks* for use by military government
officials (Richard 1957:I, 50–51; OPNAV 1944). After the last *Handbook* was
finished in September 1944, the Unit was posted to the Pacific command in
Hawaii, where it became part of the rather heterogenous staff of "regular Navy
officers, former college professors, policemen and orientalists" engaged in planning and setting up military government on captured islands (Worden 1945:11;
Richard 1957:I, 51; Walker 1945). Accompanying the invasion of Okinawa in
April 1945, the Unit worked under hair-raising conditions in unsecured areas
(Ford 1950), with Murdock supervising political affairs and public safety in
the principal area of native settlement (IHR: GPM/MM 7/29/45). The day
after V-J Day, Murdock, still on active duty in the Pacific, reported back to
Mark May, director of the Institute of Human Relations, that his war experi-

ence had convinced him "of the need of selling social science by demonstrating its practical utility": "We'll have a lot more to say on this score when we return" (IHR: GM/MM 9/3/45).

Early in January 1946, Murdock was back in Washington setting up plans for a meeting of the National Research Council Committee on the Anthropology of Oceania, and lobbying naval officials for new research (NAS3: Handy/Harrison 1/22/46; NAS5: Minutes 4/20/46, p. 9). Meanwhile, at the Research Council, three plans for the scientific exploration of Micronesia were already in circulation, one of which was closely in line with Murdock's own formulations (NAS4). Drafted the previous summer by the Harvard Peabody Museum anthropologist Douglas Oliver, it was premised on the "assumption" that "Micronesia will remain a kind of government 'reserve' for a long time, . . . requiring close control over [the] activities of civilian visitors—in regard to mobility and access to native populations." Under these circumstances, the plan called for the establishment of a "post-hostilities organization for systematic scientific exploration," which "besides possessing intrinsic scientific value," would "assist powerfully in the administration and development of the area" (NAS4: "A Plan to . . ." [6/45]).

Actually, in this immediate postwar period, two broad scientific constituencies were offering competing visions of the future of scientific research in Micronesia. The first was an emergent network of academic veterans of the war agencies, based for the most part in major East Coast universities, which Murdock drew together behind Oliver's plan for a centrally coordinated investigation. In the committee structure of the Research Council, this group was represented by the Committee on the Anthropology of Oceania, which had been formed under Murdock's chairmanship in February 1942 (NAS2: 1942–43), and included Ford, Mead, Linton, Cora Du Bois, Fred Eggan, and Lauriston Sharp—all now newly discharged from work related to the war effort (NAS: NRC, *Organization & Members*, 1941–47). At the first postwar meeting in March 1946, a Pacific Science Conference—at which delegations from the Army, the Navy, "and probably" the Departments of State and the Interior would be presented with an elaborated version of Oliver's proposal—was put on the Council's calendar for early June. Murdock attempted to limit the Conference program to "the geographical and human sciences (including public health)," as promising "the greatest help to practical administration," but was overruled—temporarily, in the event (NAS2: Murdock/Miles 2/6/46; Revitalization, 1946; NAS5: Minutes 4/20/46, p. 9; NAS3). The conference was broadened to include the biological and other sciences, and a Harvard zoologist, Harold Jefferson Coolidge, was appointed to administer the conference organization (NAS3: Merrill/Harrison 3/25/46). Coolidge, however, deferred exclusively to Murdock on matters anthropological, becoming almost an administrative factotum for Murdock when he resumed a full teaching schedule at Yale.

There was an alternative vision. Notwithstanding its formidable connections in Washington, in the context of Pacific science Murdock's was an upstart group, and it encountered significant opposition from a second, much older, scientific constituency, whose institutional foothold at the Research Council was the Committee on Pacific Investigations. Unlike those associated with Murdock's network, the scientists of this group—including Herbert Gregory, E. S. C. Handy, and Felix Keesing—were mostly affiliated with institutions on the West Coast and in Hawaii, and all had a strong allegiance to the Pacific Science Association, which had grown out of a series of international Pacific Science Congresses held triennially since 1920 (NAS4: 1945-46; Cochrane 1978:485-86). The style of interdisciplinary collaboration characteristic of Association research was closely akin to the approach of Boasian "historical" ethnographers of indigenous peoples of North America; like the Boasians, Association ethnologists saw the "ethnographic salvage" of vanishing artifacts and traditions as a project of the utmost urgency. Although some younger Association ethnologists had begun to consider problems of "acculturation" and "culture contact," the dominant modes of Pacific basin fieldwork were quite different from those advocated at the Yale Institute of Human Relations or the Harvard Department of Social Relations. Both these groups brought to bear a variety of social scientific theoretical perspectives on the analysis of a presumed phenomenal unity, human behavior. In contrast, the Association approach involved the analysis of substantially different phenomenal entities—myths, artifacts, languages, zoology, botany, ethnobotany, and so forth—toward a unified reconstruction of human and natural history, an approach which did not lend itself easily to producing results of any "utility" in colonial administration.

Pacific Science Association scientists were therefore alarmed by the "sociological" and "applied" angle of Murdock's plans for "overall Pacific research." Handy warned that Pacific research "will assume a very different shape if Murdock picks it up and carries on with it," and he "emphatically" opposed suggestions "that the future of research and administration in Pacific islands is to be largely a function of the U.S. Navy Department" (NAS3: ESCH/Harrison 1/22/46; NAS4: ESCH/Harrison 11/18/45). Modelled on older traditions of Pacific science, the key elements of the proposals advanced by members of the Pacific Science Association were a loosely coordinated mixture of pure science, applied science, and historical research, emphasizing the affiliation of scientific enterprise to internationalist organizations, including the newly formed United Nations (NAS4: Embree, "Proposal" [1946]; Buck, Burrows, and Keesing [proposal] [1945]).

But despite their differing goals and approaches, the two groups could at least agree on the desirability of a major research undertaking. For anthropologists and other scientists, Micronesia at the end of World War II represented "a rich, virtually untouched field" for new research (NAS4: "A Plan to . . ." [6/45]). For some Pacific Association scientists, however, the American takeover offered a chance to break the pattern by which Micronesian research had been an exclusive preserve of scientists of the reigning colonial power (Berg 1988; NAS4: Gregory/Harrison 7/11/45; Handy/Harrison 11/18/45; Embree, "Proposal" [1946]; Buck, Burrows, and Keesing [1945]). In this sense, the debate on the future of scientific research in Micronesia was linked to the colonial future of the islands themselves.

In the case of Pacific islands not considered vital to United States security, internationalization remained a live option throughout most of 1946. The Departments of State and Interior were solidly behind it, and although President Truman was more wavering than Roosevelt had been, he appeared at this point to support it as well (NAS4; Pearson 1945; *NYT*: 1/16/46, p. 1; Hitch 1946; Hayward 1950; U.S. Dept. of State 1945:127–30). Continued military control of Micronesia was seen by the more internationally minded as making a mockery of the anticolonial stance the United States had taken throughout the war, and of the high moral ground it assumed in granting the Philippines independence (Ickes 1946; Embree 1946; Amerasia 1946; Levi 1946; Rachlis 1946). Army and Navy officials, on the other hand, were loathe to relinquish hard-won Micronesian islands—useful strategically and for atomic testing—to a meddling internationalization, and numerous calls were issued for their outright "annexation" (*NYT*: 4/5/45, p. 1; 4/13, p. 18; 6/25, p. 1; 8/20, p. 11; 9/16, p. 1; 1/13/46, p. 6; 2/3, p. 1; Stimson & Bundy 1948:599–604).

In June 1946, such political disagreements plagued the Pacific Science Conference organized by Coolidge and Murdock. Referring to a request by the University of Hawaii for research access to Micronesia that had been put on the back burner at the Navy through the direct intervention of Coolidge and Murdock (NAS3: U. Hawaii 1946; NAS6: Coolidge/Ryerson 10/23/46), a high level representative of the Department of State cautioned the Conference that it was "especially important" that "international cooperation" be strongly encouraged, and that no single group of scientists, or special field, be given "a monopoly to the exclusion, or even to the limitation of others" (NRC 1946:9–10). This incident provoked complaints by Pacific Association scientists, followed up later by letters protesting Murdock's "scheme" for "monopolizing" Micronesian research (NRC 1946:50–51; NAS3: Bachman/Harrison 5/2/46).

Although eventually there was a movement toward compromise (NAS6: 1947), it was abruptly overtaken by political developments. In early October 1946, the American delegation to the Trusteeship Committee of the United Nations received intelligence that the Union of South Africa planned, in contravention of the United Nations Charter, to annex the former German colony of Southwest Africa. Some clarification of the United States' position in Micronesia was therefore imperative to prevent collapse of the new trusteeship system, and the head of the American delegation, John Foster Dulles, met extensively with Administration officials in October to try to break the nearly four-year-old policy deadlock on the question (*NYT*: 10/29/46, p. 5; 1/31, p. 6; 2/3, p. 1; Bedell 1946). Finally, on November 6, President Truman announced that the United States was "prepared to place" Micronesia under trusteeship, "with the United States as the administering authority." It was, however, to be a unique, "strategic" trusteeship that would allow the United States to fortify the islands militarily, and to continue indefinitely administration by naval authorities (U.S. Dept. of State 1947:30, 73–75; Newlon 1949:49). Dulles then served notice to the U.N. General Assembly that if other nations did not accept this, the United States would continue "de facto control" nevertheless (*NYT*: 11/8/46, p. 1; Dean 1946); but the Soviets, as it happened, pragmatically acquiesced—in order to gain bargaining power for their unmet demands for a similar trusteeship in Italy's former colony of Eritrea (Goodman & Moos 1981:69; Bedell 1946).

Although the Washington debate over the final disposition of Micronesia continued into 1948, it was now clear that the immediate future of Micronesian research lay with the Navy. At the National Research Council, planning turned decisively in Murdock's favor. A Pacific Science Board was constituted with Harold Coolidge as executive secretary, and Murdock announced at its first meeting that the Navy would soon be lodging with the Research Council a "request" for a predominantly anthropological research program in Micronesia (NAS6: Minutes, 12/12/46). The Navy indeed soon offered $100,000 for "a program of research in anthropology, human geography, linguistics, and sociology." Drawing on language in Murdock's own earlier draft proposals, and noting the Navy's "pressing need" for information relevant to "problems of island government," the formal request specified "the obscurity of the native system of land tenure and the scarcity of knowledge concerning the political and social structure of native communities" (NAS6: General, 1946–47; Lee/Bronk 12/24/46).

The resulting program, which was called the Coordinated Investigation of Micronesian Anthropology (CIMA), was structured as an ensemble of separate expeditions, each mounted by a museum or university under an agreement with the National Research Council Pacific Science Board. All in all, forty-two scientists from twenty-one institutions joined in the CIMA program, including three geographers, four linguists, and three physical anthropologists, and a majority of social and cultural anthropologists (Pac. Sci. Bd. 1947). As the first foray of American scientists into the Micronesian region, the CIMA program marked a radical expansion of American ethnographic interests in the Pacific (Marshall & Nason 1975).

The agreement between the Pacific Science Board and Navy was clear in emphasizing "the importance of the freedom of science"; it reserved to CIMA

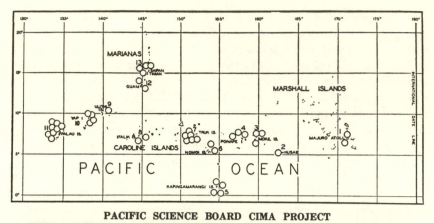

PACIFIC SCIENCE BOARD CIMA PROJECT
FIELD LOCATIONS OF PARTICIPANTS IN THE COORDINATED INVESTIGATION OF
MICRONESIAN ANTHROPOLOGY (1947-48)

1. **MARSHALL ISLANDS**—
   Majuro Atoll — Chicago
   Mus. of Nat. Hist.
   (Spoehr); Univ. of Hawaii (Chave)
2. **KUSAIE**—Univ. of Penn.
   (Lewis)
3. **MOKIL** — Clark Univ.
   (Murphy); Univ. of S.
   Calif. (Weckler & Bentzen)
4. **PONAPE**—Amer. Museum

of Nat. Hist. (Murrill);
Univ. of Calif. (Reisenburg); Indiana University
(Garvin)
5. **KAPINGAMARANGI** —
   Bishop Mus. Honolulu
   (Buck, Emory, Elbert,
   Lathrop)
6. **NOMOI** — Columbia Univ.
   (Tolerton, Rausch)
7. **TRUK ATOLL**—Yale Univ.
   (Murdoch, Gladwin, Good-

enough, Lebar, Dyen,
Wong)
8. **IFALIK**—Univ. of Conn.
   (Burrows); Northwestern
   Univ. (Spiro)
9. **ULITHI**—Univ. of Chicago (Lessa)
10. **YAP** — Harvard Univ.
    (Hunt, Kidder, Schneider,
    Stevens)
11. **PALAU**—Univ. of Oregon

(Barnett, Murphy); Milwaukee Public Mus. (Ritzenhaler); U. of Wis.
(Useem, Vidich, Mahoney,
Uyehara)
12. **GUAM** — Stanford Univ.
    (Greulich, Greulich)
13. **SAIPAN and TINIAN**—
    Saipan—Inst. of Ethnic
    Affairs (Joseph, Murray);
    Saipan and Tinian—Univ.
    of Mich. (Bowers, Bowers)

The participating institutions, personnel, and research sites of the Coordinated Investigation of
Micronesian Anthropology, 1947–48. (From Pac. Sci. Bd. 1947:13.)

participants the right to study what they might and to report on any matters
not "affecting national defense" (NAS6: Naval Bulletins folder, Wright/CIMA
4/30/47; Gladwin 1956:60). But within these guidelines, there was an unmistakable attempt to give positive direction to research, which was differentially
realized in different CIMA expeditions. As a matter of policy, funds were
"allocated to projects roughly in proportion to their correspondence with administrative needs and priorities" (NAS6: Murdock/[participating institutions]
[2/47]). And an ongoing interest in topics of potential practical application
was to some extent secured by offering to all CIMA researchers, regardless
of institution, a bonus over salary of $500 for the prompt submission of a
report which would be forwarded to the Navy. It was understood that the
reports, while not necessarily scientifically polished, had to be "adequate for
administrative uses"; and for certain island groups, Murdock provided compelling specification of the "administrative uses" he had in mind. Thus "resettlement problems" in the Marianas made "geographic research imperative."
In the Marshalls, "major administrative problems" were connected to a "system of communal land tenure by matrilineal clans." For the expedition of the
Harvard Peabody Museum, Murdock specified the problem of the "rapid depopulation" of the islanders of Yap (NAS6: Murdock/[participating institutions] [2/47]; HPM: "Yap Expedition Contract," 7/24/47).

Throughout the history of Western colonialism in the Pacific, depopulation—presenting the spectre of extinction—stood as the definitive and ultimate colonial problem: What clearer indication could there be of the failure of a colonial regime to promote native welfare and advancement? The problem engaged the interest of colonial administrators, missionaries, and, not surprisingly, anthropologists. The most famous anthropological statement on depopulation was that of W. H. R. Rivers, who had argued that "underlying" the "more obvious causes" of depopulation, such as "the new diseases and poisons," was a "psychological factor": the "loss of interest in life" caused by colonial disruptions in the religious and economic institutions that had previously motivated vigorous native pursuits. Loss of interest enhanced morbidity by suggestion; it also motivated natives to practice "voluntary restriction" or abortion—that potent "instrument of racial suicide" (Rivers 1922:96, 103–5). Since in this view the ultimate causes of depopulation were European practices, the cure clearly involved ameliorative policies, including a greater emphasis on maintaining "old customs and institutions," and the restoration of native vitality by substituting "new" interests like competitive games and Christianity (Rivers 1922:107; Stocking 1988; cf. Williams 1933). But for many who accepted the Riversian diagnosis, unprogressive colonial policies merely accelerated a postulated, "inherent" decaying tendency in certain native populations (Pitt-Rivers 1927:49). Thus the major prewar textbook on *Population Problems of the Pacific*, heavily influenced by the eugenic theories of the day, argued that in certain areas, including Yap, the islanders were already "a decadent stock when the first navigators came." Operating through moral mechanisms alleged to influence the birth rate, the "unspeakable corruption" of Yapese cultural practices had brought "their inevitable retribution" in the guise of a decline in population (Roberts 1927:59–62). Viewed from a comparative perspective, the problem could be formulated as why, given a colonial presence that was presumed to be constant in many regions, the Yapese depopulated while many other peoples did not—a formulation that suggested the appropriateness of concentrating research on distinctive Yapese customs or traits of physiology.

The focus on depopulation at first led Donald Scott, the Harvard Peabody Museum director, to decline to participate in Murdock's CIMA program (HYE: Scott/Coolidge 1/21/47; Scott/Brew 6/30/48). From Scott's perspective as a museum archeologist, it was by no means clear that solving practical problems was a museum expedition's business. However, other Harvard faculty members were more sympathetic. Because Murdock had insisted that "research in physical anthropology" was "imperative" (HPM: Murdock/[participating institutions] [2/47]), the physical anthropologist Carleton Coon supported the expedition, as did the Museum's Pacific expert, Douglas Oliver, whose earlier proposal gave him a stake in realizing the CIMA program. When Oliver "added

his plea" and agreed to take responsibility for the project, Scott gave his bless-
ing to the expedition plan. Under the circumstances, a focus on depopulation was the necessary price of mounting an expedition at all, and, "as in the
case of all expeditions," other valuable "material would be gathered" (HYE:
Scott/Brew 6/30/48).

While supervising, the summer before, an economic survey of Micronesia
for the Foreign Economic Administration, Oliver had learned of the results
of Japanese medical studies (Oliver 1946; Useem 1946) that had cited gonorrhea—probably a misdiagnosed form of yaws (Hunt et al. 1954:41; McNair
et al. 1949)—as the "chief cause" of the low Yapese birth rate (Japan 1930:139,
1936:114–16), and he sought to recruit a gynecologist to the Harvard expedition. Fortunately for the Yapese, however, the gynecologist never material-
ized, and the main thrust of the expedition proceeded along other lines, partly
dictated by the pool of eligible graduate students then available for the research. A student in sociology, Nathaniel Kidder, was to analyze the demo-
graphics of "fecundity" on the basis of a census; he was advised by Samuel
Stouffer of the Department of Social Relations. Coon contributed a physical
anthropology student, Edward Hunt, Jr., to conduct an anthropometric survey and consider questions of racial origins (HPM: "Plan of Investigation of
Yap Somatology" [3/47]). In ethnology, recruitment was hamstrung by the
accelerated CIMA timetable; most social and cultural anthropology students
were not ready to begin fieldwork, having only just entered graduate school
after military service. But Oliver found one second-year student, William
Stevens, whose undergraduate training was in biology, and who proposed to
examine "the possibility of relating physique and culture." The other ethnologist was Kluckhohn's student David Schneider (HPM: "Proposed Plan and
Personnel of the Yap Study" [3/47]).

The three dissertation topics Schneider contemplated that spring and summer were all variations on the theme "the cultural patterning of X": Yapese
dreams, Yapese aggression, and Yapese sickness. Each was developed as a point
of entry into social psychological problems: the individual as conditioned by
socialization and as responsive to values and norms (HKP: DS/CK 8/6/47).
Although sickness was clearly the most pertinent topic to the applied aim
of the expedition, Kluckhohn favored the proposal to study aggression, as
did Gorer, Parsons, and Schneider himself (HKP: CK/DS 8/12/47; DSI).

While Kluckhohn appreciated the opportunity that the expedition offered
to Schneider and supported his participation, he was opposed to the more
general Murdockian project. At about the time the CIMA program was
launched, he warned pointedly that "human-relations scientists, exhilarated
by newly discovered skills and possibly a trifle intoxicated by the fact that
for the first time men of affairs are seeking advice on a fairly extended scale,
are encouraging hopes which their science is not mature enough to fulfill."

To restrain them from "irresponsible pronouncements," the profession needed "to develop sanctions comparable to those which law and medicine have developed to control irresponsibility, charlatanism, and malpractice." The real "lesson" to be drawn from past "applied human-relations science" was "humility as to what may be predicted with present instruments for observation and conceptualization" (1946:186; cf. 1949a:262, 1950:241). It was not that Kluckhohn was opposed to instrumentality *per se*; he, too, had served in wartime Washington. But he was convinced that colonial problems were usually best addressed by applying anthropological insights to the "cultures of administrators"; and he typically contrasted the role of the "social engineer," who often introduced "new complications," with the cautious advocate of minimal interference, who appreciated how even changes seen by administrators as "trivial" and "simple" might to the administrated seem "unreasonable" and "oppressive" (1946:186, 1949a:181, 187, 194–95, 1943). Suspicious of the implied standpoint of Murdockian anthropology, diffusely above and looking down on "abstracted parts of the social structure," Kluckhohn argued that the "hallmark of anthropological method" was to ask, "How does this look from their point of view?" (1949a:181, 1944a:80).

For Schneider, Kluckhohn and Murdock were contrastive archetypal figures, standing for different projects, methods, epistemologies, and politics. Avoiding in his own work problems of kinship and social structure (Parsons 1973:55), Kluckhohn was ever mistrustful of anthropological notions of "typicality," and attacked functionalism for losing sight of "actual people." He was strongly oriented then to "life history" studies of individuals (1939b, 1939c, 1944a:80, 1944b:498, 1945, 1949b), and his major ethnographic work was half taken up with informants' statements (1944a)—which Murdock literally never directly quoted. Murdock and Kluckhohn were each the other's most directly relevant critic, and although they maintained a relationship of collegiality (HPM: GPM/Brew 10/18/50; DSI), they regularly chided each other in print (Murdock 1940a:364; Kluckhohn 1939a:337–38, 342–43, 1945:141, 1950:256).

At this point, of course, Schneider's allegiance was clear, and it was imbued with fresh animus on the eve of his departure, when Murdock forbade his wife, Adeline, to join him in the field, citing a bogus Navy regulation excluding white women from the Caroline region (DSI; cf. NAS6: [Murdock]/ [participating institutions] [2/47]). But while confirmed by a potent mixture of personal sympathies and antipathies, Schneider's Kluckhohnian orientation was rooted in a profound intellectual identification. Reading Schneider's Yap field notes, one is struck by the degree to which he internalized Kluckhohn's ideals of field procedure. Kluckhohn, in his field methods seminar and a 1945 methodological handbook, urged anthropologists to document the "interpersonal" dynamic aspects of field interview situations, including the anthropologist's "'subjective' reactions to informant and interpreter," his "own motivations" and "difficulties," and his interpretations of the "motivations" and "personalities" of his informants and interpreters (1945:124-26). In conceptualizing the field rapport relationship as essentially "dual"—at once empathetic and instrumental, an affective bond and a technique—Kluckhohn modelled its ideal conditions on the "psychoanalytic interview"; the anthropologist should seek a level of empathetic understanding that allowed him to serve as both a "sympathetic friend" and a "blank screen upon which the relevant [sic] could project his fears and fancies" (122, 139).

To achieve this level of "trust" in intercultural situations, where "intransigence of whites" was often "culturally enjoined," Kluckhohn took for granted that the anthropologist, through his actions, would distinguish himself in native eyes from other ambassadors of his home culture—especially including predatory figures like colonial officials (1945:117, 122; DSI). For Schneider, of course, to stand apart from other representatives of his culture was a familiar social posture, an element of his awareness of his own social identity. But in his field research on Yap, any attempt to dissociate himself from Navy colonialism was compromised by the genesis and aegis of the Harvard CIMA expedition—indeed perhaps by the very existence of an American colonial regime. Certainly, for the Yapese, Schneider's association with the Navy was never in doubt; what was at issue was simply the terms in which it was to be construed. Thus the duality of rapport turned out to be more than that of the researcher's motivation; since for the Yapese, as for Schneider, rapport was an instrumental as well as empathetic matter. And it was ultimately they who forced upon his consciousness a deeper understanding of the dynamics of rapport in a colonial situation.

Yapese Adaptations to Colonialism, 1885-1947

The "field," of course, is an experiential haystack, and one hesitates to construe the problem as a search for a single needle. Rather, one finds a complex pattern whose coherence was largely motivated by Yapese understandings of Schneider's presence, Yapese interests in the encounter, and Yapese efforts toward structuring Schneider's relations. This need not be surprising, for the encounter was meant to be an interchange, and, obviously, in Yapese society, Schneider operated at a disadvantage. By the same token, however, the encounter presents historiographical problems closely analogous to those Schneider faced in his field experience. Events often had meanings for Yapese that were inaccessible to Schneider, although in some cases he was later told by close informants what had earlier "gone on." Events transpired at the intersection of two different schemata of cultural meanings, with both Schneider and the Yapese keenly aware of cultural difference. Furthermore, Schneider

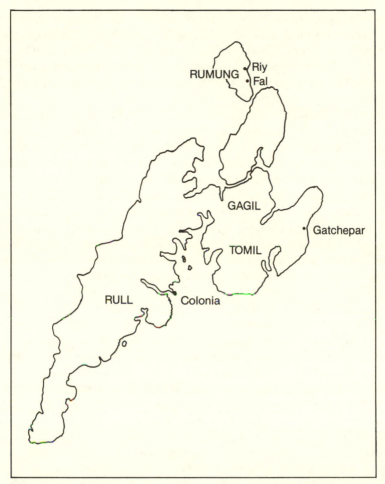

Map of Yap, including the northern islands of Rumung and Map, showing the major sites of Schneider's fieldwork.

was perceived as—and was—a significant political agent in the Yapese field of relations, and the information he received was deliberately controlled—differently, by different Yapese parties. Typically, he was "shut out" of consultations on how to deal with him, and his actions resonated politically in ways he often could not fathom, until he gained an orientation to local political situations. It might even be said that one of the most significant events of his fieldwork actually took place four months before his arrival, when the administration had destooled an impostor "king of Yap," and reallocated appointments to the chiefly offices that it recognized. Although Schneider remained largely unaware of it until he was already settled in a Yapese village, this event was a touchstone of Yapese understandings of his advent, and it crystallized the factional conflicts that defined the political context of his field encounters. With the benefit of hindsight, and of later understandings achieved by Schneider, we may explore the background of this event in the context of Yap's history of foreign rule.

On Yap, the colonial chronology begins in 1885, twenty-six years after the first European trader had landed there without being driven away or murdered (Shineberg 1971:274–78; Tetens 1958:12; Hezel 1975:6). During this interval, the small, reef-fringed archipelago became the center of the Caroline Islands trade; exporting copra and beche-de-mer (the sea slug highly valued in certain Chinese soups), it was visited in the 1870s by thirty foreign ships a year. Then Yap became the object of a dispute between Spain and Germany. Spain claimed absentee sovereignty on the basis of the Bull of Pope Alexander VI in 1493 and its role in exploring the region in the early sixteenth century; Germany, which unlike Spain carried on a substantial trade, argued that no sovereignty claim was valid without *de facto* occupation (Brown 1976; Hezel 1983:8, 306–9).

The dispute came to a head in August 1885, when two Spanish galleons landed at Yap to unload a governor, priests, soldiers, oxen, riding horses, and flags, as well as stones to build a jail, a governor's residence, and a proper church. For their new capital, christened Colonia, the Spanish selected a defensible islet guarding the mouth of Yap's central harbor. But just as they were planning a ceremony for taking possession, a German warship raced into harbor with full canvas spread and steam; its crew debarked, planted a flag, and claimed the islands for the Kaiser. Johann Kubary, who witnessed these events, reported that the "dumbfounded" Spaniards "knavishly" raised their own flag later that night, but lowered it in the morning and sailed back to Manila (quoted in Müller 1917:5–6). When the incident nearly precipitated war between Spain and Germany in Europe, the dispute was submitted for arbitration to Pope Leo XIII, who affirmed Spanish sovereignty, but enjoined Spain to grant German traders full, unprejudiced rights of access (Brown 1976:99–163; Hezel 1983:312–13; Townsend 1930:116–17; Pauwels 1936:18–19).

The Spanish administration is of more interest for what it failed to do than for what it did. To preserve Spanish "honor" in upholding its claim, Madrid was content to administer the islands at a loss, supporting missionization but not mercantile expansion. Importing Filipinos for their garrison and Christian Chamorros as domestic servants, the Spaniards had little need for native labor and were thus inattentive to Yapese chiefs (Oca 1893; Hezel 1970a, 1975; Christian 1899; Salesius 1906:156).

This changed when the Germans took over in 1899: maximal "utilization of the earth," and "above all" of its native people, became the final cause of administrative policy (quoted in McKinney 1947:96). To facilitate exploitation, the District Officer, Arno Senfft, initiated "public works"—including planting of coconut palms; building roads, piers, and a canal; and constructing a causeway from Colonia to the main Yap island—all of them undertaken entirely with drafted Yapese labor. The workers were paid in valuables earlier expropriated by the administration, and discipline was enforced by a drafted native police force and by monthly visits of German warships. Obviously, Senfft required considerable "help" from Yapese leaders, and he created a system to hold them accountable in taxation, labor recruitment, and other demands of the administration (McKinney 1947:76–77; Salesius 1906:159).

Senfft was well aware of basic features of Yapese political institutions. He knew that different kinds of Yapese "chiefs" exercised different kinds of authority, and that three main chiefly offices were recognized in every village. He understood the preeminence of the three centers, Tomil, Rull, and Gagil, and that alliances linked together villages that were not geographically "contiguous, but rather interspersed among the others over the whole" of the Yap Islands (Senfft 1903:57–59). But as these institutions were too indefinite and resistive to be efficiently controlled, Senfft regarded them, quite correctly, as impediments to exploitation. Irked by chiefly tabus impeding labor recruitment, he attempted radical measures—including forced interisland migrations—to hasten a day when "the power of the chiefs, based on nothing but superstition, [would] be broken" (quoted in McKinney 1947:107). Thus the system of "official" native chieftainships that he instituted in 1900 or 1901 was not intended to be a homologue of indigenous political structures; it was rather the familiar, two-tier "district system" employed throughout the German colonies (76).

Territorial groupings being easier to conceptualize and administer, the units of this system were defined by boundaries drawn on a map: 106 formal villages, each with a single "village chief," grouped in eight territorial "districts," each with a single "district over-chief" (McKinney 1947:76). The system did take into account one aspect of indigenous Yapese polity, inasmuch as the eight village capitals were those generally cited as "most important" in precolonial and Spanish reports (Miklouho-Maclay 1878:42; Tetens & Kubary 1873:85, 93; Oca 1893:266–67). This apparent congruence may have been a factor in the later impression of foreign observers that Senfft's system as a whole reflected the indigenous one (Yanaihara 1940:195–96, 223, 264–65; OPNAV 1944:67; Murdock 1948a:16; Schneider 1962).

Indeed, each of Yap's first four ethnographers, in German, Japanese, and American times, had to rediscover for himself the separate existence of indigenous Yapese political institutions (Müller 1917:132, 242, 254, 330; Yanaihara 1940:223, 263–66; Useem 1946:16; SFN). Whereas the common pathology of colonial administration is that indigenous offices become redefined when their occupants are drafted into the colonial framework, Yap's indigenous institutions were well defended against such subversion by the native cultural logic of chiefly authority. Indigenous political relationships were not constituted as relationships between people or groups of people but as historically sanctioned relationships between pairs of places, or land estates. Thus Yapese myths are mostly stories of initiatory progressions between places, beginning at superordinate locations and passing to subordinate locations; the specifics of the progression—what moved, how, why, and when—indicated (or were deduced from) the customs of the relationship between those places, which was spoken of as a "pathway" (*tha*) between a pair of land estates. The alliances were networks of pathways, for which the Yapese image was a string fishing "net" (*nug*), held up by one of the knots. People acted politically as representatives of land estates, speaking with the voice of a particular land estate; "they keep saying," Schneider reported, "that it is not the person but the land" which has authority. A "chief," (*pilung*, literally, "a strong voice") exerted authority in "remembering," or calling upon, the myth-historically sanctioned relationships between his estate and others; as offices, the chieftainships always referred to land parcels (SFN: 637, 670; cf. Müller 1917:242, 245; Lingenfelter 1975:25, 77–80; Labby 1976:94–113; cf. Parmentier 1987). When a person was chief to two land estates, he was understood to speak for either one or the other, depending upon the context. Similarly, where a person occupied simultaneously a colonial and a Yapese office, the two chieftainships remained distinct—separate capacities of action sanctioned in different lands. In the case of the colonial chieftainships, this land was the colonial capital, to which the district chiefs were summoned monthly to receive orders from the administration, which then travelled outward along pathways radiating from Colonia. Populated by foreign officials and heavily Christianized Chamorro compradors, Colonia, the islet, was clearly a place of foreign customs; from the perspective of Yapese it was not even a part of Yap (SFN; cf. Kirkpatrick & Broder 1976:201; Marksbury 1982:24). Hence, its "voices"—the colonial chieftainships—were seen as "customs of the foreigners" (SFN: 1206): a view continually resubstantiated by the uses to which they were put.

For themselves, then, the Yapese explicitly recognized the sanction of the colonial chieftainships as an extension of the power (warships) of the foreigners. But fearful in general of contradicting foreign opinions, the Yapese had good reason actually to promote foreign misunderstandings of the colonial offices. In the indigenous context, the highest chiefs were sacred figures, often aged and largely immobile, whose dignity was ill-served by running errands for the foreigners. The foreigners, for their part, wanted foremen and not oracles, and preferred to deal with Yapese who were able to speak their language; most of Senfft's appointees had been high-middle-level only, younger figures in local Yapese hierarchies (Müller 1917:254, 228, 330; Yanaihara 1940: 264; SFN). Whereas foreigners saw these men as active, executive authorities,

the Yapese saw them as messengers, bearing messages from Colonia; in practice, colonial chiefs returned to consult with their indigenous chiefly superiors,
who convened councils to chart responses to the initiatives of the administration (SFN; Useem 1946, 1947:1). Ultimately, this interposition of communal
deliberation between colonial order and implementation strengthened Yapese attempts to minimize foreign interference—which may account for Yap's
reputation in German, Japanese, and American colonial circles as the most
"stubbornly resistant" and "primitive" society in all of Micronesia (Peattie
1988:89; OPNAV 1948:44; Salesius 1906:161; Yanaihara 1940:125; Japan 1928–
37; Weller 1949). In foreign eyes, the principal sign of enduring "backward-
ness" was native loincloths and bare breasts. But for Yapese, the maintenance
of loincloths and grass skirts was deliberate resistance; by order of their chiefly
councils, Yapese wore Western clothing only on visits to Colonia (SFN).

In Japanese times, the emphasis was on settler colonial expansion, and
Yapese lands were expropriated for plantations run by Japanese nationals
(Yanaihara 1934, 1940; League of Nations 1928–37; SFN). But the focal point
of antagonism between the Yapese and the Japanese was the dramatic acceleration of Yapese depopulation. Regularly, beginning in 1924, the Japanese
delegation to the League of Nations Permanent Mandates Commission was
criticized regarding the "alarming" danger of "extinction" of the Yapese native
population (PMC 1931:80, 1924:11, 1928:204, 273, 1929:49–50, 1930:65, 211,
1932:109, 119, 1933:91–92, 1935:142–43, 201, 1936:191, 1937:120, 135). Nevertheless, the upshot on Yap of these manifestations of international sympathy
was a redoubled administrative effort to wipe out Yapese "age-long evil habits,"
and two separate series of Japanese medical studies, in each of which over
four-fifths of the indigenous population (men and women) was subjected to
forced genital inspections in notoriously semipublic settings (Japan 1928:204,
1929:145–46, 1936:114–16; SFN:704, 941; DS/[CK] 10/7[–11]/47). Amid suggestions that the "utilitarian" administration policy was in fact "to leave the
natives to dwindle naturally and let the Japanese immigrants fill their place"
(Yanaihara 1940:298, 1934), Japanese officials apparently convinced themselves
that "psychologically, the natives were absolutely indifferent to . . . their extinction" (League of Nations 1933:91–92; cf. Harris 1934:283–87).

But obviously no one was more concerned about depopulation, ultimately,
than the Yapese. And *they* based their theories on the empirically formidable
premise that the Yapese people had been numerous before the coming of the
foreigners (Müller 1917:9; Useem 1946:6; SFN:12–14, 363, 606–7, 668–69,
876–77, 916–20). From this perspective, Japanese "counter-measures" were seen
to be part of the problem, inasmuch as most of them interdicted practices
viewed by Yapese as specifically necessary for successful reproduction. The
major fertility rituals of the islands' ceremonial calendar were branded licen-
tiousness and were prohibited, and the administration instigated "physical

drills" at which Yapese chiefs were forced to bow before Japanese health officials
and were beaten and insulted for hygienic violations (Japan 1929:140–42;
SFN:976). One can readily appreciate why Yapese chiefs sought to insulate
themselves from foreign contacts; and because the highest chiefs controlled
magic that was believed to promote the fertility, their insulation was a particular communal preoccupation.

The power to promote fertility was concentrated in Tomil, one of three
"paramount centers" of Yapese sacred and political life—each consisting of a
nucleus of leading villages heading up an islands-wide alliance net (Lingenfelter
1975). Beginning in the mid-nineteenth century, and with greatest zeal during the Japanese era, Yapese did their best to insulate the central precincts
and leading figures of Tomil from deformative foreign contact; by design, it
was the "least foreign-infiltrated" of the three major alliances (SPR: Carroll/DS
[1950]). Precisely because its preeminence consisted in a sacred authority over
the well-being of the whole of the Yapese world, Tomil served as a place of
mediation for conflicts generated elsewhere—usually in the rivalries of the other
two centers: Rull and Gagil. Much of the dynamic of Yapese-foreigner relations was driven by differences in the response to foreigners at Tomil, Rull,
and Gagil.

Of the three, Gagil was the most actively opposed to foreigners. What
made this opposition possible was that the traditional basis of Gagil's power,
although significantly eroded, was not demolished until relatively late in the
period of Japanese administration. Gagil's alliance net extended to the farthest of the Central Caroline Islands, several hundred miles to Yap's east, providing a source of native valuables whose distribution on Yap itself maintained
and mobilized alliances with numerous villages (Miklouho-Maclay 1878; Tetens
& Kubary 1873; Müller 1917; Lingenfelter 1975; Alkire 1980; Lessa 1950a,
1950b, 1962; SFN). Of these valuables, only one type (common pearl shells)
was traded widely by Europeans, leaving intact Gagil's monopoly on the distribution of new tokens of the others, while obviating a reduction in their
value through foreign-trade-induced "inflation." At the center of an "empire"
that in precontact times extended to the Mariana Islands, Gagil chiefs saw
the encroaching foreigners as a threat to their own power well before Europeans settled on Yap; in the early eighteenth century they engineered the
murder, on Ulithi atoll, of the first European missionary to enter the Carolines region (Hezel 1970b:218–19, 1983:58; Lessa 1962:351, 362).

A century and a half later, Gagil's historic opposition to foreigners determined the pattern of European contacts on Yap. Welcomed as potential allies
against Gagil, Europeans began to settle in Rull villages in 1862, fully thirteen
years before they were accommodated by Gagil (Tetens 1958; Hezel 1975; Kling-
mann & Green 1950:224, 242–43). True, in these early years, pearl shells pro-
cured from Europeans powered a revitalization of Rull's alliance network,

leading to a civil war with Gagil in 1867 (Tetens 1958:97). But as the foreign trade settled into the pattern it retained for half a century, the traders, beginning with the American David O'Keefe, usurped the Rull chiefs' monopoly on new "stone money" from Palau, significantly undercutting the traditional bases of Rull's power (SFN:948; Hezel 1983:263–89). Chiefs of Rull became the closest Yapese associates of German and Japanese officials; and in Rull, unlike in Tomil or in Gagil, the highest-ranking indigenous chief—holding its most sacred land estate—had by the end of the German period assumed the colonial district chieftainship (Müller 1917:249; Yanaihara 1940:124–25; Lingenfelter 1975:163–65).

The great vulnerability of this arrangement became apparent when this chief died, and Rull's highest council selected a successor. Their choice was overruled by the Japanese officials; upholding the presumably "hereditary" character of the colonial chieftainships, they policed the successsion using a rule of patrilineal primogeniture (Yanaihara 1940:214; Lingenfelter 1975:165). The Japanese appointed a man named Ruwepong, the son of the deceased chief, who "stubbornly refused to capitulate" when the council asked him to resign (Lingenfelter 1975:165). Fluent in Japanese, Ruwepong became the foreigners' agent, and the leader of an emergent faction of Japanese-educated younger men, who favored the adoption of certain foreign "customs" (Yanaihara 1940; SFN). But even he still obediently consulted with Rull's council, until shortly after the transition to American naval rule (SFN).

That transition followed a period of unprecedented privation. During World War II, the Japanese drafted Yapese labor to build airstrips, bases, and a long defensive seawall (SFN:25, 884; Gilliland 1975:10; Peattie 1988:251–53), and they garrisoned the islands with over 6,000 Japanese troops, bringing the total foreign population to well over 7000, compared to a Yapese population of less than 2,500—down from an estimated 28,000 to 34,000 before the islands' foreign penetration (Richard 1957:I, 19; II, 50; III, 566; OPNAV 1948:59; Hunt et al. 1954; Schneider 1956:6). When the Americans besieged Yap in 1944, and people went hungry, Ruwepong provided food to the family of a Gagil man named Fani'ch'or; after the surrender and repatriation of the Japanese, Fani'ch'or supported Ruwepong in dealing with the Americans. Ruwepong had anticipated that the new American commander would inquire as to the identity of Yap's high chief, and made sure that he and Fani'ch'or stayed close to Colonia; the commander inquired, Ruwepong stepped forward, and Fani'ch'or confirmed that he and Rull were "number one." Fani'ch'or was appointed the new district chief of Gagil, and the Americans invested Ruwepong with a novel title: hereditary "king of Yap" (SFN:28, 76, 157, 1036; Trumbull 1946:60).

Yapese initially accepted this arrangement as simply an extension of the patterns of the Japanese era. Having proven themselves adept at manipulat-

Exchanging Japanese yen for U.S. dollars on an outer island. (From Richard 1957:I, 231.) In the late 1940s, Yapese often told dollar-peddling American visitors that they had seen Spanish reals, German marks, and Japanese yen each come and go (Wright 1947:149; Weller 1949:127).

ing foreign rulers, Ruwepong and Fani'ch'or were convenient front men for long-protected indigenous chiefs, who were fearful that the Japanese might return, and in no hurry to step forward. When the Americans held an election in the summer of 1946, the "hidden powers"—Yapese councils—instructed voters how to vote, and Fani'ch'or and Ruwepong retained their colonial positions. But by the end of the following summer, the arrangement had broken down (Lingenfelter 1974:56; SFN).

It was by then evident that the Americans were there to stay, and some Yapese attributed to the American "gods" the reversal of the depopulation trend in the spring of 1947, when births officially outnumbered deaths (SFN: 13, 28–29, 986; DS/[CK] 10/7[–11]/47; HYE: Andrus memo [7/47]). In contrast to the Japanese, the Americans distributed substantial material benefits through the chiefs—relief food, lumber, tinsheet, and a "whale boat" for each district. This made the colonial chieftainships viable as independent power bases, and soon Ruwepong and Fani'ch'or had "ceased to consult" with the older chiefs and chiefly councils (SFN:28, 158). Ruwepong had the ear of naval officials, visiting journalists, and congressional inspectors; he even told villagers how to answer the queries of a visiting anthropologist, John Useem (Trumbull 1946:60; Useem 1947:1; SFN:945–46, 1091). But the Japanese-style punishments Ruwepong threatened in order to gain compliance with naval orders invariably failed to materialize under the American administration. In this context, he and Fani'ch'or were increasingly resented by other Yapese, particularly in Tomil and Gagil, which Ruwepong claimed were subordinate to Rull (SFN; Useem 1946:16; cf. Richard 1957:I, 752). Redress, however, could only come from the Americans, and the attempt to gain it brought on the crisis that Schneider unwittingly stepped into on his arrival on Yap.

During the spring of 1947, a young naval officer, Lt. Kevin Carroll, was approached by a man from Tomil and told of Ruwepong's usurpation. As manager of the boat pool, Carroll was one of only three or four Americans (of a population of forty) who regularly ventured from Colonia to areas of Yapese habitation (Richard 1957:II, 210–11; SFN: DS/[CK] 10/7[–11]/47). Launching a private investigation, he conducted interviews throughout the islands, and in June took advantage of the departure of Yap's naval commander to instigate a reapportionment of the administrations's chiefly appointments.

Carroll had become aware that in terms of the "native system" the colonial districts were "artificial units" and the colonial chiefs a mere apparatus of "effective intermediaries" (SPR: Carroll, "Yap Traditional Government, Special Report," 6/8/47). But he nevertheless handled the reapportionment as if the two systems could be made to correspond: that is, he sought to appoint to colonial chieftainships the occupants of corresponding "traditional, hereditary" Yapese statuses. His decision may have reflected the statements of informants, who responded to his questions about hereditary criteria by advancing claims couched in an idiom of hereditary customs (SFN:159, 162, 1036). He may also have been influenced by his primary ethnographic reference, the *West Caroline Islands Civil Affairs Handbook* that Murdock's unit had prepared in early 1944. Largely based on German and Japanese reports, it presented the district system as "aboriginal," the village and district chieftainships as indigenous offices, and chiefly succession as "patrilineal" primogeniture (OPNAV 1944:67). But for whatever reason, Carroll maintained the colonial system, and while he did not insist that succession be patrilineal in all cases, he did attempt to link colonial chieftainships to specific chiefly land estates, thus partially subverting the traditional Yapese accommodation to colonial power. In the process, Fani'ch'or was replaced, and Ruwepong exiled to distant Guam—along with Fani'ch'or's young acolyte, Gumedak, whom Carroll arranged to have attend a school for native teachers (SFN).[2]

Four months later, in September, when the four Harvard anthropologists stopped in Guam for two weeks on their way to Yap, they were put in touch with Gumedak, who gave them lessons in Yapese. Managing for himself a two-month holiday from the school, Gumedak travelled back to Yap with

2. At David Schneider's request, I have used pseudonyms for his informants who were promised confidentiality, both in the text and in direct quotations from the field notes; the pseudonyms were drawn from a list of "typical" Yapese names contained in the report of a German

the anthropologists (HKP: DS/CK 9/27/47; SFN:28). To the Yapese, it appeared that the American anthropologists had returned Gumedak from his exile, thereby renewing the hopes of Fani'ch'or's faction in Yapese politics – into which Schneider was thus inadvertently and unknowingly plunged.

Adapting Research Strategy to a "Delicate Situation"

Schneider's first field site was Gatchepar, the leading village of Gagil, to which he and Stevens proceeded after a brief stay in Colonia. They went to Gatchepar largely because there they could work with Gumedak, the only interpreter then available on the islands – and because Carroll, now the officer for island "internal affairs," had recommended Gatchepar over Gumedak's nearby home village, apparently to lessen the political consequences of Gumedak's working with the anthropologists. Certainly, from Carroll's perspective it was best that the anthropologists study in Gagil, which with his changes had become the political showcase of the administration. Tomil had asked to be exempted from his new appointments policy, and there the colonial chief was merely a "delegated spokesman" for the chiefly council; Rull was in disarray in the wake of Ruwepong's ouster, with four chiefs installed successively in the first nine months alone (SFN:996, 1036–39; SPR: Carroll/DS [1950]). In Gagil, by contrast, the apical alliance leader was a strong "legitimate chief," and he had agreed to replace Fani'ch'or in the colonial district chieftainship. Thus on October 15, Schneider and Stevens boarded a naval landing craft for a short journey around the coast to Gatchepar's pier, while Hunt and Kidder stayed in Colonia to prepare the anthropometric survey and the census they later took to every Yapese village (SFN:17).

Although Gumedak was under orders to take them from the ship to Fani'ch'or, the two ethnographers arrived in Gatchepar while he was teaching in the Gagil school, and were greeted instead by an agent of the Gagil chief. When *he* then summoned Gumedak to interpret for the Americans, the dealings were brought decisively within the chief's political orbit, and it was with the chief, Fithingmau Niga, in consultation with the village council, that Gumedak thereafter cleared arrangements for the visitors' care and contacts (SFN:17, 83–84, 168). Such mediation was essential because Yapese houses were dispersed through the lowlands jungle, and it was not thought politic to "barge

---

colonial officer (Senfft 1903:53). I have, however, retained the actual names of Ruwepong, Fani'ch'or, Fithingmau Niga, and Fithingmau Tulug, considering them historical figures in the public realm; and to facilitate comparison with cited and other materials on Yap.

around" on people's land (SFN: DS/CK 10/14/47). Gumedak thus became a linguistic and social lifeline. Dressed in black shoes, bright yellow socks, and a loincloth cut from a Navy signal flag, he was clearly someone "caught between two cultures" (SFN:19, 189). But it was this very ambiguity that made him useful to the anthropologists, as he led them from early days of inactivity and helplessness—occasioned by intense disorientation, dehydration, failure to eat, and heat prostration—out to increasing participation in the social world around them. Schneider called Gumedak "a gem and a paragon of all the wonderful things on earth" and planned to "pump the hell" out of him before he returned to Guam in mid-November (19–20).

What they "pumped out" of Gumedak was Yapese language and ethnographic information, on a range of topics thought appropriate to their "delicate situation." On the morning he and Stevens emerged from their initial culture shock, Schneider declined to attend a meeting hastily called by the high chief's son—who planned to lecture "everybody" on Navy sanitation regulations—insisting to the Yapese that he and Stevens were not "tied in with [the] navy" (SFN:20). Although the Yapese postponed the meeting, and made no further overt references to the anthropologists' presumed Navy connection, Schneider soon grew anxious again that he and Stevens might subtly be evoking colonial fears. Confiding to Kluckhohn in late October that it had taken time to "realize" that they did not have "good rapport yet," since "everyone" they encountered was "so generously polite," he was worried because "people still don't understand any satisfactory reason for our presence"— that "issue" being further "confused" by "the unfortunate coincidence that we are camped on the former japanese police station." To minimize the "risk of an irrational association with Japanese times," he and Stevens were avoiding potentially controversial investigations, including mapping village lands, which in that period had been "a police function" connected with land expropriations (HKP: DS/CK 10/28/47).

Since it required "guesswork" to know which subjects might be "touchy," they were focussing interviews for the moment on Yapese "kinship" and "old yap culture"—which Kluckhohn had recommended as "impersonal" topics useful to "win the confidence of the tribesmen" (SFN:20, cf. 303; HPM: DS/CK 1/20/48; Kluckhohn 1945:111). For Schneider, in those first weeks, gaining the confidence of the Yapese became the "paramount and immediate problem," as he and Stevens learned in Gatchepar of Fani'ch'or's intrigue with Ruwepong, of Carroll's political changes, and of how they themselves had "catapult[ed]" their interpreter Gumedak "back into politics" (HPM: DS/CK 1/20/48; SFN:28, 76–77, 156–63). And because Schneider felt that honesty and "good will" were incompatible with colonial power, the "ever present risk" of "being 'frozen out'" by the Yapese became a "twenty four hour" anxiety.

He decided, therefore, to devote his "major reflective efforts" for the "next two or three months" to efforts to ameliorate "the problem of rapport" (HKP: DS/CK 10/28/47; HPM: DS/CK 1/20/48).

From a Yapese perspective, it must have seemed evident that the anthropologists had to be somehow associated with the Navy. Back in Colonia, on the first Sunday after their arrival, Gumedak had seen them conferring with "mr. carroll," who had then accompanied them on their preliminary visit to Gatchepar, to secure the permission of the Gagil chief (SFN:6–8, 17, 1033; DS/CK 10/14/47). They had Navy food, Navy tents, Navy furniture, and Navy equipment, and they were periodically resupplied from Colonia on Navy vessels. Thus when Schneider insistently denied being "part of the Navy," Gumedak seems suddenly to have had a revelation—that the two anthropologists were in fact *superior* to the Navy: "His whole body bloomed into wreaths of understanding, smiling and agreeing motion. His eyes got slightly damp, and with heavy emotion he announced, 'oh, you very rich, very very rich'" (20). Schneider, who did not normally regard "rich" as a compliment, interpreted it as flattering polysemy ("rich used twice now as synonym for smart, wise" [11]). But since Gumedak aspired mightily to political recognition by the Navy, a more likely gloss would probably be "powerful"—the more so, since the ethnographers could requisition from the Navy what they wanted and insistently promised that on their departure they were going to talk about Yap to "the people of america" (231, 312)—that is, to some higher authority back in the United States. If the Navy then was "rich," Schneider and Stevens were "very very rich."

In this context, kinship inquiries had a different meaning for Yapese than for Schneider. In the investigations the preceding spring that had led to the political changes, Carroll had asked "specifically" for genealogies, traditions, rules of succession, and old customs (SFN:162, 1036–39). Schneider, of course, was primarily interested in the abstract kinship structure. But on Yap, kinship terms were used only in third-party reference, not in address, and thus had to be clarified by first eliciting the genealogy of an individual; a month after his arrival, Schneider still had "yet to hear a kinship term enunciated" except in response to his questions (141). To the Yapese, this method— the classic, Riversian "genealogical method"—seemed very like the foreign "custom" for legitimating chiefly appointments, the more so since Schneider's interviewees were mostly chiefs, their relatives, and their rivals (1037). Because the method highlighted the political significance of possible alternative classifications, rules, and customs as the basis of competing claims, it is not surprising that there was unusually great "confusion" even over "names" and "ideal patterns" (137) —the Yapese were waging political battles on the turf of principles of social organization (SFN). For Schneider, however, the fact that "no two" of his many "lists of terms" agreed simply meant at this point that further investigation was needed, and his vocabulary in the subject was strengthened by its frequent exercise, making it the first register of Yapese language that he controlled with any fluency. Soon when discussing "kinship terminology" he "talk[ed] directly to the people," and this line of inquiry in fact became his "extra special rapport punch" (231, 243).

Yet while motivated partly by a desire to enhance communication, in the colonial context kinship study tended to confirm Yapese impressions of the anthropologists as colonial agents. This became evident early in November, when the first typhoon in thirteen years struck the Yap Islands (Schneider 1957b). For the anthropologists, whose tent was the only dwelling in Gatchepar to blow down, the storm occasioned a six-day-long distraction, during which they waited for the Navy to deliver replacement tents from Colonia (HKP: DS/CK 11/13[-17]/47). But for Yapese, typhoons were sorceries of vengeance, invariably caused by the magic of indigenous chiefs of exceptional power; this one, it was believed, was Ruwepong's revenge for his dethronement (SFN:509, 689, 1119). And if Ruwepong could conjure a typhoon, his power was not merely an extension of colonial forces, but also had a specifically Yapese substance. In this context, the ambitions of Ruwepong's political allies were renewed, and Fani'ch'or, who thus far had had no contact with the anthropologists, made bold to approach Stevens, speaking with him briefly, while Fithingmau Tulug, the high chief's son, watched with evident "hostility" and "caution" (SFN:97, 147).

Given that Carroll had linked the colonial district chieftainship of Gagil to the sacred land estate of Gagil's apical indigenous chief, for Fani'ch'or to have had a claim upon the colonial office required setting aside the special custom by which the sacred estate was held only by members of a single matrilineal group (or *genung*).[3] Because of depopulation, only four male members of this matrilineal group were alive in 1947: the current very aged chief; another very old man; one who was too young; and another currently a stu-

---

3. The topic of the *genung* is worth a separate comment. Consisting generally of a group of people who claim descent from the same womb (at broadest range that of a mythical ancestress), its more particular constitution has been described by Labby (1976), Kirkpatrick & Broder (1976), Lingenfelter (1975), and Schneider (1984). Since its characterization by Schneider (using technical terms like "clan" and "sib") is itself at issue in the present discussion, I gloss it below as "matrigroup," a deliberately nonstandard usage, though one which conveys its essentially matrilineal constitution.

The evidence strongly suggests that before 1860 the custom of reserving ownership of a land estate to the members of one matri-group was unique to the apical land estates in Tomil, Gagil, and Rull. In Rull, to judge from recorded genealogies, a putsch displaced the *genung* owners close upon the heels of the arrival of white traders (Müller 1917:252–54; Yanaihara 1940:124–25; Lingenfelter 1975:112, 163–65). In the early stages of Schneider's fieldwork, he accepted Carroll's opinion that a transition from matrilineal to patrilineal succession was now imminent also in Gagil— although in the interests not of Fani'ch'or, but of allowing the competent Fithingmau Tulug to

dent in the naval medical school on Guam, to which he had been "railroaded" the year before by Ruwepong and Fani'ch'or. In the effective absence of available successors, some Yapese favored suspending the special inheritance custom at the death of the very aged current chief, for whose position jockeying had already begun (SFN:3, 152–60, 1039). But the special custom had broad political and social significance: looking backward, it established the connection of current leaders, wielding powers over the islands' fertility, with founding ancestresses who had first imbued the land with productivity; looking forward, any movement from matrilineal to patrilineal customs would necessarily be a highly politicized issue. In this context, Stevens recorded that Gumedak made the ethnographically "surprising statement" that matri-group exogamy was "no longer" in effect (100).

Fithingmau Tulug, however, apparently sensing that a putsch was in progress, paid a visit to the anthropologists' camp on November 9. As "a hush fell" among other Yapese onlookers (SFN:104), he pointedly recounted a myth of his father's chiefly land estate, which traced the origin of the estate's special matrilineal customs to founding journeys of ancestral female spirits (150–51). That evening the waters rose, signalling the onset of a second typhoon, and Schneider and Stevens were ushered to shelter in the house of Fithingmau Niga (78, 146). By now Schneider was convinced that he and Stevens were considered "chief-changers and chief-makers" (SFN:149, 163); back in Colonia, he had interviewed Carroll about the spring investigations, and he now appreciated why the Yapese "insisted on classing us as Navy." Realizing also that no single faction had a monopoly on "political scheming," he concluded that Fithingmau Tulug's "motivation" in offering shelter in the second storm "definitely" reflected a "fear" of American-instigated political repercussions (152, 161–62). In this context, that night Schneider "broached" to Tulug his intention of transferring to a new fieldsite on Rumung, the politically less consequential northernmost island of the archipelago. Appearing "anxious" to keep Schneider and Stevens in Gatchepar, Tulug responded by inviting them to move permanently to his father's land estate (217). But Schneider now felt that too many "mistakes" had already been made in Gatchepar, and to accept Tulug's invitation would make it impossible to start afresh (HPM: DS/CK 1/20/48).

Things came to a head one week later at a farewell party for Gumedak,

succeed his father (SFN:143, 154–60). However, Carroll later decided to uphold the older custom, and he appointed a member of Fithingmau Niga's matri-group to the colonial district chieftainship (844–45, 1039).

Similarly, on the topic of the districts (whose boundaries were redrawn late in the German administration), and in the description of Yapese adaptations to colonial domination, there are subtleties of analysis that I have not been able to incorporate in this work, which is governed by narrative requirements of relevance to Schneider's experience. I hope to explore and clarify these issues further in future publications.

who after failing to persuade the anthropologists to keep him on Yap, had now to return to the naval school on Guam. Although to increase his prestige as the Americans' "friend" Gumedak had sought to hold the party at their camp, it was held instead at the house of a fellow schoolteacher in his home village, near Gatchepar (SFN:74, 115). There, when Schneider and Stevens were seated at a "japanese-style" table and honored by a special dish of chicken, served only for them, Schneider's engrained egalitarianism led him to refuse it. Undaunted, Gumedak lectured other Yapese on how to treat "'My friends the americans'": "'anything they say, hurry up give them'" (117, 125, 128). The Yapese men eventually "got crocked to the gills," and they began to caress each other and sit upon each other's laps; later, when the anthropologists had put away their cameras, Gumedak danced drunkenly "like a burlesque queen," rubbing his "exposed" penis against the "erect" foundation pole of the house. Although older men assured the anthropologists that this was just innocent "fun," Stevens reported that his "guts turn[ed] over," and he had a "mild tussle" with Gumedak to avoid being seated on his lap (122–23, 178–80; HKP: DS/CK 11/13[–17]/47). Writing to Kluckhohn, Schneider remarked on Stevens' "overreaction to the homosexuality," which "shocked and disgusted and upset him like nothing else"–indeed, to such an extent that Stevens soon returned to Colonia and ceased to keep regular field notes (HKP: DS/CK 11/13[–17]/47; SPR: DS/Gorer 6/4/48; HYE).

For Schneider, however, it was the first half of the party that was the more profoundly disturbing. He had been "acutely uncomfortable" in the role of "exalted chicken eater," and he had shuddered at Gumedak's self-aggrandizing proclamations: "'I, gumedak, only one friend to americans'" (SFN:125). And what had made the schoolteacher's display still "more difficult to take" was that Schneider had felt that Gumedak would have been "happy," and their relationship "superb"–"if I could only act like a japanese policeman" (115–16). To avoid *that* compromising situation, Schneider would definitely remove himself to Rumung, where he planned "to keep dissociated" from "Gumedaks circle–the school teachers, the ingratiators"–the "japanese educated kids," who "dont know from nothing about their culture" and who therefore "necessarily invoke external assistance–first the japanese, now the americans" (128, 142, 224, 229).

"I Am like Your Father"–"You Are Chief over Me"

Later, when Schneider spoke of his Yap fieldwork, he mostly referred to his six months on Rumung, a small, hilly island of just 130 people, and the farthest point on the archipelago from Colonia and the Navy. He chose it because he had heard it was the part of Yap "least touched" by Japanese and American "influence" (HKP: DS/CK 12/4/47). But Yapese, unlike foreign administrators and anthropologists, did not consider Rumung properly a part of "Yap" at all, classing it instead with the distant Central Carolines, as an "outer island" vassal within the Gagil alliance "net" (SFN:463–67). To mainland Yapese, Rumung's dialect was inferior, its culture less sophisticated, and its people generally "blacker"—although Schneider could detect no difference (239, 463). In this colonial situation within a colonial situation, Rumung chiefs took orders not only from Colonia but from Gatchepar as well.

The chiefly spheres of authority were based on a complex set of divisions, the legacy of an era when the Rumung islanders probably numbered 1,500 (Schneider 1949). The six remaining villages were grouped into a northern and a southern alliance; each village had sections, and there were both village and section chiefs. The three most important kinds of chiefs, found at both levels, were associated not just with lands but also each with a different age-grade. Thus the most active type was also the lowest, the "chief of young men," who led young men's communal work and discharged all save the most important political tasks requiring travel far afield. In contrast, the "chief of lands" was older, higher, and less vigorous; expected to mostly "sit"—consult, deliberate, and speak—he was the "strong voice" of the village in its political dealings and directed the activities of the local chiefs of the young men. He in turn deferred, however, to the *pilibithir*, or "ancient voice," an extremely aged figure, soon to join ancestral spirits, who sat immobile and remote from mundane business, but was consulted in exceptional matters as a voice of "custom" and mediation (Lingenfelter 1975; Labby 1976; SFN). Besides Fithingmau Niga, who, though off in Gatchepar, was *pilibithir* of all Gagil, there was no single chief on Rumung with island-wide authority. The two highest villages were Fal and Riy, which headed up the southern and northern alliances. But which was higher was controversial in late 1947.

Traditionally, it had been Fal. Although Fal's old men's house was no longer standing, in principle it served the entire Rumung island, and its meeting ground was the mythic terminus of pathways from Gatchepar (SFN:444). Riy, however, was then the terminus of pathways from Colonia, which passed through Lirau, Riy's chief of young men, who was also the colonial district chief. First appointed by the Japanese, Lirau had retained the colonial office under American administration, distributing Navy "gifts" so as to build up Riy's prestige (672). In his investigation, Carroll had learned that Lirau was subordinate, but the older chiefs were too old for frequent journeys to Colonia—and less resentful of Lirau's arrogance than they were terrified of the foreigners (467, 974–76, 1235). Thus in Colonia, and to the important constituency of Chamorro and Navy delivery men, Lirau was seen as the "chief of all Rumung" (218, 288). Schneider's arrival, however, shifted power to Fal.

Although as yet unaware of Rumung's internal politics, Schneider was de-

"A village chief [herein called Tannengin] posed in the manner of his choosing. His comb is decorated with two feathers; he holds his tridacna shell and brass areca nut pounder firmly; his heirloom necklace rests on his chest" (Schneider 1949:256). (Photograph courtesy of David Schneider.)

termined to arrange his move through Yapese, not colonial, channels; briefed by Carroll, he specifically avoided Lirau, and instead waited for a favorable opportunity to consult directly with Fithingmau Niga, who unhesitatingly arranged for two men to canoe him to Rumung. On Fithingmau Niga's instructions, they landed at Fal and first sought Tannengin, who was Fal's village chief of lands and the highest chief in Fal's old men's house. Marvelling that the foreigner had followed the traditional pathway, Tannengin asked how Schneider had known to ask Fithingmau Niga "where to come"—and, rhetorically, why had Schneider not gone first to see Lirau. That "seemed to clinch the whole thing," Schneider recorded in his field notes (SFN:217–23).

While Schneider was back in Gatchepar picking up his gear, Tannengin called a meeting of all the island's villages, at which it was agreed that Schneider would stay in Fal, but also be visited by "northern" people. Explaining that Schneider wanted to write down "on paper" the language and customs of Rumung, Tannengin reminded the young people that old customs were better recounted by the old men; the young could teach Schneider language, learning English in exchange (SFN:240, 911–12). Early in their first conversation, Tannengin had requested that Schneider "teach the children american," and although Schneider had resisted on the grounds that speaking English would slow his progress in Yapese, Tannengin was adamant (232–33)—because (as he later confided to Schneider) it would lessen Rumung's dependence on any one person, like Lirau, for mediating relations with the island's newest colonial governors (845, cf. 19, 84, 806–8).

When Schneider's boat arrived on December 10, Tannengin was ready to start the "school rumung" and "school merikan." Schneider put him off, while straightening up his camp and typing field notes from the move, until early on the third day, when Tannengin positively insisted that they begin. They worked thence daily from morning to midnight: Tannengin, his Riy counterpart, other old men, and several teenagers. When working on "the language of Rumung," Schneider would venture a word and all the old men would correct him, until Tannengin shut them up with his official toothless version. Studying "merikan," they sat with notebooks, reviewing the Yapese words Schneider had recorded on cards (SFN:240–41, 245, 256). Although Schneider hoped that this "artificial situation" would in time break down, he was pleased by his warm reception, which seemed "open and of common interest"—not "servile and all out to fence me in with kindness" (235, 241). One welcome sign was that Rumung women did not avoid him, as had all but the very oldest and very youngest in Gatchepar (223). There was thus breast-feeding to observe, and behavior of and toward young children—mainstay Freudian data Schneider thought critical to his aggression research. When a sexually mature young woman, "mystified at the typewriter" on which he was recording notes, actually ventured unafraid into his tent, Schneider broke the flow of his notes to type: "this moment . . . marks a milestone in rapport" (279).

This did not mean that rapport problems had vanished, but his experience in Gatchepar suggested to Schneider that it was a question of alliance. On one hand was Tannengin, a repository of local cultural knowledge and a connection to other old men, to whom everyone openly deferred. He was himself dignified but deferent, spoke calmly but was heeded, and under his wing, conforming to Yapese proprieties, Schneider did not "make people" avoid him (SFN:314). To side with Lirau, on the other hand, would likely "antagonize the old men"—and also yield "unreliable" information (231, 311). Educated in Japanese schools and ashamed of Yap's "bad customs," Lirau had insisted, one night when Tannengin was not around, that Yapese kin terms worked the "same way" as kin terms in America (231). It was satisfying when Schneider's more traditional conception of Yapese kinship was vindicated by the older chiefs. But the social logic of his position was nonetheless disquieting to his egalitarian American predispositions.

He was able to dismiss the problem of associating with "high ranking people," which might have shut him out from "the other side," if that side had been like a "union membership" and the chiefs like "union big shots" (SFN:313). But he worried that the "other side" seemed in fact to be full of "deviants like Gumedak and Lirau," whom in a different political or cultural context he might have empathized with or pitied (311). Here, however, they were humiliated—"fawning"—colonial subjects, asking Schneider which of their traditional customs to change "immediately"; and here Schneider himself was the hoped-for instrument of their colonial ambitions (232). Wrestling with this situational and cultural ambiguity produced pages of catharsis, self-justification, and self-doubt:

> [H]ow conservative the ethnologist becomes out of his own culture, how he despises the radicals, the break-aways, the deviants. Or just ethnologist schneider? . . . no doubt in my own culture I'm a bit of a deviant too. the judgement is not mine to make but I keep catching myself making it. (231)

On Yap, "the deviants" seemed "exploitative": Lirau had announced to him, "'I am chief of rumung'"; in Gatchepar, Gumedak had mistranslated, inventing demands on his own behalf (234, 250). Even so, it was "wrong" to simply neglect "gumedaks kind of deviant," if only because such behavior was a patterned deviation from Yapese cultural norms (314).

> [A]nd I must admit that gumedaks exploitation outraged and surprised me a little bit unduly. After a bit of consideration I realized that I must be living in some kind of fantasy world of my own to expect to come and plump down in the midst of a going concern like yap culture and expect them to rush around to my tent all day long and every night supplying me with exhaustive accounts of everything from their hidden fantasies to the technique of mat weaving. I know what's in this field trip for me; what I didn't stop to consider was what was in [it] for the yap people. Hence I should not have been either outraged or surprised that they had motivations too and that theirs should be no less selfish than mine. . . . I'm here to pump them dry and to get home; the more I pump the happier I'll be when I'm home. In other words, how different is my

behavior from gumedaks or liraus and on what grounds my outrage (except for
the frustration it would cause me to come here and learn nothing). (301–2)

It seems a clear and out and out case of being either a human being *or* an ethnologist, and you take your choice knowing you cant be both simultaneously.
In this situation of course we choose the latter—but only . . . after we know
there is no other way out of it and only . . . towards the end of the field trip. . . .
So far as is possible, that is, and that qualification is a very big one since in
the end the whole job is like walking into an unfamiliar dark room the dimensions of which are only vaguely known and the distribution and disposition
of obstacles and items which aren't obstacles is quite unknown. You just tread
gently so as not to bark your shins and so as not to ruin the china. (303)

Already sensitive to this in Gatchepar, he and Stevens had been "over-
generous" with gifts "to the point of eccentricity," and they had "carefully—
clumsily of course, but as carefully as we were capable of—explored before
we entered, felt out before we questioned, [and] sensed before we conducted
inquisitions" (SFN:302–3). In Gatchepar the "situation" had been "almost wholly
a blank," and it had "always seem[ed] to hang by a balance so fine as to be
tipped at the slightest misstep, the initial contact with a people." At least here
in Rumung, Schneider felt he was no longer "wandering around in the same
pitch black room":

Here, although the room is still largely unlit, corners and spots have been illuminated. I know this kind of deviant, and I know what to expect, and I know
what two alternative courses of action would ultimately mean for the field work.
I know, that is, that if I give lirau the attention and the response he wants tannengin will just kind of evaporate and I'll not be able to find him and he'll be
afraid of me. And tannengin is my contact man with the old men. . . . That
one fact, that tannengin is my contact with the old men, means more to me
now than anything I can think of. (312–13)

Tannengin gave Schneider a month to learn the language, then pressed
on to the "customs" of each Rumung village (SFN:312). Clearly taken aback
by the "grueling pace they set," Schneider wanted to "procrastinate on the
ethnography" until he had better fluency in Yapese (265, 432). But Tannengin
had already arranged for old people to visit, by rank order of the villages,
and on January 5 they began with "the customs of the village of Fal" (406ff.,
431). Ultimately, Schneider sought to probe social psychological dynamics
that turned on "their definitions of right and wrong," on their cultural "phras-
ing of sex roles," on Yapese ways of treating children, on Yapese "compulsions
and obsessive behavior," and on the Yapese "life-cycle pattern of intimacies"
in its "ideal" formulations and actual, behavioral instantiations (HYE: DS/CK
1/20/48; SFN:306, 320, 378). By temperament and situation, he was of course
interested in politics, which also meant learning what his position was and

who were his informants. But for Schneider, an odor of the museum clung to "esoteric subjects like myths," of which the old German ethnographer Müller had collected "enough to fill a boat"; Schneider merely spot-checked that these were "accurate and authentic" (152, 400). In contrast to Schneider's modernistic psychological ethnography, Tannengin was himself more inclined to an old-fashioned, early Boasian salvage mode. Now that under the American administration culture change was "voluntary," which "customs" to change and how much to change them was widely debated throughout the islands. Most young people — by no means only "Gumedak's circle"—were sympathetic to a movement then underway to relax the segregation of eating by rank; but this change was opposed by many chiefs, and even by old men like Tannengin who favored changes in many areas (Stevens 1949; SFN). Tannengin applauded Schneider's "little speech" about cultural relativity: American customs were good for Americans, but "customs of american people not so good for yap people." Recalling Gumedak's earlier emphatic disagreement, Schneider was pleased (76–77, 249).

However, a vision of "culture change" as loss only began to approximate the view of Tannengin, who had seen the changes worked by four successive colonial administrations. Annually performing ceremonies that no one else remembered, he regarded the forgetting of customs as an actual threat to Yapese survival, because words to be spoken to the spirits were "lost and cannot be recovered." Lamenting depopulation—the people had died around him—he wondered if the spirits of fertility had not already "all gone away from Yap" (SFN:606, 918, 1130). Tannengin deplored particular colonial policies that had severed lines of cultural transmission. Under the Germans and Japanese, young men had been removed to Palau to mine phosphates; under all four administrations, pacification had ended wars in which few were killed, but which also had been occasions when the young sought skills and magic from their elders. In attempting to "solve" depopulation by accelerating "civilization," Japanese teachers had in fact ordered children not to listen to their parents and had beaten them for conforming to "bad" and "crazy" Yapese customs (606–7, 1608, 1634–35). Against this long experience of cultural dissolution, Tannengin felt a strong appreciation for the remembering power of "the paper"—which was Schneider's project—and was sorely anxious about what was recorded on it.

Back in December, on the first day of the "school rumung," one of the words they "hit on" happened to be a kinship term, and Schneider decided to pursue the "whole [kinship] business again" more systematically. The next afternoon, after a break, Tannengin arrived at Schneider's tent "perturbed, sweating, and standing up" on his bad leg, and said he'd given Schneider "the wrong names for the kinship." Pointing to Schneider's file box, he urged Schneider to redo the word cards, but soon "got twisted up and confused" again, and they let it go until evening when Schneider took the genealogy of Tannengin's estate—"and the terms straightened out mightily" (SFN:242–43). But in fact confusion continued as to the meanings of the terms, which (as in Gatchepar) were never spontaneously employed (251–53, 256). Indeed, because none of his informants seemed to "know the terms off hand"—"they get confused, correct themselves, argue among themselves"—Schneider wondered "how much functional relevance" the "kinship relationship" actually had (461). But it was hard to say, because similar problems arose in researching customs that were still practiced. Tannengin also came back anxious to "fix" the paper soon after they had discussed the areal division of responsibilities between Fal's two chiefs of young men, and on various issues different informants would defend different answers to Schneider's questions (431, 461). At this point, however, Schneider was inclined to interpret such disagreements optimistically in "freudian" terms, thankful that their "ego-involvement" in "different theories" led to a concern that his "record be right" (403).

And at this point Schneider still thought that "freudian" topics were his primary ones. When a typhoon on January 13 forced him to take refuge in the nearby house of Fal's *pilibithir*, he saw it as a wonderful opportunity to observe family roles: "the baby," he wrote, was the "most important character" in his research, and the "merit of typhoons" was that he could "see them in people's houses" (SFN:478). The issue of focus surfaced again shortly thereafter, when a summons from Kidder brought Schneider to Colonia, where the Harvard "team" discussed a letter from Douglas Oliver and their advisors, who (except for Kluckhohn) had met in Cambridge for an end of year "stocktaking." Reminding the four students that Harvard had accepted "substantial grants from the Navy," the letter quoted the group's March 1947 proposal to Murdock, which had emphasized research on the causes of depopulation (554; HKP: "Committee"/HYE 12/47). Although professing surprise that depopulation was a "binding obligation" rather than merely a "pregnant" research "suggestion," each of them submitted by letter a brief report (HYE: Kidder/Scott 1/20/48). Schneider's was the only one not to mention depopulation, focussing instead on language and rapport, which still required close attention to informants' "motivations" and "expectations" (HKP: DS/CK 1/20/48).

These again became problematic on his return to Rumung Island. When he took a break from his "godforsaken typewriter" to accept an invitation to go fishing with some Yapese men (SFN:531, 543), his young assistant "insisted" that the small fish he caught be given to Tannengin. Sharing it with the *pilibithir* of Fal, Tannengin the next morning handed Schneider an ear clip and a shell (570). Schneider at first saw the gifts as artifacts, which he had in fact requested from Tannengin for the Peabody Museum (573). But clearly the Yapese, too, were concerned with a problem of rapport, which in their version was to bring Schneider, however ambiguously, into the sphere of Yapese relationships. Two days later, at a village distribution of Navy relief food, Tannengin announced that Schneider had caught a fish and given it to the *pilibithir*, and that he in turn had given Schneider an ear clip and a shell. Schneider was now a "person of Fal" and henceforth would confine his "benefits" to Fal's villagers; Tannengin repeated several times that Schneider was "no longer [to] give tobacco to the people of Riy" (580–82). That he had somehow been "appropriated" seemed "clear" to Schneider—and in fact to Yapese as well (582).

That night a house was burned in Fal—a traditional method of Yapese vengeance. It was apparently ignited by Ralop, who as the son of Tannengin's dead older brother was the likely heir of Tannengin's land estate—the old chief being a widower without living sons (SFN:632, 689). But because of an old grudge, Tannengin and Ralop were not on speaking terms, and the burned house belonged to Mo'on, whom Tannengin had, though still only informally, adopted as a replacement heir (443, 618, 653, 909). Although Yapese played down the significance of the fire to Schneider, it had destroyed the exceptionally valuable *gau* necklace Mo'on had probably meant to give Tannengin, in exchange for his land, to seal the adoption. The very next day Mo'on's wife's father died in a village on the main Yap island, to which Schneider's informants went three days later for the funeral (626, 632–34).

Discouraged from attending, Schneider stayed in Fal and "got the kinship terminology cleaned up." He was pleased that "it really pans out nicely," and thought it "the 'polynesian' type of cousin terminology" (Murdock's Hawaiian type), though he was still "not certain" (SFN:626; Murdock 1949:223). Tannengin, the week before, had hit on the idea of having him use a deep but politically inconsequential genealogy for establishing the terms and had brought Schneider to a very old man in one of the lower-ranking villages (SFN:605). Even so, when Schneider reviewed the genealogy with Tannengin and Fellan, his second main informant, there were important disagreements. As the "higher" of Fal's two chiefs of young men, Fellan was Tannengin's extremely devoted helper, despite the fact that, following the Japanese injunction not to follow his parents' "crazy" customs, he had married within his matri-group—which, by traditional belief, should have led to the deaths of his offspring (607, 668). Of the thirty-four terms Schneider collected on the genealogy of the old man, Tannengin and Fellan, in separate interviews, disagreed on nine of them—all of which were of course affinal relations (621). Fellan refused to let Schneider inscribe his version on "the official paper with the more than supernaturally validating machine"—not until first checking with Tannengin (609, 620). In the end, then, the terms were Tannengin's, and on this basis Schneider drew a neat kinship diagram (622)—which looked "of a piece" and "that's what counts" (626).

Soon after, and late at night, Tannengin announced that he would tell Schneider about Yapese customs of marriage exogamy—apparently a ploy to get rid of Fellan, for whom the topic was embarrassing (SFN:668–70). When

Schneider and his second main informant, herein called Fellan, seated together in native posture at Schneider's tent site on Rumung. (Photograph courtesy of David Schneider.)

Fellan quickly left the tent, Tannengin, with "great conspiratorial mien," slipped Schneider a present, urging him to tell nobody; it was one of the valuables of his estate, and he was dispossessing Ralop of it (674). "The pot boils," Schneider entered in his journal:

> Why does tannengin give me these invaluable presents? Why does he do it in that conspirator's way? Why does he stay until 4 a.m. tired and exhausted as he is? I don't know the answers yet. But I would hazard this guess; there's something very valuable . . . that I'm giving tannengin by our relationship. (675–76)

Sensing that Schneider was not getting the point, Tannengin organized an interview at which he spoke of the father-son relationship. On Yap, a son fished for his father in exchange for learning customs; the father, "a sort of teacher," fed the child when he was small, and then when he was old, he was fed by his grown son (693). Schneider had been feeding Tannengin fairly regularly since the typhoon, which had destroyed Tannengin's house, and he had caught the fish, which cemented the relationship. Ever concerned with "distinguishing real from ideal," Schneider checked Tannengin's account with other informants—without yet consciously realizing that in this case *he* was the "real": that he was becoming Tannengin's heir unapparent (694–95).

During this period, the two continued to see delegations of old men, and Schneider began a project to map village lands throughout Rumung. In Gatchepar, no one had spoken to him of chieftainships as having "sanction" in land "estates," as Schneider had seen noted in "older" ethnographic sources; the people of Gatchepar being more accustomed to foreign inquiries, informants had simply portrayed chiefly succession as based on customs of heredity—save for Gumedak, whose account Schneider had discounted because of his "miserably ambitious position and our relationship to him as political assets" (SFN:156). But on Rumung, where he had seen informants illustrate chiefly customs by drawing sketch maps of village lands, it dawned on Schneider that "land" was "a cornerstone to yap culture" (718). Now the delegations from the villages listed customs by estate, and Schneider went out with young men and mapped estate and village divisions.

The work on customs of village lands crystallized the problem of conflicting testimony. Different Yapese knew (and were expected to know) about different aspects of "their culture," and when they disagreed head on, there were often ulterior motivations. These were not so easily grasped in the context of an ostensibly "neutral" subject like kinship. Fellan knew perfectly well on which terms he differed from Tannengin—he listed them for Schneider before Schneider's interview with the old man. Fellan was in effect using Schneider to propose changes to Tannengin—who rejected them because he regarded Fellan's marriage within the matri-group as an abomination. But Schneider had simply thought that Fellan was just "not sure" of the terms. In the case of customs, however, the political logic was less culturally obscure; it came out vividly in discussing the chieftainships of Riy village.

Each of Riy's two sections had a land estate sanctioning a chieftainship of lands. But the question was which section chief was the chief of the whole village. From the perspective of Fithingmau Niga in Gatchepar, who was the relevant indigenous legitimating authority, the Lanturow section was higher because it had "long ago" been higher, and Gatemangin, its chief of lands, was the chief of lands of Riy. But the local "traditional" logic had it that the Lendri section was higher, because in Lanturow there was no longer a meeting ground (an abode of village-protecting spirits). What gave the local argument force was the personalities involved. Gatemangin was a senile old man who was rumored to have broken serious tabus in having had sexual intercourse with his wife while preparing her body for burial. Folebu, chief of the Lendri section, still had his wits, and he therefore acted as the village chief in most actual contexts, while Gatemangin was treated as *pilibithir*. In practice it was possible to sustain diplomatic ambiguities, but writing things on paper forced the issue of competing claims—all the more so as paper, to the Yapese, was a primary symbol of foreign power. Since Spanish times, foreign officials had posted codes and pointed to rulebooks; and recently the Navy had issued its chiefs appointment letters, with Carroll telling Yapese, "You are a chief because you have a paper" (SFN:1084; OPNAV 1948:104). Schneider's often-posed question—Who is really chief?—could only be asked by an outside observer concerned with problems of legitimacy, and as an American who was known to have been sent by Fithingmau Niga, he himself was associated with not one but two recognized higher authorities.

The drama unfolded throughout January and February, from the first session on Riy customs to the completion of the Riy map, and the one thing to emerge with clarity was that Riy "functioned" without a consensus. True, whenever Gatemangin was within earshot, everyone agreed that Lanturow section was higher and that he was chief of Riy (SFN:437–47, 730–31). But when he departed, responses varied significantly. His main opponents were Folebu and Lirau, who pressed Schneider to "correct" all papers listing Gatemangin as chief (555). Tannengin and Fellan initially supported Gatemangin—until late January, when it had become clear that Schneider did not report back to Fithingmau Niga (437–47, 555–56, 575, 689). When the two then changed sides to that of Lirau, this forced Schneider to reevaluate Lirau, who his investigation had also revealed was "rightly and properly" the chief of young men in Lanturow. Indeed, given the precedence of age criteria, it was actually somewhat ambiguous which estate "really" sanctioned which section chieftainship, so that Lirau also seemed Gatemangin's likely successor (434; cf. 555–56, 731): "The picture I had sustained previously of him as an interloper, a climber . . . just didn't hold together as well as I had thought it did." Perhaps his arrogant manner was "something called 'personality' first and culture a little later": "what the hell did I really know for sure?" (434). Bringing together politics and personalities, the "Infamous Affair of the Chieftainship of Ri Village" ended with Schneider beset by methodological doubts (730).

In a sense, he was rediscovering the Kluckhohnian problem of "typicality." But as the tabular roster of Riy chiefs and their chieftainships in his dissertation would later suggest, he still felt an imperative to adjudicate in matters of "basic" ethnography (Schneider 1949:250–52). Here, as with his investigation of kinship, it was the problem of "fixing the reliable" that transformed a preliminary study of backround ethnography into a prolonged, ego-invested "affair" (SFN:459). But in this context, kinship seemed actually all the more attractive, because there Schneider's model of alternative viewpoints was simpler and apparently apolitical.

[In studying customs] you take the essence of the interview and re-do it with tannengin and gatemangin. . . . And find what: find that its essentially slightly different . . .; what do you do then; you say, well, either . . . we warped the

responses in writing them or the different people in different statuses gave different responses. Not equipped with a coin to toss, you are left with a messy sack.
To take one is dishonest; to take the other equally so. To take both leaves a
quandary. To write it off as a mistranslation seems shamefully [a] waste. You
then think, am I anthropologist or what; can I come home and report well look
here I got some confusing stuff. [No,] a scientist gets the facts. . . . Well, the facts
are confusing. So we take things which can be "established" fairly easily; the
yap term for mothers brother is what; you ask around and no matter what you
get its good, for it shows either [a] that they know, or b) that they dont know,
or c) that they dont use that term or d) that the kinship system is a little secondary to other things and has somewhat less social importance on yap than
is generally found elsewhere. thats good, clearcut, sizeable. (460)

But in psychological contexts, where Schneider *was* concerned with idio-
syncrasy as itself a theoretical problem, there were anxieties about his rapport
relationships, about their attendant anxieties, and about his limited insight
in evaluating subjective phenomena in the Yapese context. And not long after
revising his earlier "mis-estimates" of Lirau (SFN:436), he also reevaluated
Tannengin—although here significantly at a psychodynamic rather than a conscious methodological level. While in Colonia to resupply, he had insomnia
on his last night there and stayed awake until dawn, thinking about home:

> particularly of my father. It was immediately afterward that I went through the
> simple and almost infantile fantasy of catching a very big fish to give to tan-
> nengin. With that fantasy came the phrasing which I have learned in yap and
> heard so often; when the child is young the mother and father feed it and care
> for it and when the child grows up it feeds and cares for the father and mother
> and they teach it the customs of yap.

That morning he returned in a small boat to Rumung, fishing the whole way;
and when it arrived in Rumung waters he hooked a twenty-five-pound barra-
cuda. He did give it to Tannengin, who was indeed pleased. It fulfilled "the
yap formula to the letter except for the 'actual' kinship relationship": "So that
my 'bias' is clear, then, I record that apparently I've managed to identify my
chief informant with my father" (779–80).

A week later, after Schneider had given Tannengin a parcel of rice and
sugar, Tannengin surprised him by making the transference reciprocal: "You
have no father here and so I am like your father. You always give me food"
(SFN:859). Tannengin proceeded then to teach him of the fertility rites for
girls—first menses ceremonies that had only recently been revived after having been banned under the Japanese, as one of their "solutions" to the problem of depopulation. Clearly, here was another "milestone" of rapport: "I first
claimed [Tannengin] for a father surrogate and now he has claimed me for
a son" (SFN:859). But given the nature of Schneider's research, this identifica-
tory impulse seemed methodologically ambiguous. Aware that his relation-

ship with his "real" father had been stormy and complex, Schneider might have searched back in his notes for emergent patterns of rebellion against Tannengin. He had in fact been acutely sensitive to the old man's slightest repulse and jealous of his loyalties to other Yapese. Already in early February, Schneider had exploded with resentment on overhearing Tannengin tell other Yapese to move on past a point Schneider was having difficulty grasping: "never mind, never mind, he will go back to american after a while and we will not have to worry about explaining these things to him. just say you dont know." Likening Tannengin to the hustlers "who inhabit Kleins 14th street," Schneider had lamented then that to them he was only "a sign of their prestige": Yap was "not one of those anthropologically idyllic places where people are just dying to tell you of their customs" (697–98; cf. 279, 926–27, 1046).

All the while, however, Schneider had been growing doubtful of the Freudian explanatory paradigm. Back in America, an anthropologist who had been to Yap (John Useem) had suggested that male homosexuality might have been the cause of depopulation. Gumedak's party had seemed to confirm this, and Schneider even suggested to Kluckhohn a theory along these lines (HKP: DS/CK 11/13[–17]/47; SFN:106–7, 215–16). But before receiving Kluckhohn's reply, which urged analytic caution, Schneider regretted getting "jerked" on that "bum steer," attributing his "hypersensitivity" to male affection to his "own miserably american backround" (HKP: CK/DS 12/5/47; SFN:306–7). Because ultimately the Yapese "seemed to pan out on the heterosexual side if anything," the party more appropriately posed the problem of "defining sexuality in terms of [Yapese] culture" (306–7). Schneider continued through December to think that he could deploy "psychoanalytic theory usefully," when "some other people, try as they might," just could not "seem to make it pay" (318). Observing that Yapese men frequently adjusted their loincloths, he had wondered if this was not a way to assuage "castration anxiety" (275–77). But by February, he had begun to question such Freudian musings: when his assistant feared a centipede, he rejected "bug-equals-penis" as "wrong"—and in retrospect "the castration anxiety" was "wrong" as well (666). His "entire collection" of psychological observations began to seem "quite useless," because each observation was "limited to the incident as I saw it," while "what it mean[t] to the participants"—"why they acted as they did"—was with "a few scattered exceptions" almost entirely "unknown," without "a picture of the culture against which to view the episodes" (HYE: DS/CK 1/20/48).

There was a parallel disillusionment in Schneider's ideas on method. Back in Gatchepar, he had had some firm commitments, and he had outlined plans to administer Rorschachs and Thematic Apperception Tests, at least to all the children in Gumedak's Gagil school (SFN:31). But those plans were put on hold as his contempt grew for Gumedak and the other progressivist school teachers; in April the tests were "still hang[ing] fire" (HKP: DS/CK 4/25/48).

Like any standardized research technique, they required the standardization of a specific social situation, and for "rapport reasons" Schneider was wary to exert "force" or impose his "will" (SFN:242). Later, however, writing to Gorer, Schneider said he did not "believe" the tests were "such super-hot stuff," but he could not yet "afford" to proclaim "out loud" this "heresy" (SPR: DS/Gorer 7/7/48).

So what remained in March of Schneider's psychological "method" were simply his own human entanglements, epitomized by Tannengin's—or was it Schneider's?—patrifiliating counter-transference. Here, Schneider was ambivalent—such entanglements were "so difficult to manage" (Schneider 1949:14)—even when accomplished in the Yapese terms that were the object of his research. Writing to Kluckhohn two days after Tannengin's moving acknowledgment, Schneider confessed to "less and less hope of getting the psychological materials" (HKP: DS/CK 3/8/48); soon after, he sent Kluckhohn a revised thesis proposal, which reformulated the "aggression" problem with greater emphasis on ideal patterns. Kluckhohn and Gorer had "both agreed," before he left the United States, that "more than a bit of spectacular baby watching" was needed for his research, and feeling now that the "time allotted" was too short for achieving adequate psychological "coverage," Schneider took "pains" in the new prospectus "to exclude matters psychological." For "rational and irrational reasons" he wanted "to become a professional anthropologist, and not a deviant psychoanalyst or a stranger in someone else's domain" (HKP: DS/CK 3/11/48).

Although Kluckhohn did not respond to this comment, he could well appreciate the self-doubt that was projected in the fieldnotes when Schneider saw Yap's deviants as interlopers, climbers, rebels eager to be co-opted, and despised them as illegitimate, opportunistic, and misguided. Kluckhohn knew also of Schneider's worries over postwar teaching prospects (HKP: DS/CK 8/6/47), and of the anxieties aroused when he himself had encouraged Schneider to send his masters thesis on Yir-Yoront dreams to psychoanalysts like Géza Róheim, who had responded critically to the treatment of psychoanalytic questions by a person not yet analyzed (HKP: DS/CK 9/3/47; DSI). Finally, Kluckhohn himself had sent a letter that crossed Schneider's in the mail, expressing concern that while Schneider's "stuff" had "all the 'reality' . . . of clinical [psychoanalytic] data," it had a similar "'intangibility'," an "elusive, non-scientific character" (HKP: CK/DS 3/3/48). It was surely not lost on Schneider that what Kluckhohn praised without qualification was his "filling in of the ideal patterns" of "kinship and political organization"—there he was bringing home "some real meat" in a "first-rate" set of notes (HKP: DS/CK 12/5/47, 3/3/48).

In the same mail came a follow-up communiqué from Oliver addressed to all four students, affirming that the "emphasis" on depopulation was indeed an "obligation" that they had assumed "in accepting the Navy funds," and that their individual thesis projects should therefore remain only "secondary considerations." Oliver also made it clear to Schneider and Stevens that it was a part of their particular obligation to the Navy to develop a "clear picture" of "Yap social organization"—not like *Naven*, in which Gregory Bateson "had not carried out his responsibility to his readers," but more like Reo Fortune's *Sorcerers of Dobu*, which although offering perhaps "too pat an analysis," at least "tied together [the] material into a coherent and plausible system" (HPM: Oliver/Stevens 3/4/48). Nor was this admonition really news to the anthropologists, who had already heard "from various sources"—presumably other CIMA anthropologists—that they had better "fill the categories of the cross cultural survey," or their "findings" on depopulation would not be "acceptable" to Murdock (HPM: Stevens/Oliver 1/20/48). At the beginning, Schneider had apparently thought he could do this and at the same time investigate "subjectivity." But another feature of the CIMA program was its compressed, inflexible schedule, designed to hasten the reporting of anthropological "findings" to the Navy. Now, forced to choose how he would allocate his last three months, Schneider grew "depressed" by the thought that he needed another year (SFN:907). In justifying to Kluckhohn his decision to drop psychology, Schneider had in fact pointed to the "priority" of collecting "the standard and full ethnographic materials" (HKP: DS/CK 3/8/48)—as defined in Murdock's *Outline of Cultural Materials*. The institutional context of Schneider's research was thus not intellectually neutral, but channelled his interests and energies in a Murdockian direction.

Institutional pressure was magnified by group dynamic processes. Although his "teammates" Hunt, Kidder, and Stevens left Schneider alone with his "psychology," where ambiguity was known to be endemic, they were all anxious to satisfy Murdock as to kinship and social structure, where positivistic preconceptions suggested that data were either "right" or "wrong." In a Murdockian epistemology, the team format conduced to "truth," since the likely source of error was thought to be the investigating subjectivity; while Schneider by no means accepted this, he did feel a competitive impulse. Despite the fact that he thought that he had got the kinship firmly fixed in February, he rechecked his work twice more when the "half-assed ethnography" of his fellows produced differing versions, raising the spectre of being contradicted by a "vote" of "three to one" (SFN:1067, 1236, 1239, 1338). The first recheck was crucial, for it in fact reoriented his interpretation of the importance of the matrilineal customs. Working from Tannengin's information, Schneider had decided in late January that "descent" was "strictly" matrilineal (624), but by late March Stevens was disputing this finding. When Kidder and Hunt brought their census and anthropometric survey to Rumung, Schneider designed a questionnaire and interviewed every Rumung adult, taking people aside after they had finished with Kidder's census. Tannengin had warned him that a person's matri-group was considered intimate and kept a secret, and Schneider was aware that even asking about this was a step away from "human being" toward "ethnologist." But it was "so easy" in the census context "to do a survey on a larger sample," and the focus of concern shifted to what to do with the results (1267). Having been exhorted to do so by Tannengin, "at least 50%" divulged the name of their matri-group; but the other half (including Fellan) professed ignorance – leaving Schneider in a quandary. Although still "very very unsure," he was inclined to think that people had "answered 'honestly'" – the mixed result implying then that the matri-group was of "little functional importance." He had, after all, had the older men's consent, the interviews had been "private," and by now he had "good rapport" (1048-68, 1265-67).

Schneider continued to record psychoanalytically relevant observations, but by mid-April his psychological ambitions had come to seem dubious and impractical. Their most valued product and promising vehicle was the rapport he had created with specific informants. But now, abruptly, the integrity of that rapport seemed compromised by colonial associations. The moment of revelation – the second pivotal moment of his fieldwork – was another drunken party, on April 21.

Because his informants had been clamoring for whiskey, pointing out that Stevens "gave" it, Schneider had brought two bottles back from Colonia (SFN:1158), and the celebration began at the house of Tannengin's daughter, where Tannengin, growing tipsy, invited Schneider "to stay forever in Fal." He could bring his wife, or take a new one, and Tannengin would give him land – thereby making Schneider his heir, his real (not "fictive") Yapese son – and "everyone would come" to build him a house. There were "much worse fates," Schneider thought then, than "living the rest of my life in Fal" (1158-59). But when the party moved later to Schneider's tent, the mood shifted as well. Drunk now on beer, Tannengin averred that Schneider was "high high high up" and "he and all rumung people were . . . low low" – the lowest Yapese class. When Schneider demurred, Tannengin was furious. Continuing, he "bellowed" that Schneider was "his chief": "I, Dave . . . , was chief over him" (1163).

Himself still sober, Schneider "writhed" at this revelation (SFN:1168). The traditional Freudian terms of transference had been cut and repasted in a new colonial arrangement: his "father" was his subject; the son was the authority, and all of his rebellions had been ridiculous, if not malicious. Although Schneider had been mindful of his own exalted status, with Tannengin his rapport had seemed at worst hierarchically ambiguous, the old man retaining superiority as a father and Yapese chief. But when Tannengin now called him "chief over rumung" (1163), Schneider had to reevaluate his romantic egalitarian notions. His marginality in America was meaningless to the Yapese; there *was* no simple community of the oppressed (1174–77; SPR: DS/Gorer 6/4/48).

As in Gatchepar, so on Rumung: his rapport techniques had only raised his colonial status higher. At a canoe-launching in December, wanting desperately "to be liked," Schneider "got tight" on toddy to avoid the appearance of "alignment" with the Navy's blue laws for natives. But if "refusing to drink" meant Navy, drinking also had implications: if Schneider broke laws willingly and with impunity, it could only mean that he was above them. To every subsequent ceremony, Tannengin had Schneider bring two bottles of beer, which he would insist that they drink at a climactic moment (SFN:315, 330, 582, 635–37, 898). Wondering "why tannengin ostentatiously drinks beer with me," Schneider noted in February the old man's "advertising" that "I am of even higher rank than the navy" in Colonia (636, 670).

The problem, for Schneider, was that what Tannengin said was true. His team's interim CIMA report, prepared in December, had come to the attention of Admiral Carleton Wright, with its "finding" that "all foreign people" could "leave Yap immediately," with no adverse effect on "the pattern of [native] life" (NAS6: CIMA Interim Reports, 1947–48). In late January, when Yap's naval complement was reduced to just nine men (HYE: Kidder/Scott 2/1/48), Schneider discussed these changes with his informants; they knew that his actions had provoked them (SFN:673, 764–65, 810, 840). In late March, when Admiral Wright visited Yap to supervise the deportation of the last Chamorros, Schneider went to Colonia, thereby confirming his involvement (Richard 1957:III, 156; SFN:844, 1072–75). He had also helped to get the Navy to cancel road construction, to which Yapese objected (336, 1312; DS/Carroll [n.d.]). It was obvious that he had great power—power which they lacked.

He also had great wealth, which, distributed for rapport purposes, posed in stark terms the limitations of rapport "technique." Because Yapese conceptions of social relationships highlighted exchanges of objects, Schneider simply had to be generous to be liked. But his largesse had repercussions. Funnelled primarily through Tannengin and Fellan, it elevated their position and that of Fal. Already in February, Schneider was conscious of the resentment of other villages; in March, Riy moved to "control" the Rumung visit by Kidder's CIMA census and the distribution of Navy lumber, in order to counterbalance the privileged access of Fal villagers to gifts from Schneider (SFN:810, 891). When Schneider gained permission for Fellan to scavenge a decommissioned Navy landing craft—for "my own evil ethnographic purposes," in order to see how the booty was later distributed—it was clear that his generosity could overwhelm any effort of reciprocity (1032, 1048–53).

During his speech at the April party, Tannengin had said that it was because "they had nothing" that the people of Rumung were "low," whereas

Schneider was "great and high" because he "had things"—"high" things—and "gave everybody everything": tobacco, prestige foods, "high [tools] from the [Navy] boat" (SFN:1163). Discomfited at being named "chief over everybody," and recalling the "earlier drunk with Gumedak," Schneider again objected to his imputed loftiness. In response, Tannengin began to debase himself, mustering incidents to prove his lowliness: he was not even chief, but only regent. Soon, he, Lirau, and Fellan were arguing passionately, each claiming that he of all was the very lowest (1163–64), and when the argument turned eventually to "aggressive" mutual accusations, one was made against Schneider for passing information to Carroll (1166–72). "The experimental administration of beer to a native population sure as hell" brought up "things" that were "not welcome" (1174–75). It marked the second (and decisive) turning-point in Schneider's fieldwork.

From that drunken party until the end of his Yap field stay, changes in Schneider's views of rapport crystallized a shift in the focus and method of his research, setting the lines of his future scholarship. Rapport, now that he had it, was suddenly onerous, a false grail. Far from opening up possibilities for empathetic understanding, it constrained him: he was "isolated" at the "center of a series of concentric rings" (SFN:1380, 1423). In the aftermath of the party, Schneider became "disgusted" by Yapese "greed" (1302). He now felt himself "scrounged off . . . mercilessly" by "selfish and grasping" informants; themselves "exploitative," they had "built" him into a "role of being exploited" (1422–24, 1603). No longer a wise father, Tannengin now seemed "just like" Gumedak, out for "a bigger share"; far from being deviant, Gumedak had been "typical" (1177, 1380). Complaining of the daily and nightly "conferences," once welcome in his tent, now Schneider wrote: "goddamnthemoneandall" (1372).

Such resentments cloud his field notes through May and June. Aware that they were in part his own "paranoid suspicions," he saw their compartmentalization in the notes as a constructive, cathartic process (SPR: DS/Gorer 7/7/48; SFN:1313). Still, he was growing anxious over the value of "all that material" which in March he had been optimistic might allow the correction of his evidence (HKP: DS/CK 3/16/48). Increasingly, it was becoming clear that the problem of "bias" was interactive, involving not only the selectivity of his observing subjectivity but also alterations that he induced in the objects of study: Yapese people. They were not transparent, and he was no "blank screen"; how they saw him had been revealed, layer upon layer, in a process by no means complete, and neither painless nor itself unreactive. He suffered insomnia and ceased to dream; what was he hiding from himself? Linking this "datum" in early May to uncertainty over his revised plan of research (SFN:1248), he wrote despairingly two weeks later that his aggression project was finally "up the creek": most of the aggressive behavior he had witnessed had been partly instigated by him (1399).

Left directionless, he turned to Murdock's framework—a decisive step, in retrospect, from anxiety to method (cf. Devereux 1967). The CIMA-issued *Working Manual* of Murdock's *Outline of Cultural Materials* now helped him to "think" and to "organize," Schneider recorded in mid-May, adding that he now "kicked himself" for having failed to bring his kinship notes from Murdock's lectures (SFN:1398–99). He used Murdock's theoretical vocabulary— the terms concisely defined in the *Manual*—in reconsidering his March interview survey on the matri-group. Adopting the Murdockian term "sib" for the group he had formerly called a "clan," Schneider suggested that its "minor importance" in Yapese "social structure" was "demonstrated" by the "fact" that half of his respondents had not known their "sib affiliation." Troubled about the facticity of this fact—the real "fact," he reminded himself, was that many had "answered 'i dont know'"—Schneider pressed Tannengin on the question of whether people had told "the truth." His suspicions were aroused by Tannengin's suspiciously emphatic confirmation (". . . as if there was actually some doubt . . . "), but Schneider dismissed them on the naïvely rationalistic basis that a "hypothesis" remained "legitimate" until explicitly "rejected" (1265–67). Clearly, Schneider was losing patience with the subtleties of interaction.

Although he made wry remarks on quantification—the "reporting of meaningless data with a statistical accuracy beyond reproach" (SFN:1370)—he began in mid-May to conduct four further surveys—polls on insanity, medical ailments, copulation, and criminal cases. He also deployed the one standardized "projective" psychological technique of his fieldwork, an adaptation of the Stein sentence completion tests. Tannengin wanted to teach about ceremonial and exchange, which Schneider was now "convinced" was a "central theme" of the culture; but although he felt it deserved "complete and detailed" treatment such as Bunzel and Benedict had given Zuñi ceremonial "business," time was "wasting," and he had done nothing on depopulation (1254). He began to interview women, whose victimized "tenderness" he now contrasted with the men's "coldly empirical a-morality." Although noting that his own "bias" was a sensitivity to "'injustice,'" Schneider toyed with a theory—later disproven demographically (Underwood 1973)—that young women sought to "delay" male-imposed "responsibilities of adulthood," and that the abortions they induced were a cause of depopulation (SFN:1402–5, 1582–90; cf. Schneider 1955; Hunt et al. 1954). The need to bring back something on depopulation also motivated Schneider's poll of the frequency of copulation—which unfortunately coincided with the opening of trochus-fishing season, when men were customarily enjoined from either having or discussing intercourse (SPR: DS/Gorer 7/7/48). The poll provoked resentment, and many from Riy refused to participate. But Schneider now "didn't care if the men got sore"; he was cashing in his chips by finally "risking bad rapport" (SFN:1422)—choosing, as he had predicted, to be "an ethnologist," not "a human being" (303).

Or, perhaps, "good rapport" and "bad rapport" seemed not so different after the party, when Schneider gave up trying to dissociate himself from the Navy and broke out of the isolation of those "concentric rings" by borrowing Carroll's Navy motorboat (SFN:1215–18, 1550–51). He did not forget, however, that it was the Navy that seemed to be the source of his rapport problems, and he launched his survey of criminal cases as an "investigation" of the administration, and Carroll in particular, in retaliation for having leaked to the Yapese word of some of his own "leaks" to Carroll (1551). Discovering that Carroll had inadvertently furthered Yapese intrigues with his jail sentences, Schneider in his investigation explored the politics of the American colonial administration (and although not carried to fruition, that investigation contributed substantially to the possibility of the present essay). Only the Americans, Schneider decided, saw Yapese customs as "fixed" rules; Yapese, among themselves, rearranged customs to suit circumstance. In fact, there was no determinate "traditional" order, and the more Carroll intervened in the attempt to "reestablish" one, the more he made himself the instrument of particular Yapese factions (1036–38, 1180, 1575ff.). Schneider himself had experienced something analogous, as his romantic expectations were undercut by limits enforced by the colonized Yapese; because no Yapese were politically "neutral" in the situation of domination, no real involvement—no rapport— could shut out these realities, save by invoking colonial power to silence their expression.

In this context, then, Schneider wrote to Gorer before his departure that in fact he had "good rapport," but no longer "labored under" the "misconception" that rapport was "like being loved" (SPR: DS/Gorer 6/4/48). True, he was still not reconciled to being defined by his gifts and "things." His informants' statements during the last days of his stay that they would miss him for his tobacco, coffee and sugar, Spam and biscuits, rice and beef stew, did not strike the warmest chord in Schneider's American cultural consciousness; liking him only for his gifts, he complained, they "de-personalized" the relationship (SFN:1604; cf. Schneider 1949:341–42). Having read Malinowski but not Mauss, Schneider had no confirmation, beyond his own uncertain experience, that the food gifts were the vehicles for fully authentic Yapese sentiments, making his rapport largely a relationship on their terms. Indeed, back in March, when Tannengin had likened himself to his father, Schneider had wondered if "love on yap" was not "an exchange of concrete objects" (859). And because such exchange in fact betokened love, the major "problem" of rapport from the perspective of Yapese was not honesty, as for Schneider, but reciprocity—or its breakdown in the face of Schneider's overwhelming stores.

The Yapese themselves solved this problem on the day before his departure, gathering at his tent in the early afternoon with gifts of watermelons, chickens, taro, coconuts, yams, and fish. Schneider was "disturbed" at the "unparalleled collection of perishables." But in speeches, his informants praised Schneider's generosity, and when later that night Schneider grumbled about the gifts' unportability, Tannengin—shocked—silenced Schneider with a final commentary on the dynamics of rapport: "But it is food! Everybody likes you!" (Schneider 1949:231–32).

Schneider flew to Guam on June 17 and was in New York on the twenty-seventh. A few days later, Carroll took over on Yap as the naval commanding officer, until he was transferred from the islands in October (SPR; cf. Gladwin 1979:245). At that point Ruwepong, who had meanwhile been pleading his case to the naval High Command in Guam, returned to Yap, where he and Fani'ch'or were soon afterwards reinstated (SPR: Carroll/DS [1948–50]). In August of the following year, the Yale linguist Isidore Dyen visited Fal village, and on Schneider's behalf presented five cartons of cigarettes to Tannengin. The old man had been living in Schneider's tent since his departure. Some months later, he passed away (SPR: Dyen/DS 8/21/49; Ramos/DS 11/26/49).

From Cross-Cultural to Native Categories in the Study of Kinship

Schneider was a romantic with a realistic, even pessimistic eye. Far from ideal-izing his field experience, he regarded it as troubling. The Yapese surveillance of him—as intimate as his of them—had been an unexpectedly oppressive aspect of the fieldwork situation; so also, its "emotional sterility": he had not seen his wife, not seen his friends, not gotten "drunk or laid" or, in public, even "mad." His "compulsive" typing of notes had often gotten him "down"; now at home, he found himself "horribly tender" and suspicious: "overreacting . . . damn it, without any provocation" (SPR: DS/Gorer 7/7/48).

Nor did he idealize the Yapese. They seemed liberated from nothing, neither their own psychological nor American colonial repression. They were not blissfully sexual, nor loyally communal, nor politically easygoing, and not by a long stretch were they egalitarian. Nor did their psychological charac-teristics seem easily amenable to analysis from a culture and personality per-spective. Although there was plenty of suppressed aggression, its significance was not clearcut; as Tannengin had pointed out, in a final interview the old man had arranged, the culturally sanctioned contexts for expressing aggres-sion openly were warfare and mock warfare, both of which had been abol-ished under colonial administration (SFN:1608–10; 1634–35). When Schneider found out in New York on his return that the Social Science Research Coun-cil had turned down his application for a fellowship to write a dissertation on aggression, that made it definite; he would change his thesis topic (HKP: DS/CK 6/26/48).

Back in Cambridge on July 8, the first thing he had to handle was the Peabody team's CIMA report, most of which he wrote himself. Aware of the problems generated by the best-intentioned interventions, he decided to compose a "very, very anonymous report" in order to protect his informants from becoming objects of Navy attention (SPR: DS/Gorer 7/7/48). As forwarded by Murdock to the Navy, the report was short on politics, long on descriptive generalities, and made no policy recommendations whatsoever (Hunt et al. 1949:60, 115, 220). On the problem of depopulation, it noted that the population had begun a "slow, but steady" increase, and advanced Schneider's theory of abortion to explain the past decline: under earlier administrations, the incentive for abortion had been increased by "repressive" colonial measures, but the Yapese suffered no Riversian "loss of the will to live" (29, 187–92, 215).

Schneider's contribution to the report included an analysis of Yapese kinship, which when augmented and revised became the first half of his dissertation (60–116; cf. Schneider 1949:22–165). To write the dissertation, he coded his field notes with the numbers of topic categories in Murdock's *Outline*. After having the numbered materials retyped, he sorted them by subject, and then wrote "segments" for the important subjects, which were "clumped into 'chapters'" (HKP: DS/CK 11/21/48). Obviously, the process filtered out methodological doubts, cathartic outbursts, Schneider's daily concerns and emotions. In terms, then, of the project that gave his field notes their distinctive character—as Kluckhohn had put it, like "a friend's private diary" (HYE: CK/DS 3/3/48)—this was the point of actual disengagement, at which Schneider in effect "pulled" *all* the "paranoid material" and turned to subjects which seemed impervious to "observer's bias" (HKP: DS/CK 3/16/48). From that point on, he referred primarily to the subject-coded series, interposing method, again and decisively, between his field anxieties and his ethnography (cf. Devereux 1967).

Completed in August 1949, the dissertation was entitled "The Kinship System and Village Organization of Yap, West Caroline Islands, Micronesia: A Structural and Functional Account." The two halves of the text looked forward to two later phases of Schneider's career. The first, on kinship, rigorously applied Murdock's theoretical vocabulary in describing the Yapese "system" as one of "double descent." On the one hand, a principle of matrilineal descent was recognized in the relatively functionless Yapese "sib." On the other, patrilineal principles, as modified by certain "unusual features," governed membership in and the inheritance of the multifunctional *tabinau*, or land estate, which was described as a Murdockian "compromise kin group," neither quite "patrilineage" nor "patrilocal extended family" (Schneider 1949:25–30, 164, 199; cf. Murdock 1940b, 1949; Hunt et al. 1949:71). Although written more under the influence of Parsons than of Radcliffe-Brown (whose work Schneider had encountered after returning from the field), this first part reads like a conven-

tional social anthropological treatment, with descriptions of marriage, the life
cycle, and roles in "the nuclear family." By contrast, the second part, on the
village, contained mostly material that had been volunteered by Tannengin;
it dealt with the *tabinau* as "a piece of land to which a group of persons, who
happen to be related, are attached" (Schneider 1949:8). This, Schneider emphasized, was "the actors' definition," as opposed to the "a priori" definitions
he had employed in the first part, where he had distinguished the nuclear
family as "an analytically useful unit," although it had no "recognition as an
entity" in Yapese culture (5, 8, 190).[4]

It was, however, the first half of the thesis that Schneider developed in
years to follow. In 1950, he took a Fulbright teaching fellowship to the London School of Economics. While there, he maintained a background interest
in psychological questions – the "neglect" of "motivational aspects" in his thesis having gone "strongly against" the grain of his "personal inclinations"

---

4. The thesis incorporated little of Schneider's material on colonial relations, except in a
discussion of abuses of chiefly authority. There, Schneider explicated the avenues of political
intrigue that were opened up by "foreign administrators," including the pressing of charges, "either
true or false," which administrators were likely to punish with imprisonment or deportation,
and the arrogation of new spheres of political authority, on the basis of rules actually "promulgated by the chief himself," but "pronounced as emanating from the foreigners" in Colonia. The
latter "device" built, of course, upon "much common feeling between the chief and the members
of his village about the unpredictability, the irrationality, and the obnoxiousness of the foreigners and their rules, and [upon sentiments] that the day will come when Yap will be free of un-
wanted foreigners" (Schneider 1949:273–74).

On two important points, Schneider's thesis account diverged from the materials in his field
notes, raising problems of interpretation which may be indicated briefly. Having learned of,
and formulated, in the last months of his fieldwork, the distinction Yapese maintained between
colonial and indigenous chieftainships, Schneider nevertheless confused the issue in his thesis,
presenting "the district chieftainships" as indigenous Yapese positions and describing succession
as "matrilineal" in "certain" of the districts (Schneider 1949:160; cf. 1962:7–8). Apparently, he
had in mind the example of Fithingmau Niga (simultaneously a district chief and Gagil's *pilibithir*),
which he reconciled with the case of Lirau by contrasting district chieftainships (indigenous positions) with "messengers" who went to Colonia (colonial positions) (Schneider 1949:289–90). Thus
just as Fithingmau Niga (who was old and semiparalyzed) was "spoken for" in Colonia by his
son, Fithingmau Tulug, Lirau spoke in Colonia for the older Rumung chiefs, including Tannengin
– whom Carroll had meanwhile recognized as the "legitimate" district chief (SFN). Schneider
apparently took the districts themselves for granted as political units (Schneider 1957a, 1957b,
1962). On the question of the three chieftainships within the village, here again Schneider described the matter clearly in his notes, save for some confusion over whether the *pilibithir* was
a "chief" or simply a respected "old person"; however, in his thesis and later essays he focussed
almost entirely on the "village chief" (or chief of lands) (Schneider 1949:297, 326), for which he
has been critized by later ethnographers of Yap (Lingenfelter 1976:103; Labby 1976). Naturally,
here Schneider thought mostly of Tannengin, and his relationship with Tannengin was perhaps
also the model of another of his subsequently criticized interpretations: that the chief's authority
was sharply delimited (Tannengin was a modest ruler), leaving the "father" (or "father surrogates")
the primary figure with "real authority" (Schneider 1949:343–45, cf. Lingenfelter 1975:119).

(Schneider 1949:8–9). But the British were suspicious of culture and personality anthropology, viewing it as a distinctively American bit of "nonsense," and it made Schneider uncomfortable to be cast in the "role" of "Kluckhohn Spokesman" (HKP: DS/CK 10/15/49, 6/21/50). Visiting Manchester to give a seminar in March 1951, he found Max Gluckman's students "armed to the teeth" with "What is Wrong with Gorer-Mead-Benedict"; sidestepping the attack, he tried to prove himself "almost as structural as they, in showing why psychology could be helpful in anthropology" (HKP: DS/CK 3/29/51). Pursuing the structural line after his return to Harvard's Department of Social Relations in autumn of 1952, he reworked material from his thesis into an essay on Yapese kinship (Schneider 1953a), and began two projects with George Homans, one on the "American Kinship System" (Schneider & Homans 1955), and another that resulted in a critique of the theory of preferential cross-cousin marriage recently advanced by Claude Lévi-Strauss (Homans & Schneider 1955).

If in a British context he had represented American psychological currents, now, back in America, where these currents were losing force, Schneider was increasingly identified with British structural-functional theories. In 1954 he organized a conference on "matrilineal kinship" that produced a "Kroeberized" structural-functionalism: a "kinship system" was like a language, a scheme of classification, "patterning" kin relationships by partitioning the human universe. But this attenuation of the emphasis on kinship as a social "institution" did not preclude attention to "rules" of residence, group membership, and inheritance or descent; nor did it substantially reconfigure the basic structural-functionalist typology of societies, which was instead subtly reconceptualized as a "typology of patterns of lineage structure" (HKP: DS/CK 9/7/54; Schneider & Gough 1961). And of course the very theme of "matrilineal kinship" was a counterpoint to developments across the Atlantic, where the British had already "done patrilineal," and "bilateral" kinship was to be saved "for later" (Stocking/DS interview, 3/9/78).

However, matrilineal kinship was also emerging as a key issue in Schneider's analysis of his Yap materials, where the functional salience he was ascribing to the "patrilineal lineage" (the *tabinau*) contrasted with a kinship terminology suggesting matrilineal descent (1953a:232–33), as well as with matrilineal systems found everywhere else in Micronesia—including that of nearby Truk, which Schneider analyzed for the conference volume (Schneider & Gough 1961). Although Schneider emphasized his "psychological" work in letters to Kluckhohn (HKP; cf. Kluckhohn et al. 1953), and insisted that kinship was "NOT an obsession," at the conclusion of this conference he had "still not had enough of it" (HKP: DS/CK 11/28/54).

Accepting a fellowship the following year at the newly established Center for Advanced Study in the Behavioral Sciences, he drafted four chapters for a book on Yapese "patterns" of kinship and the effects of depopulation—although the manuscript broke off where it would have been natural to begin a chapter on the matri-group (SPR). Moving then to Berkeley, Schneider taught kinship and Parsonian "systems" theory (DSI), and was on hand for the Kroeber-Parsons "summit" of 1958, at which the "relational system" of "society" was distinguished from "culture," defined as an ensemble of "symbolic-meaningful systems" (Kroeber & Parsons 1958:583).

By this time Schneider had consolidated a reputation as a leading American exponent of structural-functionalism (Murphy 1971:209). But he was soon to undergo a dramatic reorientation. In terms of the distinctions that the Kroeber-Parsons "summit" established, he shifted from the "sociological" study of kinship as a "functioning" social institution, to a "cultural anthropological" study of kinship as a "system of symbols and meanings" (Schneider 1965a, 1968b, 1972, 1976a). No doubt, this shift was promoted by his personal re-engagement with psychoanalysis between 1958 and 1960, which highlighted issues of symbolism and the subjectivity of human experience. But an equally relevant context was the recent literature from Britain, where Edmund Leach, delivering the inaugural Malinowski Lecture, had condemned the "typology making" project of "followers of Radcliffe-Brown," and questioned the value of classifying whole societies as "matrilineal" or "patrilineal"; instead, Leach urged attention to "ideas" of matri- and patri-filiation that were "present" conjointly in any one society (Leach 1961:2–4, 7, 17).

Taking Leach's problem to his Yap materials in a 1962 essay, Schneider drew on information provided by Carroll (in earlier letters commenting on his dissertation) to reconceptualize the matri-group or "clan," concluding that matrilineal and patrilineal ties were radically different in "symbolic value" (SPR: Carroll/DS [1949–50]; Schneider 1962:20–21). Symbolized by a kind of "biological relatedness" (clansmen were said to have been born "'of the same belly'"), matrilineal ties sanctioned inalienable bonds of "undifferentiated solidarity." By contrast, patrilineal ties were essentially "political"; symbolized, like village "alliances," by "the gift and its return," they were in no way "believed" to be based on "consanguinity." Thus while patrilineal "units" were "most conspicuous" from the viewpoint of political function, they were problematic as "descent" groups—raising questions of the applicability of structural-functional "descent theory" (Schneider 1962:1, 14–15, 20–21).

This was in fact Schneider's last essay to adopt the perspective of "descent theory," which he soon attacked directly in a 1963 paper entitled "Some Muddles in the Models." There he embraced the French structuralist "alliance theory" of Louis Dumont and Lévi-Strauss, which was congenial with the Kroeber-Parsons viewpoint in emphasizing problems of the "symbolic order" in cultural study (1965a:40). Criticizing Radcliffe-Brown and Murdock for "imposing our way of thinking on their system" of thought (28–29), the paper clearly signalled Schneider's "defection" from structural-functionalism (Murphy 1971:210). Although it offered no *mea culpa*, that was yet to come—as "the sixties" moved forward, and a "crisis" struck anthropology.

In a context of unprecedented disciplinary concern with colonial issues, the once-regnant structural-functionalist "paradigm" was attacked from numerous viewpoints, and many anthropologists linked its rejection with developments outside the discipline: political struggles in the universities and abroad, including the wars of independence of colonized peoples (Leclerc 1972; Murphy 1971; Hymes 1972; Asad 1973). In characteristically depicting native societies as functionally integrated, autonomous "micro-worlds" (Wolf 1970:3), structural-functionalists, it was now argued, had maintained "a certain agreement" between anthropology and colonial ideologies of "indirect rule" (Leclerc 1972:116, 135–36).

Amid this disillusionment, Schneider heralded an alternative to sociologically oriented functionalisms (with their clear potentials for instrumentality) in the "symbolic anthropology" that was exemplified by his resumed and expanded study of contemporary American cultural ideologies of kinship (Schneider 1968b, 1969a; Schneider & Smith 1973; Dolgin et al. 1977; Murphy 1976:15–17). The research had quite definite political implications, in radically compressing the distance between "anthropologist" and "other," and it illuminated the ethnocentrism of structural-functionalist kinship theory (Schneider 1984:175, 197, 1968a, 1969a, 1976a). From this perspective, Schneider more systematically called into question his own original Yapese research (1969b, 1972, 1984).

Published shortly before his retirement from Chicago to Santa Cruz in 1985, Schneider's fullest self-critical statement was a broadside attack on the comparative study of kinship as a "tenable or a legitimate endeavor" (1984:177). Although Murdock's theories were not extensively discussed, those of Murdock's more enduringly loyal students were, and his conceptions might be said to haunt the book's pages; *Social Structure* was prototypical of "the theory" Schneider attacked (viii, 7). But the "defects" of "conventional" kinship study were "exemplified" by a somewhat caricatured précis of Schneider's own early, Murdockian writings on Yapese kinship (1984:6, 38; cf. 1949, 1953a, 1955, 1957a). In effect, these were now repudiated.

Schneider compared his earlier work with a revised "description" of Yapese culture which reflected his later theoretical project and was partly inspired by a more recent study of Yap by his student, David Labby (1976; Schneider 1984:viii, 8; cf. 1969b). The sharpest difference was in the depiction of the Yapese matri-group. Labby's research had revealed that Yapese conceptualized land inheritance as a transaction between matri-groups: in exchange for the garden labor that a woman invested in an estate owned by the matri-group of her husband, her sons, who were of her matri-group, received the estate in the next generation (Labby 1976; Schneider 1984). In practice, however, this resembled patrilineal inheritance, as qualified by the inelegant "unusual features" Schneider had described in his dissertation (1949:25–30; cf. 1953a, 1956).

Schneider cast his retrospective self-critique in terms of the philosophy of science, arguing that the "faulty" theoretical "paradigm" of the "conventional wisdom" of kinship studies—which "put" many of his Yapese "data in an ambiguous or anomalous position"—had guided his perceptions while in the field, his "sort[ing]" of materials back at home, and finally his efforts at "translation" and representation (1984:3–7, 58–59). The theories of this paradigm were not only "wrong," they were at bottom "ethnocentric" (4, 197); by applying a European conception of consanguinity as a texture of blood- and marriage-based relations "arising out of the processes of human sexual reproduction," they imposed characteristically European "'biologistic' ways of constituting and conceiving human character, human nature, and human behavior" (174–75). Schneider now "indicted" his own Yapese research for having violated the "one most sacred canon" of anthropological study, by placing a "blinding" prior commitment to the study of an "a priori" construct of "kinship" ahead of the "sensitive perception" and "appreciation" of the "understandings" of "the other" (1984:77, 196–97). Shoehorning Yapese conceptions into the "a priori categories" of the "genealogical grid," his first description had distorted "how the world exists in Yapese culture" (77). Eschewing this all-too-easy "cross-cultural" reference point, the revised description sought instead to explicate "native conceptions": "their groups and how they structure them," the "shared understandings," the "system of categories and units," that imbued action with "meaning" in the Yapese cultural context (75, 77, 174, 196).

From a different perspective, however, one might argue that there was more to Schneider's "inadequate" depiction of matrilineal customs than a paradigm-driven projection of a "dubious" and ethnocentricly "biologistic" conception of "kinship" (1984:viii, 8). His doctoral dissertation had contained not one but two discussions of the questionably "patrilineal" *tabinau*: the first used "a priori" assumptions to categorize it analytically, but the second aimed to interpret "its conception in the native mind" (1949:5, 8). That he had proceeded subsequently to elaborate only the first of these analyses speaks to the intellectual force of disciplinary conventions; that he had created the analysis in the first place recalls the articulation of such conventions with colonial priorities. But there was still more to it than that.

Indeed, had the problem been simply the subordination of Yapese to Western concepts, one might actually have expected the Yapese matri-group to appear strikingly salient, since its constitutive symbols—ties of blood and parenthood—closely resembled the primary Western symbols of kinship, and its associated behavioral proprieties, like those of Western kinship, prized a segregation of kin relationships from the competitive realm of politics (Schneider 1962). In the Yapese colonial situation, however, this segregation had in fact tended to cloak the matri-group from Schneider's view; as a foreigner, scribe, and significant political power, he was for Yapese a consummately political figure. Twenty years later, when Labby worked on Yap, matri-group customs had largely fallen into desuetude and could be spoken of freely as a matter of almost purely historical interest (Labby 1976:7–11). But in Schneider's time, they were still powerfully sensitive, not only as customs of fertility recently attacked by a foreign power, but inherently—one's matri-group being as intimate as one's mother's vagina, to which informants emphasized it in fact referred (SFN:1265–67). From a colonial perspective such customs were thus at the very limit of obscurity, and one can readily understand why Schneider's poll survey had been misleading. If anything had been a "touchy subject," requiring the best possible rapport to probe, it had been the matri-group, its customs, and its potent affective meaning.

Its meaning had been potent even for Fellan, who had himself transgressed the rule of matrilineal exogamy, having been encouraged to do so by the teachers in a Japanese colonial school. On Schneider's next to last night on Yap, Fellan's wife gave birth in Schneider's borrowed powerboat; when Fellan went ashore to get a ritual coconut, he had a horrific vision of the ancestress of his matri-group—confirmation that the infant was endangered as the issue of an incestuous union (SFN:1120, 1598–1602). Tannengin, too, as Schneider had in time learned, was "unwilling" to speak of matri-group customs of land inheritance (1038): partly because he was in fact only regent (for Fellan), and partly because the customs sanctioned inheritance of his own estate by the despised son of his older brother—when he would rather have had Schneider receive those lands upon his death (SFN). As it happened, Schneider's only informant to tell of matrilineal land inheritance was Gumedak, who was clearly not as despicable as Schneider had thought, and whose older brother in his home village held a chiefly land estate, making the matrilineal tie his most promising conduit to an indigenous chiefly office (37–38, 56, 116–18). But since Schneider regarded Gumedak as an index of acculturation, he reported that the "inheritance of land from the mother" was a "new" cultural "feature" (Schneider 1949:200–201; cf. 1956:IV, 32–34).

So we are led back to the specifics of Schneider's relationships with informants in the colonial situation he encountered on Yap. He had entered the field an ideological egalitarian, whose humanistic impulses impelled him toward just such an empathetic "appreciation" as he later advocated. But his egalitarian ideals were extremely problematic in the Yapese context, where a culturally valued hierarchy was complexly implicated in a hierarchical system of colonial relationships from which, try as he might, he could not dissociate himself. Nor could he engage issues of cultural conceptualization apart from the

IRA BASHKOW

subjective conceptions held—and voiced—by specific informants, and outside the charged context of their subjective responses to him—within the colonial situation which defined central issues of their lives. They consistently thrust upon the investigator of their subjectivities the range of their own subjective human concerns. From a certain perspective, this might be viewed as a conduit to understanding, rather than as obscuring the "objective" facts of the matter. And ultimately, Schneider's most enduringly valuable insights (into Yapese understandings of colonial politics and into the political importance of land and exchange) were in fact products of his "compromised" rapport relationships. Yet where he had instead denied the influence of the specific qualities of his rapport on his results—as in the poll surveys of sexuality and Yapese "knowledge" of the matri-group—his methodologically "cleansed" findings were seriously misleading.

The centrally important relationship of Schneider's fieldwork on Yap was that with Tannengin.[5] From a certain perspective, it could be argued that, in effect if not intention, Schneider's move toward defining kinship—"real" kinship—as a biological relationship was a way of negating the reality of his troubling bond with Tannengin: "I am like your father"—"you are chief over me." From a similar perspective, it could be suggested that his later critique of the biological definition of kinship was a retrospective legitimation of that same bond. But just as the relationship was given different meanings by its principals at the time, so may it, and the others that surround it, be given various meanings from different retrospective points of view; this discussion has only begun their exploration. But from whatever perspective it may be offered, no interpretation of Schneider's ethnography can ignore the dynamics of rapport in the particular colonial situation he faced on the islands of Yap.

Acknowledgments

The research and writing of this essay were supported by a National Science Foundation Graduate Fellowship, but the "opinions, findings, conclusions or recommendations expressed in this publication are those of the author, and do not necessarily reflect the views of the National Science Foundation." An early, inchoate version of this paper was discussed in 1989 by the History of Human Sciences Workshop at the University of Chicago, sponsored by the Morris Fishbein Center for the History of Science and Medicine. I am also grateful to the Fishbein Center for a research travel

5. With a certain measure of distance, Schneider had been able to learn from, and theorize, his complex and troubling experience of adoption by Tannengin, deriving an understanding of the interweaving of patrilineal ties with politics; the "essence" of both being gift exchange, neither was inconsistent with affective content (Schneider 1962:14–15).

grant which enabled me to interview David Schneider, and to the Century and Searle Funds at the University of Chicago for additional support during the writing of this essay. I wish to thank Nancy Munn, Marshall Sahlins, and Daniel Rosenblatt for significant inspiration and encouragement along the way. Others who have helped include Justine Cassell, Nahum Chandler, Kate Chavigny, Alan Chester, Raymond Fogelson, Ward Goodenough, Richard Handler, Leesa Hubbell, Timothy O'Leary, Michael Silverstein, and Fred Strodtbeck. I owe warmest thanks to George Stocking for his tireless encouragement, patience, and numerous helpful comments, and to David Schneider for his open-minded and generous support—and for providing the inspiration and foundation of this project. I would also like to thank the librarians and archivists who have assisted in my research.

References Cited

Alkire, W. 1980. Technical knowledge and the evolution of political systems in the Central and Western Caroline Islands of Micronesia. *Can. J. Anth.* 1:229–237.

Amerasia. 1946. Trusteeship versus annexation; controversy over the future of the former Japanese-Mandated Islands. [Editorial]. *Amerasia* 10(5): 147–52.

Asad, T., ed. 1973. *Anthropology and the colonial encounter.* London.

Bedell, J. 1947. In trust we annex. *New Republic* 116 (3/17/47): 31.

Benedict, R. 1934. Anthropology and the abnormal. In Mead 1959:262–83.

Berg, M. L. 1988. "The wandering life among unreliable islanders." *J. Pac. Hist.* 23: 95–101.

Bierstedt, R. 1981. *American sociological theory.* New York.

Brown, R. G. 1976. Germany, Spain, and the Caroline Islands, 1885–1899. Doct. diss., Univ. Southern Mississippi, Hattiesburg.

Caffrey, M. 1989. *Ruth Benedict: Stranger in this land.* Austin.

Christian, F. W. 1899. *The Caroline Islands: Travel in the sea of the little lands.* New York.

Cochrane, R. 1978. *The National Academy of Sciences: The first hundred years, 1863–1963.* Washington, D.C.

Connor, S. 1950. The Navy's entry into military government. *Ann. Am. Acad. Pol. & Soc. Sci.* 267:8–18.

Darnell, R. 1984. Personality and culture: The fate of the Sapirian alternative. *HOA* 4:145–83.

———. 1990. *Edward Sapir: Linguist, anthropologist, humanist.* Berkeley.

Dean, V. M. 1946. Trusteeship: Military model. *Nation* 163:547–48.

Devereux, G. 1967. *From anxiety to method in the behavioral sciences.* The Hague.

Dolgin, J. L., D. A. Kemnitzer, & D. M. Schneider, eds. 1977. *Symbolic anthropology.* New York.

Dollard, J., L. Doob, N. Miller, O. H. Mowrer, & R. Sears. 1939. *Frustration and aggression.* New Haven.

DSI. See under Manuscript Sources.

Eggan, F. 1968. One hundred years of ethnology and social anthropology. In *One hundred years of anthropology,* ed. J. O. Brew, 119–64. Cambridge, Mass.

Embree, J. F. 1946. Micronesia: The Navy and democracy. *Far Eastern Survey* 15:161–64.

Fischer, J. L. 1979. Government anthropologists in the Trust Territory of Micronesia. In *The Uses of Anthropology*, ed. W. Goldschmidt, 238–52. Washington, D.C.

Fischer, J. L., & E. Z. Vogt. 1973. Introduction. In Taylor et al. 1973:1–13.

Ford, C. S. 1950. Occupation experiences on Okinawa. *Ann. Am. Acad. Pol. & Soc. Sci.* 267:175–82.

———. 1970. Human Relations Area Files: 1945–1969. *Behav. Sci. Notes* 5:1–27.

———. 1971. The development of the *Outline of Cultural Materials*. *Behav. Sci. Notes* 3:173–86.

Freud, S. 1900. *The interpretation of dreams*. New York (1965).

FSI. See under Manuscript Sources.

Gillilland, C. L. 1975. *The stone money of Yap*. Washington, D.C.

Gladwin, T. 1956. Anthropology and administration in the Trust Territory of the Pacific Islands. In *Some Uses of Anthropology*. The Anthropological Society of Washington. Washington, D.C.

Goodman, G., & F. Moos. 1981. *The United States and Japan in the Western Pacific: Micronesia and Papua New Guinea*. Boulder.

Harris, W. B. 1934. *East again: The narrative of a journey in the Near, Middle and Far East*. New York.

Hayward, E. J. 1950. Co-ordination of military and civilian civil affairs planning. *Ann. Am. Acad. Pol. & Soc. Sci.* 267:19–27.

Hessler, W. 1943. Military government in the Navy. *U.S. Naval Inst. Proc.* 69:1471–74.

Hezel, F. X. 1970a. Spanish Capuchins in the Caroline Islands. Micronesian Seminar Bulletin rexograph. In SPR box 10.

———. 1970b. Catholic missions in the Caroline and Marshall Islands. *J. Pac. Hist.* 5:213–27.

———. 1975. A Yankee trader in Yap: Crayton Philo Holcomb. *J. Pac. Hist.* 10:3–19.

———. 1983. *The first taint of civilization: A history of the Caroline and Marshall Islands in pre-colonial days, 1521–1885*. Honolulu.

Hitch, T. K. 1946. The administration of America's Pacific islands. *Pol. Sci. Quart.* 61:384–407.

HKP. See under Manuscript Sources.

Homans, G., & D. M. Schneider. 1955. *Marriage, authority, and final causes*. Glencoe, Ill.

HPM. See under Manuscript Sources.

Hughes, D., & S. Lingenfelter, eds. 1974. *Political development in Micronesia*. Columbus, Ohio.

Hull, C. 1948. *The memoirs of Cordell Hull*. New York.

Hunt, E. E., Jr., N. R. Kidder, & D. M. Schneider. 1954. The depopulation of Yap. *Hum. Biol.* 26:21–51.

Hunt, E. E., Jr., D. M. Schneider, N. R. Kidder, & W. D. Stevens. 1949. The Micronesians of Yap and their depopulation. Coordinated Investigation of Micronesian Anthropology, Report no. 24. Washington, D.C.

HYE. See under Manuscript Sources.

Hymes, D., ed. 1972. *Reinventing anthropology*. New York.

Ickes, H. 1946. The Navy at its worst. *Collier's* 118 (8/31/46): 22–23, 67.

IHR. See under Manuscript Sources.

Japan. South Seas Bureau. 1922–37. *Annual report[s] to the Council of the League of Nations on the administration of the South Sea Islands under Japanese mandate.* Tokyo.

Kennedy, R. 1945. The colonial crisis and the future. In Linton 1945:306–46.

Kirkpatrick, J. T., & C. R. Broder. 1976. Adoption and parenthood on Yap. In *Transactions in kinship,* ed. I. Brady, 200–27. Honolulu.

Klingman, L., & G. Green. 1950. *His Majesty O'Keefe.* New York.

Kluckhohn, C. 1927. *To the foot of the rainbow.* Glorieta, N.M. (1967).

———. 1939a. The place of theory in anthropological studies. *Phil. Sci.* 6:328–44.

———. 1939b. Studying the acquisition of culture. *Man* 39:98–103.

———. 1939c. Some social and personal aspects of Navaho ceremonial patterns. In Kluckhohn 1962:97–122.

———. 1943. Covert culture and administrative problems. *Am. Anth.* 45:213–29.

———. 1944a. *Navaho witchcraft.* Boston (1967).

———. 1944b. The influence of psychiatry on anthropology in America during the past one hundred years. Reprinted in *Personal character and cultural milieu,* ed. D. Haring, 485–512. Syracuse (1956).

———. 1945. The personal document in anthropological science. In Soc. Sci. Res. Council *Bulletin* 53:77–173.

———. 1946. The social scientist's responsibility. *Commentary* 2:186–87.

———. 1949a. *Mirror for man.* Tucson (1985).

———. 1949b. Two Navaho children over a five-year period. In Kluckhohn 1962: 150–67.

———. 1950. Anthropology comes of age. *Am. Scholar* 19:241–56.

———. 1962. *Culture and behavior: Collected essays.* New York.

Kluckhohn, C., H. A. Murray, & D. M. Schneider, eds. 1953. *Personality in nature, society, and culture.* New York (2d ed., revised).

Kroeber, A. L., & T. Parsons. 1958. The concepts of culture and of social system. *Am. Sociol. Rev.* 23:582–83.

Labby, D. 1976. *The demystification of Yap.* Chicago.

Leach, E. 1961. *Rethinking anthropology.* London (1966).

League of Nations. Permanent Mandates Commission. 1928–37. Minutes.

Leclerc, G. 1972. *Anthropologie et colonialisme.* Paris.

Lessa, W. 1950a. Ulithi and the outer native world. *Am. Anth.* 52:27–52.

———. 1950b. The place of Ulithi in the Yap empire. *Human Organ.* 9(1): 16–18.

———. 1962. An evaluation of early descriptions of Carolinian culture. *Ethnohistory* 9:313–403.

Levi, W. 1946. The United States and Pacific bases. *Fortnightly* 166 (September): 165–71.

Lingenfelter, S. 1974. Administrative officials, Peace Corps lawyers, and directed change on Yap. In Hughes & Lingenfelter 1974:54–71.

———. 1975. *Yap: Political leadership and cultural change in an island society.* Honolulu.

Linton, A., & C. Wagley. 1971. *Ralph Linton.* New York.

Linton, R., ed. 1945. *The science of man in the world crisis.* New York.

McKinney, R. 1947. Micronesia under German rule, 1885–1914. M.A. thesis, History, Stanford Univ.

McNair, P. K., R. R. Garison, J. H. Gilpin, et al. 1949. Report of a medical survey of the Yap District of the Western Caroline Islands of the Trust Territory of the Pacific Islands. *Hosp. Corps Quart.* 22(4): 5–19.

Marksbury, R. A. 1982. Legislating social order: An example from the Yap Islands. *Oceania* 58:19–28.

Marshall, M., & J. D. Nason. 1975. *Micronesia 1944–74: A bibliography of anthropological and related source materials.* New Haven.

May, M. A. 1950. *Toward a science of human behavior: A survey of the work of the Institute of Human Relations through two decades, 1929–1949.* New Haven.

———. 1971. A retrospective view of the Institute of Human Relations at Yale. *Behav. Sci. Notes* 6:141–72.

Mead, M. 1928. Coming of age in Samoa. New York (1973).

———. 1959. *An anthropologist at work: Writings of Ruth Benedict.* Boston.

Mikloucho-Maclay, N. N. 1878. The island of Yap. Trans. J. Honigmann, in Human Relations Area Files. New Haven (1968).

Morawski, J. G. 1986. Organizing knowledge and behavior at Yale's Institute of Human Relations. *Isis* 77:219–42.

Müller, W. 1917. Yap. In G. Thilenius, ed., *Ergebnisse der Südsee-Expedition, 1908–1910,* II, B, 2. Hamburg. (English ed., 1942, in Human Relations Area Files, New Haven.)

Murdock, G. P. 1940a. The Cross-Cultural Survey. *Am. Sociol. Rev.* 5:361–70.

———. 1940b. Double descent. In Murdock 1965:167–75.

———. 1948a. Anthropology in Micronesia. *Trans. N.Y. Acad. Sci.,* 2d ser., 11:9–16.

———. 1948b. New light on the peoples of Micronesia. *Science* 108:423–25.

———. 1949. *Social structure.* New York (1965).

———. 1965. *Culture and society: Twenty-four essays.* Pittsburgh.

Murdock, G. P., et al. 1938. *Outline of cultural materials.* New Haven (1982).

———. 1945. *Outline of cultural materials: Working manual. Yale Anth. Studies,* vol. 2.

Murphy, R. F. 1971. *The dialectics of social life.* New York.

———. 1976. Introduction: A quarter century of american anthropology. In *Selected Papers from the American Anthropologist, 1946–1970,* ed. R. F. Murphy, 1–22. Washington, D.C.

NAS1-6. See under Manuscript Sources.

Newlon, R. E. 1949. Evolution of the United States' position in Micronesia. M.A. thesis, International Relations, Univ. Chicago.

NRC (U.S. National Research Council). 1946. *Proceedings of the Pacific Science Conference.* (= NRC Bulletin no. 114).

NYT. *New York Times.*

Oca, José Montes de. 1893. Western Carolines. Trans. for Human Relations Area Files. New Haven (1942).

Oliver, D. 1946. *Summary of findings and recommendations.* Vol. 1 of U.S. Commercial Company 1946.

OPNAV (U.S. Office of Naval Operations). 1944. *West Caroline Islands Civil Affairs handbook (OPNAV 50E-7).* Washington, D.C.

OPNAV (U.S. Office of the Chief of Naval Operations). 1948. *Handbook on the Trust Territory of the Pacific Islands.* Washington, D.C.

Oren, D. 1985. *Joining the club: A history of Jews at Yale.* New Haven.

Pacific Science Board. First [and subsequent] annual report[s], 1947–. Washington, D.C.

Parmentier, R. J. 1987. *The sacred remains; Myth, history, and polity in Belau.* Chicago.

Parsons, T. 1956. *The Department and Laboratory of Social Relations at Harvard; Report of the chairman on the first decade: 1946–1956.* Cambridge, Mass.

——. 1962. Clyde Kay Maben Kluckhohn. *Am. Anth.* 64:140–61.

——. 1970. On building social systems theory: A personal history. *Daedalus* 99: 826–81.

——. 1973. Clyde Kluckhohn and the integration of social science. In Taylor 1973: 30–57.

Parsons, T., E. Shils, et al. 1951. Some fundamental categories of the theory of action. In *Towards a general theory of action,* ed. T. Parsons & E. Shils, 3–27. Cambridge, Mass.

Pauwels, P. C. 1936. *The Japanese mandate islands.* Bandung, Indonesia.

Pearson, D. 1945. The Washington merry-go-round. *Wash. Post* 10/15/45, p. 8.

Peattie, M. R. 1988. *Nan'yō: The rise and fall of the Japanese in Micronesia, 1885–1945.* Honolulu.

Pitt-Rivers, G. 1927. *The clash of cultures and the contact of races.* London.

PMC. See under League of Nations.

Rachlis, E. 1946. Navy rule in the Pacific. *New Republic* 115:755–56.

Rattan, S. 1972. The Yap controversy and its significance. *J. Pac. Hist.* 7:124–36.

Richard, D. E. 1957. *United States naval administration of the Trust Territory of the Pacific Islands.* 3 vols. Washington, D.C.

Rivers, W. H. R. 1922. The psychological factor. In *Essays on the depopulation of Melanesia,* ed. W. H. R. Rivers, 84–113. Cambridge.

Roberts, S. H. 1927. *Population problems of the Pacific.* London.

Roe, A. 1953. A psychological study of eminent psychologists and anthropologists. *Psychological Monographs* 67(2).

Salesius, Fr. 1906. The Carolines island Yap. Trans. for Human Relations Area Files. New Haven (1963).

Sapir, E. 1934. The emergence of the concept of personality in a study of cultures. In *Selected writings of Edward Sapir,* ed. D. Mandelbaum, 590–97. Berkeley (1949).

Schneider, D. M. 1946. The culture of the army clerk. *Psychiatry* 9:123–29.

——. 1947. The social dynamics of physical disability in army basic training. *Psychiatry* 10:323–33.

——. 1949. The kinship system and village organization of Yap, West Caroline Islands, Micronesia: A structural and functional account. Doct. diss., Harvard Univ.

——. 1953. Yap kinship terminology and kin groups. *Am. Anth.* 55:215–36.

——. 1955. Abortion and depopulation on a Pacific island. In *Health, culture and community,* ed. B. Paul, 211–35. New York.

——. 1956. Yap. (Unpublished partial manuscript on depopulation, in SPR.)

——. 1957a. Political organization, supernatural sanctions and the punishment for incest on Yap. *Am. Anth.* 59:791–800.

——. 1957b. Typhoons on Yap. *Hum. Organ.* 16(2): 10–15.

——. 1962. Double descent on Yap. *J. Polyn. Soc.* 71:1–24.

——. 1965a. Some muddles in the models: or, How the system really works. In *The relevance of models for social anthropology.* ASA Monographs 1:25–85. London. (Paper presented in 1963.)

————. 1965b. Kinship and biology. In *Aspects of the analysis of family structure*, ed. A. Coale et al., 83–101. Princeton.

————. 1968a. Rivers and Kroeber in the study of kinship. In W. H. R. Rivers, *Kinship and social organization*, pp. 7–16. London.

————. 1968b. *American kinship: A cultural account*. Chicago (1980).

————. 1969a. Kinship, nationality, and religion in American culture: Toward a definition of kinship. In *Forms of symbolic action*, ed., R. F. Spencer, 116–25. Seattle.

————. 1969b. A reanalysis of the kinship system of Yap in light of Dumont's statement. (Unpublished lecture; in SPR.)

————. 1972. What is kinship all about? In *Kinship studies in the Morgan centennial year*, ed. P. Reining, 32–63. Washington, D.C.

————. 1976a. Notes toward a theory of culture. In *Meaning in anthropology*, ed., K. Basso & H. Selby, 197–220. Albuquerque.

————. 1984. *A critique of the study of kinship*. Ann Arbor.

Schneider, D. M., & G. Homans. 1955. Kinship terminology and the American kinship system. *Am. Anth.* 57:1194–1208.

Schneider, D. M., & L. Sharp. 1969. *The dream life of a primitive people*. Washington, D.C.

Schneider, D. M., & R. T. Smith. 1973. *Class differences and sex roles in American kinship and family structure*. Englewood Cliffs, N. J.

Schneider, D. M., & K. Gough, eds. 1961. *Matrilineal kinship*. Berkeley.

Senfft, A. 1903. Ethnographic contributions concerning the Carolines island of Yap. Trans. for Human Relations Area Files. New Haven (1942).

SFN. See under Manuscript Sources.

Shineberg, D., ed. 1971. The trading voyages of Andrew Cheyne, 1841–1844. Honolulu.

Smith, R. J., 1974. Introduction. In *Social organization and the applications of anthropology: Essays in honor of Lauriston Sharp*, ed. R. J. Smith, 7–19. Ithaca.

SPR. See under Manuscript Sources.

Stevens, W. D. 1949. A study of depopulation on Yap Island. Doct. diss, Harvard Univ.

Stimson, H. L., & McG. Bundy. 1948. *On active service in peace and war*. New York.

Stocking, G. W., Jr. 1968. *Race, culture, and evolution*. Chicago.

————. 1988. Before the falling out: W. H. R. Rivers on the relation between anthropology and mission work. *Hist. Anth. News.* 15(2): 3–8.

Taylor, W. W., J. L. Fischer, & E. Z. Vogt, eds. 1973. *Culture and life: Essays in memory of Clyde Kluckhohn*. Carbondale, Ill.

Tetens, A. 1958. *Among the savages of the South Seas: Memoirs of Micronesia, 1862–1868*. Stanford.

Tetens, A., & J. Kubary. 1873. The Carolines Island Yap or Guap. Trans. for Human Relations Area Files. New Haven (1942).

Townsend, M. E. 1930. *The rise and fall of Germany's colonial empire, 1884–1918*. New York.

Trumbull, R. 1946. A swing around our Pacific "empire." *N.Y. Times Mag.* 5/19/46, pp. 13, 59–60.

Underwood, J. H. 1973. The demography of a myth: Abortion in Yap. *Hum. Biol. Oceania* 2:115–27.

U.S. Commercial Company. 1946. *Economic survey of Micronesia conducted for the U.S. Navy, 1946.* Washington, D.C. (Lib. of Cong. microfilm, 5 reels.)

U.S. Department of State. 1945. *Charter of the United Nations; Report to the President on the results of the San Francisco Conference.* Washington, D.C. (Department of State Publication 2349.)

————. 1947. The United States and non-self-governing territories. Washington, D.C. (Department of State Publication 2812.)

Useem, J. 1945. Governing the occupied areas of the South Pacific. *Appl. Anth.* 4(3): 1–10.

————. 1946. *Economic and human resources—Western Carolines.* Vol. 5 of U.S. Commercial Company 1946.

————. 1947. Applied anthropology in Micronesia. *Appl. Anth.* 6(4): 1–14.

Walker, C. 1945. Anthropology as a war weapon. *Am. Mercury* 61 (July): 85–89.

Wallace, S. C. 1944. The Naval School of Military Government and Administration. *Ann. Am. Acad. Pol. & Soc. Sci.* 231:29–33.

Weller, G. 1949. That stubborn island called Yap. *Sat. Eve. Post* 221 (5/14/49): 42–43, 124–29.

Whiting, J. W. M. 1986. George Peter Murdock (1887–1985). *Am. Anth.* 88:682–86.

Williams, F. E. 1933. *Depopulation of the Suau District.* Port Moresby, Papua New Guinea.

Wolf, E. 1970. American anthropologists and American society. *West. Can. J. Anth.* 1(3): 10–18.

Worden, W. 1945. Our dubious new empire. *Sat. Eve. Post* 217 (3/17/45): 9–11.

Wright, C. H. 1947. Let's not civilize these happy people. *Sat. Eve. Post* 219 (5/3/47): 23, 149–50.

Yanaihara, T. 1934. Nanyo-gunto-min no kyoiku ni tsuite. (The educational system in the south sea islands.) *Rin-ri Koen-shu* (May): 67–85. Human Relations Areas Files archives, trans. Ms. no. 1576. New Haven.

————. 1940. *Pacific Islands under Japanese mandate.* London.

Yans-McLaughlin, V. 1984. Science, democracy, and ethics: Mobilizing culture and personality for World War II. *HOA* 4:184–217.

————. 1986. Mead, Bateson, and "Hitler's peculiar makeup"—Applying anthropology in the era of appeasement. *Hist. Anth. News.* 13(1): 3–8.

Manuscript Sources

In writing this essay I have drawn on research in several bodies of manuscript materials, which are cited by the following abbreviations:

DSI   David Schneider interviews, conducted by the author, August 17–18 and 22–23, 1989, Santa Cruz, Calif. I have also used this form to include personal communications.

FSI   Fred Strodtbeck interview, conducted by the author, January 28, 1991, Chicago, Ill.

HKP   Harvard University Archives, Clyde Kluckhohn Papers.

HPM   Harvard Peabody Museum, accession files 48–51, 48–51A, and 48–51B.

HYE   Harvard Yap Expedition Papers at Harvard Peabody Museum. The collection includes a carbon copy of David Schneider's field notes, as well as notes by expedition colleagues Edward Hunt, Jr., William Stevens, and Nathaniel Kidder.

IHR   Institute of Human Relations Papers, Yale University Archives. Group no. YRG-37-V, box 11, folder 95.

NAS   National Academy of Sciences Archives, Washington, D.C. Text citations are to branches of the NAS Archives as follows:

NAS1   NAS Archives, Exec. Bd., Ethnogeographic Bd.

NAS2   NAS Archives, NRC Div. of Anth. and Psych., Com. on Anth. of Oceania.

NAS3   NAS Archives, NRC Central File, Exec. Bd., Pac. Sci. Conf.; also NRC Central File, Pac. Sci. Conf.

NAS4   NAS Archives, NRC Central File, Foreign Relations, Com. on Pac. Investigations.

NAS5   NAS Archives, Div. of Anth. and Psych., Meetings.

NAS6   NAS Archives, NRC Central File, Exec. Bd., Pac. Sci. Bd.; also NAS Archives, Exec. Bd., Pac. Sci. Bd., CIMA.

SFN   Schneider Field Notes. In box 1, David M. Schneider Papers, Department of Special Collections, Regenstein Library, University of Chicago.

SPR   Schneider Papers Regenstein. Boxes 7 and 10, David M. Schneider Papers, Department of Special Collections, Regenstein Library, University of Chicago.

MOIS AND MAQUIS

The Invention and Appropriation of
Vietnam's Montagnards from Sabatier to the CIA

OSCAR SALEMINK

In April 1926 Léopold Sabatier, the French *résident* in the province of Darlac in the Central Highlands of Vietnam, was forced to resign from office and barred from the province. During twelve years in office, Sabatier had facilitated colonial rule in the Protectorate of Annam by a policy of transforming the culture of the Rhade people and excluding ethnic Vietnamese influence from the Highlands. In addition to the creation of *coutumiers*, or customary law codes, he provided a romanized Rhade script, established a Franco-Rhade school, transformed a ritual new year's celebration into an oath of loyalty by Rhade "chiefs," and incorporated Rhade and other Montagnard warriors into the colonial militia of the *Tirailleurs Montagnards*. Paradoxically, the very success of his pacification and administrative policies—as embodied in roads constructed by Montagnard corvée labor—opened up the fertile but hitherto hardly accessible Darlac Plateau to rubber plantations which Sabatier feared would destroy Rhade society. Sabatier found himself caught in the contradictions between two dominant concepts of French colonial ideology, *mise en valeur* and *mission civilisatrice*. On the one hand, there was the commitment to capitalist exploitation of natural resources, which might be contrary to the economic interests of the indigenous population—as in the case of the Highland rubber plantations. On the other hand, there was the effort to spread the "blessings" of French civilization to subjugated peoples through education, medicine, the imposition of Western law, and more generally the contact with the "superior" French culture. Because this effort implied some interest in the indigenous population, it relied on the ethnographic discourse of men like

---

Oscar Salemink, a researcher at the Instituut voor Moderne Aziatische Geschiedenis of the University of Amsterdam, is the author of *Ethnografie en Kolonialisme: Minderheden in Vietnam, 1850–1954*, and in 1991 did further research there.

Sabatier. Although Sabatier was unsuccessful in opposing colonization in the 1920s, he set the pattern for an ethnographic discourse and an ethnic policy in the Central Highlands that would become dominant from the later 1930s on through three decades of colonial warfare, when the French and later the Americans sought the support of the Montagnards against the nationalist movements of the Vietnamese.

Missionary and Military Models of the Montagnards in the Penetration of the Central Highlands

Although consisting of more than twenty different language groups, the autochthonous population of the Central Highlands was known to the Vietnamese simple as *Moi*—a word which may be glossed as "savage," but with servile connotations added by the slave trade that was concentrated in the Highlands. The French adopted the term, and it was only in World War II that Sabatier's proffered alternative, *Montagnard*, came into general use (Boudet 1942:II). Before the French arrived, the Montagnards were mainly agriculturalists, growing wet rice where they could, but more often dry rice by the method of shifting cultivation. They had little political organization beyond the village level, and it was only after the French used language groups as the basis for administrative divisions that these peoples took on an ethnic identity—a process which has since been described as "tribalization" (Condominas 1966:168). Despite this decentralization, there had always been contacts among the different groups living in the valleys, the slopes, and the plateaus of the Annam Cordillera, as well as between the Montagnards and the lowland civilizations. These contacts were primarily economic, and although there was a formal recognition of the foreign overlordship of the Khmer, Cham, and Viet states, the Montagnards maintained a real political autonomy.

The first Europeans to make contact with the Montagnards were French missionaries, at a time when Vietnam was still independent, but when tensions with France were growing. Seeking to escape the persecution of Catholics by the Vietnamese mandarins, the missionaries founded a station (*mission des sauvages*) at Kontum in Bahnar territory in 1850. To facilitate conversion, they carried on ethnographic studies, focussing on Montagnard religion, which they regarded as based on fear and terror inspired by sorcerers (*beidjao*) who were accomplices of the devil. To combat them the missionaries were "quite ready to fight the pagan impostor with his own arms" (Guerlach 1887a:455), by posing as the "great *beidjaou* of the Christians" and presenting Western technology as magic. Another adaptation to local custom was participating in a pledge of alliance by animal sacrifice, in order to enhance their status with the Bahnar and neighboring groups. Once a Christian community had been firmly established, the missionaries facilitated conversion by modifying Bahnar rituals to fit into Christian dogma. But most of their success was probably due to the weapons and organization they offered to the Bahnar and Rengao, which enabled them to resist more aggressive neighboring groups (Guerlach 1887a:514–16; Guilleminet 1952:448–56; Simonnet 1977:34–35).

In the 1880s, the missionaries began to be more directly involved in the military activities and the politics of French colonial expansion. French military explorers began to penetrate the Highlands from Cochin-China (the southern portion of Vietnam), which had been turned into a French colony between 1862 and 1867. After the establishment of the French protectorate over Annam and Tonkin between 1882 and 1885, the missionaries passed along their ethnographic knowledge to French officials involved in the first attempts at "pacification" in the Highlands. Between 1885 and 1887, during the heyday of the royalist Cân Vu'o'ng (Save the King) movement—an early expression of Vietnamese resistance against French occupation—the missionaries, supported by Bahnar villages, were able to defend their station against a blockade which lasted almost three years (Guerlach 1887b:538–89; Maitre 1912: 519–32).

In 1888, when the Belgian adventurer Mayréna was sent by the French governor of Cochin-China on a mission of exploration, and tried instead to found a Catholic Sedang kingdom, the missionaries created a scandal in French colonial circles by supporting him—and then made up for the mistake by putting their "Bahnar-Rengao Confederation," allied with Mayréna's Sedang kingdom, formally under French authority (Guerlach 1906:129–40; Maitre 1912:523–25; Leger 1977:236–42). Between 1890 and 1893, the mission actively supported the members of the Mission Pavie, which succeeded in winning Laos for the French and ousting the Siamese from the Central Highlands (Guerlach 1894:241–43, 1906:100–105; Cupet 1893:177–247; Maitre 1912:526–36; Hickey 1982a:237–45). From 1898 till 1907 the missionaries were allowed to administer the Kontum area in the name of the colonial régime. After the establishment of a regular colonial administration, relations with the colonial officials deteriorated somewhat, because of competition over spheres of influence and competence. In general, however, the Mission aided the colonial administration not only by the direct transfer of ethnographic knowledge, but also insofar as military and civil colonial officials drew upon ethnographic notes of missionaries in their dealings with the local populations (Le Jarriel 1942; Salemink 1987:20–29).

The success of the mission, however, remained restricted to some Bahnar and Rengao groups near Kontum, and when the missionaries promoted the immigration of Christian Vietnamese to Kontum after 1900, it became increasingly an enclave of ethnic Vietnamese. In contrast to the Montagnards, who tended to remain aloof and autonomous, and whom the missionaries regarded as violent, unpredictable savages, incapable of development and civilization, the Vietnamese were considered to be "trustworthy" and loyal to the French, and their presence was seen as a way to force the Montagnards to change their ways and accept conversion (Durand 1907:1158–71; Kemlin 1922; Simonnet 1977:259–61; Salemink 1987:20–25).

During this period, French military and political organization of Indochina developed apace. Leading members of the Pavie Mission had pleaded for an immediate occupation of the Central Highlands, which, together with all the territory east of the Mekong River, came formally under French authority only after the 1893 treaty with Siam. Arguing that a firm hold on the mountains was necessary to avoid insurgencies in the Annamese plains, captains Cupet and De Malglaive of the Mission Pavie envisaged a "peaceful conquest" of the area through a *politique des chefs*, establishing a military and political organization through existing leaders or "chiefs" chosen by the French, coupled to a control of the trade in the area (Cupet 1893:248–56; Cupet in Pavie 1900:417; De Malglaive in Pavie 1902:xxvi). However, the Governor-General of French Indochina at that time, De Lanessan, was more concerned with the pacification of the mountain areas of Tonkin, the northern part of Vietnam, where the military was pursing policies antithetical to his own. De Lanessan's "associationist" policy, which sought to rule through the Vietnamese mandarins, using the existing political structure, was strongly criticized by the French colons and other "assimilationists" for being too "annamitophile" (Lanessan 1895:56–112; Yersin 1893a:42–51; *Histoire militaire* 1931:9–10; Hickey 1982a:255–58). In contrast, the colonels in charge of the pacification of rebellious areas in the *territoires militaires* of Tonkin advocated the "oilspotmethod." This plan called for areas to be pacified from forts situated at strategic sites, from which roads and military posts would be constructed, and markets supervised, leaving local potentates in power so long as they did not bother the French. In this context, Colonel (later Marshall) Galliéni formulated an explicit ethnic policy, connecting political control with the ethnography of a region:

> It is the study of the races who inhabit a region which determines the political organization to be imposed and the means to be employed for its pacification. An officer who succeeds in drawing a sufficiently exact ethnographic map of the territory he commands, has almost reached its complete pacification, soon followed by the organization which suits him best. . . . Every agglomeration of individuals—a race, a people, a tribe or a family—represents a sum of shared or opposed interests. If there are habits and customs to respect, there are also rivalries which we have to untangle and utilize to our profit, by opposing the ones to the others, and by basing ourselves on the ones in order to defeat the others. (1941:217)

This argument for a divide-and-rule policy on the basis of ethnographic knowledge was not immediately implemented in the Central Highlands, because of the resistance of the Governor-General and the lack of political and economical incentives to penetrate the area. But it provided a reference point for those involved in that penetration, including most notably Henri Maitre, who conducted a series of expeditions in the Darlac area between 1905 and 1914, when he died at the hands of a Mnong chief. Maitre left behind an impressive ethnographic oeuvre, culminating in his *Les Jungles moi* (1912), which is still considered a standard work on Montagnard culture and history. Directly relating pacification with ethnography, he spoke of the Central Highlands as "the refuge of troubling and plundering tribes which I shall, perhaps soon, have the honor of studying and subjecting to our yoke, just like I have subjected the Mnong of Cambodia, the Cop and the Dip of Donnai, for the glory of a greater France" (Maitre 1912:558). His plea for the administrative penetration of the Highlands, reflecting the model set by Galliéni, was to be very influential after World War I. But until that time, the process of penetration was not continuous, depending upon the ad hoc policies of subsequent colonial administrations.

Although they viewed the Montagnards in the same Eurocentric evolutionary terms as did the missionaries, military men like Cupet tended to regard them as "barbarians" rather than "savages." Insofar as they were contrasted with the civilizations in the plains, resisting violently and refusing to submit like the Vietnamese, the Montagnards remained barbarians, whose harmful habits — shifting cultivation, slavery, superstitions — had to be eliminated. But as agricultural peoples with a rudimentary political system, they could be approached through a *politique des chefs*, playing not only on fear but on the self-interest of individuals (Cupet 1893; Cupet in Pavie 1900; De Malglaive in Pavie 1902). The contrast reflects the different context of military and missionary penetration, which was also evident in their respective ethnographic practices. Leading an awkward existence among the population which they sought to convert, without power to enforce change, the missionaries had to persuade by showing that their religion was superior, and focussed foremost on the religion of the local population. By characterizing it as "savage," they not only legitimized their efforts at conversion, but helped to convince a Catholic European audience of the hardships they suffered, and the need of compassionate financial support. But for the military, who wanted to enter the Central Highlands for strategic reasons, and who augmented military force by alliances with local leaders, the political system became the focus of research. This entailed a somewhat higher evaluation of Montagnard culture, which was labelled "barbarian."

In Indochina, however, "barbarian" had a specific meaning by virtue of the contrast between the tribes of the mountainous areas and the civilizations of the plains. The Montagnards, who were generally thought to be the original population of Indochina, supposedly had been forced to retreat before more civilized "races." Theirs was a "vanishing race," incapable of further evolution, that would in time be replaced by the more prolific Vietnamese race. The French had only to make sure that they controlled the Montagnards in the beginning, and according to the social Darwinist formula of the survival of the fittest, over the longer run they would simply disappear. In the meantime, they would "remain a useless force for the civilizing action," and should be encouraged to "merge with the neighboring peoples" (Lavallée 1901:291). Thus the spread of civilization inevitably would entail the arrival of ethnic Vietnamese in the Highlands.

It is against this background of evolutionary assumption that the work of Sabatier must be considered. It was his contribution to argue that the Montagnards and their culture were valuable in themselves and capable of development. It was he who provided an alternative administrative and ethnographic model.

Léopold Sabatier and the
Invention of Montagnard Tradition

Sabatier was born in a lower middle-class family on April 1, 1877, in Grignan in the mountainous Drôme region in the south of France. Not especially well educated, he had difficulty finding a job after military service, and decided to look for adventure in French Indochina, where he was appointed to a low-ranking job as civil servant in 1903. A man of somewhat difficult and suspicious character, he found it hard to adapt to the routine of an administrative job supervised by others. Coming from a mountainous region himself (he would retire to the Pyrenees), he applied for a job in the still-unruly Central Highlands (Boudet 1942; ANSOM D 3201, Dubois 1950:3–5). After a three-year service as assistant of Guénot, French *résident* of the province of Kontum, Sabatier was appointed head (*délégué*) of the autonomous district of Darlac in 1913. In Kontum province the *résidents* followed the lines set by the missionaries, who until 1904 had administered the region, basing themselves primarily on the Christian community of ethnic Vietnamese (Lechesne 1924: 9–13). But in Darlac, which was two hundred kilometers to the south and shunned by most colonial officials, the new *délégué* enjoyed considerable autonomy of action. There he could "live his dream" to liberate the *Mois* from barbarism and to make human beings of them rather than coolies (Bourotte 1955:94; Dorgelès 1944:18). But although he was later to be known as "the apostle of the Rhade" (Boudet 1942), Sabatier was certainly unconventional —and controversial—within Indochina at that time.

Not only did Sabatier keep out the Vietnamese and Chinese traders, but

Léopold Sabatier. (From Boudet 1942.)

French missionaries and businessmen as well, in an effort to create a "human reserve" to protect the Montagnards. He worked primarily with the Rhade ethnic group on the plateau of Darlac, regarding them as big children ("grands enfants") whom he, as a stern father, must bring up ("guider et gronder") (Dorgelès 1930:26). In 1915 he founded the Franco-Rhade school, where children from the colonial center of Ban Me Thuot and the surrounding villages got instruction in French language, history, and geography, as well as Rhade culture. At first the courses were taught by a Cambodian and a Vietnamese teacher; later, by Rhade teachers under a French headmaster, Dominique Antomarchi. Although Darlac officially belonged to the protectorate of Annam, no Vietnamese was taught. Antomarchi instead developed a Rhade script after the fashion of Quôc Ngu, the romanized Vietnamese script (Monfleur 1931:18, 25; Antomarchi 1946; Bourotte 1955:94–95).

After a few years Sabatier became fascinated with the oral poetic tradition

of the Rhade, which regulated rituals and relations between individuals and
social groups. Already by 1913, when an indigenous law court had been established in Kontum, he must have been aware of the existence of a Montagnard "law." The court was presided over by a judge, usually a powerful
man who knew the traditional customs, who after hearing the parties involved,
would chant the traditional verses he deemed relevant for the case. Sabatier
started to note down the verses, and composed a *coutumier*, after the model
of the written law code which every Vietnamese village possessed. In 1923,
when the delegation of Darlac was made a separate province with Sabatier
as *résident*, an indigenous law court was formally established. The indigenous
"laws" that had been collected and translated by 1919 were posthumously
published in 1940, together with the jurisprudence that developed within the
law court.

Sabatier's presentation of the *coutumier* touched upon a number of questions of ideology and policy. The key issue, he suggested, was how to protect
the Rhade against the lowlanders and Europeans who would be after their
land: "[The foreigners] think that you don't have laws, but that is not true,
for you have them like your ancestors had before; they had designed them
to protect the land, the soil and the populations of Darlac" (Sabatier & Antomarchi 1940: preface). But the laws were being forgotten, or misused by their
own chiefs: "the few—if any—among you who know them, use them to con-
fuse and repress the inhabitants." This failure of collective memory in fact
accounted for the current sorry state of the Rhade: "you have become cow-
ardly and fearful; your villages are depopulated, your race is vanishing." It
was only by the establishment of the *coutumier* that their future could be
guaranteed:

> Tomorrow or after the foreigners will come to plunder your residences, grab
> your lands, and you, you will become their slaves. To prevent that from hap-
> pening, I decided with all the Chiefs of Darlac to write down your laws in order
> to preserve them forever. . . . So if you don't want to be deprived of your lands,
> if you don't want to be the slaves of strangers, if you want your villages to be-
> come large and populated as in the past, then learn your laws, obey them al-
> ways. (Ibid.)

The foreigners referred to were of course the ethnic Vietnamese, who were
depicted as the main threat to Rhade society: the French, in contrast, posed
as the protectors of the Rhade and their putative tradition.

Sabatier's *coutumier* may have been expressed in a traditional idiom, but
like many such efforts of codification of native law, it was not always traditional in content. The poetic language of Rhade oral tradition was very fluid
and never unambiguous. Describing the proper behavior of kinship groups
toward the spirits and to each other, it was used to mediate in case of conflicts

between groups. But it was never used as a law code as we know it, representing a central authority of king or state, and certainly did not define any rules of obedience toward official village heads, who were a French invention. There had been "big men" in the Central Highlands, who were very influential in one or even several villages by virtue of their position in the networks of long distance trade that linked the Montagnards to the Vietnamese, Laotians, Siamese, and Chinese. Contrary to the French view of the Montagnards, they had not been "isolated" before European contact; rather, it was the French who had isolated the Central Highlands in order to establish their own influence in the area. Since the "big men" had been the most outspoken opponents of French penetration, their political power had been destroyed by the French; so also their economic power, by French efforts at preventing the long distance trade in the region (Maitre 1909:161–62).

Like other such codifications of customary law—notably the *adat* in the Netherlands East Indies—Sabatier's efforts rigidified social relations which often bore the mark of French colonial rule, despite the fact that they were presented as "traditional." Many "laws" were modified or even invented in a way which benefited French colonial rule. Thus Sabatier pretended that the village heads appointed by the French had existed in the past, but had lost their authority, which the French had simply restored. Other laws newly formulated in the traditional idiom concerned relations with groups and villages that did not acknowledge French authority or pay taxes—the "insoumis" (who were not yet pacified) and the "pirates" (rebels against French rule) (EFEO: MSS Europ. 138; Sabatier & Antomarchi 1940: passim).

The one highland leader who benefited from the French penetration was Ma Krong, better known by his Lao-Siamese title Khun Jonob. Of mixed Lao-Mnong descent, Ma Krong controlled the capture and trade of elephants in the region surrounding the center of Ban Don, and initially opposed French penetration. Sabatier, however, was able to ally himself with Ma Krong, using his influence on the Mnong and Rhade to improve the collection of the poll tax. This tax and another levied on the elephant trade enabled Sabatier to establish an administrative infrastructure in Darlac, financially independent of the colonial center. In addition to education and medical assistance, he was able to fund the construction of a network of roads built by corvée labor of Montagnards and forced labor of convicts—as well as a telephone line between the new administrative center of Ban Me Thuot and Ma Krong's seat at Ban Don. Ma Krong saw his economic power enhanced by the formal political power that French authority bestowed upon him, including his service as judge in the Ban Me Thuot law court from its inception in 1923 until after World War II (Monfleur 1931:15–19; Bourotte 1955:94; Hickey 1982a: 297–308).

Sabatier created a middle-range category of indigenous supra-village officials, the *chefs du canton*. Elected by the village headmen and assisted by graduates from the Franco-Rhade school, they saw to the execution of his commands and reported any irregularities. After he started recruiting Rhade warriors in 1915, Sabatier was also able to rely on a *Garde Indigène*, which in Darlac consisted primarily of Montagnards. Although it was remarked that the recruits for these *Bataillons de Tirailleurs montagnards du Sud-Annam*, or simply *Tirailleurs mois*, were often marginal young men who had been evicted from their village because of some moral or physical defect, their remarkable fighting qualities fitted well into the French efforts to control the Highlands and to have a loyal, non-Viêt force at its disposal, by pitting one ethnic group against the other (Daufès 1933–34:190; Maurice 1941:226).

Sabatier's most celebrated co-optation of "traditional" Montagnard culture was the *palabre du serment*, a ceremony in which village chiefs and other influential men in Darlac swore an oath of allegiance to the French. The *palabre* was actually a transformation of an older ritual that took place at the beginning of the new year, when the rich and powerful men gathered to reinforce their alliances and relations of dependency. There is disagreement when the ritual was held for the first time, but it became famous with the well-described celebration of January 1, 1926, in the presence of Louis Finot, director of the Ecole Française d'Extrême-Orient, and of Pierre Pasquier, the senior French official (*résident-supérieur*) of Annam. Sabatier made a speech exhorting the chiefs and others present to obey the traditional law (as interpreted by himself) and the village heads (selected by him); to stop the slave trade; to avoid and isolate rebels; to heed the prescriptions of French medical care; to contribute corvée labor for road construction; to send the young men to the militia; to send the children to school; and to take good care of the land out of respect for the *po lan*, the ritual female keeper of the land. Each time, the chiefs had to touch a bracelet in token of their obedience (Sabatier 1930).

The ceremony was concluded by the ritual sacrifice of a buffalo, donated by the most influential participant (now Sabatier himself, as the French *résident*), which created obligations for the others present. Claiming to be the preeminent connoisseur of Rhade (and Mnong) history, and the protector of their culture, Sabatier put himself in a direct line with the ancestors whose will he pretended to know:

> You must obey me because I know the past, yesterday, today and tomorrow. You must obey me because then you do what the spirits want, who are all with me for the prosperity, the health, the freedom of you all, for the peace of the great land of Darlac. You have to obey me because if you do not, I shall leave you and with me all the spirits of Darlac and of your ancestors whom you follow. You will always be wild dogs and you will become the slaves of foreigners. Do you understand? . . . The foreigner robs you, exploits you, subdues you, despises you, and you say nothing. Some help him for their private profit against

Montagnard village chiefs affirming their loyalty to a French official at a *palabre du serment*, c. 1940. (From Antomarchi 1941:12; courtesy of the John M. Echols Collection, Cornell University Library.)

the common interest. I protect you, and this does not please many. (Sabatier 1930:33, 41)

The *coutumier* and the *palabre du serment*, being purposeful modifications of traditions, may be considered as inventions of tradition for political goals (cf. Hobsbawm & Ranger 1983). As Governor-General Brévié noted in 1937 (ANSOM 137.1240), it was deliberate French policy to modify the *coutumiers* in a way suitable for the administration. The issue was specifically addressed some years later, when the Ecole Francaise d'Extrême-Orient announced that

Marcel Ner, one of the ethnographers of this stronghold of French oriental-
ism, would separate the "really traditional" Rhade laws from Sabatier's political wishes (Ner 1940b:3). On the basis of the testimony of "the elderly who
dictated the *coutumier rhade,* and the teachers who transcribed it," Ner concluded that Sabatier had "requested that it would be adapted to the demands
of the Administration and to the rule of hygiene; but [that] its expression
remain archaic" (Ner 1952:49). More recently, Jacques Dournes, who served
as a missionary in the area until the 1960s, made it clear that Sabatier's *coutumier*
deprived women in the matrilineal Rhade society of many rights by ignoring
their role in practical and ritual affairs (Dournes 1977:188).

From a pragmatic point of view, however, Sabatier's efforts were quite successful. He was able to create an administrative and geographical infrastructure for Darlac which in those days was unique for the Central Highlands
(Monfleur 1931). His achievement depended on an intimate knowledge of
Montagnard culture, which if properly handled would make the Montagnards
not only amenable to French colonial rule but also politically and militarily
useful. In the process, however, Sabatier created an ethnographic image of
the Montagnards quite different from that of the early missionary and military ethnographers—an image that might be called "relativist" insofar as,
"recognizing the values set up by every society to guide its own life, [it] lays
stress on the dignity inherent in every body of custom" (cf. Herskovits 1973:
76–77). In the specific context of the Central Highlands this implied that the
culture of mountain dwellers, and especially the Rhade, was equally as valuable as Vietnamese culture. Breaking away from the evolutionary discourse
that characterized Montagnards by what they lacked, Sabatier showed that
they had a law code, a script, a political system, and that they were good
soldiers, and amenable to colonial government and education. Most important, he defended their right to the land, based on clan ownership, and their
agricultural practice of shifting cultivation, in the face of the general condem-
nation of such "primitive," "destructive," and "lazy" methods by most of his
contemporaries. Sabatier showed that the Montagnards, far from being irre-
deemably "savage" or "barbarian," were capable of Western-style development—
"perfectible," as the French called it, without any involvement of the ethnic
Vietnamese in the process. Their race would not vanish and their cultural
identity would be preserved, on condition that it was protected by direct French
rule, and that ethnic Vietnamese were denied free access to the Highlands.

It has been argued, however, that there is a direct connection between
cultural relativism and an established colonial rule: cultural relativists tended
to be conservative in their protection of indigenous values and traditions,
thereby accepting existing inequalities and legitimizing colonial rule (Lemaire
1976:174–81). And Sabatier's ethnographic oeuvre not only legitimized French
rule in the Highlands; it also made a special policy with regard to the Mon-

tagnards possible. Already in 1918 Sabatier's policy was noticed favorably by the central colonial authorities in Hanoi as an example to follow (AOM Gougal 19.188: Programme de travaux et projet d'organisation administrative de l'Hinterland moi, 1918), and in 1923 it influenced Pasquier, then *résident-supérieur* of Annam, in formulating a policy for the Central Highlands (Pasquier 1923). However, Sabatier's "policy of attraction and peace" was far from being undisputed, and its full realization was to be delayed by Sabatier's forced resignation from office in April 1926, in the face of accusations that he resisted the opening of Darlac province for European colonization. It was precisely his defense of traditional land rights which made his position untenable. For the next decade the economic exploitation of the Central Highlands was to be sustained by an evolutionary view dismissive of the Montagnards and neglectful of their interests.

The Rubber Boom and the Conflict of Economic and Political Interests

About 1900, tests in the Highlands of eastern Cochin-China demonstrated the suitability of the red and grey soils of its basaltic plateaus for the cultivation of rubber, which in the next few years was to command record prices on the world market. During this first of two early-twentieth-century rubber booms, large areas already "pacified" were confiscated for the benefit of large European enterprises like Michelin, as well as for private colonists who established rubber plantations. In Cochin-China the power balance was such that the indigenous Montagnard population was simply evicted from their lands and employed on the new rubber estates, without much effective protest (Montaigut 1929:65ff.; Thompson 1937:130–63; Murray 1980:255–313).

A second rubber boom followed the decision of the major rubber-producing states to limit rubber production in order to keep the price artificially high after World War I. French financial circles soon became interested in the soils of the Central Highlands of Annam, which were not yet entirely pacified and where a colonial administration was just developing. This led to a clash between the protagonists of economic colonization and those of political and strategic colonization. Those associated with major rubber companies and financial circles in the metropole and in Saigon wanted a rational exploitation of the land, regardless of the consequences for the local population who lived off this land. According to still-current evolutionist opinion, economic colonization of the Highlands would be in the best interest of the Montagnards, who would simply "vanish" as a race if they did not give up their "backward and harmful" agricultural practice of shifting cultivation, and start working on the rubber plantations. Sabatier's successor, Giran, who in 1926 opened Darlac for colonization, put the matter succinctly: "a handful of French-men living in the midst of the population would do more for their evolution than all the most eloquent official palavers"–clearly a reference to Sabatier's *palabre du serment* (Monfleur 1931:20; trans. in Hickey 1982a:308).

Opposing this *mise en valeur* option was that of the *mission civilisatrice* favored by the military and some officials within the colonial bureaucracy. Typified by Sabatier, they sought to develop an efficient ethnic policy, informed by ethnographic knowledge and based on immediate contacts between the French and the Montagnards to the exclusion of the ethnic Vietnamese. To strengthen the hold of the French on Indochina, the strategic Central Highlands were to be made into a "friendly" military base in hostile surroundings, in case there was a Vietnamese insurrection in the plains, or an attack from abroad. In the process, France would fulfill its civilizing mission by protecting the autoch-thonous populations, respecting their cultures and encouraging their gradual development.

The conflict between the interests came to the surface around 1923, when the French *résident-supérieur* of Annam, Pierre Pasquier, had to formulate a policy regarding colonization of the Central Highlands and the immigration of ethnic Vietnamese. His initial plan was based on an inquiry among local officials, among whom Sabatier was most influential, but others also tried to influence Pasquier with reports or publications. These neatly reflected the interests that were at stake: the colonial administration arguing from the per-spective of political control; the Catholic mission, from the perspective of conversion; the army, from a military point of view; the colonists and busi-nessmen, from an economic point of view.

In 1922, Monseigneur Kemlin of the Catholic mission of Kontum, who enjoyed a reputation as ethnographer and correspondent of the prestigious École Française d' Extrême-Orient, published a pamphlet on Vietnamese im-migration to the Highlands. Accepting the inescapability of European col-onization, with its attendant appropriation of Montagnard lands and ex-ploitation of their labor, Kemlin insisted that the real issue was the ethnic Vietnamese. The experience of the Vietnamese Christians in Kontum showed that the Montagnards could learn from the Vietnamese community in the fields of agriculture (by abandoning shifting cultivation), commerce (by the introduction of money), industry (by introduction of a work ethic), hygiene, education, and religion (by the elimination of superstition). Furthermore, the Vietnamese presence would enhance the political security of the area, insofar as the Montagnards could take Vietnamese deference toward European au-thority as an example, while the Vietnamese could provide the administra-tion with information in case of Montagnard unrest (Kemlin 1922). That same year an anonymous article in a French journal representing business interests in the colonies argued in favor of Galliéni's "oil-spot method." Recalling

Galliéni's suggestion that a sufficiently accurate ethnographic map was almost equivalent to pacification, the author suggested that administrative divisions should follow ethnic and linguistic lines. As French influence spread through political means and the provision of services (e.g., using the scarcity of salt as an economic means to curb rebelliousness), the Montagnards would have to give up shifting cultivation, and the area would be opened for European colonization, after the example already set in the highlands of Cochin-China. Although Vietnamese, Khmer, and Lao merchants, whom the author saw as cheaters, would be evicted, the Vietnamese would be admitted as coolies on the European plantations (M. C. 1923:548–64). In contrast to the missionary and business interests, a classified study by Lieutenant-Colonel Ardant du Picq emphasized the strategic value of the Highlands in case of a foreign attack or a revolt in the Vietnamese lowlands. Drawing largely on Sabatier, he anticipated the possibility of a guerrilla war in which the Montagnards might act as partisans, if the colonial administration could gain their confidence: "These proud peoples with their spirit of independence will provide us with elite troops, as safety valves in case of internal insurgency, and as powerful combat units in case of external war" (AOM Gougal 49.506: Du Picq, Etude du pays Moy au point de vue militaire, 1923:110–11).

An intermediary position was taken by Paul Lechesne in a booklet published early in 1924. Although apparently an outsider (i.e., not a colonist, a civil servant, a military man, or a missionary) from the coast of Annam, Lechesne's presence at the *palabre du serment* of 1924 testifies to a lively interest in the Highlands. Acknowledging the political and military value of Sabatier's policy in Darlac, he compared the utilization of Rhade warriors with the British use of Gurkhas and Sikhs in India. But he also insisted on the economic value of opening the land for colonization and immigration, as *résident* Fournier had done in Kontum, where the presence of the Catholic mission had prepared the way for colonial administration. Sabatier, the apostle of the Rhade, was not Christ and would not live forever, and a flexible policy would leave room for both perspectives (Lechesne 1924).

Faced with such opposing interests and viewpoints, sustained by different images of the Montagnards as either backward savages or as useful protégés, Pasquier in his circular of July 30, 1923, attempted a synthesis of political paternalism and economic liberalism along lines previously suggested by former Governor-General Sarraut. Pasquier followed Sabatier in seeking to protect the Montagnards against their more developed and powerful neighbors. In line with the slogan "to all their own chiefs—to all their own judges—to all their own laws," he proposed that a *coutumier* should be established for every ethnic group, and that every year the chiefs should swear a ritual oath of loyalty to the French resident—Sabatier's *palabre du serment*. The Highlands would be divided into three zones in which policy would be adapted accord-

ing to the degree of pacification and evolution of the local population, and
Vietnamese traders should be eliminated as much as possible by the establishment of supervised markets. This "well-oriented racial policy" would allow
for a gradual evolution, avoiding the stagnation that allegedly characterized
the Indian reserves in the United States (Pasquier 1923; *Variétés* 1935:220–64).

But in regard to colonization, Pasquier took a different line than Sabatier.
Acknowledging that in the Highlands all land was claimed by the Montagnards, Pasquier nevertheless felt the need to "intervene in their conventions
in order to find formulas reconciling the interest of the colonists with the
customs of our protégés" (Pasquier 1923: Préliminaire de l'arrêté no. 1085-D).
Europeans were to be allowed to obtain "temporary" concessions in the free
zones, up to a maximum of 99 years. But since allocation of the concessions
was left to the provincial *résidents* (who would also determine policy on the
issue of Vietnamese immigration for the plantations), the effective right of
the autochthonous population to the land was drastically limited, and they
would gradually have to give up shifting cultivation.

The issue, however, was not settled by Pasquier's circular. In 1925, Sabatier
objected to the projected colonization, insisting that no concession be granted
without asking the permission of the native group claiming the land. He supported his plea by a study of traditional Rhade land tenure systems, symbolized by ritual landownership of the female *po lan*. In a second report, he
urged the restriction of concessions and the recruitment only of Montagnard
laborers on the plantations, in order to forestall Vietnamese immigration
(EFEO: MSS Europ. 138; Hickey 1982a:305–6). Even after the division of Darlac into zones, when European companies made requests for concessions to-
talling 167,845 hectares, Sabatier stubbornly resisted, refusing to lease out the
concessions. His attitude created a scandal among French colonists, with repercussions even in the metropole. He was severely attacked in the colonial
newspapers, and rumors spread that he even tried to keep out land prospectors by destroying a bridge. Some Rhade, including Sabatier's ally Ma Krong,
complained of the amount of corvée labor he demanded for his projects, of
the school that "swallowed" their children, of his habit of sleeping with Rhade
girls, and of his authoritarian manner in general. The opposition gained in
strength, and only four months after his apotheosis, the *palabre du serment*
of 1926, Sabatier had to leave office, and was denied future access to Darlac.
The interests of the "colons" had overriden the politico-military interest in
appeasing the Rhade (Monfleur 1931; Boudet 1942; Dorgelès 1944:28–32;
Hickey 1982a:307–9).

In 1927, Sabatier left Indochina for Paris, where again he found himself
a target of accusations by colonial pressure groups. Successfully defended in
the French parliament by his friend, the belletrist Roland Dorgelès, he was
rehabilitated by Doumergue, president of the French Republic, and returned

to Indochina to take up office as inspector of administrative affairs in the Central Highlands—only to resign disappointedly in 1929, when he was still denied access to Darlac. At the request of his friend Pasquier, now Governor-General in Hanoi, he published an official account of the *palabre du serment* (1930). Returning disappointedly to France with his daughter H'ni, he soon retired to Montsaunès in French Pyrenees, where he died in 1936 (Boudet 1942; Dorgelès 1944:28–32; Dubois 1950:225–26). His successor Giran opened Darlac province for colonization, and soon its entire surface was claimed by financial groups and individual colonists. The irony, as a later *résident* noted, was that Sabatier's effective indigenous policy and his impressive infrastructural achievements had made Darlac ripe for colonization (Monfleur 1931:19).

It was expected, however, that Sabatier's achievements would vanish with him, especially when it soon became clear that the regulations concerning the concessions were not implemented, and that the land rights of the Rhade were systematically violated. Resisting the expropriation of their lands, they were unwilling to work on the plantations, and the resulting conflicts and the lack of an adequate labor force made most aspiring concessionaires abandon their claims. The eight concessions that remained, owned by three major capital groups, covered only a limited area, and when the economic crisis of 1929 prompted a decline of the rubber price, clearing and cultivation slowed down considerably. The colonization process exacerbated relations between the French and the Montagnards, who stopped sending their children to the Franco-Rhade school. In 1929 there were even a few armed attacks by Montagnards on rubber plantations and trucks—to which the army responded by air assaults on insurgent villages (ANSOM Gougal 268.2342; ANSOM 271.2397; AOM Gougal 53.659). Thus European colonization threatened the "pax gallica," jeopardizing the administrative structure of the Central Highlands.

Characteristically, troubles occurring in the Highlands were attributed to the presence of ethnic Vietnamese, generally depicted as nationalist or communist "pirates," cheaters, and land grabbers. To avoid an unfettered Vietnamese immigration, the colonial administration would have preferred alternative sources of labor. The use of Javanese coolies, who would be politically harmless and closer to the Montagnards ethnically and linguistically, might have been a solution, but after an early migration in the first decade of this century, the colonial administration of the Netherlands East Indies did not permit further emigration. And since Chinese labor was by comparison too expensive, the plantations had to fall back on the Vietnamese, although now under a strictly regulated access to the Highlands. Vietnamese coolies were not allowed to leave the plantations during their contractual term, and had to return to the plains thereafter. Every area not supervised by a European was forbidden to Vietnamese; contact with the Montagnards could only take place in the supervised markets and the areas with an already existing Vietnamese settlement. In this way the colonial administration tried to reconcile the economic interest of a Vietnamese labor force on the plantations with the political interest of isolation of the Central Highlands (ANSOM 137.1240: Brévié 1938; Brenier 1929:184; Monfleur 1931:47; Robequain 1944:66–67, 237; Thompson 1937:150–51; Murray 1980:270–71; Trân Tu Bình 1985).

The Defense of the Colony and the Revival of Ethnography

As the world economic crisis slowed the plantation process in the 1930s, a series of events inside and outside the Central Highlands shifted the balance of colonial interest from the economic to the political, leading to a revival of ethnographic activity after the lapse of a decade. A decision to end the "state of anarchy" within the boundaries of French Indochina led to a renewal of pacification campaigns against Highland groups that had resisted since the turn of the century—from Cochin-China to subdue the Mnong and Stieng groups to the south; from Annam to subdue the Sedang, Katu, and affiliated groups to the north of Kontum. The ethnographic descriptions generated by the military offered an image of the Montagnards similar to that of earlier military explorers and the proponents of economic exploitation—as fierce, independent, and untrustworthy "savages." The notable exception to this image was Sabatier's Rhade, who were presumed to be more civilized on the basis of their adaptation to French rule and their incorporation in the French colonial troops, where they were used to subdue other Highland groups (ANSOM 137.1239: Pénétration 1931–35; Pagès in *Variétés* 1935:209–16; Salemink 1987:72–82).

Outside of the Highlands, the same period witnessed the rise of Vietnamese nationalism. In 1930, two uprisings challenged the French hold on the Vietnamese plains. In Yên Bái, where the Vietnamese Nationalist Party organized a mutiny among indigenous troops in the colonial army and tried to poison the French garrison, the movement was severely repressed. In the provinces of Nghê An and Hà Tinh, peasants revolted against the mandarins and the French, forming the Nghê Tinh Soviets, which came to be supported by the newly founded Indochinese Communist Party. When this movement was also repressed, the Communist Party had to go underground, and throughout the 1930s, the French secret police, the Sûreté, held such movements in check, arresting and sending nationalists to detention camps.

Internationally, French Indochina was threatened from abroad by Japan, which after occupying the north of China from 1931 on, turned its attention to the south, coming closer to the border of Indochina. In the west, the military government of Japan's ally Siam had expansionist ambitions, aspiring to incorporate all Thai-speaking nations and to reconquer the territories it had been forced to cede to France in 1893. With the rise of nationalism, fascism, and communism in Asia, the tension mounted, and the French colonial government had to take measures to defend the colony. Since the densely populated areas (the deltas, the coastal strip, and the Mekong Valley) were narrow and vulnerable in case of attack or uprising, the colonial government and army turned their attention to the strategic Central Highlands, from which most of Indochina could be controlled.

The situation in the Central Highlands suddenly worsened in 1937, when a widespread millenarian movement threatened the French administration. When a village chief by the name of Sam Bam announced that his daughter had given birth to a python, the rumor spread that the mythical Python-God had appeared to proclaim the coming of a cataclysm that would destroy all foreigners in the Central Highlands. Montagnards who possessed a bottle of magic water distributed by Sam Bam and who heeded his prescriptions would be saved and enjoy eternal life in an earthly paradise. Some ethnic groups stopped cultivating their land; others, thinking themselves invulnerable, attacked the French posts. Repressing the movement with force, the French arrested several "leaders" of the rebellion, including Sam Bam. At first, the rebellion was attributed to discontent of the Montagnards with the French presence — an interpretation which called into question the myth of a special relationship with the Montagnards in the inimical surrounding of colonial Vietnam.

However, on the basis of a report of the Catholic mission regarding the ethnographical and political content of the movement, this view was quickly replaced by the old theme of outside Vietnamese involvement. Seeing the movement as a religious rival, the mission blamed sorcerers for stirring it up, but also suggested that its organization must be in the hands of Vietnamese Communists (AOM Gougal F 03.79: Annexe du rapport politique de l'Annam, 9/1937). Although there was in fact no trace of Vietnamese involvement, in the increasingly tense climate characterized by the rise of nationalism in Vietnam and the threat of war in Asia, the colonial administration found this interpretation convenient, since it enhanced the myth of a special relationship between the Montagnards and their French protectors. Comparisons with other millenarian movements, however, indicate that the Dieu Python Movement must be considered an indigenous political protest in religious idiom against French colonial rule in the Highlands (Salemink 1987: 83–106).

Responding to criticisms of French colonial rule, in 1937 the recently elected Popular Front government commissioned the "Guernut Committee" to study conditions in the colonies. This investigation speeded up the process of assessing the consequences of the Dieu Python Movement, and of formulating a policy with respect to the Montagnard population. As increasing political tension highlighted the political and military value of the area, the colonial adminis- tration became concerned with the effects of unfettered colonization on the attitude of the autochthonous population of the Central Highlands, and began once again to encourage ethnographic work. Within this context both the policy and the ethnography of Sabatier were rediscovered, and his image of the Montagnards eventually came to dominate ethnographic discourse.

Practiced mostly by colonial officials, the ethnographic research concen- trated on the possibilities of political management of ethnic groups, by com- bining economic development with a conservative indigenous policy that played on ethnic sentiments in order to exclude Vietnamese influence. This ethnographic discourse provided the administration both with tools for cul- tural management and an appropriate ideological legitimation for their direct rule policy. Ethnographic practice was increasingly institutionalized, notably within the framework of the prestigious Ecole Française d'Extrême-Orient, where an ethnographic branch headed by the respected French ethnologist Paul Lévy had been established in 1937. The Institut Indochinois de l'Etude de l'Homme, a joint venture of the Ecole and the medical faculty of the Uni- versity of Hanoi, was founded to cover research in the fields of ethnography and physical anthropology. In Saigon, the Société des Etudes Indochinoises turned again to ethnography, in which, around 1880, it had taken an earlier interest (Salemink 1987:107–26).

As early as 1923, the colonial administration had instructed the *résidents* to see to it that *coutumiers* were compiled for every ethnic group in the Cen- tral Highlands, in collaboration with the Ecole, which undertook to guide research by their members and correspondents, and to edit their publications, avoiding the usual evolutionist terminology. In this atmosphere the composi- tion of a *coutumier* became the aspiring ethnographer's test of his ability. As late as the 1960s French anthropologists were still publishing *coutumiers*, often complete with the jurisprudence of the colonial court (Lafont 1963). Ethno- linguistic research was also promoted, with the goal of transcribing the various Montagnard languages and producing school primers. Anthropological work continued during World War II, after the Decoux administration in French Indochina allied itself to the Pétain regime in France and to Japan. Physical anthropology, which had become a field of interest for physicians and offi- cers, developed increasingly racist overtones. Feverishly constructing strate- gic roads in the Highlands, the Decoux administration also promoted con- ferences on the Highlands policy. Claiming a special relationship to the Montagnards, Decoux himself attended a revival of the *palabre du serment* in 1943 (Salemink 1987:127–70).

The revived ethnographic interest not only facilitated French rule in the Highlands, but also presented an image of the Montagnards as constituting—

Montagnard tribesmen in warrior dress. (From Boudet 1942.)

despite ethnic differences—a single group, to be opposed to the ethnic Vietnamese. Their languages, belonging to the Malayo-Polynesian and Mon-Khmer language groups, were grouped together and opposed to the Vietnamese tonal language. Their *coutumiers*, although varying considerably, made them comparable to each other to the exclusion of the Vietnamese. Symbolized by such cultural features as the oath-swearing ceremonies and the ritual buffalo sacrifice, a common Montagnard cultural identity was produced, reified, and bureaucratically prescribed by the colonial state (cf. Miles & Eipper 1985). As defined by the French, Montagnard culture was considered valuable in itself, needing no adaptation to Vietnamese civilization. Under French protection Montagnard culture would be respected and even perfected by an appropriate development policy, designated *faire du Moi* after the populist slogan of *faire de l'ouvrier* (ANSOM 370.1240: Réplique du Gougal à Résuper, 9/1940). Ethnographic discourse provided the arguments to exclude the ethnic Vietnamese from the region, to counter Vietnamese claims of the Highlands, and even to separate the Highlands from Annam. Montagnards were likened to children, perceived as credulous, naïve, often violent, but very loyal if one knew how to handle them; they needed the firm but just guidance of France to move into the twentieth century (Salemink 1987:107–26). Loudly proclaimed dur-

ing World War II, when writers close to the colonial administration glorified
Sabatier's oeuvre as a model to follow, this image was to be very persistent
(Antomarchi 1946; Boudet 1942; Ner 1943).

Professional Anthropology and the French Indochina War

In March 1945 the Japanese forces in French Indochina staged a coup against
the French, who seemed unreliable allies once metropolitan France had been
liberated from occupation by Nazi Germany. When the Japanese surrendered
to the Allies five months later, power was seized by the Communist-led Viêt
Minh front under Hô Chí Minh—the only force in Vietnam that had resisted
both the French and the Japanese. When the French sent an expedition army
the following year to reconquer Indochina, the Central Highlands became
a strategic asset, which the French tried to keep out of the negotiations with
the Viêt Minh by disconnecting it from Vietnam. At negotiations at Dalat
between France and the Viêt Minh in 1946, a Montagnard "delegation," headed
by Ma Krong, demanded an autonomous status from Vietnam, under direct
French rule. In 1948 the Central Highlands, formerly known as the "pays Moï,"
was rebaptized as Pays Montagnard du Sud-Indochinois. When this formal
disconnection proved untenable, the Highlands, as Emperor Bao Dai's hunting ground, formally became his Crown Domain, but actually continued to
be administered directly by the French (ANSOM 137.1241; Hickey 1982a:
385–405; Salemink 1987:129–35).

In this context, the inhabitants of the Highlands underwent a few name
changes:

> The administration and the ethnographers abandoned the term "savages,"
> which was considered vague and insulting. First, they adopted the term "Moï"
> which they borrowed from the Vietnamese, while specifying it and stripping
> it of its pejorative connotations. More recently, the "policy of consideration"
> [politique d'egards] was prescribed. One tried "Indomalais," and then "popula-
> tions montagnardes du Sud-Indochinois," whose initials produced "Pemsiens."
> (Ner 1952:45)

The term Pémsien, enthusiastically propagated by Dournes in France/Asie (Dam
Bo 1950), was soon replaced by Condominas's Proto-indochinois (1953), which
is still being used.

In a special ethnographic issue of the semi-official Revue Education (1949),
edited by the then inspector of the Pays Montagnard, the action civilisatrice
of the French was glorified and contrasted with the "barbarism" that puta-

tively characterized the Viêt Minh. There were even articles by Montagnards testifying to their appreciation of the benefactions of colonization:

> From plundering and warring tribes, without laws or beliefs, France has made them . . . a race which is almost ready for modern civilization. But in many respects, the Montagnards lag behind, and their evolution remains incomplete. If the realizations continue, the Montagnards will not be destined for extinction, but on the contrary will become a strong and beautiful race, worthy of its educators. (Y-Bih-Nie-Kdam in *Revue Education* 1949:90)

The parallel themes of French concern for the Montagnards and denial of legitimacy of Vietnamese claims to the Highlands permeated French ethnography in this period—not only shallow and obviously ideological publications like the *Revue Education*, but also publications of a more seriously scientific character. In the first serious postwar monograph—a detailed description of Rhade funeral rituals published by the Institut d'Ethnologie in Paris—the medical doctor of Ban Me Thuot, Jouin, insisted that although "insignificant" borrowings from the Laotians and Cambodians were evident in Rhade ritual, "in no respect, however, is an Annamese [Viêt] contribution perceivable" (Jouin 1949:207). It was up to the French to save the rich Montagnard culture by fighting disease, laziness, carelessness, and superstition. Only by developing to the same level as the neighboring nations would the Montagnards be able to resist invasions from them. Similar strains were echoed elsewhere in early postwar ethnography in the work of Paul Guilleminet, former resident of Kontum province (1941, 1942, 1952); of Marcel Ner, a former civil servant who became Professor of the Ethnology of Indochina at the Ecole nationale de la France d'Outre-Mer (1940a, 1940b, 1952); and of Albert Maurice, an officer serving with the Bataillons Montagnards (1941).

Such themes, however, were not limited to elder colonial civil servants doing ethnographic research or turning into retrospective ethnographers. The same image was cherished by a new generation of professional ethnographers—some of them academically trained in the metropole (Georges Condominas, Pierre-Bernard Lafont), others amateurs who gradually assumed a professional status (Jacques Dournes, Jean Boulbet). The new generation took their lead from the newly founded Centre de Formation aux Recherches Ethnologiques and the posthumously published *Manuel d'Ethnographie* of Marcel Mauss (1947), who back in 1901 had proposed instruction for ethnographic research at the founding congress of the Ecole d'Extrême-Orient in Hanoi (Mauss 1903). In prewar France, fieldwork never received the attention it got in Anglo-American anthropology—although in French Indochina the composition of a *coutumier* played a somewhat similar role. The Centre de Formation therefore looked across the Channel, even across the Atlantic, to find the model of participant observation, and the ideas of functionalism, structuralism, or cultural relativism that soon came to permeate the research of its graduates. And because the Centre de Formation was sponsored by different parts of the postwar "Union Française," its graduates did their fieldwork in the "associate states" that had once been colonies of the "Empire Française." Thus the process of institutionalization of ethnographic practice, beginning in the 1930s with the Ecole de Extrême-Orient, was followed by a process of professionalization after World War II.

The most productive ethnographer until 1954 was Jacques Dournes, a Catholic missionary sent to the Central Highlands immediately after World War II, who soon found himself engaged in all kinds of ethnographic work, including ethnolinguistics (1950) and, of course, the composition of a *coutumier* (1951). Well aware of anthropological theory and practice, Dournes gradually shifted away from the church and by the 1970s had become a professional anthropologist. Although based on research among the Sré of the province of Haut-Donnaï, his first major monograph was presented as a description of the culture of all "Pémsiens." Justifying this unity on geographical, ethnic, and racial grounds, he argued that the Montagnards belonged to the "Indonesian race," which would be as different from the "Yellow" as from the "White" race. Despite the contested character of the Pays Montagnard du Sud-Indochinois, Dournes denied that the term *Pémsien*—his own invention—had any political connotation. The Pémsiens were, in short, quite distinct from the Vietnamese, who constituted the main threat to their existence (Dam Bo 1950:5–6, 19).

Like the other postwar anthropologists, Dournes presented his relation with the Montagnards in terms quite different from those of his prewar predecessors. He published his first major monograph under the pseudonym Dam Bo, the name given to him by the Sré. Others of the postwar group also adopted indigenous names, among them Condominas (Yo Sar Luk) and Boulbet (Dam Böt). Twenty-five years later, Dournes was aware of the ambiguous significance of this practice:

> Yo Sar Luk, Dam Böt . . . and myself, Dam Bo at the time, publicized our "savage" names as the program of our dreams: this was the integration into a people quite different from our community of origin, knowing well that we remained the Whites in the eyes of those who, we pretended, had adopted us—although we had been imposed upon them—and for whom our strangeness excused our marginal lives and our privileges, within a context of colonization. (Dournes 1977:76)

Dournes evidently loved the Montagnards, and was concerned about their eventual disappearance. But although critical of aspects of French rule, such as the use of straw men as village heads, he promoted direct rule as the best guarantee against a Vietnamese "invasion" of the Highlands.

The first professional anthropologist after World War II to conduct modern fieldwork in the Central Highlands was Georges Condominas. Sponsored by the Office de la Recherche Scientifique et Technique d'Outre-Mer, he began work in Indochina in 1947 under the general supervision of the director of the Ecole Françoise de Extrême-Orient, the ethnologist Paul Lévy. By agreement with colonial officials, the isolated Mnong Gar village of Sar Luk was chosen as location for an acculturation study, which Condominas felt "must be the main concern of the 'colonial' anthropologist" (1952:305). Practiced within the framework of new institutes like the Office de la Recherche d'Outremer and the Centre de Formation aux Recherches Ethnologiques, and financed by the colonies or associated states, postwar ethnography geared itself to the demands of the newly formed "Union Française," stressing problems of acculturation, education, and economic development. In the two-volume *Ethnologie de l'Union Française* (1953), to which Condominas contributed an article on the ethnology of Indochina, it was argued that "only anthropology can form a valid basis for a policy":

> It would be vain to pretend to advise and direct an indigenous society without proceeding with the methodical study of its habits and mentality . . . French anthropological research, then, seems to be of national interest; formerly, colonization could not do without it, and now it is one of the vital conditions of the Union. (Leroi-Gourhan & Poirier 1953:897)

Condominas, however, soon became aware of the less positive effects of colonial rule on local populations: notably, recruitment for the army, the régime in the plantations, and exploitation of local populations by French-appointed chiefs (Condominas 1957:459). Stimulated by the anticolonial anthropologist Michel Leiris, Condominas became sensitive to the "colonial situation," and to what he called the *préterrain*—the local colonial milieu from which the ethnographer set forth and which offered itself as a haven of rest when he came out of the field (Condominas 1972:9–10). When he published his ethnographic monograph of the Mnong Gar in 1957, after the French withdrawal from Indochina, it was in the form of a diary, which included his own role in the society.

Although the published ethnography of this postwar group appeared too late to be of use for the Action Psychologique which accompanied the military struggle against the Viêt Minh (cf. Boulbet 1957, 1967; Lafont 1963), ethnographic knowledge had nonetheless played a role in the attempt to win over the Highland population for the French cause. Medical and social work, economic development and promises for political autonomy were the tools, and schools were transformed into "formation centers for Montagnard propagandists" (Pagniez 1954:135–42). The effort was backed by a colonization program for retired French military, who were supposed to form a protective buffer against Vietnamese insurgents (ANSOM 386.3167; Boulbet 1967:2; Salemink 1987:131–33). Even a small-scale village resettlement scheme was initiated, heralding later American efforts (Nguyên Dê 1952:21–22). The most important development, however, was the *maquis* or Groupements de Commandos Mixtes Aeroportés. Led by European officers or soldiers expected to adapt to local life styles, in order to gain the confidence of these ethnic groups, these irregular armies were skillful in action behind enemy lines (Fall 1963b:185–250; Trinquier 1976).

Notwithstanding these efforts, the first Indochina war made two things very clear. First, despite the "esteem" of the French for Montagnard culture, symbolized by their ethnographic practice and ethnic policy, they could not win Montagnard affection in the face of taxes, corvée labor, and forced labor under horrible conditions on the plantations (Lewis 1951; Condominas 1957). Second, the French could not prevent the ethnic Vietnamese from establishing contact with the Montagnards. Trân Tu Bình, for example, has described how Vietnamese plantation workers got in touch with ethnic groups living near the Phu Riêng plantation in order to secure their support during strikes (1985:28–31, 66). The result was that many Montagnards, sometimes entire ethnic groups, joined the nationalist struggle, and by 1954, a large part of the Central Highlands was controlled by the Viêt Minh (Fall 1963a:127, 1983b:185–250; Hickey 1982a:408–13).

After the French defeat and withdrawal from Vietnam, French ethnography stood in a different relation to the Montagnards than it had under colonialism. The old colonial *préterrain* of officials, missionaries, and planters lost its force (Condominas 1965:95–101). Because the new *préterrain* of American experts, military officers, and advisors did not impinge directly on French anthropology, it was now free to develop along more independent lines. This was reflected in the 1960s in the founding by Condominas of the Centre de Documentation et de Recherches sur l'Asie du Sud-Est et Monde Insulindien, which dropped the *coutumier* the Ecole Français de Extrême-Orient had requested in the past, devoting attention instead to ethnolinguistic studies and ethnoscience. But although ethnographic discourse was now conditioned more by professional interests in France than by administrative interests in Vietnam, it continued to be dominated by a cultural relativist viewpoint reminiscent of Sabatier. Like Sabatier, French professional anthropologists dealing with the Montagnards stressed the value of their culture and its distinctness from that of the Vietnamese. They saw the Montagnards as victims of the Vietnamese, much in the same way French colonial officials had depicted them before. During the second Indochina war, however, it seemed that the Montagnards would be forced to take sides, and eventually be assimilated by the Vietnamese, either those of the Saigon régime or those of the National Liberation Front.

Ethnographic Discourse and Strategic Options in the United States Vietnam War

The context of American domination of South Vietnam from 1954 to 1975 was very different from French colonial rule.[1] Since direct American rule was impossible, the United States had to rely more on their Vietnamese counterparts. And because the Americans had no important economic interests in plantations or industry in Vietnam, there was no sharp contradiction between economic and politico-military interests. However, other contradictions developed, as the strategic options represented by different military and political institutions became vested interests: the army and navy wanting increased and modernized firepower; the Central Intelligence Agency concerned about the attitude of the population; The United States Agency for International Development (USAID) busy developing the countryside in order to counter peasant insurgency.

The model for the American experience with the Montagnards had been set in World War II by George Devereux, a Hungarian-born ethnopsychologist who studied ethnology in France before coming to the United States. In the early 1930s, Devereux conducted ethnographic fieldwork among the Sedang, near Kontum, commissioned by the Institut d'Ethnologie. During World War II, he served in the Far East Bureau of the Office of Strategic Services, the predecessor of the CIA, developing a plan "to establish friendly relations with the mountain tribesmen—whose long-standing hatred of the French, the Japanese, and the Vietnamese was well-known—and organize them into guerrilla bands," by parachuting in a group of twenty special agents (including anthropologists and psychologists). Although organizational difficulties and political arguments with the "Free French" caused cancellation of the plan late in 1943, a pattern of direct contact with the Montagnards to the exclusion of other than American influence had been set (Spector 1983: 23–27; NSA: Admiral Miles Records, Naval Group China).

Although Devereux published his views on the role of the Montagnards in Indochina in 1947, for some time policy moved in other directions. In the view of Rostow's influential modernization school, which focussed on economic development in nation building, the Montagnards were regarded as minor obstacles to an integral Vietnamese nation-state, and some even saw them doomed as a distinct ethnic group (Wickert 1959:126–35). When an American colonel of the famous Lansdale Mission, the French-born Lucien

---

1. This section is a preliminary exploration of American discourse concerning the Montagnards, not a balanced, chronological account of their subsequent history. It does not deal with Vietnamese communist views of the Montagnards, which were much less influenced by the French ethnographic discourse.

Conein, proposed in 1955 to adopt the French program of recruiting Montagnards for special battalions, his plans were rejected by his superiors without argumentation (Dassé 1976:166–78; Conein Interview, 5/10/90). Considered strategically unimportant during the 1950s, the Montagnards did not receive much attention from Americans, whose opinions generally reflected and rationalized South Vietnamese practice. But when the American-backed nation-building policy of South Vietnam's Diêm régime was expressed in land-grabbing, exploitation, discrimination, and repression of ethnic cultures and languages, it provoked resentment among the Montagnards. The suppression of the Bajaraka Movement (*Bahnar, Jarai, Rade, Koho*) in the late 1950s helped to create support among the Montagnards for the National Liberation Front. The Kennedy administration's response to the insurgency was counterinsurgency, which – informed by Mao's well-known metaphor of the fish and the water – was intended to isolate the guerrilla from the rural population by borrowing from Communist guerrilla methods. Much to the dismay of the South Vietnamese government, the approach brought the Americans into closer contact with the Montagnards.

From 1962 onward, after initial successes with a Village Defense Program started by the CIA, the U.S. Army Special Forces "advisers" recruited Montagnards into Civil Irregular Defense Groups (CIDG), which were expected to provide village defense and border surveillance from camps in their home regions. Despite "all the enmity between the Montagnards and the South Vietnamese government," the Americans were able to establish "a warm relationship" with the Montagnards – so close, according to the later recollection of General Westmoreland, that "many Vietnamese were quick to suspect American motives in the Highlands" (Westmoreland 1976:78–79).

Direct American involvement with the Montagnards awakened an awareness of the consequences of South Vietnamese nation building. The influence of ethnic Vietnamese in the Highlands came to be seen as detrimental to the political security situation, in that it drove the Montagnards to the National Liberation Front's Montagnard Autonomy Movement, headed by a former Bajaraka leader, Y Bih Aleo. In this context, American institutions like the Special Forces, the CIA, and USAID, informed by often classified social science research, stressed Montagnard cultural identity in opposition to the Vietnamese of either the Viêt Công or the Saigon régime. Apart from the Special Forces involvement with the CIDG groups, the most telling example was the CIA involvement after 1961 with the Bureau of Highland Affairs and its successors, the Directorate and the Ministry of Development of Ethnic Minorities (Hickey 1982b:122). Thus did American counterinsurgency practice converge with French ethnic policy before 1954 insofar as both had an interest in an appeasement policy toward the Montagnards in a rebellious country which seemed as hostile to foreigners as to its minorities.

Montagnard troops of a Civil Irregular Defense Group unit being given a pre-attack briefing by a U.S. Army Special Forces "adviser." (From Kelly 1973:109.)

In its dealings with the Montagnards and the Vietnamese in general, American counterinsurgency practice often drew upon French experience (as well as the British experience in Malaya and previous American experience in Greece and the Philippines), trying to transform this experience into applicable concepts. Some French experts like Bernard Fall worked directly in American service, either in Vietnam or in the United States. American experts read French material, which was being collected in American universities and research organizations, and American anthropologists and army researchers translated French ethnographic publications. When Condominas was in Saigon in the 1960s he even found an illegal translation of his monograph on the Mnong Gar—apparently classified as "For Government Use Only" (1973:15). The knowledge thus gleaned would be used, for example, in the Special Forces handbooks, which gave descriptions of the major ethnic groups, largely based on French ethnography, and prescriptions of how to deal with them effectively, in chapters on "Political Subversion," "Psyops [psychological operations] Considerations," "Civic Action Considerations," "Paramilitary Capabilities" (*Montagnard Tribal Groups* 1964) or "Communications Techniques," "Civic Action Considerations," and "Suggestions for Personnel Working with the Montagnards" (*Minority Groups* 1966).

At the operational level, the Special Forces adopted the tactics developed by Colonel Trinquier of the French army for the *maquis* who operated behind

Viêt Minh lines during the first Indochina war, in which specially trained soldiers lived with the Montagnards and adopted their life styles, copying the successful methods of the Communist cadres. Further developed by the Special Forces, the *maquis* constituted a *faire du moi* policy par excellence, in that it adapted to local customs in order to use the local population for political goals which transcended their social space. This did not imply, however, that the Montagnards had much influence on ethnic policy, for this policy was motivated by interests beyond their control. For this reason, Colonel Trinquier refused to work with the Americans, fearing that the "tribes" would be sacrificed again for ulterior goals (Fall 1963a:195–96; 1963b:117–18; Kelly 1973; Stanton 1985; Trinquier 1952:85–88).

The character of the American Montagnard policy might best be demonstrated by their response to FULRO (Front Unifié de la Lutte des Races Opprimées), which was considered a Montagnard autonomy movement, although it pretended to represent the Khmer and Cham minorities in Vietnam as well (FULRO 1965). The rank and file of the movement, however, were the Montagnard CIDG units headed by the American Special Forces. The main grievances of FULRO were the Viêt immigration and landgrabbing in the Highlands, the lack of Montagnard representation in the higher levels of the South Vietnamese administration and army, and the disdainful attitude of many Viêt toward the "Moi" (savages) in general; in short, they wanted a return to the *statut particulier* which they enjoyed under the French. In September 1964, FULRO rose against the Saigon government by taking over four Special Forces camps, killing Vietnamese troops and taking many hostages. Although Saigon wanted to repress the rebellion severely, American anthropologists, Special Forces officers, and CIA agents tried to avoid a clash that would turn the Montagnard population against the government, and negotiated a solution between Saigon and the less radical rebel leaders at a conference of Montagnards and South Vietnamese held in Pleiku (Sochurek 1965: 38–64). Gerald Hickey, an anthropologist who had played a role in the negotiations, observed that the Montagnards saw the Americans as a protective buffer against the Vietnamese, who in turn were annoyed by American interference (Hickey 1982b:83, 98–109). In a book intended to devise a winning strategy in Vietnam, Herman Kahn, director of the Hudson Institute on National Security and International Order, noted with some concern that "many U.S. military or political officials have, in effect, supported the FULRO movement among the Montagnards, which, given some of its objectives (the attainment of relative or complete independence of the mountain people), really represents a kind of subversive movement" (Kahn et al. 1968:327).

In line with official American policy of support for the Saigon régime, General Westmoreland issued strict orders to cut off all contacts with FULRO by the Special Forces. However, many military and civil officials tried to remain in touch with FULRO in the years after the revolt, hoping to prevent them from allying with the National Liberation Front, which had its own minorities organization. FULRO even seemed to offer opportunities for countering Viêt Công insurgency in areas that were "acknowledged" FULRO territory. The CIA, which had an outstanding Montagnard intelligence network in the Highlands in the early 1960s, almost succeeded in winning over Y Bih Aleo, vice-president of the NLF, only to be obstructed by the Saigon army (Layton Interview, 5/7/90). American organizations like the CIA and USAID were involved in the Directorate of Development of the Ethnic Minorities, which in 1966 was raised to the status of Ministry, and pressure was exerted to bring the Saigon government to accept Montagnard candidates for the 1967 elections. Some FULRO leaders, including Paul Nur, Touneh Han Tho, Nay Luett, and Touprong Ya Ba, were incorporated into government agencies, and in 1969 FULRO was persuaded to surrender formally to the Saigon government, after it had made some concessions concerning the recognition of Montagnard land titles, primary education in their own language, and representation in parliament. USAID had many programs running in the Highlands, although these were not very successful, because of South Vietnamese non-cooperation (U.S. General Accounting Office 1973).

On the other hand, the Saigon government, suspicious of American motives in the Highlands after the 1964 uprising, managed to bring the CIDG units under formal control of the Vietnamese Special Forces, which had the effect of reducing direct American contacts with the Montagnards. Many Bajaraka and FULRO adherents outside these units, viewing the concessions by the Saigon government as merely cosmetic, remained in exile in Cambodia or took sides with the NLF. In 1972 FULRO was in fact reestablished outside the CIDG forces, and eventually took sides against the Saigon government. And in March 1975 it was the non-cooperation of the Montagnards with the South Vietnamese authorities that would make possible the Communist surprise attack at Ban Me Thuot, capital of Dak Lak (Darlac) province – an event which eventually triggered the fall of South Vietnam as a separate state.

Some American institutions working with the Montagnards developed a perspective resembling that of the French, promoting discord between Montagnards and the ethnic Vietnamese in an effort to discredit the Viêt Công, and posing as trustworthy protectors. Their success was evident in April 1975, when a group of pro-American Montagnards, mainly associated with the Ministry for Development of Ethnic Minorities, made a deal at the American Embassy to continue fighting in exchange for American support after the Communist take-over. Under the banner of FULRO they kept on fighting, although the American support did not materialize (K'Bruih Interview, 4/15/90; Sprague Interview, 5/17/90). Their influence, however, was limited, because of the build-up of a conventional U.S. military presence in Vietnam.

Increasingly, American counterinsurgency doctrine became geared to the demands of conventional strategy, which coupled a reliance on abundant fire-power and the efficacy of the air force to the belief that guerrilla warfare was supported from without, if not actually imported by the North Vietnamese regular army. In order to facilitate the use of conventional tactics, free fire zones were created by the forced resettlement of populations to "strategic hamlets" or other guarded, "secure" areas, in an attempt to separate the water from the fish. The Special Forces, the main American instrument for direct contact with the Montagnards, were increasingly curtailed, not only by South Vietnamese suspicion of American motives in the Highlands but also by their progressive incorporation into the conventional army, which was also suspicious of the strategy of irregular warfare developed by the CIA for the Special Forces (Kelly 1973:151–75; Blaufarb 1977:243–95; Cable 1986:141–57).

In 1969 the two positions clashed over the issue of forced relocation of Montagnard villages, which had been resumed by the South Vietnamese army with support of the U.S. Military Assistance Command/Vietnam, despite earlier agreements with both FULRO and the Ministry of Development of Ethnic Minorities. Protests of the Civil Operation/Rural Development Support, the civil pacification body, and the Ethnic Minorities Council, in which the anthropologist Gerald Hickey and USAID specialists participated, were to no avail, and despite reconciliation efforts by Ambassador William Colby, some AID personnel resigned (MACCORDS: MACJ3-032, March 1969; Colby 1989:284; Colby Interview, 4/20/90). By 1971, however, Colby, advised by Hickey and John Paul Vann, decided to stop the relocations temporarily (Hickey 1982b:223).

This conflict was reminiscent of the conflict over Sabatier in the 1920s, with the outcome much the same. In both situations the culture and the life style of the Montagnards, symbolized by their traditional land rights, were threatened by foreign claims to the lands, and the land rights were ignored for ulterior goals. In the 1920s the land was claimed in order to establish plantations in the Highlands; in the 1960s the Montagnards were driven off their land in order to establish free fire zones (which all too often were turned into plantations again by rich Vietnamese).

Despite the differences over strategy and tactics, American officials were generally in agreement that Vietnamese society could be managed and steered in the desired direction if the right tools were used—specifically, those of applied social science and social engineering. In contrast to French ethnography before 1954, American anthropology was already thoroughly institutionalized and professionalized, and in the context of the Vietnam War, research for the military was oriented toward the needs of counterinsurgency, a new field in which careers could be made. And since "the Department of Defense could obtain most of the information it required on minority groups from literature of scholarly anthropological research" through the Cultural Information Analysis Center (CINFAC) and the Defense Documentation Center, it was "only when vital gaps exist[ed] in academia's knowledge of strategically located minority peoples [that] the Pentagon found it necessary to sponsor original research in this field" (Klare 1972:111).

Research for the army, navy, and air force was either performed in house or on a contractual basis by research institutes like the RAND Corporation and the Simulmatics Corporation, or by universities. Counterinsurgency research programs like Project Agile and CINFAC were set up within the framework of army thinktanks, and, to reduce the risk of bias, the research was spread out over a number of research institutes (Deitchman 1976).

Regarding the Montagnards, there were three sources of information: American representatives in the field, who acquired practical knowledge of the ethnic groups; past research by anthropologists/ethnographers, mostly French; and sponsored research on specific topics deemed vitally important. Usually, these sources were used simultaneously, as is reflected in the *Montagnard Tribal Groups* volume (1964), prepared by the Special Warfare School at Fort Bragg; in the *Minority Groups in the Republic of Vietnam* volume (1966), prepared by the Center for Research in Social Systems of the American University; and in an extremely well-informed, anonymous, secret study, *The Highlanders of South Vietnam 1954–1965*, prepared in 1966, on political developments among the Montagnards (Bajaraka, FULRO, and the Viêt Công), which included over one hundred biographies of Montagnard leaders (NSA: CIA–Vietnam Station, June 1966). Generally, such studies emphasized the strategic importance of the Central Highlands for the control not only of Vietnam, but all of Indochina. According to both North Vietnamese revolutionary and United States counterinsurgency doctrine, the control of a geographic area presupposed the control of the indigenous population. Any successful policy not only had to be respectful of Montagnard tradition and custom, but had to take the grievances and aspirations of the Montagnards into account, as expressed by their political organizations. Thus, military strategy and tactics, politics, and ethnographic knowledge had to go hand in hand in the Central Highlands.

The outstanding American expert on the Montagnards was and is the anthropologist Gerald C. Hickey, who along with Bernard Fall became one of the main links between the French and the American discourse. As a graduate student at the University of Chicago, Hickey in 1953 received a fellowship to study the ethnology of Indochina in Paris, where he was impressed by the wide range of ethnographic material on the Montagnards (Hickey 1988:xxvii). After travelling to Saigon in 1956 as a member of the Michigan State University Vietnam Advisory Group, he wrote a report encouraging the South Vietnamese government to accommodate to the "highland people's desire to preserve their ethnic identity." Barred from further travel in that region by high-ranking Vietnamese officials who reacted negatively, he carried out his first research in the lowlands. But between 1964 and 1973, with funding from the RAND Corporation, he did extensive field research in the Highlands (1964, 1967a, 1967b). His reports and later publications stressed the differences between the lowland Vietnamese and the Highlanders—who, "although divided into many ethnic groups," shared "many sociocultural characteristics that historically have set them apart from the more advanced Cham, Khmer, and Vietnamese" (Hickey 1982b:xiv).

Hickey's research reports mainly dealt with the "Highlanders" in general, and his *Ethnohistory* (1982a, 1982b) recounted the attainment of a common ethnic identity and the rise of ethnonationalism among the Montagnards. His strong sympathy for the Montagnards was expressed in an ethnographic discourse that borrowed heavily from cultural relativism, stressing the value of the original Montagnard culture and avoiding political implications. In his description of the Dieu Python Movement for example, Hickey did not follow French sources that had blamed Vietnamese Communists for the revolt, but instead adopted Ralph Linton's rather apolitical, voluntaristic conceptualization of a "magical nativistic movement"—in contrast to Jacques Dournes, who paid more attention to both the mythological and political content of the movement (Dournes 1978:85–108; Hickey 1982a:343–58). Hickey was equally indulgent toward FULRO, which he considered as the genuine expression and culmination of Montagnard ethnonationalism, whereas French anthropologists like Dournes and Condominas, as well as critical American scholars, saw it as a movement of tribal mercenaries organized and supported by the CIA. While there is no indication that FULRO was actually organized by the CIA, despite evidence of considerable support, close contacts, and mutual exploitation, it must be kept in mind that the distinction between FULRO and the CIDG, organized by the U.S. Special Forces, was slight; even Brigadier General S. Marshall remarked that the Montagnards were mercenaries paid by the United States (Marshall 1967:22).

During the Vietnam War, Hickey was the main academic expert on the Montagnards, and being sympathetic to their cause as he perceived it, developed into their major spokesman (1971). Considering himself an "action anthropologist" in the Sol Tax tradition (Hickey Interview, 4/5/90), he became increasingly critical of the conventional warfare tactics advocated by the regular Army and the Air Force, which proved detrimental to the Montagnards and their way of life. Hickey sided instead with those segments within the American camp that stressed the political rather than the military aspects of the struggle—organizations like the Special Forces, the CIA, and USAID, which were inclined to achieve pacification through a more balanced counterinsurgency program, taking account of the social, economic, and political situation of the population to be pacified. He tried to influence American advisors in the Central Highlands to refrain from the use of indiscriminate firepower and herbicides, and opposed the forced relocation programs, which resettled thousands of Montagnards into guarded camps in order to create "free fire zones" (Hickey 1988:196–207).

Hickey was not the only anthropologist working among the Montagnards. Ethnolinguistic research was conducted by the Summer Institute of Linguistics/Wycliffe Bible Translators, an organization committed to converting all ethnic groups in the world to Christianity by translating the Bible into local languages. Entering Vietnam in 1957 through an introduction by President Magsaysay of the Philippines to President Diêm, the Summer Institute had a contract with the Ministry of Education to provide school primers in the ethnic languages, and from 1967 on, USAID provided extensive funding for bilingual education programs. Although the Summer Institute claimed to be nonpolitical, it tended to see the American war effort in Vietnam as part of an anticommunist missionary crusade. Often working in Special Forces camps or provincial capitals for security reasons, its researchers were part of the information network that surrounded the American counterinsurgency efforts in the Central Highlands (Stoll 1982:86–92). In addition to school primers and Bible texts, it published ethnolinguistic and ethnographic studies focussing on folklore items, with Hickey's encouragement (Gregerson 1972; Gregerson & Thomas 1980). While the Summer Institute workers seemed harmless and apolitical, their very superficiality served to reify Montagnard cultural identity as "traditional" and antithetical to communist doctrine.

In general, American ethnographic research with respect to the Montagnards was relativist insofar as it insisted on the value of Montagnard culture and stressed the need to respect their traditional landrights. But inasmuch as the questions being asked were designed to render the ethnic groups amenable to counterinsurgency, they fitted with one of the alternative strategic options in Vietnam. Social scientists were free to write critical reports with respect to alternative strategies, as Hickey demonstrated when he criticized the conventional warfare strategy of the U.S. Army in Vietnam. However, such critical opinions had limited force. Seymour Deitchman, an insider in research sponsored by the Department of Defense, noted that only opinions which remained within the boundaries of the established discourse about the origins of communist insurgency and the preferred course of counterinsurgency had any influence on policy. Dissenting opinions outside the accepted discourse were either dismissed as immaterial or simply not read (Deitchman 1976:328–44), and once the commitment to conventional warfare was no longer open to question, relativist discourse became irrelevant.

Given the interest of the South Vietnamese government in asserting control in the Highlands, relativist discourse had political as well as strategic implications. Insofar as the Americans pictured the Montagnards as loyal warriors and victims of warfare among the ethnic Vietnamese, this led to friction between Americans—posing as protectors of minorities—and ethnic Vietnamese in the Highlands. But as the use of abundant firepower, the defoliation, the forced urbanization, and the resettlement schemes provoked an adverse response among the Montagnards, the NLF and the North Vietnamese were able to reap the profit, as was shown by the Spring Offensive in 1975, which started in the Central Highlands, leading to the unification of Vietnam under the Hanoi government.

In the 1920s and the 1930s French reports and publications on the Montagnards frequently alluded to the fate of the American Indians who had been forced onto reservations. This ran counter to the ideals of *mise en valeur* and *mission civilisatrice*, on the one hand insofar as reservations failed to stimulate development or allow investment, on the other, insofar as they prevented contact with civilization. And since indigenous peoples were thought to live miserably on reservations, the French could hardly think of themselves as the protectors of minorities if they adopted such a policy. Later on, French anthropologists like Condominas and Dournes, although remaining within the boundaries of the same relativist ethnographic discourse, were highly critical of United States policy with respect to the Montagnards, blaming the Americans for not protecting them, indeed for destroying their societies and cultures with their indiscriminate warfare. Condominas in fact coined the term *ethnocide* (by analogy with *genocide*) to designate American strategy (Condominas 1965:469).

On the American side, some historians and sociologists blamed the French for their racism, their colonial exploitation, and their "divide and rule" policy with regard to the different ethnic groups. They saw French colonial policy concerning the Montagnards not as humanitarian protection but as self-interested exploitation. However, among American anthropologists there was more ambivalence. Hickey especially showed considerable sympathy for the position of Sabatier, whom he called the "hero of Darlac" (Hickey 1988: 186). Hickey saw a continuity in the French and American presence in the Highlands, and so, in a broader historical context, may we. Just as the nation-building discourse of the Rostow school resembled the earlier evolutionist discourse of prewar French colonialism, so did the ethnographic discourse of American counterinsurgency resemble the cultural relativist discourse of postwar French anthropologists. And insofar as American relativist discourse was in fact continuous with the latter, there was in fact a certain continuity of assumption, practice, and policy that endured for more than half a century. During that period, the underlying opposition of economic and political priorities, of *mise en valeur* and *mission civilisatrice*, was replaced by an opposition of strategic priorities within an anticommunist *mission civilisatrice*. But from Sabatier to the CIA, there was an evident thread of continuity in the invention and appropriation of the highland groups that he first designated "Montagnards."

Acknowledgments

I would like to thank Talal Asad, Peter Kloos, Dick Kooyman, Ken Post, and George Stocking for their valuable comments on earlier drafts of this essay. In 1989, a first version was discussed at a workshop at the Centre for Asian Studies in Amsterdam of the University of Amsterdam, for which discussion I would like to thank the participants. This essay is in part an adaptation of my thesis on the colonial era, to which I refer the reader for more detailed references to French sources. Follow-up research in France and the United States has been made possible by grant no. W 52-456 from the Netherlands Foundation for the Advancement of Tropical Science.

References Cited

Abbreviations:

ASEMI	*Asie du Sud-Est et Monde Insulindien*
BAVH	*Bulletin des Amis du Vieux Hué*
BEFEO	*Bulletin de l'Ecole Française d'Extrême-Orient*
BSEI	*Bulletin de la Société des Etudes Indochinoises*
CEFEO	*Cahiers de l'Ecole Française d'Extrême-Orient*
TIIEH	*Travaux de l'Institut Indochinois de l'Etude de l'Homme*

AID. See under Manuscript Sources.
ANSOM. See under Manuscript Sources.
Antomarchi, D. [1946]. *Premier livre de lecture en Rhadée. 1ʳᵉ année – Cours enfantin.* N.p.
AOM. See under Manuscript Sources.
Blaufarb, D. 1977. *The counterinsurgency era: US doctrine and performance.* New York.
Boudet, P. 1942. Léopold Sabatier, apôtre des Rhadés. *Indochine* 3(113):i–vii.
Boulbet, J. 1957. Quelques aspects du coutumier (N'dri) des Cau Maa. *BSEI* 32(2): 110–78.
———. 1967. *Pays des Maa': Domaine des génies.* Hanoi.
Bourotte, B. 1955. Essai d'histoire des populations montagnardes du Sud Indochinois jusqu'à 1945. *BSEI* 30 (1): 17–116.
Brenier, H. 1929. L'Indochine économique. In *L'Indochine, un empire colonial français,* ed. George Maspéro, 137–216. Paris/Bruxelles.
Cable, L. 1986. *Conflict of myths: The development of American counterinsurgency doctrine and the Vietnam war.* New York.
Colby, W. E. 1989. *Lost victory.* Chicago/New York.

Condominas, G. 1952. Rapport d'une mission ethnologique en pays Mnong Gar (PMSI). *BEFEO* 46:303–13.

———. 1957. *Nous avons mangé la forêt de la Pierre-Génie Gôo.* Paris (1977).

———. 1965. *L'exotique est quotidien.* Paris.

———. 1966. Classes sociales et groupes tribaux au Sud-Vietnam. *Cah. Int. Sociol.* 40:161–70.

———. 1973. Ethics and comfort: An ethnographer's view of his profession. Distinguished lecture, American Anthropological Association. *Annual Report, 1972.* Washington, D.C.

———. 1980. *L'Espace sociale à propos de l'Asie du Sud-Est.* Paris.

Cupet, P. 1893. Chez les populations sauvages du Sud de l'Annam. *Tour du Monde* 12–16:177–256.

Dam Bo [Dournes, J. T.]. 1950. Les Populations Montagnardes du Sud-Indochinois. *France/Asie* 49–50 (special number).

Dassé, M. 1976. *Montagnards, révoltes et guerres révolutionnaires en Asie du Sud-Est continentale.* Bangkok.

Daufès, E. 1933–34. *La garde indigène de l'Indochine, de sa création à nos jours, t. II: Annam.* Avignon.

DDRS. See under Manuscript Sources.

Deitchman, S. 1976. *The best-laid schemes.* Cambridge, Mass.

Devereux, G. 1947. Potential contribution of the Moï to the cultural landscape of Indochina. *Far Eastern Quart.* 6(4): 390–95.

Dorgelès, R. 1930. *Chez les beautés aux dents limées.* Paris.

———. 1944. *Route des tropiques.* Paris.

Dourisboure, P. 1857. *Les sauvages bah-nars (Cochinchine orientale).* Paris.

Dournes, J. 1950. *Dictionnaire Srê (Koho)-Français.* Saigon.

———. 1951. *Nri, recueil des coutumes Srê du Haut-Donnai.* Saigon.

———. 1977. *Po'tao. Une théorie du pouvoir chez les Indochinois Jo'rai.* Paris.

———. 1978. Sam Bam, le Mage et le Blanc dans l'Indochine centrale des années trente. *L'Ethnographie* n.s. 76(1): 85–108.

Dubois, P. 1950. *Notes sur L. Sabatier, résident du Darlac, 1913–1916.* Mémoire présenté a l'Ecole Nationale de la France d'Outre-Mer. ANSOM Bibliothèque D 3201.

Durand, E. 1907. Les Moy du Son-phong. *Rev. indochinoise* 6:1055–68, 1158–71.

EFEO. See under Manuscript Sources.

Fall, B. 1963. *The two Vietnams: A political and military analysis.* New York.

———. 1963b. *Street without joy: Insurgency in Indochina, 1946–1963.* London.

FULRO. 1965. *Historique du Front Unifié de Lutte de la Race Opprimée (FULRO).* Phnom Penh.

Galliéni, J. 1941. *Galliéni au Tonkin, 1892–1896, par lui-même.* Paris.

Gregerson, M., ed. 1972. Ethnic minorities of Vietnam. *Southeast Asia* 2(1).

Gregerson, M., & D. Thomas, eds. 1980. *Notes from Indochina on ethnic minority cultures.* Dallas.

Guerlach, J. 1884. Chez les sauvages bahnars. *Les Missions Cathol.* 16:22–466 passim.

———. 1887a. Moeurs et superstitions bahnars. *Les Missions Cathol.* 19:441–527.

———. 1887b. Deux ans de captivité chez les Bah-nars. *Les Missions Cathol.* 19:538–89.

———. 1894. Chez les sauvages de la Chochinchine orientale: Bahnar, Reungao, Sedang. *Les Missions Cathol.* 26:9–243.

———. 1906. *L'oeuvre néfaste.* Saigon.

Guilleminet, P. 1941. Recherches sur les croyances des tribus du Haut-pays D'Annam, les Bahnar du Kontum et leur voisins, les magiciens. *TIIEH* 4:9–36.

———. 1943. Ebauche d'une classification des Moïs au point de vue culturel. *Indochine* 169:21–25.

———. 1952. *Coutumier de la tribu Bahnar, des Sedang et des Jarai de la province de Kontum.* Hanoi.

Herskovits, M., ed. 1973. *Cultural relativism: Perspectives in cultural pluralism.* New York.

Hickey, G. C. 1964. *The major ethnic groups of the South Vietnamese Highlands.* Santa Monica, Calif.

———. 1967a. *The Highland people of South Vietnam: Social and economic development.* Santa Monica, Calif.

———. 1967b. Some aspects of hill tribe life in South Vietnam. In *Southeast Asian tribes, minorities and nations,* ed. P. Kunstadter, 2:745–70. Princeton.

———. 1971. *Some recommendations affecting the prospective role of Vietnamese Highlanders in economic development.* Santa Monica, Calif.

———. 1982a. *Sons of the mountains: Ethnohistory of the Vietnamese Central Highlands to 1954.* New Haven.

———. 1982b. *Free in the forest: Ethnohistory of the Vietnamese Central Highlands, 1954–1976.* New Haven.

———. 1988. *Kingdom in the morning mist: Mayréna in the Highlands of Vietnam.* Philadelphia.

Histoire militaire. 1931. *Histoire militaire de l'Indochine française des débuts à nos jours,* par les Officiers de l'Etat-Major du Général de Division Aubert. 2 vols. Hanoi.

Hobsbawm, E., & T. Ranger, eds. 1983. *The invention of tradition.* Cambridge.

Jouin, B. 1949. *La mort et la tombe.* Paris.

Kahn, H., et al. 1968. *Can we win in Vietnam? The American dilemma.* London.

Kelly, F. 1973. *U.S. Army Special Forces, 1961–1971.* Washington, D.C.

Kemlin, J. 1922. *L'immigration annamite en pays moy, en particulier dans la province de Kontum.* Quinhon.

Klare, M. 1972. *War without end: American planning for the next Vietnams.* New York.

Lafont, P.-B. 1963. *To'Lo'i Djuat, coutumier de la tribu Jarai.* Paris.

Lanessan, J. L. de. 1895. *La colonisation française en Indochine.* Paris.

Lavallée, A. 1901. Notes ethnographiques sur diverses tribus du Sud-Est de l'Indochine. *BEFEO* 1:291–311.

LCTR. See under Manuscript Sources.

Lechesne, P. 1924. *L'Indochine seconde, régions moïs.* Quinhon.

Leger, D. 1977. A propos des missionnaires de Kontum, "dupes et complices" dans l'affaire Mayréna en 1888. *ASEMI* 9:231–47.

Le Jarriel, R. 1942. Comment la mission catholique a servi la France au pays Moï. *BAVH* 29:37–53.

Lemaire, T., 1976. *Over de waarde van kulturen: Een inleiding in de kultuurfilosofie.* Baarn, Holland.

Leroi-Gourhan, A., & J. Poirier. 1953. *Ethnologie de l'Union Française.* Paris.

Lewis, N. 1951. *A dragon apparent.* London.

M. C. 1923. Pénétration et organisation de l'Hinterland moï. *Rev. Pac.* 5:548–64.

McAlister, J., Jr. 1967. Mountain minorities and the Vietminh: A key to the Indochina war. In *Southeast Asian tribes, minorities, and nations,* ed. P. Kunstadter, 2:771–845. Princeton.

MACCORDS. See under Manuscript Sources.

Mac Du'ò'ng. 1978. Chu nghia thuc dân mó'i cua My và các dân tôc thiêù sô o' miên nam nu'ó'c ta. *Tap Chí Công San* 2:89–96.

Maitre, H. 1909. *Les régions moïs du Sud-Indochinois: Le Plateau du Darlac.* Paris.

———. 1912. *Les Jungles moï.* Paris.

Marshall, S. 1967. *Battles in the monsoon: Campaigning in the Central Highlands, Vietnam, summer 1966.* New York.

Maurice, A. 1941. Rudiments de l'anthropologie des Mnongs du Lac (Mnong Rlam). *TIIEH* 4:225–26.

Mauss, M. 1903. Essai d'une instruction pour l'étude sociologique des sociétés indochinoises. In *Premier Congrès International des Etudes sur l'Extrême-Orient,* 115–16. Hanoi.

———. 1947. *Manuel d'ethnographie.* Paris (1989).

Miles, D., & C. Eipper, eds. 1985. Special volume: Minorities and the state. *Canberra Anth.* 8(1–2).

Minority Groups. 1966. *Minority groups in the Republic of Vietnam.* Washington, D.C.

Monfleur, A. 1931. *Monographie de la Province du Darlac (1930).* Hanoi.

Montagnard tribal groups. 1964. *Montagnard tribal groups of the Republic of Vietnam.* Fort Bragg, N.C.

Montaigut, F. de. 1929. *La colonisation française dans l'Est de la Cochinchine.* Limoges.

Murray, M. 1980. *The development of capitalism in colonial Indochina (1870–1940).* Berkeley.

Ner, M. 1940a. Rapport sur les coutumiers. *CEFEO* 22:4.

———. 1940b. Rapport sur les coutumiers. *CEFEO* 23:3.

———. 1943. La France en Pays Moï: Humble constructeurs de l'Empire. *Indochine (hebd. illus.)* 4 (144): i–vi.

———. 1952. Psychologie des populations archaiques (Moi) du Sud de l'Indochine. *Rev. Psychol. des Peuples* 1:44–61, 157–77.

Nguyên Dê. 1952. *Plan de développement économique pour les Pays Montagnards du Sud du Domaine de la Couronne.* Saigon.

Pagniez, F. 1954. Sur les plateaux d'Indochine, guerre psychologique. *Rev. Deux Mondes,* January: 135–42.

NSA. See under Manuscript Sources.

Pasquier, P. 1923. Les principes directeurs de l'administration des regions mois. In *Variétés* 1935.

Pavie, A. 1900. *Mission Pavie: Géographie et voyages,* vol. 3. Paris.

———. 1902. *Mission Pavie: Géographie et voyages,* vol. 4. Paris.

Revue Education. 1949. *Revue Education* 16: numéro spécial consacré aux populations montagnardes du Sud-Indochinois, sous la direction de l'Inspection des Colonies.

Robequain, Ch. 1944. *The economic development of French Indochina.* London.

Sabatier, L. 1927. *La Chanson de Damsan.* Paris.

————. 1930. *Palabre du serment au Darlac.* Hanoi.

Sabatier, L., & D. Antomarchi. 1940. *Recueil des coutumes rhadées du Darlac.* Hanoi.

Salemink, O. 1987. *Ethnografie en kolonialisme: Minderheden in Vietnam, 1850–1954.* Amsterdam.

Sarraut, A. 1923. *Mise en valeur des colonies françaises.* Paris.

Simonnet, Ch. 1977. *Les tigres auront plus pitie.* Paris.

Sochurek, H. 1965. American Special Forces in action in Viet-Nam. *Natl. Geog.* January:38–64.

Spector, R. 1983. *Advice and support: The early years.* (The U.S. Army in Vietnam Series.) Washington, D.C.

Stanton, S. 1985. *Green Berets at war: U.S. Army Special Forces in Southeast Asia, 1956–1975.* London.

Stoll, D. 1982. *Fishers of men or founders of empire?* London.

Thompson, V. 1937. *French Indochina.* New York.

Trân Tu Bình. 1985. *The red earth: A Vietnamese memoir of life on a colonial rubber plantation.* Athens, Ohio.

Trinquier, R. 1952. *Les maquis d'Indochine: Les missions spéciales de service action.* Paris (1976).

————. 1961. *Modern warfare: a French view of insurgency.* New York (1964).

U.S. General Accounting Office. 1973. *Progress and problems of U.S. assistance for land reform in Vietnam: Report to the Congress.* B-159451, AID, Dept. of State. Washington, D.C.

Variétés. 1935. *Variétés sur les pays mois.* Saigon.

Westmoreland, W. 1976. *A soldier reports.* New York.

Wickert, F. 1959. The tribesmen. In *Vietnam: The first five years,* ed. R. Lindholm. East Lansing, Mich.

Yersin, Dr. 1893a. Sept mois chez les Moi. In *Variétés* 1935:166–205.

————. 1893b. Les Moïs de la Cochinchine et du Sud-Annam. *Revue indochinoise illus.* 2(2): 52–81.

Manuscript Sources

This essay is based on research in various archival collections in France, the United States, and Vietnam. The cited materials are found in archives collections which have been abbreviated as follows:

AID — Agency for International Development library, Rosslyn, Va.

ANSOM — Archives Nationales, Section d'Outre-Mer. This collection was recently moved from Paris to Aix-en-Provence, France.

AOM — Archives d'Outre-Mer, Aix-en-Provence, France.

DDRS — Declassified Documents Reference System (microfilm collection published by the Carrollton Press), Library of Congress, Washington, D.C.

EFEO   Ecole Française d'Extrême-Orient, Paris.
LCTR   Library of Congress, Technical Reports (declassified, microfilm), Science Reading Room, Washington, D.C.
MACCORDS   Military Assistance Command/Civil Operations and Revolutionary Support files, U.S. Military History Institute, Carlisle Barracks, Pa.
NSA   National Security Archive, Washington, D.C.

Interviews

Colby, William E. April 20, 1990.
Conein, Col. Lucien. May 10, 1990.
Hickey, Gerald C. April 5, 1990.
K'Briuh, Pierre. April 15, 1990.
Layton, Col. Gilbert. May 7, 1990.
Sprague, Edmund. May 17, 1990.

REPRESENTING, RESISTING, RETHINKING

Historical Transformations of Kayapo Culture and Anthropological Consciousness

TERENCE TURNER

First Encounter: Gorotire 1962

The Brazilian Air Force mail plane bearing my wife and me arrived in the Kayapo village of Gorotire late one afternoon in 1962. It was in the rainy season, and as it happened the climactic day of a women's naming ceremony. At the airstrip we were met by a large crowd of Kayapo, many of whom had run out from the village in their ceremonial regalia. We presented our papers to the Brazilian in charge of the Gorotire Post of the government's Indian Protection Service, who subjected them to a minute examination while the plane unloaded cargo and refueled. Then, as it rose into the sky, he frowningly returned them, announcing that he could not accept them, since they were addressed only to "the *encarregados* [chiefs] of all Indian Posts in the Third Inspectorate" (which included Gorotire), and not directly to him by name. He regretted, he said, that we would therefore have to leave for Rio by the next plane, scheduled to arrive the following week, and could return only if we could have the documents "properly addressed." Our protestations that the papers in question had actually been drawn up by the office of the director of the *Serviço pela Proteção aos Indios* (hereafter, SPI) in Rio, and were plainly intended to serve as a general permission to conduct research in any of the Kayapo villages in the Inspectorate, fell on deaf ears.

Fortunately for us, the "weekly" plane did not return the following week,

---

Terence Turner is Professor of Anthropology at the University of Chicago. Since 1962 he has worked with the Kayapo people of the Brazilian Amazon. He is presently at work on a critique of American cultural anthropology entitled *A Critique of Pure Culture*.

nor indeed for the following three months. This allowed us ample time to learn why the *encarregado* had been so eager to get rid of us. The Chief of the Regional Inspectorate of the SPI, with the collaboration of the local *encarregado*, had for the past several years exhorted the Gorotire Kayapo to collect Brazil nuts, a valuable cash crop. The arrangement was that the Regional Inspector would market the nuts in Belem and return the proceeds to the Kayapo in the form of manufactured goods (guns, ammunition, clothes, cooking pots, metal tools, and beads). For two years, however, the Kayapo had seen little of the promised goods. Two months after our arrival, and immediately after the grudging completion of yet another nut harvest, the Regional Inspector himself flew in to Gorotire, and in an address to the villagers assembled in and around the communal men's house explained that no more goods would be forthcoming because the last year's harvest had been stolen from the warehouse by "a bad man."

This brazenly dishonest cover-up of the embezzlement of the Gorotires' hard-earned money by the Inspector and his lackey, the *encarregado*, was greeted with disbelief and outrage by the mass of Kayapo listeners, but the two village chiefs, supported by the native "chief of police," successfully kept the people's anger from spilling over into acts of violence against the Director, the *encarregado*, or the Post buildings. Owing their position to appointment by a previous SPI *encarregado* rather than to the indigenous institutional procedure for designating "ritual chanters" (*benhadjuoro*), the same chiefs acted as foremen in organizing the collection of the Brazil nuts and all other work projects for the SPI Post. Their loyalty was maintained by periodic presents of goods from the *encarregado* and by occasional trips to Conceição do Araguaya or Belem in one of the Air Force planes that supplied the SPI Post. The *encarregado* always took care to make a show of funnelling all presents of food and goods brought in to the village by the SPI through them, thus allowing them to play the role of dispensers of *largesse* to their followers. The "native police" were another recent creation of the SPI: five Kayapo men provided with blue fatigue uniforms and billy clubs, on whom the *encarregado* had conferred the right to throw anyone vaguely defined as misbehaving into a locked room in the SPI bunkhouse overnight.

The episode of the stolen Brazil-nut money and its aftermath epitomized the oppressive and corrupt aspects of the control exercized by the SPI over the Gorotire and other Kayapo communities. The Gorotire put up with these degrading arrangements out of desperation and lack of alternatives. They had made their first peaceful contact with members of the regional Brazilian population twenty-five years before, in 1938. Then over eight hundred strong, they had just split off from a much larger community, whose other offshoots were pursuing and attacking them. Sheltering first in the Brazilian river town of Nova Olinda, and then at an SPI Post built for them nearby, they had lost all but one hundred of their population to disease, further internal schisms, and starvation resulting from administrative incompetence and neglect. Their devastation by disease emphasized their radical dependence on any source of Western medicine, which the SPI could only sporadically and partially supply, owing to its general inefficiency, corruption, and incompetence. The alternative source of medical support was the Unevangelized Fields Mission, which established a Mission Post as a rival to the SPI's Gorotire Post in 1938–39, and remained with Gorotire ever since (more recently, as the *Missão Cristão Evangélica Brasileira*). The missionaries were competent, honest, diligent, and compassionate; without their medical aid the Gorotire probably would have become extinct. But they were also proselytizing evangelists, especially in the first two decades of their mission. They were out to convert the Kayapo and to suppress aspects of their culture they deemed works of the Devil, including nudity, various sexual and ritual practices, infanticide, and the men's house (which at one point they actually burned down).

The Kayapo, however, were not amenable to conversion, and clung tenaciously to their traditional social and cultural values. Because their communal ceremonies had little to do with theistic or supernatural beliefs, they did not in essential respects conflict with the missionaries' creed. The conflict came at a more fundamental level, in the incompatibility of the missionaries' Protestant emphasis on individualistic conscience and conversion and the Kayapo cultural emphasis on the person as collective social product—the underlying theme of their communal ceremonial system. By the time of our arrival, the missionaries had withdrawn from active evangelization and were concentrating on linguistics and Bible translation. Although about 25 percent of the village attended Sunday services to sing the hymns (some adapted as ceremonial dance songs in communal rituals), the missionaries themselves did not feel that they had made a single definite convert in twenty-odd years of effort. The one tantalizing possible exception was indicative: one of the two village chiefs was shrewdly capitalizing on the long-standing rivalry between the missionaries and the SPI by pretending to be teetering on the brink of conversion while using the threat of realignment with the mission to extract better treatment from the *encarregado*. It was a performance that might be the envy of many a Third World leader attempting to play off rival superpowers in the heyday of the Cold War.

From the Kayapo point of view, another problem with the missionaries was that they were not a satisfactory source of trade goods. They did offer some work (cutting wood, drawing water, helping with the construction of buildings in the mission compound, etc.), for which they paid reliably and relatively well. But these opportunities for remuneration-through-work fell far short of the demand for Brazilian goods in the community as a whole, and the missionaries were in fact ideologically opposed to a policy of buying the Indians' support or allegiance by bestowing large quantities of material goods on them as "presents." The SPI, on the other hand, was committed to precisely such a policy, seeking to induce the Indians to stay at the Post and remain dependent on the governmental agency, rather than satisfying their commodity wants by resuming raids on the local settlers. Unfortunately, however, the incompetence, corruption, and chronic under-budgeting of the government agency rendered it incapable of implementing its policy at a level satisfactory to the Kayapo.

Short of breaking off peaceful relations and resuming full-scale raiding, the Gorotire had no alternative but to depend on the two rival institutional representatives of the Western world system in which they were becoming ever more inextricably embedded for the satisfaction of their medical and commodity needs. Monopolizing all opportunities for the remuneration of labor by goods or money, these two agencies also monopolized control of, and access to, all means of transportation and communication linking Gorotire to the outside world: airplanes, motor launches, the village short-wave radio, the electric generator that powered it, audio tape recorders, cameras, literacy and the use of the mails, and the arithmetical skills needed to use money and buy and sell in the market, from the purchase of a fishhook to the marketing of a Brazil-nut crop. No more than a third of the Gorotire (including only one woman) had some command of spoken Portuguese, and only a few were fluent.

The Gorotires' enforced dependence on the Brazilians and missionaries gave powerful leverage to the efforts of both of these agents of Western civilization to change those aspects of Kayapo culture overtly incompatible with integration into Western society. Among these was the traditional form of the Kayapo village, built in a circle with its men's house or houses in the center. The SPI had made the Gorotire rebuild their village at the site of the SPI Post in the form of a "street" formed of two parallel lines of houses. This was a deliberate attempt to suppress the cosmological and ceremonial aspects of the indigenous culture, with which the circular village plan was directly connected, and which a zealous *encarregado* had recognized as obstacles to the assimilation of the Kayapo into Brazilian society. The missionaries, as previously noted, had attempted to get rid of the men's house in an *auto da fé*; but the Kayapo rebuilt it, not in the "center" of the "street," but at one end, between the two rows of houses, so that it opened directly out onto the empty space between them.

An even more flagrant obstacle to social intercourse between the Kayapo and representatives of Western civilization, Brazilian or missionary, was the traditional Kayapo bodily adornment. Both sexes went nude, except, in the case of men, for penis sheaths and large wooden plugs in the lower lip. All adults wore their hair long in back but shaved in front up to a point at the crown; the shaved area, along with most of the rest of the face and body, was usually covered with bold designs in black and red paint. The Kayapo had learned from their earliest contacts with Brazilians that nudity, lip plugs, body paint, and penis sheaths were inconsistent with minimal Brazilian standards of social intercourse. Recognizing that some social intercourse with Brazilians had become essential to their survival, they needed little urging from SPI agents and missionaries to adopt minimal clothing and discard other flagrantly "savage" aspects of their traditional appearance. By the time of our arrival in 1962, most men had removed their lip plugs, had their hair cut short Brazilian style, and had taken to wearing shorts and occasionally T-shirts in the village, although some still appeared in long hair, lip plugs, and penis sheaths. Although perhaps one in five still went entirely nude, most of the women wore dresses of the typical interior Brazilian style, with scoop necks to free the breasts for nursing. The chiefs and most of the older men possessed complete Brazilian-style outfits (shoes, sometimes even socks, long pants, and long-sleeved shirts) for wear on trips to Brazilian towns, visits to the village by Brazilian officials, or attendance at the missionaries' Sunday services; with such fancy-dress outfits no body paint or Kayapo ornaments were worn.

As we discovered on the evening of that first day in Gorotire, however, the rules of dress were still quite different on traditional ceremonial occasions. After our gear had been carried in from the airstrip and stowed in the tiny room in the SPI workers' bunkhouse which the *encarregado* had allotted us until the next plane arrived, we walked out to the broad village "street" to watch the final dance of the women's naming ceremony that had been interrupted by our arrival. Although the Gorotire themselves had given us a friendly welcome, we were depressed, upset, and confused, even more by Gorotire's failure to live up to our idea of what a Kayapo village should look like than by the *encarregado*'s hostile reception. As we gloomily considered our situation, women, girls, and a few men began to assemble at one side of the street near the men's house. They were nude, their bodies painted and covered between the knees and the neck with parakeet feathers, their cheeks decorated with crushed blue eggshell stuck on with resin, their earlobes distended with large mother-of-pearl earrings made of freshwater mussel shells, and their torsos hung with ornamental sashes and baby-slings. Many wore gorgeous feather capes of macaw plumes that covered their backs and stuck out like halos around their heads and shoulders. Others wore feather headdresses identical to those of the Tupinamba in the woodcuts in Hans Staden's sixteenth-century account of his captivity among the savages of Brazil.

As the dancers were assembling, an elderly man began to declaim an oration from the middle of the "street," gesturing flamboyantly with his Winchester rifle and shouting with obviously exaggerated intonation. When per-

Old-fashioned uniforms: smartly outfitted Kayapo leader (Toto'i of Gorotire) with shirtless author, 1963. (Photograph by J. Bamberger.)

haps a hundred dancers had assembled, they formed into a double column, led by two husky young women beating time with large rattles, and began to move counterclockwise around the street, chanting a slow processional hymn. We realized that despite the "civilized" rectangular "street" plan, the Kayapo had managed to lay out a "circular" (actually elliptical) dancing path in the "street" in front of the men's house. As dusk gave way to darkness, huge bonfires were lit at the two poles of the ellipse, and the rhythm of the dance changed from the stately slow march of the opening processional to a series of more vigorous steps, each with its accompanying song, all sung and danced in unison by the massed dancers of the column.

Those not dancing (mostly men and young children) stood just outside the dancing track in front of the houses, watching. Several people were working frantically to prepare a huge earth-oven filled with great manioc cakes stuffed with fish and game, while others were busily hacking holes in the lower shells of large tortoises, perhaps fifty of which lay lashed to long racks near the fire. To our horror, hot rocks were dropped into these holes, and the wretched creatures, writhing in agony, died boiled in their own blood. All of this was in preparation for a feast to be held when the dancing finally stopped at dawn. As the sun finally rose over the exhausted column of dancers, armed men suddenly appeared and began seizing girls and women from the line (we later learned these men were the personal "ritual companions" or god-kin of the women). As they raced away, dragging their captives toward the houses, they were pursued by older women (mothers and grandmothers of the girls, who stand in a joking relation with their daughters' and granddaughters' ritual companions), who brandished burning logs, with which they beat the backs of the retreating warriors. All this was greeted with hilarious laughter by the spectators; a solid hit on a bare back with a blazing log drew the loudest cheers. When the column of dancers had been sufficiently depleted in this way, an orgy of tortoise-eating began. We felt too exhausted to cope. As we dazedly made our way back to our hammocks, a beaming, Portuguese-speaking Kayapo called out to us, "Wasn't it beautiful?" We had attended our first Kayapo ceremony.

Ethnographic Presence and Ethnographic Present: Objective Observer and Subjected Native

The experiences of this first day in the field were to be a paradigmatic frame that oriented our research for the rest of that first field trip. It was apparent that historical pressures of contact and coexistence with the Brazilians and missionaries had imposed a number of changes on the outward forms of Kayapo life and culture. These changes had been forced upon the Kayapo as part of a situation over which they had no control, and within which they were dependent for survival on those imposing the changes. The changes had no intrinsic meaning for the Kayapo, but had been imposed because of the meanings they held for the dominant outsiders, the whites. They simply seemed an alien overlay beneath which the authentic Kayapo culture still persisted, manifesting itself in collective ritual events like the ceremony we had witnessed that first night in Gorotire, and in enduring social institutions like the men's house and the stubbornly matri-uxorilocal extended-family households that bordered the village "street." The native social and cultural forms, however, appeared to have persisted in spite of their encompassment by the situation of inter-ethnic contact, rather than because of any stable or harmonious accommodation with it. While in many cases the native forms had been eroded or suppressed by the Western forms, there appeared to be no positive synthesis, syncretism, or adaptive accommodation of either set of forms to the other. The anthropological interest in the situation thus seemed to lie in discovering the authentic Kayapo social and cultural system beneath the corrosive overlay of imposed political, social, and ideological forms constituting the situation of contact, and in analyzing how this system might work, or might have worked, in its own terms. From this point of view, anthropology, like Kayapo culture itself, defined itself in abstraction from the "situation of contact," as the antithesis of "change" and the enemy of "history."

The essential historical condition of the plausibility of this view was the apparent lack of any endogenous Kayapo political or cultural response to the situation of peaceful coexistence with Brazilian society. As a successful raiding people, the Kayapo had become dependent on Western commodities, above all firearms and ammunition, *before* their "pacification." Their annual raids on Brazilian settlers and itinerant gatherers of rubber and Brazil nuts were undertaken to satisfy the commodity needs they had built up following their initial exchanges with Brazilians or hostilities with other native groups who had acquired firearms or other Brazilian goods. Raiding had been a Kayapo political solution, of sorts, to the political-economic crisis posed by the historical encounter of the Kayapo with Western society. Raiding, however, was a relatively risky, arduous, and unreliable way of obtaining needed commodities. Many Kayapo groups therefore responded with alacrity to the overtures of Brazilian pacification teams, which offered as inducements quantities of "presents," consisting for the most part of the very commodities the Kayapo had up to then been obliged to resort to raiding to acquire. Peaceful coexistence on the terms the Brazilians offered (essentially, the exchange of trade goods for the cessation of hostilities) accomplished the same ends as raiding had done. Peace, in short, appeared as a continuation of war by other, and decidedly easier, means.

The problem was that once the Kayapo were peacefully settled at an SPI Post, the primary motive for the Brazilian "presents" was removed. The flow of presents tended to diminish and become more unreliable, and desperately needed medical assistance all too often failed to materialize. The Kayapo had no means of compelling the Brazilians (or missionaries) to provide more "presents" or medical help other than threats of violence against Post personnel or buildings, or the ultimate threat to abandon the Post and go back to raiding from the forest. The longer a Kayapo group remained in peaceful contact, however, the less credible this threat became. In particular instances, threats of violence within the Post context could be effective in extorting compliance with Kayapo demands, but they were no long-term solution, since they did not address the basic problem of acquiring some measure of direct Kayapo control over the means of acquiring commodities.

The lack of a viable political response to their subordination to, and dependency upon, the representatives of Western society was one limiting parameter of the predicament of Kayapo groups like the Gorotire in the early 1960s. Another was a lack of consciousness of the political significance of their own culture in the new context of inter-ethnic coexistence: a lack, in other words, of an awareness of the ambivalent import of their "ethnicity" as a pretext for subordination by the dominant society, but also as a potential basis for the assertion of collective autonomy and communal self-determination.

In this context, the continuing vitality of Kayapo social institutions like the matri-uxorilocal extended family household, the men's house, the age-set system, and such communal *rites de passage* as naming and initiation appeared to me, as an anthropological observer, to draw its force from their role in reproducing basic Kayapo social relations, values, and persons. Communal institutions like the age-set system and ceremonies brought about the reproduction of basic social groups such as the family and household through the transformations of social relations effected by recruitment to collective groups and the associated rites of passage. It was apparent to me that the system continued to function because it continued to produce the cultural values to which the Kayapo oriented their personal lives and identities: the "beauty" or completeness and dominance of the senior men and women who fulfilled the roles of heads of households and ceremonial leaders.

The system served, in sum, as a collective apparatus through which the Kayapo could control the reproduction of themselves as social persons and their community as a social universe, and imbue both with the highest values of their culture. More than merely a cultural system of "symbols and meanings," it was an instrument of social empowerment in the most fundamental sense, an organized process through which individual and community could concretely produce themselves and the social values that made life worth living. To abandon this complex system of social and ceremonial institutions, either because it interfered with the demands of the *encarregado* for increased cash crop production or because it embodied values irrelevant or inimical to those of Brazilian society or the missionaries, as the Gorotire were under chronic pressure to do from both sources, would have been not only a cultural loss but a political catastrophe.

In 1962–64, however, the Kayapo of Gorotire did not seem to understand the issues in these terms, at least not in a consciously articulated way. To them, their ceremonies and social institutions were simply the ways they had always done things. Their most inclusive term for their traditional corpus of cultural forms, ceremonial patterns and social institutions was *kukradja*, "something that takes a long time [to tell]"; they thought of it simply as the prototypically human way of living, a body of lore and ways of doing things created and handed down by mythical ancestors and cultural heros. They had no notion that this body of institutions and ideas were the products of social actors like themselves or that they served specific social purposes like the reproduction of families, households, and persons. They had, in short, no notion that their assemblage of received customs, ritual practices, social values, and institutions constituted a "culture" in the anthropological sense, nor any idea of the reflexive role of that culture in the reproduction of their society and personal identities.

The Kayapo, in sum, had not yet developed forms of social consciousness appropriate to their new historical situation as part of an inter-ethnic social system, in which their culture not only served to define them as an "ethnic group" distinct from and opposed to the dominant group but also provided a potential basis for uniting in struggle to protect the internal autonomy of their own communities. This lack of forms of historical, cultural, and political consciousness commensurate with the requirements of their new situation was oddly consonant with the lack of political, inter-ethnic, and historical dimensions of the anthropological concepts of cultural and social structure I was attempting to apply to the analysis of their situation. What did not occur to me at the time was that the structural-functionalist, structuralist, and Boasian-Kroeberian-Kluckhohnian culturalist theoretical perspectives upon which I was attempting to draw might contain homologous lacunae to those of the Kayapo perspective, derived from the corresponding limitations in the perspective of dominant groups in analogous situations of colonial and inter-ethnic domination.

In the quarter century that passed before I returned to Gorotire, the Kayapo did develop new forms of social consciousness appropriate to the orientation of political resistance in their "situation of contact," and put them into practice with spectacular results. To understand how this came about and the cultural transformations it involved, it is necessary to have an idea of the traditional Kayapo world view and the specific ways it changed as the Kayapo struggled to create a viable place for themselves in their new historical circumstances.

From Cosmology to Ethnicity: Transformations of Kayapo Social Consciousness

The structure of the Kayapo conception of the world in the period when the individual village still functioned as a relatively self-sufficient and autonomous social unit can be most easily grasped from the spatial layout of the traditional village itself. A circle of extended-family houses surrounded an open central plaza, which was the locus of communal ceremony and social activities. In the plaza stood two men's houses, one in the east and one in the west, respectively called the "lower" and "upper" men's houses. The land immediately surrounding the circle of houses was called the "black" or "dead" ground, and was conceived as a transitional zone between the social space of the village and the natural domain of the savannah or forest. In this zone were located the cemetery and various ritual seclusion sites used in rites of passage. The village was thus organized along two intersecting spatial dimensions, one of concentric and one of diametrical (east-west) contrast, the latter also being conceived in terms of the vertical contrast between lower and upper, or in the other pair of terms employed by the Kayapo, "root" and "tip." This spatial polarity of the village circle is retained in extant Kayapo villages with only one men's house.

The model of cosmic space-time embodied by the ideal village plan can be seen as a model of the process of social production and reproduction, in which the life cycle, defined as a reversible alternation of socialization and death, is subsumed as an ultimately irreversible but infinitely replicated linear process of growth. East is the "root" of the sky, the beginning of the sun's journey, and metaphorically also of the life cycle. West is the "tip" of the sky, the end of the sun's journey, and metaphorically of the human life cycle or the growth cycle of a plant. "Vertical" space thus defines a temporal process, which is linear and irreversible but infinitely replicable. The concentric dimension of space is conceived as the form of the cyclical, reversible process of transforming natural energy and raw materials into social form (epitomized by the process of socialization) and the breaking down of social forms by natural energy once again (epitomized by death, which is ritually referred to by the Kayapo as "transformation into an animal"). The village is the center point of both dimensions, the focus of social space, which gives way on all sides to the "natural" space inhabited by animals and inferior, non-Kayapo peoples. All levels of social organization, from the village as a whole through the domestic household to the individual person, are conceived as replicating this same socio-cosmic model. The process of social (re-)production is thus recursively embodied in the structure of its products. All levels of the social whole are equally conceived as products of the single, cyclical, and infinitely replicated process of social production it embodies.

The cosmological terms in which this traditional Kayapo view of the social world were cast left no room for a consciousness of the structure of this integral process of social production as itself a social product. It was, rather, seen as the natural structure of the cosmos. Kayapo society was conceived both as the central focus of this cosmic process and as the society that most fully conformed with the cosmic pattern. Other, non-Kayapo societies and peoples were accordingly conceived as both less "social," that is, less than fully human by Kayapo standards, and as less fully exemplifying the "natural" pattern of what a society should be. In concrete terms, this meant that the Kayapo saw

them as at once more animal-like (thus, in this sense, more "natural") and
less "beautiful" or complete (less fully realized instances of the "natural" pattern of humanity, and thus, in this sense, less "natural" as well). This pejorative assessment was epitomized in the Kayapo term for non-Kayapo peoples, *mē kakrit* or "people of little worth or beauty" (other Ge-speaking peoples, with their similar social organizations and languages, were sometimes exempted from the status of *mē kakrit*, and included with the Kayapo in the category of *mē mētch* or "beautiful people").

With the integration of the Kayapo into the polyethnic society of Brazil, however, this traditional cosmological view underwent fundamental modifications in several respects. These changes tacitly add up to a new "world view," as totalizing in its scope and explanatory power as the old. This new formulation, like the old, expresses the relation between the Kayapo and non-Kayapo societies in terms analogous to the internal structure of Kayapo society. But there has been a fundamental change in the conception of "society." The isolated Kayapo village has been replaced, as the exclusive model for social humanity, by the situation of contact, in which Brazilian society, on the one hand, and indigenous societies, on the other, confront each other in a relationship of ambivalent interdependence. Not only are Brazilians admitted into this new conceptual scheme as fully human, social beings, but the Kayapo have come to see themselves as one "Indian" people among others, with a "culture" of the same order as their own. The political corollary of this new level of cultural self-awareness is that the Kayapo have begun to see the preservation or loss of their cultural identity as a matter for conscious concern and concerted political action. From seeing themselves simply as the prototype of humanity, in other words, the Kayapo now see themselves as an ethnic group, sharing their ethnicity on a more or less equal footing with other indigenous peoples in their common confrontation with the national society.

The most fundamental alteration underlying these specific changes is the shift of the central focus of the system of social consciousness as a whole from the internal structure and reproduction of Kayapo society, considered as an autonomous system complete in itself, to the relation between Kayapo society and the national society. The correspondence between the internal structure of Kayapo society and the structure of this focal level of inter-ethnic relations still obtains, as in the old system, but runs, as it were, in the opposite direction, with the internal order of Kayapo society now tacitly seen as motivated or determined by the structure of relations across the inter-ethnic frontier. It is important to note that this "decentering" and its concomitant changes in social consciousness appear to have begun to take definite shape as a collective cultural pattern only when the Kayapo began to interact at the level of concerted communal organization with the national society to contest and change the terms of their relationship with it. The new view thus cannot be regarded as a "reflection" of an existing state of relations, but consists of the forms of pragmatic activity through which the new system, as a specific pattern of conflict and interdependence, was brought into existence through the actions of the Kayapo themselves.

The basic structural principles of the new view are still recognizably the same as those of the old. The key relationships which determine the internal structure of the social domain continue to be modelled on the processes of (re-)productive transformation that link the social and the encompassing natural domain. Within the social sphere, this same structure is seen as repeated on the successive levels of society as a whole, the segmentary household unit, and the construction of the individual social person. The relations and structures themselves, however, have changed dramatically both in form and content.

The universe is still seen as a series of concentric zones of nature and society, but in contrast to the old view, with the Kayapo as the exclusive occupants of the social center and other indigenous peoples and Brazilians in more peripheral, "natural" positions, the new view posits a "social" totality encompassing both Kayapo and Brazilian elements. In this outlook, an "Indian" core (including not only the Kayapo themselves but other indigenous peoples as well) is encompassed by Brazilian society, which is nevertheless accepted as a complementary constituent of the fully social domain. The opposition between Indian and Brazilian society thus combines, or collapses, the meanings carried by the distinct modes of diametrical and concentric contrast in the older, exclusively Kayapo-centered formation of social consciousness.

Each group within this divided social field relates in opposite ways to the surrounding zone of "nature." The Indians' way is constructive, consisting in the traditional processes of transformation of natural energies and materials into social powers and forms, in ways that permit the renewal of nature and its powers. That of the Brazilians, on the other hand, is destructive: the chopping down of forests and their conversion to grassland, the pollution of rivers, the mining of the earth, or the damming of rivers and flooding of the surrounding land, all of which permanently despoil nature and render it unfit for habitation or agriculture, hunting or fishing. The complementarity of these opposing relations to nature thus partakes of the properties of the "vertical" opposition in the old cosmology between the parts of an irreversible process: beginning and end, growing root and exhausted tip. At the same time, it retains the essential significance of the concentric opposition between the domains of human society and nature in the older view. Here again, then, the vertical and concentric modes of opposition, which in the older view were counterposed as distinct and complementary dimensions of contrast, are collapsed into a single, composite but ambivalent mode of opposition.

The relation between native and Brazilian society which constitutes the structure of this new social totality is replicated at all levels of social organization, including the household and the individual person. Just as the social totality is now seen as made up of a native side and a Brazilian side, with the boundary between them defined by the movement of commodities and by the struggle to assert autonomy against the source of those commodities, so the household and the individual have likewise become double beings, diametrically divided between an internal, indigenous Kayapo core and an external façade composed wholly or in part of Brazilian goods and forms. The prototypical commodities involved are clothes, in the case of the person, and in the case of the domestic group, the Brazilian-style house and other items of private property such as cooking pots and suitcases for storing possessions.

At all levels of the social totality, in sum, from the individual to the relation between Kayapo and Brazilian societies as wholes, a Kayapo part or aspect ambivalently defines itself in contrast to a "Brazilian" aspect, struggling to assert the separateness and autonomy of its indigenous aspect, while assimilating to itself a veneer of Brazilian-derived commodity property that it can no longer do without. The new view has not replaced the old, but exists alongside it and as it were on a different level, being specifically focussed on the interface between Kayapo and Brazilian society, whereas the older view is primarily concerned with processes and relations within Kayapo society itself. The new view, moreover, is not formulated in the same terms of ritual and myth, nor as clearly articulated with the structure of village space, as the traditional cosmology; rather, it is implicit in new social forms, attitudes, and rhetoric relating to interaction with Brazilian society, in particular the usage of Brazilian commodities.

This division within the structural units of Kayapo society between an indigenous and a Brazilian component, like that between Kayapo society as a whole and Brazilian society, is a focus of both dependency and struggle. The indigenous social entity (individual or collective) depends on Brazilian commodities and property forms not merely for their practical uses, but to confer a necessary cachet of viability and acceptability within the new, composite, indigenous Brazilian social totality. At the same time, the indigenous Kayapo component of the resulting composite social entity struggles to assert its continuing autonomy and validity against the alien Brazilian aspect. Many features of the social use of commodity property are symptomatic of this ambivalence: body painting of areas of the skin concealed beneath Brazilian clothing; the condescending reference to the new Brazilian-style houses by their owners as "unreal" or "ersatz" (kaygô); and even, at Gorotire, a double village, with an "authentic" traditional circular village for the "real" (older, more traditional) Kayapo, built in the mid-1970s alongside the original Brazilian "street"-style village as an effort to reassert traditional Kayapo cultural patterns.

This process can be seen working itself out in the evolving patterns of use of key commodities. Clothing is a good example. Replacing the penis sheath, shorts were the first form of Brazilian clothing to become standardized in Kayapo communities. The Kayapo also acquired both short- and long-sleeved shirts, long pants, and jackets, and many today possess these items. In the 1960s, it was normal for the chiefs of Gorotire to dress up in long pants and long-sleeved shirts to meet with official visitors, and other Kayapo would don similar "civilized" apparel to have their pictures taken. Short Brazilian haircuts became the norm, and lip plugs were discarded.

Today, however, the same chiefs and other men are again wearing their hair long. In Mentukti and Mēkranoti, a number of older men continue to use lip plugs, and boys' lips are still pierced. Lip plugs have not returned at Gorotire, but both there and in these other two villages, when chiefs go to a Brazilian city, they make a point of wearing shorts (or sometimes long pants) and shoes, but no shirt or jacket. Their faces, arms, and upper bodies are painted, and they wear traditional shell necklaces and bead earrings. The whole ensemble is often topped off with a feather headress. The shift away from full Brazilian clothing for official or formal dress back to a half-and-half compromise between Brazilian and Indian costume reveals more vividly than anything else the recent shift in the local social, political, and cultural balance of power between Brazilians, and Kayapo, and the concomitant development of a new assertiveness and pride in Indian identity.

This new structure of social consciousness may be seen as a complex transformation of traditional Kayapo cosmology, but it is no mere twist of a cognitive kaleidoscope in the structuralist sense. Rather, it embodies the form of the central social process in the new situation of inter-ethnic confrontation in which the Kayapo find themselves. In contrast to the older, cosmological world view based on the internal process of reproduction of Kayapo society, this process is one of struggle and contradiction between the Kayapo and other native ethnic groups, on the one hand, and the Brazilians and other Western nations of the capitalist world system, on the other. Like the older view, the new view not only represents the pattern of this process but provides a charter and ideological framework for action and political struggle within it. In place of the older view of the Kayapo as the autonomous and supreme paradigm of humanity, it defines them as one of a category of ethnic groups ("Indians") locked in struggle with a dominant, alien ethnic group, the whites. In place of the ahistorical and acultural vision of Kayapo society offered by the traditional world view, it defines the very survival of their society and culture as contingent on their successful resistance to the destruction of their natural environment by the dominant whites. The new view constitutes, in short, the sort of formation of social consciousness that the Kayapo seemed to lack, but sorely needed, when I first visited them in the early 1960s.

Changing times, changing shirts: conventionally draped author with bare-chested Kayapo chief (Rop-ni of Mentuktire), Altamira meeting, 1989. (Photograph by Alex King.)

This new Kayapo social and political view was developed as an integral part of the Kayapo struggles of the 1970s and 1980s to take control of the technological capacities, political institutions, and ideological agencies that defined their subordination to the national society. Before proceeding to consider these struggles in more detail, however, it is important to recognize the role played by anthropology in these cultural and political transformations.

From Postcolonial Situation to Postmodern Eco-Politics: The Kayapo Resurgence and Its Implications for Anthropology

Missionaries and Indian Service workers were not the only outsiders to play a role in the new situation of interethnic coexistence. Following the establishment of peaceful relations with the national society, the Kayapo were visited by a series of anthropologists, photographers, ethnozoologists, ethnomusicologists, museum collectors, journalists, cinematographers, and others who may be grouped for convenience under the generic heading of "anthropologists."

Unlike the other representatives of the dominant society with whom the Kayapo came into contact, these visitors came in a relatively deferential and suppliant role, to learn and record Kayapo "culture." The cumulative effect of these contacts was to catalyze the development of an awareness on the part of the Kayapo of the potential political value of their "culture" in their relations with the alien society by which they found themselves surrounded. The discovery that their traditional social institutions, practices, and beliefs constituted something which that society, or at least that sector of it from which anthropologists came, called a "culture," and that rather than a justification of subordination or exploitation, this sector of the dominant society saw Kayapo "culture" as a resource of great value in which it had an interest, was of great political importance for the Kayapo. As a general point, for many native peoples, the fact that anthropologists and other relatively prestigious outsiders, who plainly disposed of impressive resources by local Brazilian as well as native standards, were prepared to spend these resources, not to mention much of their lives, on the study of native "cultures," may have done more than anything else to convey to these peoples the awareness that their traditional way of life and ideas were phenomena of great value and interest in the eyes of at least some sectors of the alien enveloping society. It was realized, in sum, that the difference that had seemed to constitute the greatest obstacle to coexistence with the dominant society might after all represent a valuable resource for such coexistence. This effect was reinforced when anthropologists and others whose primary motive was the documentation of culture contributed material goods and medical assistance, or undertook to act as mediators of concern and concrete support from the metropolitan centers from which they came.

The point here is not the effectiveness of such assistance in itself, but the cumulative effect of such external contacts and information on the reflexive cultural and political consciousness of the Kayapo themselves. In the situation of most Amazonian peoples in the first half of this century, where even those elements of the dominant society that offered support against an overwhelmingly hostile world (the government Indian agency and the missionaries) were committed to assimilationist ideologies that explicitly or implicitly held native cultures in contempt and relegated them to dependent or tutelary roles, simply doing anthropological fieldwork in the modern sense of participant observation became a tacitly political act fraught with radical implications for the positive valuation of native cultures and their right to equality and self-determination. If anthropologists themselves often remained oblivious to these political implications of their activities, Brazilian Indian service workers and missionaries rarely missed the point, as their chronic ambivalence, suspicion, and hostility toward anthropologists in the field attests.

However this may be, it seemed clear to me as I began to study the political struggles of the Kayapo during the period of resurgence in the late 1970s and 1980s that in their takeover of political and technological functions in their own villages and in their political confrontations with Brazilian and international society, the Kayapo were guided by a new level of consciousness of their "culture" as a focus of political struggle.

Kayapo struggles to create and defend a sphere of relative autonomy for their communities and lands have taken place on two fronts, one internal and the other external. Internally, they have sought to gain control of every feature of village/Indian Post society that constituted a point of control by or dependency on the national society and culture. Externally, they have repeatedly confronted threats emanating from the dominant national society and world system at their source, in national and international centers of political and economic power.

With respect to the internal sphere, the Gorotire exemplify the achievements of the other larger Kayapo communities. During the 1970s and 1980s, they systematically took over every major institutional and technological focus of dependency on Brazilian society within their community and reserve. A Gorotire has displaced the Brazilian FUNAI agent as chief of the Gorotire FUNAI Post (the old Brazilian Indian Protection Service, or SPI, was replaced in 1969 by the present agency, the National Foundation for the Indian, or FUNAI). Gorotire run the short-wave radio. Gorotire paramedics staff the new dispensary, which was built and stocked by the Gorotire themselves. Gorotire mechanics maintain the community's fleet of motorboats, truck, tractor, and automobile, which are driven by licensed Gorotire drivers. The Gorotires' own airplane (flown by a salaried Brazilian pilot paid by the community) patrols the frontiers of the Gorotire reserve and takes serious medical cases out to hospitals in nearby Brazilian towns. Gorotire manage their own communal bank account and individual accounts for the village chiefs, which receive money from mahogany and gold concessions on communal land negotiated by the Gorotire themselves. A Gorotire convert now runs the missionaries' Sunday services, attended by a dwindling group of followers, now down to about 10 percent of the village population. In short, the Gorotire have not so much overthrown as made their own the architecture of dependency which comprised these functions, when monopolized by representatives of the national society. They have converted it into the foundation of internal communal autonomy and local control over the principal nodes of articulation with the encompassing national and world system.

These political and cultural conquests at the intra-communal level have been accompanied by a cooperative, inter-communal political offensive directed against threats from the national society and the world economic system in which the Gorotire have participated in alliance with other Kayapo groups. This Kayapo political offensive is without parallel, in its scope, style, substance, and achievements, in the history of Amazonian native societies. Over the past half-dozen years, the Kayapo have staged a series of demonstrations against a variety of threats to their political, social, and territorial integrity and their economic subsistence base. In chronological order, these have included the successful recapture of the gold mines illegally opened up near Gorotire village; a sit-in in the presidential palace in Brasilia against the dumping of radioactive waste on the western frontier of Kayapo territory; the recapture and official demarcation of the territory of the Metuktire Kayapo on the northern border of the Xingú Park; the demonstration at the Brazilian constitutional convention in 1987–88 against the attempts of right-wing forces to insert clauses damaging to indigenous rights and interests into the new constitution; the large and spectacular demonstration in Belem against the arraignment of Gorotire leader Kuben'i on politically inspired charges in 1988; and as the culminating triumph of the series, the great inter-tribal rally at Altamira against the building of a hydroelectric dam scheme on the Xingú River, which played a major role in forestalling a World Bank loan to Brazil that would have made the project possible. As this is written, the Kayapo are awaiting the demarcation of a large new reserve for the remaining Kayapo communities and territories which still lack a legally constituted reserve. This demarcation was promised by the Brazilian government as the result of an international campaign by the Kayapo and non-Kayapo supporters, notably the rock singer Sting, on behalf of the projected reserve.

From Abstract to Concrete:
Cultural Politics and Theoretical De-Alienation

At the time of my first fieldwork, I did not think of the stance of methodological objectivity and non-interventionist "participation" that I adopted as a function of the alienating colonial relation of the Kayapo to Brazilian society. In retrospect, however, it seems clear to me that the underlying factor that made this alienated perspective seem so appropriate and compelling was the apparent radical cultural and political disparity between the Kayapo and the Western society that had encompassed them. In this perspective, Kayapo culture and society, with no prospect of reversing the terms or evening the odds of political and cultural domination, appeared already objectified and abstracted in relation to their encompassing social and political context, in the sense of being held apart from any culturally meaningful or politically constructive engagement with the encompassing alien society.

The historical and political determinants of my initial anthropological perspective on the Kayapo were highlighted for me as I followed the successes of the Kayapo political resistance and cultural resurgence of the next two decades. It was only when I returned to Gorotire in 1987 to make my first "Disappearing Worlds" film (1987), however, that I fully realized what a long way the Kayapo, and I, had come since my first arrival in the village in 1962. The exuberance, optimism, and outgoing warmth of the Gorotire, and their confidence in themselves in relation to the Brazilians, in the wake of their successful takeovers of the political administration and technological functions of their own village and their bold series of political confrontations, made me realize how comparatively dispirited and desperate they had been in the early 1960s.

The change in morale, however, was less striking than the change in social and cultural self-consciousness. In 1986–87, and even more in 1989, it was common to hear Kayapo leaders and ordinary men and women speaking about continuing to follow their cultural way of life and defending it against assimilative or destructive pressures from the national society as the animating purpose of their political struggle. Many, including otherwise monolingual speakers, had begun to use the Portuguese word "cultura" to subsume their mode of material subsistence, their natural environment as essential to it, and their traditional social institutions and ceremonial system. The native term for the body of lore and custom of a society, *kukràdjà*, was now also commonly used in the same way, in speaking of Kayapo customary practices and lore as requiring conscious efforts on the part of the community as a whole to preserve and reproduce.

I emphasize that this new consciousness is not merely a defensive conservatism couched in moralistic terms, as in "We should follow the ways of our ancestors." Rather, it tends to be positively expressed in terms of the necessity of following the culture, frequently concretely identified with traditional modes of subsistence and diet, or the performance of ceremony, in order to preserve the "life," "strength," and "happiness" of Kayapo social communities. Again and again, I have heard Kayapo say that eating Brazilian food, having sex with Brazilians, and especially drinking Brazilian alcoholic drinks, makes one "weak." This belief is often offered as the reason why the environment must be defended, since its destruction would destroy the basis of native subsistence. This in turn would undermine the "strength" and "happiness" of the Kayapo by forcing them to abandon the traditional diet and rely on imported Brazilian food. Kayapo who have travelled and encountered more acculturated native peoples tend to describe them as "sad" and "weak" as a result of their loss of their ancestral *cultura* or *kukràdjà*. The essential idea underlying these expressions is that "culture" is the means by which a society maintains its morale and capacity for action, including both political action vis à vis the national society and the reproduction of its own pattern of life.

The point for present purposes is that by making their culture a political issue, and self-consciously making the dissemination of their cultural image in public demonstrations and news media a key aspect of their political struggle, the Kayapo not only transformed the meaning and content of their culture itself but also the political significance of documenting it and communicating about it to the non-Kayapo public. In the 1980s, to publish or otherwise communicate publicly about Kayapo culture was to become, willy-nilly, a part of both the political and cultural dimensions of the phenomenon about which one was attempting to speak as an anthropologist.

Nor was this any longer merely a case of conveying to the Kayapo a concept of their "culture" as such, or of respect or positive valuation of it, in the sense of my earlier comments on the political implications of anthropological fieldwork in the Amazon. The changes in Kayapo culture and in the social and political relation of the Kayapo to national and international society that have been described involved not only changes in structure and level of reflexive consciousness but also fundamental changes in the relation of the anthropologist to Kayapo culture and society. These changes included (here I speak for myself) a raising of consciousness on the part of the anthropologist of the historical conditions and political implications of his own role analogous to the raising of Kayapo social and cultural self-consciousness that has been described. They also included a shift in methodological and political stance from that of objectively detached "participant observer" to that of an observing and communicating actor, aware that his very activities of observation and communication had become integral parts of the process he was struggling to observe and understand.

These transformations in my relationship as anthropologist to the Kayapo were exponentially intensified as I became more involved in the use of visual media in the field. Beginning with a relatively conventional series of ethnographic films for the BBC filmed in 1976 (1978a, 1982), I went on to make two films in the "Disappearing Worlds" series with Granada Television in 1987 and 1989 which attempted to break with received approaches to ethnographic film by focussing on the ways internal political debate over how to deal with the situation of inter-ethnic contact with a Western society can stimulate the development of cultural self-consciousness, and the ways traditional social and cultural patterns may be drawn upon in such situations as effective resources for empowerment and resistance (1987, 1989a, 1989b). These developments in my own work (and that of my colleagues on the BBC and Granada film crews) were in turn primarily made possible by the fact that the Kayapo had already begun to use visual media in the same way.

By the mid 1970s, representational media (photography, audio recording, and in the mid 1980s, film and video) had begun to play a key role in the Kayapos' objectification of their own culture. As the most concretely accessible and most technologically glamorous aspects of the recording of their culture by outsiders, visual media conveyed to the Kayapo more vividly and

Controlling representation, representing control: Kayapo video cameramen Kuben'i of Gorotire and Kinhiabieti of Mentuktire shooting at Altamira beside British television cameramen. (Photograph by Alex King.)

directly than any other form of communication that their "culture" had value in the eyes of some puzzling but potent part of the alien society from whence the culture recorders emanated. The power of representation through these media thus became associated with the power of conferring value and meaning on themselves in the eyes of the outside world, and reflexively, in new ways, in their own eyes as well. The technology of representation thereby assumed the character of a power to control the terms of this meaning- and value-imbuing process. The acquisition of this technology, of both hardware and operating skills, thus became an important part of the Kayapo struggle for self-empowerment in the situation of inter-ethnic contact. Control over the power and technology of representation, even more than over the image *per se*, became a symbolic benchmark of cultural parity.

The significance of the acquisition of media capability for the cultural politics of empowerment is manifest in the prominence the Kayapo give to their camerapersons in their confrontations with the national society and the world press. The role of Kayapo camerapersons in situations such as the Altamira encounter is not only to make an independent Kayapo documentary record of the event itself, but also to be seen and represented in the act of doing so by the non-Kayapo media. The point is thus made that the Kayapo are not dependent on the outside society for control over the representation of themselves and their actions, but possess to a full and equal extent the means of control over the image, with all that implies for the ability to define the meaning and value of acts and events in the arena of inter-ethnic interaction.

Audio and above all visual media thus become, not merely *means* of representing culture, actions, or events and the objectification of their meanings in social consciousness, but themselves the *ends* of social action and objectification in consciousness. The Kayapo have passed rapidly from the initial stage of conceiving video as a means of recording events to conceiving it as the event to be recorded, and more broadly, conceiving events and actions as subjects for video. The recent inter-tribal meeting at Altamira, which the Kayapo organized to protest a Brazilian project to build a hydroelectric dam scheme in the Xingú river valley, was planned from the outset as a demonstration of Kayapo culture, and of political solidarity among the different Kayapo villages and non-Kayapo native peoples, that would lend itself to representation by informational media, above all film, video, and television.

The documentary film made by Granada Television, "The Kayapo: Out of the Forest" (1989a), for which I served as anthropological consultant, was planned in close consultation with the Kayapo organizer of the Altamira meeting, Payakan, and formed an integral part of Payakan's plans for the demonstration. The idea for the film, in fact, originated in discussions between Payakan and me during his tour of North America in November 1988, when I served as his translator and host in Chicago. Payakan explained that the Kayapo wanted a complete documentation made of all phases of the organization of the meeting, including the preliminary preparations in the Kayapo villages, and that they saw this as an important part of their presentation of the event to the outside world. He accordingly undertook to secure our entry into two of the main Kayapo villages involved in the project, as well as the cooperation of the villagers in enacting their ritual and other preparations before our cameras. He also invited us to accompany him and a delegation of thirty Kayapo leaders to inspect the huge hydroelectric dam at Tucurui, which formed an important part of the initial phase of the organizing for Altamira. All of these subjects were duly represented in our film.

The staging of the Altamira meeting itself was comprehensively planned with a view to its appearance on film and video media. The daily sessions were in effect choreographed with gorgeous mass ritual performances which framed their beginnings, ends, and major high points. The encampment of the Kayapo participants was created as a model Kayapo village, complete with families, traditional shelters, and artifact production, all on display for the edification of the hundreds of photo journalists, television and film camera crews, and video cameras. The Kayapo leaders saw Altamira as a major opportunity to represent themselves, their society, and their cause to the world, and felt that the impact it would have on Brazilian and world public opinion, via the media, would be more important than the actual dialogue with Brazilian representatives that transpired at the meeting itself. At the same time, they shrewdly realized that the production of a huge and gaudy confrontational event would draw large numbers of journalists and documentary makers from the Brazilian and world media, and that the presence of these witnesses, and through them, their mass audience ("the whole world is watching") would be their best guarantee that the Brazilian government would feel compelled to send its representatives to the meeting and to do its best to prevent violence against the indigenous participants. In the event, they were proved correct on all of these points. These, then, are further dimensions of the Kayapo use of media. They are also, by the same token, further dimensions of the role of the anthropological film maker among the Kayapo, and thus of the ways in which he or she becomes part of what he or she films.

The reflexive relationship of the participant observer to the reality he or she records is of course common to all modes of anthropological fieldwork. In attempting to document the role of audio and video media themselves in the cultural transformation and self-conscientization of the Kayapo, however, the reflexive dynamic of this relationship is greatly intensified. One not only becomes part of the process one is trying to record, but directly affects it in numerous ways, some intended and some not.

What happened during the making of the first Granada "Disappearing Worlds" film on the Kayapo is a case in point. I had planned the film as a comparative study of the reactions of two different Kayapo communities to the challenges presented by the encroachments of Brazilian society. I wanted to show that the Kayapo were successfully drawing on their common stock of social institutions and cultural values to resist and adapt to the national society, and at the same time that they were, in the process, actively debating and revising the meaning of their own culture. The general point was that the "cultures" of simple societies like the Kayapo are not homogeneous, internally oriented, closed systems of "collective representations," but active processes of political struggle over the terms and meanings of collective accommodation to historical situations involving interaction with external conditions, including other societies. I was aware of the Kayapo use of audio cassette recorders and video cameras, and planned to include this along with other forms of newly acquired technological expertise in the film as instances of this general point.

When our crew was preparing to leave the first of the two villages to go to the second, the leader of the community asked us to record a message from him to the second community on one of our audio cassette recorders. The message criticized the second community for allowing too much Brazilian exploitation of tribal land and resources, and generally for going too far in the direction of acculturation to Brazilian ways. We duly carried the tape to the second community, where it was played by that community's leading chief to the assembled population. They reacted angrily to the criticisms by the first community's leader, and several made speeches justifying their own approach to coexistence with the Brazilians, insisting that in their fashion they were remaining true to their culture. We filmed this dramatic and revealing encounter, and it became the pivotal scene of our film, linking the sections on the two communities as expressions of opposing positions in the historic debate taking place among the Kayapo over the meaning of their culture in the present crisis of inter-ethnic confrontation.

As a prime example of the way the second community was attempting to use Brazilian technology to defend and preserve its Kayapo culture, we filmed their use of video to record their own ceremonies and encounters with the Brazilians, actually incorporating sections of videos they had shot in our film. In order to do this, however, we had to clean, restore, and recopy Kayapo video tapes which had been damaged by mildew and hard use. These in due course again became available to the community for showing on its own monitor. Meanwhile, our desire to film the Kayapos' use of video stimulated them to video-record our crew filming their camerapersons video-recording certain ceremonies. In all of these ways, our activity of video- and audio-recording the Kayapo became a material part of their own use of video and audio media for their own political and cultural purposes. This material participation became, in an unplanned and spontaneous but therefore perhaps even more significant way, the organizing structure of our audio-visual representation of their cultural reality: the first "Disappearing Worlds" Kayapo film. Our presentation of a video camera to the community was merely a further instance of this reflexive involvement in their use of audio-visual media.

When these reflexive dimensions of audio-visual documentation of contemporary cultural reality are considered together with the ways the Kayapo have begun to incorporate audio-visual media and the physical activity of audio-visual recording (e.g., the presence of Kayapo camerapersons and non-Kayapo film crews) into their own collective acts of political confrontation and cultural self-definition, it becomes apparent that the use of audio-visual media has taken on dimensions of meaning without close parallels in traditional anthropological methods of fieldwork. The quantitative shift certainly approaches, if it has not already reached, the point of qualitative transformation. For the anthropological film maker, the change becomes a shift from participant observation to observant participation.

This shift involves a change in the traditional terms of ethical responsibility in fieldwork. As a participant (like it or not) in processes of cultural self-conscientization and sociopolitical empowerment, the anthropological user of media has some control over the terms of his or her participation. He or she can consciously plan documentary activity so as to encourage, augment, or otherwise support those aspects of the documented phenomena that promote the empowerment of its subjects to reflect upon, control, and transform according to their own lights the cultural, political, and material aspects of the reality in focus.

However, the change wrought by the use of contemporary media technologies, including their ability to reach mass audiences and exert instantaneous influence on public opinion by way of worldwide television networks, affects not only the role of the anthropologist and documentary maker, but the nature of the reality being documented. If the Kayapo are any indication, the processes of cultural and ethnic self-conscientization that have been catalyzed by the new media and their use in worldwide networks of communication are becoming more important as components of "culture" (or, by the same token, "ethnicity") and more central to basic social and political processes in many "primitive" and "traditional" as well as "modern" cultures. This comes to the same thing as saying that the nature of "culture" itself is changing together with the techniques we employ to study and document it.

The essence of this change is that the process of defining cultural reality — ostensibly by "representing" it, but in the process creating specific interpretations and modes of consciousness — is becoming ever more important as a focus and determining element of that reality. This rapidly increasing importance is manifested in the greatly augmented political role of media and the political importance of control over the definition and interpretation of political as well as cultural meaning that media afford. This is a phenomenon that calls for more study and documentation — and more participation — by anthropologists than it has thus far received. When they get around to it, they will find that they have much to learn from peripheral, culturally alien peoples like the Kayapo, who perhaps because of their very alienness have proved quicker studies of our own changing culture in these respects than most Western anthropologists.

Just as the use of representational media by the Kayapo played a key role in the transformations of Kayapo culture and social consciousness in the 1980s, so I found that it also played a similar role in the transformation of my relation as an anthropologist to Kayapo social and cultural reality. Not only did I find myself, as a film maker, becoming involved in the events I was filming, but I found that the Kayapo were increasingly attempting to influence and direct the filming so as to control the content and cultural meaning on the filmic representation, and were even planning some of their political actions from the standpoint of how they would be represented in film and news media. As an anthropologist, in short, I had become a cultural instrument of the people whose culture I was attempting to document.

Realizing the way the wind was blowing, I decided that the Kayapo were ready to dispense with representational middlemen and could proceed directly to making their own films. I obtained a grant from the Spencer Foundation to assist in the training of several Kayapo camerapersons in video-editing techniques. The first round of training was completed in the summer 1990, with the assistance of Vincent Carelli of the Centro de Trabalho Indigenista in São Paulo. Two edited videos were produced by a Kayapo cameraman from Mēntuktire, and a Kayapo video archive was established at the Centro as a repository for the original videos and produced video films (only copies will be returned to the villages). Further training and editing sessions are planned, and several Kayapo communities have indicated a keen interest in participating. One goal of the project is to compile a comprehensive video archive of Kayapo culture, including traditional knowledge, ceremonies, myths, oral history, and contemporary political issues and actions. Another is to provide a number of Kayapo communities with the capacity to plan and execute self-representations of their own cultural and social-political reality. My own role as an anthropologist in this project, in addition to providing the necessary organization and funds, is to observe how the Kayapo use this capacity to represent their culture and their contemporary political-historical situation. The project, in sum, is an attempt at both furthering the development of cultural and social self-consciousness and studying the forms it takes.

When I returned to film the Kayapo in 1987, and again in 1989, when I accompanied and filmed their demonstration at Altamira, I found myself part of a situation of inter-ethnic confrontation and struggle radically different from that of the Gorotire in 1962. The Kayapo were now consummate ethnic politicians: fully engaged, defiantly confrontational, coolly calculating how far they could go without giving a plausible pretext for violent repression by the army or police, and extremely self-conscious of the cultural dimensions and meanings of their struggle for themselves. They organized their demonstrations and political confrontations using adaptations of traditional ritual, mythical, and social forms which infused them with meaning for the monolingual and monocultural Kayapo participants as well as for the leadership; at the same time, they had become expert in articulating these traditional notions with the ideas, values, and causes of Western environmentalist, human rights, and indigenous support groups. These creative adaptations, and the bold policies and acts of political resistance and collective cultural assertion of which they formed part, are authentic manifestations of Kayapo culture. At the same time, they presuppose the supportive involvement of non-Kayapo opinion, organizations, and individuals, including anthropologists and documentary film makers such as myself. I have repeatedly found myself scripted by Kayapo planners and leaders for supporting roles as courier, tour organizer, translator, foreign news bureau, and documentary film maker, in the very events I was attempting to study and analyze. The line between observer and observed, I realized, had shifted, and now passed somewhere through myself, in ways not always easy to follow. The colonial situation that had made my original detached posture of methodological objectivity seem "natural" had been transformed by my original objects of study into a quintessentially modern struggle to control the cultural terms of collective identity and the means to represent and reproduce it. In the process, we had become coparticipants in a project of resisting, representing and rethinking, and both their "culture" and my "theory" had become, in some measure, our joint product.

Acknowledgments

I began fieldwork among the Kayapo of Central Brazil in 1962, and have continued to work on and among them down to the time of this writing. My research has included seven field trips to Kayapo communities (1962–64, 1965–66, 1976, 1986–87, 1989, 1990, and 1991, for a total of twenty-four months in the field), and an additional five months' research on unpublished reports and historical documents on the Kayapo located in various Brazilian archives and research institutions. My first field trip was supported by a grant from the National Institutes of Mental Health; the second by a grant from the Harvard Laboratory of Social Relations; the third by the British Broadcasting Company; the fourth and fifth by Granada Television; and the sixth and seventh by the Spencer Foundation. Additional documentary research was supported by two Fulbright Visiting Professorships in the Programa de Pôs-Graduação em Antropologia Social at the Museu Nacional in Rio de Janeiro.

I am greatly indebted to Fernando Coronil for a close reading and critique of an earlier paper on which the last section of the present paper is largely based (Turner n.d.:1). Jane Fajans has also made a number of helpful suggestions which have been incorporated in the text.

Further information on Kayapo society, history, and politics is contained in the following sources: Turner 1978b, 1979, 1980, 1988, 1989b, 1989c, 1989d, n.d.1, n.d.2, n.d.3, and n.d.4.

References Cited

Turner, Terence. 1978a. Face values. Seven-film series on social anthropology including Kayapo material. Various directors; T. Turner, General Consultant. BBC TV. London.

———. 1978b. The Kayapo of Central Brazil. In *Face values*, ed. Anne Sutherland. BBC TV. London.

———. 1979. Kinship, household, and community structure among the Northern Kayapo. In *Dialectical societies*, ed. D. Maybury-Lewis. Cambridge, Mass.

———. 1980. The social skin. In *Not work alone*, ed. J. Cherfas & R. Lewin. London.

———. 1982. Other People's Lives. Three 20-min. films on Kayapo: Politics and leadership among the Kayapo of Central Brazil; The jaguar: Myth and ritual in a Kayapo community of Central Brazil; and The struggle to survive: Contact, adaptation, and conflict between the Kayapo Indians of Central Brazil and national Brazilian society. BBC TV. London.

———. 1987. Disappearing worlds: The Kayapo. Film, 52 min. M. Beckham, Director; T. Turner, Anthropological Consultant. Granada.

———. 1988. Myth, history, and social consciousness among the Kayapo. In *Rethinking history and myth: Indigenous South American perspectives on the past*, ed. J. Hill. Urbana, Ill.

———. 1989a. The Kayapo: Out of the forest. Film, 52 min. M. Beckham, Director; T. Turner, Anthropological Consultant. Granada.

———. 1989b. Kayapo plan meeting to discuss dams. *Cult. Survival Quart.* 13(1): 20–22.

———. 1989c. Five days in Altamira: Kayapo Indians organize protest against proposed hydroelectric dams. *Kayapo Support Group Newsl.* 1.

———. 1989d. Amazonian Indians lead fight to save their forest world. *Lat. Am. Anth. Rev.* 1(1): 2–4.

———. N.d.1. De cosmologia a história: Resistência, adaptaçõ, e consciência social entre os Kayapó. To appear in *Rev. Antropol.* (São Paulo).

———. N.d.2. The role of indigenous peoples in the environmental crisis: The example of the Kayapo of the Brazilian Amazon. To appear in *New Perspect. Biol. & Med.*

———. N.d.3. Altamira: Paradigm for a new politics? Paper presented to the Annual Meeting of the American Anthropological Association, Washington, D.C. 1989. To appear in *The Kayapo offensive*, ed. T. Greaves & T. Turner.

———. N.d.4. *Os Kaiapó do Suleste do Pará.* Vol. 8, pt. 2 of *Povos Indígenas do Brasíl.* São Paulo.

AFTERWORD

From the History of Colonial Anthropology to the Anthropology of Western Hegemony

TALAL ASAD

I

The story of anthropology and colonialism is part of a larger narrative which has a rich array of characters and situations but a simple plot.

When Europe conquered and ruled the world, its inhabitants went out to engage with innumerable peoples and places. European merchants, soldiers, missionaries, settlers, and administrators — together with men of power who stayed at home, they helped transform their non-European subjects, with varying degrees of violence, in a "modern" direction. And of course, these subjects were not passive. The story recounts how they understood initial encounters with Europeans in indigenous cultural terms, how they resisted, adapted to, cooperated with, or challenged their new masters, and how they attempted to reinvent their disrupted lives. But it also tells of how the conditions of reinvention were increasingly defined by a new scheme of things — new forms of power, work, and knowledge. It tells of European imperial dominance not as a temporary repression of subject populations but as an irrevocable process of transmutation, in which old desires and ways of life were destroyed and new ones took their place — a story of change without historical precedent in its speed, global scope, and pervasiveness.

It was in this world that anthropology emerged and developed as an academic discipline. Concerned at first to help classify non-European humanity in ways that would be consistent with Europe's story of triumph as "progress"

Talal Asad is Professor of Anthropology and chair of the Anthropology Department at the New School for Social Research in New York. He is currently at work on historical problems of religion and power in Christian and Muslim traditions.

314

(Stocking 1987; Bowler 1989), anthropologists then went out from Europe to the colonies in order to observe and describe the particularity of non-European communities, attending to their "traditional" cultural forms or their subjection to "modern" social change.

There is nothing startling today in the suggestion that anthropological knowledge was part of the expansion of Europe's power, although there is a general consensus that the detailed implications of this bald statement need to be spelled out. The question then arises as to whether we want to fill in the broad picture of anthropology's growth that is already familiar to us or to illuminate through anthropology aspects of the transformation of which this discipline was a small part.

It is possible, at any rate, to deal straight away with some vulgar misconceptions on this subject. The role of anthropologists in maintaining structures of imperial domination has, despite slogans to the contrary, usually been trivial; the knowledge they produced was often too esoteric for government use, and even where it was usable it was marginal in comparison to the vast body of information routinely accumulated by merchants, missionaries, and administrators. Of course, there were professional anthropologists who were nominated (or who offered their services) as experts on the social life of subjugated peoples. But their expertise was never indispensable to the grand process of imperial power. As for the motives of most anthropologists, these, like the motives of individuals engaged in any collective, institutional enterprise, were too complex, variable, and indeterminate to be identified as simple political instrumentalities.

But if the role of anthropology for colonialism was relatively unimportant, the reverse proposition does not hold. The process of European global power has been central to the anthropological task of recording and analyzing the ways of life of subject populations, even when a serious consideration of that power was theoretically excluded. It is not merely that anthropological fieldwork was facilitated by European colonial power (although this well-known point deserves to be thought about in other than moralistic terms); it is that the fact of European power, as discourse and practice, was always part of the reality anthropologists sought to understand, and of the way they sought to understand it.

II

What preexisting discourses and practices did anthropologists enter when they went at particular imperial times to particular colonial places? What concepts of dominant power did they assume, modify, or reject, as they tried to observe and represent the lives of "traditional" populations being transformed in a "modern" direction? All of the contributions to this volume attempt, in their different ways, to address these questions.

Stocking's fascinating essay traces the unfamiliar story of European colonial interventions and ethnographic concerns that preceded Malinowski in New Guinea, and in response to which he formulated many of his views about the study of culture. It was in this context, we discover, that Malinowski acquired his moral ambivalence regarding the consequences of modern change, and his predisposition to credit colonial authorities with good intentions. Stocking makes it clear that Malinowski either suppressed the presence of colonial powers and interests from his account of Trobriand life or represented them as essentially disintegrative of "tradition." Thus in an early passage that represents the classic functionalist doctrine, Malinowski writes:

> every item of culture . . . represents a value, fulfils a social function. . . . For tradition is a fabric in which all the strands are so clearly woven that the destruction of one unmakes the whole. And tradition is . . . a form of collective adaptation of a community to its surroundings. Destroy tradition, and you will deprive the collective organism of its protective shell, and give it over to the slow but inevitable process of dying out. (Cited in Stocking, this volume, p. 51)

This Burkean notion of tradition has been subjected to critical scrutiny by anthropologists and historians in recent decades. The point has been made repeatedly that in a world subjected for centuries to the forces of European capitalism and imperialism anthropological assumptions about cultural continuity, autonomy and authenticity must be questioned. Much of what appears ancient, integrated, and in need of preservation against the disruptive impact of modern social change is itself recently invented. Salemink's article in this volume on Montagnard identity belongs to this subversive genre. He demonstrates not only the recency of their so-called traditions but the framework of colonial practices, interests, and representations within which they were constructed and manipulated.

There is clearly much to be learned from such scholarly histories of the particular colonial contexts of anthropological practice. I propose that it is worth pursuing even further the critical inquiry they initiate. For in an important sense the concept of tradition employed in them is still the one espoused by Malinowski, and the disagreement is over which existing social arrangements qualify as "genuine" traditions and which as "invented" ones (Hobsbawm & Ranger 1983). Real tradition—so the assumption goes—is a matter of the unreasoning reproduction of custom, and it is therefore opposed to radical change. However, one may note here that this particular conception extends well beyond the writings of functionalist anthropologists and has its origins in the political response of European conservatives to the threat of the French Revolution.

The eighteenth century in Europe witnessed the development of a bourgeois social and moral order based on the principle of individual private property (Hill 1969; Porter 1982). Especially in England, this meant underwriting de facto class privileges through the systematization of law as precedent. The rhetoric of revolutionary France, with its attack on inherited privilege and prejudice in the name of universal reason and justice, was clearly a threat to conservative England. This was how Edmund Burke, the great spokesman of English class privilege, conceptualized the ideological danger facing that class, and how he theorized his counterattack. What made justice, and coherent social life itself, possible, was "tradition," and "tradition" consisted in a reverence for unbroken continuity, for the prejudices of the past, and it *was* indeed antithetical to the irresponsibility of free reason and the disruption of radical change.[1] Thus for Burke "the past" is not a particular (and changing) *conception* of one's inheritance—including those parts that are argued as being relevant to the present as compared with others that are not. "The past" is a palpable point of authority to which one is either linked by mimetic action or from which one is forever severed.

What are the implications of such a political genealogy for the way anthropologists have addressed change in precolonial, colonial, and postcolonial societies? One implication, I would suggest, has been the difficulty of theorizing the place of non-Western traditions within the contemporary scheme of things, except perhaps when they are depicted as "myths" that help people cope with disorientation or resist oppression. Indeed, such depictions often reinforce the assumption (even where this is not explicitly argued or intended) that traditions in the contemporary world may be regarded as functionally valuable insofar as they "empower the weak," but only because the universal principles of the Enlightenment project have not yet been fully realized.

A prominent example of this is the reaction of Western social scientists and Orientalists to the contemporary growth of Islamic rhetoric and practice

1. Thus it is with reference to this historical construction that MacIntyre (1980:63) writes: "from Burke onwards, [conservatives] have wanted to counterpose tradition and reason and tradition and revolution. Not reason, but prejudice; not revolution, but inherited precedent; these are Burke's key oppositions. Yet if [my] arguments are correct it is traditions which are the bearers of reason, and traditions at certain periods actually require and need revolutions for their continuance. Burke saw the French Revolution as merely the negative overthrow of all that France had been and many French conservatives have agreed with him, but later thinkers as different as Péguy and Hilaire Belloc were able retrospectively to see the great revolution as reconstituting a more ancient France, so that Jeanne D'Arc and Danton belong within the same single, if immensely complex, tradition."

in the Middle East. Thus, since the nineteenth century, it has not been common to find Western writers expressing the need to *explain* processes of Europeanization and secularization as opposed, that is, to *describing* them. The reason is that those processes are taken to be natural. The political invocations of Islamic traditions in that region have, on the other hand, been the object of a swelling stream of anxious explanation in recent years. What explains the recurrent political assertiveness of Islamic tradition? Typically, the answers tend to be given in terms of the localized failures of modernization,[2] or in terms of an irrational reluctance to abandon tradition.[3] But while there can be no doubt that Muslim societies have changed radically over the past two centuries, and that this has involved the adoption of Western institutions, values, and practices, it is not at all clear that every form of re-argued Islamic tradition must be seen either as an anomaly or as a spurious claim to historicity. The need to explain such developments as anomalies in the modern world indicates something about the hegemonic discourses of "progress," and about some of the fears underlying them in the contemporary West.

III

In an earlier period, when "progressive" Western scholars were less anxious about developments in the societies they studied, there was also a concern to *explain away* what appeared to be anomalies in the process of modernization experienced by colonized populations. An interesting example from the history of British anthropology is the attempt by members of the Rhodes-Livingstone Institute in central Africa to explain the persistence of "tribalism."

It is sometimes forgotten that functionalist anthropologists were as interested in analyzing "modern" change in colonial Africa as they were in reconstructing "traditional" cultures. The Rhodes-Livingstone Institute, in what is now independent Zambia, was a well-known research center devoted from the late 1930s on to documenting economic, political, and religious changes affecting African populations. In spite of all the social problems involved, the

---

2. For example: "Contrary to their expectations, however, education (even higher education) fails to provide them with the keys to modernity. It is from these circles that the heavy battalions of the Islamicist movement are drawn. They are the living symbols, and their numbers are massive, of the failure of the independent state's modernization project" (Kepel 1985:218).

3. Thus the eminent Middle East specialist, Leonard Binder (1988:293): "From the time of the Napoleonic invasion, from the time of the massacre of the Janissaries, from the time of the Sepoy mutiny, at least, the West has been trying to tell Islam what must be the price of progress in the coin of the tradition which is to be surrendered. And from those times, despite the increasing numbers of responsive Muslims, there remains a substantial number that steadfastly [stubbornly] argue that it is possible to progress without paying such a heavy cultural price." Binder's own closely argued book conveys the same Western message to Islam.

move from a "primitive" life toward "civilization" (Wilson 1945) was conceptualized as a progressive development.

When Max Gluckman succeeded Godfrey Wilson as the Institute's second
director, the basic categories for apprehending that transformation were altered from "primitive" and "civilized" to "tribal" and "industrial." These categories were central to the administrative discourses of various colonial interests,
including the copper mining company of Northern Rhodesia. (Many of the
studies by Institute researchers were carried out in response to specific administrative problems [e.g., Epstein 1953, 1958].) A major preoccupation of
the Institute, Gluckman wrote in 1961, was to understand the persistence of
"tribalism," especially in the mines and townships which represented the most
modern sectors of social life. "Tribalism," unlike "nationalism," was not intrinsic to modern life, and its presence needed explaining. Gluckman and his
associates (notably Mitchell and Epstein) insisted that "tribalism" in urban
areas was nothing more than a form of reconstructed group identity, something that would later be renamed "ethnicity." Since identities were inevitably
determined by the economic conditions of towns as contemporary "social fields"
(the phrase is Gluckman's), their compatibility with modernity was assured.
Such tribalism was not a relic of the (traditional) past but a function of the
(modern) present.

> Tribalism acts, though not as strongly, in British towns: for in these Scots and
> Welsh and Irish, French, Jews, Lebanese, Africans, have their own associations,
> and their domestic life is ruled by their own national [sic] customs. But all may
> unite in political parties and in trade unions or employers' federations. Tribal-
> ism in the Central African towns is, in sharper forms, the tribalism of all towns.
> (Gluckman 1961:76)

Thus even for functionalist anthropologists of the colonial period the normality of colonized peoples was sometimes affirmed by arguing that their life
was essentially the same as that of the metropole, albeit perhaps a little less
developed along the universal path to modernity.

It is not only what historical events are felt to need explaining but also
the terms in which they are thought to be persuasively accounted for that
reveals the force of hegemonic discourses. Kuklick's story of the archeological
disputes over the origins of the famous ruins of Zimbabwe, in the former British colony that adopted that name, is a revealing illustration of this point.
Kuklick describes in detail how,

> seeking to legitimate their rule, British settlers and African nationalists sub-
> scribed to very different accounts of the building of the ruins, basing their
> construction alternatively in ancient times and the relatively recent past, and
> identifying the builders—or, at least architects—either as representatives of some
> non-African civilization or members of the indigenous population. (This vol-
> ume, pp. 137–38)

Yet what emerges strikingly from her account is the fact that Rhodesian settlers and Zimbabwean nationalists shared the basic terms of a historical argument. They accepted and used the modern European language of *territorial
rights* and its essential preconditions: only long, continuous, *settled* association with a given territory could give its inhabitants exclusive title to it. Indeed, that was precisely the point of difference—according to the classical European law of nations—between a wandering "tribe" and a settled "nation." Thus
the influential eighteenth-century *philosophe* Emer de Vattel:

> It is asked whether a Nation may lawfully occupy any part of a vast territory
> in which are to be found only wandering tribes whose small numbers can not
> populate the whole country. We have already pointed out, in speaking of the
> obligation of cultivating the earth, that these tribes can not take to themselves
> more land than they have need of or can inhabit and cultivate. Their uncertain
> occupancy of these vast regions can not be held as a real and lawful taking of
> possession; and when the Nations of Europe, which are too confined at home,
> come upon lands which the savages have no special need of and are making
> no present and continuous use of, they may lawfully take possession of them
> and establish colonies in them. (Curtin 1971:44–45).

Furthermore, both colonialists and nationalists seem to agree that evidence
of a relatively sophisticated urban life in its past indicated some capacity for
social progress in a colonized people—*and that proof of such capacity was essential to the credibility of its claim to independence.* Imperial administrators might
deny the existence of such capacity in the populations over whom they ruled,
or insist that at any rate the capacity was too feeble to justify an immediate
transfer of sovereignty, but the point is that this was central to the discourses
legitimating independence—for colonizers and colonized alike. As they enter
the political arena, archeologists and anthropologists too have found themselves inevitably involved in these hegemonic discourses. Gluckman and his
colleagues at the Rhodes-Livingstone Institute were by no means exceptional
in this regard.

Feit's excellent contribution provides another example. He shows that
Speck's case for the existence of the principle of private property in Algonquian culture was the product of a local "colonial situation," including government policies and settler claims. What emerges from his account is that the
defense of Algonquian interests in the face of predatory white settlers was
felt to be credibly made only in terms of Western legal concepts. Whether
it was Speck himself who conceived this defense, or the Algonquians whose
claims he forwarded, the result was an account fully situated in Western discourses of power.

Feit draws on the recent work of Bishop and Morantz which apparently
challenges that discourse. This is a work of revisionist history very much of
the kind we need if we are to develop an anthropology of Western imperial

hegemony. But in resorting to it we should remember to distinguish between legal facts and social practices that might be relevant to the law, for the former have an institutional force that the latter lack. Western legal discourse participates in processes of power by creating modern realities of a special kind, and it should not be thought of as a form of representation that can be subverted by scholarly argument. The realities are special in part because they define social relationships—for individuals as well as for corporate groups—in terms of legal "rights" and "duties" within the modern state.

When Europeans acquired imperial control over subject societies, they set up law courts to administer justice in a radically new way. Thus a legal historian of colonial Africa has recently described how the judicial system instituted there by the British gave some Africans new weapons to fight for their interests in profoundly changed social circumstances, as judicial individuation accompanied an emerging economic individualism. But more important, "defined legal rights and duties, enforceable through institutions, replaced ongoing relationships containing their own sanctions. The general sharpening of rights and sanctions were [sic] a result of 'disintegration' expressing itself through institutional change. 'Rights' were replacing both physical force and compromise" (Chanock 1985:44). The mere presence of a government-instituted law court (including so-called customary courts) meant that resort to it required the treatment of vague claims and dissatisfactions in accordance with precise rules—that is, as "rights." The concept of "custom," which previously had the status of persuasive instances, now became grounds for judicial decisions, which possessed an entirely different authority, linked to the coercive character of the modern colonial state.

The writings of influential British anthropologists dealing with African law and custom failed to note this transformation in the direction of modern Western institutions (e.g., Gluckman 1955). Instead, they reproduced the hegemonic discourse of colonial administrators (which also later became the discourse of African nationalists), according to which "customary law" under the British was simply a more evolved form of "custom" in the precolonial era. As Chanock rightly points out, they did not recognize that the *representation* of conventional practice as a form of "customary law" was itself part of the process that *constituted* it as a legal instrument. That this was a colonial legal instrument is made plain in the way its effectiveness was defined—most notably, perhaps, in the rule that a "custom" cannot achieve the force of law if it is "contrary to justice and morality":

> Of all the restrictions upon the application of customary laws during the colonial period, the test of repugnancy "to justice or morality" was potentially the most sweeping: for customary laws could hardly be repugnant to the traditional sense of justice or morality of the community which still accepted them, and it is therefore clear that the justice or morality of the colonial power was

to provide the standard to be applied. Of course, customary law evolved, as the sense of justice and morality of the community evolved; old rules might appear repugnant to new standards of justice and morality derived from colonial authority or other Western influences. (Read 1972:175)

The uncritical reproduction of administrative-legal discourse by anthropologists of the colonial period was not confined to those who studied the functioning of African tribal courts. In much anthropological theory of that time the primary form of *all* social relationships in colonized societies was talked about in quasi-legal terms as "rights" and "duties."[4] The indeterminate, contradictory, and open-ended character of social structures was reduced in this way to the status of a precisely articulated and consistent legal-administrative document.

IV

The essays by Tomas (on Radcliffe-Brown in the Andamans) and Bashkow (on Schneider's intellectual biography) are valuable contributions to our knowledge of the history of colonial anthropology. But I have been arguing that we also need to pursue our historical concerns by anthropologizing the growth of Western imperial power, because unless we extend our questions about the cultural character of that hegemony, we may take too much for granted about the relationship between anthropology and colonialism. A number of scholars have begun to address themselves in interesting ways to this extended enquiry (e.g. Cooper & Stoler 1989). It needs to be stressed, however, that it is not enough for anthropologists to note that that hegemony was not monolithic, or that Western power continually evoked resistance. It is not enough because conventional political history of colonial times and places has always been a record of conflict: between different European interests, between different groups of non-Europeans, as well as between colonizers and colonized. We do not advance matters much conceptually if we simply repeat slogans about conflict and resistance in place of older slogans about repression and domination. An anthropology of Western imperial power must try to understand the radically altered form and terrain of conflict in-

---

4. Thus Radcliffe-Brown (1950:11): "An important element in the relations of kin is what will here be called the jural element, meaning by that relationships that can be defined in terms of rights and duties. . . . Reference to duties or rights are simply ways of referring to a social relation and the rules of behaviour connected therewith. In speaking of the jural element in social relations we are referring to customary rights and duties. Some of these in some societies are subject to legal sanctions, that is, an infraction can be dealt with by a court of law. But for the most part the sanctions for these customary rules are what may be called moral sanctions sometimes supplemented by religious sanctions."

augurated by it—new political languages, new powers, new social groups, new desires and fears, new subjectivities.

Turner's contribution in this volume is an anthropological account of aspects of precisely that transformation. He documents a profound change in Kayapo perspectives over the three decades of his involvement with them. Faced with white power, there is now not only a new assertiveness about their ritual life and conventional dress, but a new conception of their collective identity. Instead of seeing themselves as the autonomous paradigm of humanity, the Kayapo now present themselves as part of a dominated ethnic group (the Indians) engaged in political struggle with a dominant ethnic group (the whites). Turner notes that "over the past half-dozen years, the Kayapo have staged a series of demonstrations against a variety of threats to their political, social, and territorial integrity and their economic subsistence base" (this volume, p. 303), and goes on to describe how Kayapo traditions have become politicized and how his own conception of their culture was altered as a consequence of his involvement in their struggles. This involvement came through his use of audio-visual media. Resorted to at first for narrow documentary purposes, audio-visual media soon assumed a critical role in the Kayapo struggle against encroaching white power. "The Kayapo have passed rapidly from the initial stage of conceiving video as a means of recording events to conceiving it as the event to be recorded, and more broadly, conceiving events and actions as subjects for video" (this volume, p. 307).

Turner's account of the changing concept of "culture"—from a closed system of mutually referring symbols and meanings to practices of collective identity that are technologically representable and legally contestable—is a substantial contribution to the anthropology of Western imperial hegemony that I am urging. It also illustrates the importance of some points I have argued above, including the ways in which contest and conflict are increasingly relatable to *legal* forms (even when governing powers seek to deny their legality). But in addition it deals with something that needs to be pursued more systematically: the role of Western technologies in transforming colonial subjects. Just as modern modes of locomotion (railways, motorcars, etc.) have altered concepts of time and space (Schivelbusch 1986), so Turner reminds us that modern modes of representation (e.g., film and video) have helped to reconstitute colonized subjectivities. All these things have certainly been very important for the changes that Western hegemony has brought about. It is necessary, however, to extend the concept of technology to include all institutionalized techniques that depend on and extend varieties of social power.

Right through modern imperial times and places, Western techniques for governing subjects have radically restructured the domain we now call society— a process that has reorganized strategies of power accordingly. This process has been extensively written about (and not only by Foucault and his followers) in the context of modern European history, but far less so in the context of Europe's imperial territories. In fact the difference between the processes of transformation in the two contexts remains to be properly explored. Grasping that difference seems to me to require in part a closer examination of the emerging discourses of "culture" (cf. Asad 1990). Until we understand precisely how the social domain has been restructured (constituted), our accounts of the dynamic connections between power and knowledge during the colonial period will remain limited.

References Cited

Asad, T. 1990. Multiculturalism and British identity in the wake of the Rushdie affair. *Polit. & Soc.* 18(4): 455–80.

Binder, L. 1988. *Islamic liberalism.* Chicago.

Bowler, P. 1989. *The invention of progress.* Oxford.

Chanock, M. 1985. *Law, custom and social order: The colonial experience in Malawi and Zambia.* Cambridge.

Cooper, F., & A. L. Stoler, eds. 1990. Tensions of empire. *Am. Ethnol.* 16(4): 609–765.

Curtin, P. D. 1971. *Imperialism: Selected documents.* London.

Epstein, A. L. 1953. *The administration of justice and the urban African.* London.

———. 1958. *Politics in an urban African community.* Manchester.

Gluckman, M. 1955. *The judicial process among the Barotse of Northern Rhodesia.* Manchester.

———. 1961. Anthropological problems arising from the African industrial revolution. In *Social change in modern Africa,* ed. A. Southall, 67–82. London.

Hill, C. 1969. *From reformation to industrial revolution.* Harmondsworth.

Hobsbawm, E., & T. Ranger, eds. 1983. *The invention of tradition.* Cambridge.

Kepel, G. 1985. *The prophet and pharaoh.* London.

MacIntyre, A. 1980. Epistemological crises, dramatic narrative, and the philosophy of science. In *Paradigms and revolutions,* ed. G. Gutting, 54–74. Notre Dame.

Porter, R. 1982. *English society in the eighteenth century.* Harmondsworth.

Radcliffe-Brown, A. R. 1950. Introduction to *African systems of kinship and marriage,* ed. A. R. Radcliffe-Brown & D. Forde. London.

Read, J. S. 1972. Customary law under colonial rule. In *Indirect rule and the search for justice,* ed. H. F. Morris & J. S. Read, 167–212. Oxford.

Schivelbusch, W. 1986. *The railway journey: The industrialization of time and space in the nineteenth century.* Berkeley.

Stocking, G. 1987. *Victorian anthropology.* New York.

Wilson, G., & M. Wilson. 1945. *The analysis of social change; Based on observation in Central Africa.* Cambridge.

INDEX